ARISTOTLE'S EMPIRICISM

ARISTOTLE'S EMPIRICISM

Experience and Mechanics
in the Fourth Century BC

Jean De Groot

PARMENIDES
PUBLISHING

Las Vegas | Zurich | Athens

PARMENIDES PUBLISHING
Las Vegas | Zurich | Athens

© 2014 Parmenides Publishing
All rights reserved.

This edition published in 2014 by Parmenides Publishing
in the United States of America

ISBN soft cover: 978–1–930972–83–4
ISBN e-Book: 978–1–930972–84–1

Library of Congress Cataloging-in-Publication Data

De Groot, Jean.
Aristotle's empiricism : experience and mechanics in the fourth century BC / Jean
De Groot.
    pages cm
ISBN 978-1-930972-83-4 (pbk. : alk. paper) -- ISBN 1-930972-83-0 (pbk. : alk.
paper) -- ISBN 978-1-930972-84-1 (e-book) -- ISBN 1-930972-84-9 (e-book)
1. Science, Ancient. 2. Science--Philosophy--History--To 1500. 3. Aristotle. I.
Title.
Q124.95.D43 2014
509'.014--dc23
                                    2013050403

In Figure 2.5b, the illustration of a skeletal arm and muscle was drawn by the author from Figure 1–6 in *Basic Machines and How They Work*. The figure is used with the permission of Dover Publications.

Figures 5.4 and 5.5 are from the Teubner edition of Hero of Alexandria, *Automatopoietica*, Figure 87, in *Opera Omnia*, vol. 1, 334–453, edited by Wilhelm Schmidt. The figure is used by permission of De Gruyter Publishing, the copyright holder of the work.

Part of Chapter 5 appeared first in the author's article, *"Dunamis* and the Science of Mechanics: Aristotle on Animal Motion," published in *Journal of the History of Philosophy* 46, no. 1 (2008): 43–68.

Part of Chapter 8 appeared first in the author's article, "Modes of Explanation in the Aristotelian *Mechanical Problems*," in *Early Science and Medicine* 14 (2009): 22–42, published by Brill. The paper is reprinted in *Evidence and Interpretation in Studies on Early Science and Medicine: Essays in Honor of John E. Murdoch*, edited by William R. Newman and Edith Dudley Sylla, also published by Brill.

Typeset in OdysseaUBSU and Futura
Printed and lay-flat bound by Documation Inc. | www.documation.com

www.parmenides.com

To the memory of my parents

Carl and Vera Christensen

Table of Contents

List of Illustrations

Figures

Charts and Tables

Acknowledgments

I wrote most of this book in the course of a year's sabbatical leave and then another semester of university leave. Sadly, this time coincided with my care giving for my parents during the time of their decline and deaths. I am grateful for their patience and their encouragement of my intellectual project. They were the most generous of souls, and this book is dedicated to them.

I have been fortunate to be part of the faculty in the School of Philosophy at The Catholic University of America. The combined expertise and collegiality of this body of philosophers has made it possible for me to learn a great deal of classical philosophy from my colleagues and also to absorb something of the phenomenological perspective in contemporary philosophy. I am especially grateful for conversations with Robert Sokolowski, John Wippel, Kevin White, Richard Hassing, William A. Wallace, Angela McKay Knobel, Cristina Ionescu, and Philosophy Dean Fr. Kurt Pritzl, O.P., now deceased. Dean Pritzl's battle with cancer took place in the same time period as my work on this project. I am grateful for Fr. Pritzl's confidence in me and his continual encouragement of my work. Thanks belong also to Dean Emeritus Jude Dougherty for his insights into philosophy of science and for his giving me the initial opportunity to teach in the School of Philosophy. I am grateful to John Rist, holder of the Kurt J. Pritzl, O.P. Chair in Philosophy at Catholic University for consultation on Aristotle and for stimulating conversations about ancient philosophy in general. I thank our present Dean John C. McCarthy whose support has made my work on this book so much easier.

Among professional colleagues, I owe much to Edith Sylla, of North Carolina State University, who along with William Newman of Indiana University organized meetings of the Medieval Science Colloquium, where those of us who study early science could compare our work and perspectives. Sylla's learning and discernment have more than once corrected some incipient excess in my thinking through of the new material on which I was working. I am also grateful for conversations with Mark Schiefsky and Barry Mazur, both of Harvard University, about the character of ancient mathematical science. Mazur affirmed for me the generally topological nature of Aristotle's appropriation of proportional thinking in physics. He suggested the term "descriptive mode" for the invariance carried through different subject matters in Aristotle's treatment of change (Chapter 9). Any missteps in execution of the concept of a descriptive mode in that context are very evidently my own. I wish to thank also the anonymous referees of the book who offered valuable insights on weaknesses that I could correct in various chapters and for pointing out clarifications that needed to be made.

As always, my thanks are owed the most to my husband, Simon, who has done so much to give me the time to finish this work and whose wit has always lightened the load of historical research and philosophical problems. I am also grateful to my three daughters who cheered on the work, never in doubt of my eventual success in producing something worth reading.

I also wish to thank the graduate students who have helped me at various stages of my research. They are Brian Fox, Joshua Potrykus, Richard Berquist, and Steve Stakland. Richard and Steve have borne the burden of proofreading and indexing. I am grateful to Parmenides Press for seeing the significance of the project and for pursuing it early on. The editors, Sara Hermann and Eliza Tutellier, as well as Gale Carr, were always responsive and encouraging. I wish to thank Derryl Rice for his vectoring of the diagrams and equations into the finished text. I am especially grateful to Parmenides Publishing for their readiness to include all the diagrams in the appropriate places in the text. A Faculty Grant-in-Aid from my university assisted me in the final stage of completion of the book, for which I am most grateful to the Office of Graduate Studies and Dean James Greene.

Jean De Groot
Arlington, Virginia, October 2013

Introduction

This book was written during a period of roughly five years from the fall of 2008 to spring 2013. The seeds of the present interpretation of Aristotle and of ancient mechanics, however, were sown much earlier in my work in the history of early physics as a graduate student in the History of Science department at Harvard University. I studied ancient, medieval, and Arabic science with John E. Murdoch and Abdelhamid I. Sabra. A course in nineteenth century physics taught by Erwin Hiebert made an enduring impression on me. I saw that truthfulness to nature in classical mechanics had a distinctive character, evident both in the questions pursued and in the logical method. Building upon this insight over a period of years, I came to discern in antiquity the footprint of mechanics as a way of thinking about natural movement and as an empirical method.

Studying the thought of Ludwig Wittgenstein reinforced my sense of the philosophical fruitfulness of (what I understood as) the *minimalism* of mechanics. Mechanics makes few assumptions. Its concepts are structural or relational in character, and their meanings are linked very closely to what has or can transpire. The concepts of mechanics remain close to the very changes of which they give an account. This was to me the most intriguing feature of mechanics, which was remarkably universal to the science throughout its history. There is a similar minimalism and empiricism in Aristotle's way of analyzing things in natural philosophy.

It seemed to me that this minimalism made Aristotle's works especially hospitable to explication by ordinary language philosophy during its golden era from about 1945 to 1985. I refer to the philosophy and scholarship of Ryle, Owen, Ackrill, Austin, Anscombe, Geach, and others. The approach to Aristotle by way of philosophy of language was striking for its brilliance and penetration but also because it never seemed completely to capture Aristotle's own way of thinking. My historical training made me sensitive to the unlikelihood of Aristotle's physical science and biology being mainly dialectical and endoxic. The puzzle of the uncaptured Aristotle provided the impetus for me to look for the source of Aristotle's minimalism in what is universal to mechanics. I believed the mechanics of Aristotle's own time could be one of the mainsprings of his investigations into nature and movement and could thus bring us closer to Aristotle's own way of thinking in these areas of investigation.

The Platonist Atticus complained that Aristotle is hard to catch because like the squid he escapes using darkness.[1] The allusion is to the squid's inky defense. This book is for anyone who has ever felt after close study of Aristotle that he still slips away. I provide a new point of entry for some of the most basic concepts of Aristotle's philosophy, in particular *dunamis* and *archê*. I argue that these concepts had a strong physicalistic meaning at their inception. I believe that this fact should be relevant to the evaluation of Aristotle's philosophy more generally.[2]

The connection I have undertaken to establish—between mechanics and Aristotle—would have been unthinkable for centuries, since modernity early on claimed mechanics as its own. A mechanical philosophy (as exemplified in Robert Boyle's corpuscularian philosophy) came into being in the early modern period after the efflorescence of mechanics proper. The mechanical philosophy provided an alternative to the persistent vein of causal teleology that runs through Aristotle's scientific thinking. My study does not address that teleology, which has been the subject of many fine studies already. The best tactic, it seemed to me, for uncovering the source of Aristotle's natural philosophy in ancient mechanics was to pursue it independently without continual reference to teleological issues in biology or cosmology.

With respect to the mechanical philosophy, it became clear to me that, with the possible exception of Newton's pragmatic formulation of it, the mechanical philosophy of the early moderns does not follow very closely

---

1   Atticus took the obscurity to be intentional. I do not. The passage is quoted by Barnes, "Metacommentary," in Barnes, *Method and Metaphysics*, 195. It comes from Eusebius' *Preparatio Evangelica* XV, ix, 13.

2   Aristotle develops more than one line of thought and, in his lecture notes that are our record of his thought, sometimes leaves standing philosophical conclusions that do not form a systematic whole. (For affirmation and clarification of this judgment, I am grateful to conversations with John Rist.) This fact only reinforces the need for a more complete understanding of the influences on Aristotle.

how mechanics actually works. Like the theory of Epicurus, early modern mechanical philosophy is dogmatic philosophy. On the other hand, some aspects of Aristotle's procedure in natural philosophy do match up rather neatly with the rudimentary but perennial mechanics he knew. My studies of *Movement of Animals* 7 and *Physics* IV.8 and VII.4 have a bearing on this claim (Chapters 5 and 9) and lay the groundwork for my account of what is minimal about mechanics and what are the philosophical implications of this minimalism in antiquity (Chapter 11).

One benefit of doing the present work has been the occasional glimpse into the archeological layers of interpretation of Aristotle, which extend from late antiquity all the way up through modern philosophy. These interpretive layers have *remade* the philosophy of the Peripatetic and remain part of our present day understanding of Aristotle. The unacceptability of natural teleology by modern scientific standards is certainly one of these interpretations. Another is the default to metaphysics—the nearly irresistible tendency to commence study of Aristotle's natural philosophy with a standard metaphysical meaning for key terms like potency and form. For the most part, the Aristotle of the twentieth and twenty-first centuries is the medieval Aristotle viewed from a distance of many centuries.

I do not want to make present-day interpretation of Aristotle seem like a hall of mirrors. I bring up the topic of layers of interpretation of Aristotle in order to account for the wide-ranging and sometimes dense historical grounding presented here. This historical grounding is an avenue to understanding Aristotle in his ancient context. My rationale at least constitutes an alternate approach to the Peripatetic. It could contribute something of value to more metaphysical approaches. These issues receive an airing in Chapter 3.

A central theme of the book is the relation of empiricism and mathematics. The book looks first at mathematical connections in natural contexts—mathematics as it appears in nature. I contend that some mathematical connections are first *perceived*, and I develop in some detail what this would mean. That the ancient formulation of movement was primarily kinematic is a theme of the book. A specific instance central to ancient mechanics up to Aristotle, the moving radius principle and its various formulations, is explored in some depth. Using ancient sources and ordinary experiences, I argue in concert with a late fifth-century BC view that, at the least, some objects and properties of a mathematical sort just are part of nature and sometimes are principles of nature. This original mathematics is not, in the language of modernity, *a priori*. Accommodating or making use of effects of the moving radius as manifest in mechanical advantage or torque constitutes bodily knowing that fits very well Aristotle's accounts of memory, experience, and craft in *Metaphysics* A.1 and *Posterior Analytics* II.19. I show that the foundational principle of ancient mechanics was known much earlier than its mathematical formulation. It was known through kinesthetic awareness first and made conscious in connection with activities like fishing, turning a cart or a speeding chariot, and mechanical advantage in hand-to-hand combat.

This point is reinforced by another kind of historical argument. The distinction of the subject matters of mathematical science and pure mathematics, often treated as already well established in Plato and Aristotle, were only just emerging in the early to mid-fourth century BC. The subject matter of mathematics was finally taken by both philosophers to be *not* subject to change. In consequence, on a cognitive plane a door was rapidly closing on the ancient *mathêma* of mechanics,[3] the mathematical science of movement. Mathematical mechanics was about to become invisible in the philosophical reorganization of mathematical sciences in the fourth century. One might wonder why this fate befell mechanics, since even astronomy was a mathematical science of moving bodies. In the case of astronomy, however, the bodies were eternal and their movement completely recurrent. Also, astronomy did not involve the crabbed subject matter of weight. (On this topic, see Chapter 10.) Mechanics did not have the saving graces of astronomy nor its endorsement by Plato.

As an empiricist, Aristotle knew not to exclude from his science of sensible things a principle capable of explaining the balance and lever, especially since the principle had so very many manifestations in nature and craft. He imported basic notions of mechanics, as well as its dominant mathematical frame, ratio and proportion, into his physical science and biology. A primary task of the book is to substantiate this claim and the accompanying history outlined above. My argument for the influence of kinematics in Aristotle's thinking draws on material in *Physical Problems* XVI, which has not yet been the subject of much discussion. This book of

---

3   Mathematics is derived from a plural Greek word, *mathêmata*, of which the singular is *mathêma*. The singular literally means "what is learned." The word was used in the singular for each mathematical science—geometry, arithmetic, optics, astronomy, etc. Already among the fifth century BC southern Italian Pythagoreans, *mathêma* was limited to what we recognize as mathematical sciences as opposed to narrative accounts of reasons for natural occurrences.

the *Problems* casts new light on the southern Italian mathematics known at least by acquaintance to Plato and on the post-Aristotelian *Mechanics*.

Despite dealing with mathematics in Aristotle, this book is called *Aristotle's Empiricism,* because its argument bears on what Aristotle means more generally by *phainomena*—phenomena, states of affairs, what occurs in nature. I distinguish *phainomena* from *endoxa,* common opinions. One aim of this study is to unsettle the usual interpretation of Aristotle's science as naïvely empirical. The supposed naïveté is taking things just as they appear and making those appearances into causes. Aristotle's empiricism is rather a critical empiricism in the sense of using seeing, sightings, or observations as they are significant in a context. This becomes clear through understanding his use of mechanical principles.

There are three main areas in which the argument of this book will be developed. The first aim must be to elaborate the moving radius principle itself and to display its use, primarily by Aristotle but also by Archytas. Chapter 2 sets out in simplest terms the variety of expressions of the moving radius principle in Plato and Aristotle. This exposition shows that the principle was well known in the fourth century BC and also aids the explanation in the middle Chapters (5–6) of Aristotle's applications of the principle. Later Chapters (7 and 8) address in more detail expressions of the moving radius principle in *Physical Problems* XVI and *Mechanics*. A detailed interpretation of the argument of *Mechanics* 1 is included in Chapter 8. These chapters display the broader base of mechanical knowledge that could have been available to Aristotle and also make the case that the materials in *Physical Problems* XVI were discussed in his circle. The degree of interest in and the familiarity with the basic principle of the lever that is manifest in these texts show why the mechanical tropes discussed in Chapters 5 and 6 would have been on Aristotle's mind. My view is that, although *Mechanics* was written by an Aristotelian living at least several decades after Aristotle's own time, the essentials of *Physical Problems* XVI could have been put together by someone in Aristotle's own circle. It will become clear that parts of the contents of *Physical Problems* XVI were known to Aristotle. The discussion found in Book XVI thus gives some indication of the sources of the principle for Aristotle and its influence on him.

The second aim of the book is to make more precise the *physical* content and method of Aristotle's natural philosophy. Aristotle understood philosophy of nature to be something different from both dialectic and metaphysics. This interpretation takes certain basic concepts of natural philosophy, in particular potency and form, as grounded in perception and less dependent on a propositional form of knowledge than has been thought in recent decades. In connection with this thesis, it will be important to treat in some detail Aristotle's concept of experience. Chapters 3 and 4 take up this theme, sketching the origin of mechanical knowledge in kinesthetic awareness and tracing that knowledge, first presented vaguely in perceptual cognition, through to its expression in a mathematical formulation. The mathematical conception itself represents a fairly advanced stage of mechanical knowledge, insofar as it separates the basic phenomenon of circular speeds varying with distance from a stationary point into a structure of subject and *kath'hauto* attribute. Chapter 4 deals in particular with astronomical knowledge and addresses what expressions of the moving radius principle in *On the Heavens* II have to do with experience. Chapters 5–6 show explicitly the relation of the moving radius principle to Aristotle's accounts of animal motion and embryological development, focusing on the meaning of *dunamis* in *Movement of Animals* and *Generation of Animals*. I claim that, in the biological contexts where mechanical analogies appear, Aristotle is not just drawing upon mechanical examples in an episodic or ad hoc way. He has in mind a precise physical concept of natural power.

The third topic to be treated is why Aristotle saw fit to generalize (more properly, analogize) the latent power in torque and mechanical advantage so far beyond practical mechanics and to so many natural situations. My belief is that Aristotle's philosophy of nature tracks the ancient *mathêmata* more closely than has been realized. Philosophy of nature receives much of its conceptual impetus from these mathematical sciences, in particular logistic and mechanics. Really, it was the defining of mathematics away from its sources in experience that paved the way for philosophy of nature, because it was impossible to include weight in mathematics. Weight was simply too closely involved with motion. This did not mean, however, that weight could not be treated relationally. Aristotle's philosophy of nature remains mathematical, in the sense of *logistikê*, the Archytan *mathêma* concerned with relation and proportion. This topic is treated in Chapter 10.

Chapter 11 proffers a certain kind of inference as distinctive of mechanics. This inference pattern is what has been shown to be present in Aristotle's theory of motion, and I relate it to some of the earliest developments in Greek science. Chapter 11 also offers a perspective on the cognitive role of proportional analogy in narrative natural philosophy. Device as contrivance was working at a deep level in the construction of Greek intellectual culture. Device in this sense made it possible for devices (objects) to be placeholders for the things themselves, when one is searching for principles of nature. The philosophical issues of similarity and action are considered in the dual context of principles of nature and theater performance as both emerged from the fifth century BC to influence natural philosophy of the fourth century BC. The Conclusion addresses the character of Aristotle's empiricism in relation to expressions of empiricism in the twentieth century and addresses a few possible objections to the project.

The issue of Aristotle's science being naively empirical or "qualitative," a frequent characterization of his science, is brought up in Chapter 1 and resolved in Chapters 10–11. For the sake of clarity now, let me state a conclusion of the study in this regard. "Qualitative" is not an accurate description of Aristotle's natural philosophy, whether one takes "quality" in an Aristotelian sense (*Categories* 8), an early modern sense (as secondary qualities, a notion that presupposes a particular physical ontology), or a late modern sense (sense data). If one wishes to take "qualitative" more colloquially as connoting science formulated solely in terms of sight, hearing, taste, touch, and smell, then it is precisely this more conventional sense that is shown in the present study not to be a good characterization of Aristotle's natural science. Aristotle works with mathematical notions in his natural philosophy, aiming at philosophical concepts possessed of sharp boundaries because of their grounding in natural things.

A different objection to the interpretation of Aristotle's natural philosophy here offered might come from the direction of modern mathematics. What Aristotle designs and develops as natural philosophy in the instance considered is not really mathematical science, since its root notion, the moving radius principle, is not good mathematics. It is vaguely conceived, because of (among other things) the lack of knowledge of π and the absence of a notion of angular velocity. A tentative reply to this objection is that the moving radius is good enough mathematics to the extent that it depends on a geometrically correct property of the circle. Furthermore, it has the advantage of being both mathematical and experiential in as fundamental a sense as a mathematical principle can be. Finally, Aristotle's application to nature of proportional thinking drawn from the mechanics of the moving radius introduces into philosophy the mathematical idea of an invariance present throughout deformation of a state of affairs. This idea still makes an important contribution to mechanics.

The limitations imposed on mechanics by a kinematic conception dependent on the circle is another story. The aim of the present study is to make more precise the character of Aristotle's empiricism and to show what he himself understood to be the meaning of key concepts of natural philosophy that are too often treated as purely rationalistic notions. A great benefit of the study, I believe, will be to provide a more precise formulation of what pre-modern mechanics was and to remove some conventional objections to the consideration of its relation to ancient philosophy.

Note on Transliterations and Abbreviations

Important single words from the Greek texts treated in this book have been transliterated, e.g., *dunamis* for δύναμις. There are about twenty such words that appear frequently in the book. My aim has been to make the book accessible to any reader interested in the topic.

I have also included references in Greek, when these would add to the understanding of readers of ancient Greek. Sometimes transliterated words and Greek words or phrases appear in close proximity, and I apologize for any cognitive dissonance this may afford to either type of reader. It is simply a hazard of systematic practice of the two rules I have endeavored to follow.

The abbreviation *L-S* in footnotes is a reference to the ninth edition of *A Greek-English Lexicon*, compiled by Henry George Liddell and Robert Scott, revised and augmented by Sir Henry Stuart Jones, with a supplement, 1968. The Berlin edition of the Greek commentaries on Aristotle, *Commentaria in Aristotelem Graeca*, is cited as *CAG*. The abbreviation for *Complete Works of Aristotle,* ed. Jonathan Barnes, is *CWA*. Diels-Kranz refers to *Die Fragmente der Vorsokratiker* of Hermann Diels and Walther Kranz.

Chapter 1

Empiricism and Mathematical Science in Aristotle

Empiricism, the conviction that in one way or another sense experience or being acted upon by the world is the primary source of human knowledge, is a notion so broad as to be in need of continual refinement. In the history of philosophy, Plato the great rationalist is contrasted to Aristotle the empiricist. Some say, though, that Aristotle is not really an empiricist, despite his claim that all knowledge originates in sense perception and that intelligible universals arise out of memory and experience. More often, it is said that Aristotle's empiricism was exceptionally naïve, because he read the essences of physical things off of their surface appearances.[4] This book provides a platform for reevaluating the meaning of empiricism in Aristotle. I examine Aristotle's attentiveness to the practical mechanics of his day and his understanding of the rule or principle that lay behind that mechanics. The Greeks in general were cognizant of this rule in its different versions by means of experiences we still recognize and also in their use of simple machines that continue to figure prominently in daily life.

That these experiences and techniques form a dimension of Aristotle's thought is revealed by relating texts of the Aristotelian school dealing with mechanics (*Mechanics, Physical Problems* XVI) to the main body

---

4   On the difficulties of defining empiricism, see Van Fraassen, *Empirical Stance*. Van Fraassen says Aristotle was not really an empiricist but was "more empiricist than Plato" (32). Michael Frede argues that Aristotle is not an empiricist in "Rationalism." McMullin is among those who present the objection that Aristotle's empiricism simply follows the superficial appearance of things (*Inference*, 7–9).

1

of Aristotle's writings. These mechanical texts are seldom cited by scholars concerned with Aristotle's general philosophy (*Physics*, *Metaphysics*, and the logical works). This new material lends a fresh perspective on the meaning of basic concepts of Aristotle's natural philosophy, like power or potentiality (*dunamis*) and form (*eidos*). There is another side to Aristotle's natural philosophy than is usually seen, another Aristotle. It is this other philosopher, scientist, empiricist, who is the subject of this book.

The clearest path of approach to this other Aristotle and his intellectual circle is through the ancient conception of the balance beam and lever,[5] which fell at this time under the same rule of explanation. This is a mathematical principle concerning the circular movement of bodies, which appears in a variety of contexts in the writings of Aristotle and his school. This principle states a property of the moving radius of a circle or of revolving concentric circles. Both of the following two formulations are expressed verbally and diagrammatically in Aristotle' writings:

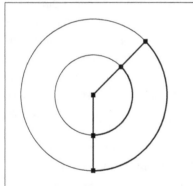

Points on a moving radius all move at different speeds proportional to their distance from the center of the circle.

Of concentric circles, a point on the circumference of the smaller circle moves in the same time a shorter distance than a point on the circumference of the larger circle.

Figure 1.1

Figure 1.1 gives a geometrical representation of the principle. A similar figure is described in the course of a demonstration of the principle in *Mechanics* 1. In *Movement of Animals* 1, Aristotle uses letters to refer to a diagram illustrating the principle when he describes the rotation of a radius about a stationary point.[6] The principle is mathematical—it treats lines, arcs, the center of a circle, and points on its radius—but the prop-

---

5   ζυγόν and μοχλός respectively.

6   *Mechanics* 1, 849a3–b18; *Movement of Animals* 1, 698a18–24.

erty of the circle on which it depends was not separated from motion.[7]
Aristotle gives one formulation of it in terms of longer and shorter arcs of
concentric circles subtended by the same two radii, but for the most part,
the principle explains why things subject to the same force (understood as
a push or blow) would move different distances in the same time.[8] Longer
and shorter arcs represent speeds. The principle was "mechanical" in a
scientific sense, because it was a mathematical rule concerned with motion. The rule described how force affects speed when forces (including
weight) influence one another or when a rigid body is rotated. The principle was taken by the author of *Mechanics* to be behind the power of
the lever, and his treatise is a tour de force of applications of the lever
principle, explained in terms of properties of the circle, to other tools and
technical devices. The principle was well known to Plato and Aristotle,
a fact placing it at least as early as the mid- to late fourth century BC.
Aristotle has recourse to some formulation of it in a number of passages
of his natural philosophy, in terms that are quite independent of the ratios
of weights, times, and distances covered that are sometimes plucked out
of *Physics* IV and VII and treated as Aristotle's mechanics.[9] Thus, there
was in Aristotle's philosophical environs an approach to mechanics as it
would come to be recognized in the early modern period.[10]

---

7   I use the English word "principle" in a general sense most of the time. It appears that
Aristotle sometimes thinks of the relation of the circle and its properties of speed in rotation
as an ἀρχή in the sense of an unmediated causal premise, but to catalog those instances is
not a main concern of my study. The word "rule" in some ways better describes the import
of the principle, because it is a sort of covering law of action revealed in practice. If we are
looking to types of expressions in words, the connection to practice makes the principle
more like a verbal command than an axiom of deduction. For more on the status of the
principle, see Chapters 3 and 4. I come back to *archê* as a principle in Chapter 11.

8   For the formulation solely in terms of arcs of concentric circles, see *On the Heavens*
II.8, 290a3–5. For the more typical formulation comparing motion along arcs, see the preceding lines, 289b34–290a2 and II.10, 291a34–b1.

9   Cohen and Drabkin (*Source Book*, 203n1–3) and Clagett treat the proportions of
force, distance, time, and resistance in Aristotle as "quantitative laws" (Clagett, *Science
of Mechanics*, 425). The practice is given a detailed criticism by Owen, "Aristotelian
Mechanics" (315–333) and De Gandt, "Force et science des machines." The latter focuses
in particular on *Physics* VII.5, where the ratios seem the least embedded in other arguments and therefore more like laws of motion presented by Aristotle himself. For a recent
schematization that better contextualizes the rules of motion, see Hussey, "Mathematical
Physics."

10   For a treatment of early modern mechanics in relation to some of the ancient texts
from which it came, see Meli, *Thinking With Objects*, especially ch.1. Historians have long
noted that the ancients had in hand the principles governing simple machines and steam

The moving radius principle has not been brought into the interpretation of Aristotle's own natural philosophy in part (it seems to me) because of its prominence in *Mechanics*.[11] Mechanics developed on a base of practice with simple machines in the 4th–3rd centuries, as *Mechanics* itself testifies. Machines are craft items, banausic in origin, and this has led scholars away from inspecting mechanics as a source for theoretical philosophy.[12] The treatise is unlikely to have been written by Aristotle himself, and the first chapter, which presents something like a proof of the principle, is vague and lacking in rigor as an argument. Furthermore, the author seems to compose circular motion from rectilinear movements. An oddity in an Aristotelian text, the treatment of circular motion as composite may be a sign that the treatise is much later than Aristotle.

A neglect harder to countenance is the scant interest in the characteristic proportion of rectilinear elements taken by the author of *Mechanics* 1 to pick out corresponding arcs covered in the same time by the ends of a balance or lever. While attempts have been made to connect *Mechanics* to the ratios of force, time, and distance found in *Physics* VII.5 in particular, the comparison has been made in terms that more or less dismember the moving radius principle in order to derive from it rules of motion that are like axioms or at least highest generalizations.[13] No notice has been taken of references to the principle peppered throughout the works held to be Aristotle's own, sometimes because the references have not been recognized as coming from the principle (*Movement of Animals* 7) and some-

---

power that brought about the industrial revolution in Europe. For a review of the continuing debate as to why the Greeks did not industrialize, see Schneider, *Technikverständnis*, 1–9, 52–62.

11   Some essays in the recent collection of Laks and Rashed, ed., *Dix études sur le De motu animalium*, correct this deficit to some extent by bringing mechanics into the interpretation of Aristotle's treatises on animal motion. In this volume, Bodnár gives reasons both in favor of and against considering the mechanical principles in *Mechanics* as influential in *Movement of Animals* and *Progression of Animals* ("Mechanical Principles," 137), before showing the connections among the treatises. He does not address the moving radius principle as such.

12   On the opposition between philosophy and the practice of the technical craftsman as a theme within classical philosophy, see Nightingale, *Spectacles of Truth*.

13   See De Gandt, "Force," 121–24, and Hussey's treatment of the movement of a balance in "Mathematical Physics," 224–225. An exception to this way of analyzing the text is the groundbreaking work of Fritz Krafft, *Betrachtungsweise*. Krafft focuses on the "concentric circles principle" in *Mechanics* and traces it back to a lost treatise of Archytas (144–146). The connection to Archytas is disputed by Huffman as outrunning the evidence (*Archytas*, 78n13).

times because the principle is overlooked as unimportant and simplistic relative to more complex mathematical accounts of celestial phenomena (*On the Heavens* II.8 and 10). *Physical Problems* XVI, which presents the principle in a variety of forms, is treated (if at all) as a footnote to *Mechanics*, when in fact it presents the principle in a different way from *Mechanics* and could, taken along with *Mechanics*, provide a revealing link between works of natural philosophy attested to be Aristotle's, on the one hand, and the science of his school, on the other.[14]

Certainly, *Mechanics* and *Physical Problems* have a form and histories that separate them from works more certain to reflect Aristotle's own teaching.[15] Nevertheless, even the works accepted as Aristotle's own are, as far as we know, notes of his lectures written by students, or by Aristotle himself and then rewritten or reorganized by others.[16] The bio-

---

14   For the footnote, see Krafft, *Betrachtungsweise*, 159n. Heath omits the key chapters 3 and 12 in his treatment of *Physical Problems* XVI (*Mathematics in Aristotle*, 264–268).

15   Both treatises are comprised of a series of questions posed, the answers to which class the puzzling phenomenon questioned under some other phenomenon taken as explanatory. *Mechanics* is most consistent in explaining almost all its chosen phenomena as examples of the lever. The books of *Physical Problems* are a very diverse collection of problems and explanations of varying historical date. Most of its problems are viewed by scholars as having little enduring scientific interest. See introductions to the translations of *Physical Problems* by Hett, *Problems*, viii, and Flashar, *Problemata*, 295–296. Mayhew is more optimistic about the value of the text for yielding information about Aristotelian science in the Lyceum after Aristotle (Mayhew, *Problems* 1, xi). My concern with *Physical Problems* is Book XVI only.

16   For a treatment of this issue in its significance for the history of science, see Grant, *Natural Philosophy*, 28–33. The literary form of the Aristotelian treatises in relation to their history has been treated mainly in relation to the *development* of Aristotle's philosophy, a topic I only touch upon. Whether cross-references in the text are all from a later period or whether some were inserted by Aristotle himself is an issue that figures prominently in discussion of the developmental thesis. This question is taken as an index of how much the writings themselves might have been reformulated. This debate detracts from the much simpler and more immediate point that the lecture note format of the writings gives reason, where the language and content justifies it, to use minor works to expand our knowledge of what are taken to be Aristotle's central writings. The literary form of the problem literature is not itself a reason for its content being considered remote from Aristotle's own interests and even authorship. For an overview of the problem of the style of writing in relation to Aristotle's development, see Rist, *Mind of Aristotle*, Preface and Chapter 1, and Grayeff, *Aristotle and his School*, 82–85. For the argument against any sort of developmental thesis as futile due to the literary character of the Aristotelian corpus, see Shute, *Aristotelian Writings*. Discussion of the developmental thesis received new impetus in the twentieth century from Jaeger, *Development*, and Düring, *Biographical Tradition*. Discussion mainly concerns whether or not Aristotle was a Platonist and seldom touches upon the problem literature of Aristotle. For a fresh discussion of the current state of the question, see Gerson, *Other Platonists*.

logical works in particular bear interpretation as incorporating the work of his associates contributed under his supervision. In fact, in the specific case we will consider, references to the moving radius principle in *On the Heavens, Movement of Animals,* and *Generation of Animals* provide very interesting points of comparison to both *Mechanics* and *Physical Problems* XVI, so that at least a few benchmarks of the relation of the problem literature to the standard Aristotelian works can be set down. Furthermore, if our interest is the history of mechanics as a natural science, then we are interested in whatever connections truly obtain among the Aristotelian treatises reasonably dated to the fourth century BC, whether those treatises are more or less strictly attributable to Aristotle, the man. Since the boundary between Aristotle and his immediate circle is already blurred historically, there is good reason to consider more neglected texts of the corpus if it can be shown that they shed light on the science and philosophy of that circle.

Qualitative Science

A cautious approach to the style of Aristotle's writings is important for establishing an unbiased history of science of the period. Decoding the evidence about mechanics as a craft and a science in classical Greece has been hampered by supposing that Aristotle's own natural philosophy was entirely "qualititative" rather than mathematical and "quantitative."[17] There has been no expectation that mathematical accounts from the problem literature will be relevant to Aristotle's own philosophy. If one looks at what falls into the categories of quantity versus relation in Aristotle, the charge of qualitativeness is seen to be anachronistic at best.[18] It hardly does justice to the ways mathematics influenced Aristotle's thinking. Nevertheless, it is the most common interpretation of his science. If the

---

17   A recent statement of this point of view on Aristotle is Dear, *Discipline and Experience*, 3. For older versions, see Gillispie, *Objectivity*, 8–16, Einstein and Infeld, *Physics*, 6–11, and Jaki, *Relevance*, ch.1.

18   For instance, Aristotle says that quantity does not admit of more and less. What has quantity is always a definite quantity. More and less, great and small, etc., are relations, instead (*Categories* 6, 5b11–16). The category of relation is usually treated tangentially in studies of substance and attribute in Aristotle. (See Mann, *Discovery*, 140–141; Wedin, *Substance*, 22n30; and Modrak, *Language and Meaning*, 37–43.) A book-length account in English is Hood, *Category of Relation*. See her Preface and Chapter 1 for some reasons for the lack of interest in the category of relation. For an extended commentary on *Categories* 7, see Oehler, *Kategorien*, 292–313.

qualitative interpretation of his natural philosophy is not correct, then comparing the more mathematical accounts in *Physical Problems* and *Mechanics* to Aristotle's treatises in narrative natural philosophy would yield a perspective from which to understand better even Aristotle the man (i.e., the philosopher).

Reassessment of the mathematical and empirical aspects of Aristotle's natural philosophy has been slowed by the predominance of the endoxic (from the Greek word *endoxa*, common opinions) interpretation of Aristotle's empiricism. This is the view that Aristotle derives his starting points in science, perhaps even his first principles, from common consensus, taken as such or analyzed dialectically. This approach became a special theme of Anglo-American interpretation of Aristotle beginning about fifty years ago. The endoxic intepretation of Aristotle's method in science drew the teeth of the charge of qualitativeness by showing that Aristotle's physics was really a work of dialectic starting from the data of ordinary language. Since ordinary language has a deep logic of its own, this type of inquiry, while not comparable to modern science, has perennial validity as the first and most doggedly persistent intellectual organization of human experience of the world.[19] In one way or another, we cannot do without it. The logical acuity of this overall approach to Aristotle fostered some of the most probing and precise scholarship on Aristotle of its generation, opening up new perspectives on his language and ways of reasoning.

Yet, where Aristotle's natural philosophy is concerned, the approach is limited. For one thing, as interpretations of *Prior Analytics* I.30 show, scholars in this tradition have understood *phainomena* in natural science as an accumulation of data from the senses.[20] This has to do with the asso-

---

19   The relevance of the analytic method to understanding Aristotle's natural philosophy was established by Owen's very influential article, *"Tithenai ta phainomena."* Owen's argument concerns the *Physics*. Bolton seeks to re-characterize Aristotle's method in physics as empirical but admits that his argument makes Aristotle's results look "crude" ("Aristotle's Method," 29). In a broader philosophical arena, Sellars gives an account of what he calls the "manifest image," a man-in-the-world characterization of reality constructed from the base of human experience that is different from the "scientific image." He regards classical philosophy as being a development of the manifest image and notes that Anglo-American philosophy since Wittgenstein "has done increasing justice to the manifest image." Sellars seeks to locate with exactitude the actual philosophical limitations of the manifest image. He would seem to be in sympathy both with the view that Greek science is qualitative and with the general strategy of analysts in making qualitative science worthy of modern interest. See Sellars, "Scientific Image."

20   Owen, *"Tithenai,"* 239, a view that perhaps goes back to Shute, *Aristotelian Writings,*

ciation of perceptual *phainomena* with astronomy, which supposedly had a relatively large base of observational data. Experience, understood as *phainomena*, is a big enough collection of observations or conventional opinions from which to draw first principles, either by induction over many cases or by inquiry involving a variety of forms of *a posteriori* reasoning. Furthermore, individual experiences, to be the basis for further inquiry, must be evident, in the sense of being agreed upon by all. There is a strong communal and conventional element to experience, regardless of its origin in sense experience. The endoxic interpretation of Aristotelian experience has reinforced the judgment among historians of science that Aristotle's science is qualitative. Historians of early modern science see Aristotelian experience as having proven unsuitable for natural science, because it gives priority to usual occurrences, rather than to the informative deviation from the usual, and because it takes its principles from appearances superficial enough to be seen at a first glance by anyone.[21]

What we find if we follow the trail of Aristotle's appropriation of a genuinely mechanical principle, the moving radius, is a different conception of experience, one that gives reasons to separate Aristotle's method in dialectic, a logical enterprise, from his procedure in dealing with sense experience, the origin of his own natural science. At least some of Aristotle's scientific experience is grounded in direct kinesthetic awareness of how bodies, including one's own, act and react subject to mechanical forces. This awareness is not always what we would call conscious awareness, and so its generalization—if that term should be used at all—is not an induction over cases in the usual sense. Nor is the principle a matter of agreement. It is both more necessary to bodily orientation in the world and more singularly personal than the notion of the conventional, or even the communal, can capture. Furthermore, this sort of knowledge comes out of thwarted expectations—a fall or a rare quickly improvised

---

4–5. Lennox moderates the Baconian interpretation but still emphasizes the importance of amassing empirical data before explanations can be attempted ("Data and Demonstration," 43). Lloyd notes Aristotle's nuanced use of the term *phainomena* (*Magic*, 137) but also assumes a bank of observations in astronomy of which Aristotle should have made better use (*Explorations*, "Heavenly Aberrations").

21   Dear, *Discipline and Experience*, 18–23, 125, 161–163; Daston, "Fact and Evidence," 109–111. Though Daston's focus on common experience rather than the unusual as the source of medieval science is disputed tangentially for Aristotle's case in the present study, her distinction between evidence and fact—the latter a modern notion implicating a particular idea of objectivity—may be valuable in interpreting Aristotle's scientific practice. Aristotle cited evidence, as we shall see in Chapter 4.

overcoming of natural forces—even more than it does out of regular occurrences. From this standpoint, what amazes or surprises (a wonder,
thauma) does not always signal a chance occurrence, the customary interpretation of Aristotle's view of the unusual, but may be the index of
a natural principle operating in such a way that we inevitably react to it.
The phenomenon captured in the moving radius principle is an interface
between conscious and sensory motor experience and is, to this extent,
of considerable philosophical interest. In the history of Greek science,
the principle externalized and conceptualized the mechanical knowledge
lying within kinesthetic awareness and experiences of un-premeditated
coping with the unusual.

The range of situations in which human understanding capitalizes
upon mechanical knowledge of this sort, expressed in the fourth century
in terms of the moving radius, is very wide. The list of applications is
nearly endless even in the cybernetic age, but I will mention only a few
ancient applications. Besides the many recognizable instances of the lever and balance used in commerce, like the steelyard, there are the axe
and hammer, the fishing line, the whip, the potter's wheel and miller's
stone, the water wheel, the wheel and axle, cylindrical rollers for moving
massive objects like building materials, conical rollers for crushing stone,
oars and rudders, as well as devices on a sailing ship, from the yardarm
and rigging to winches. There are the requirements of rotation of a linear
formation of soldiers or any other sort of parade,[22] as well as all manner
of theatrical devices, including automata that mimic the movements of
animals and humans. It might be said that these are all craft items or
applications and not natural artifacts, but ancient authors did carry the
principle into nature. The author of *Physical Problems* XVI applies the
principle to the revolving motion of projectiles of uneven weight distribution, the shape of shells and stones subject to continual buffeting, the
phenomenon of falling backward due to a blow from behind, and relates
it also to circular growth. Aristotle applies it to the movement of limbs,[23]

---

22   Τὸ ζυγόν (*to zugon*), a term meaning a yoke for oxen was used for the beam of a
balance or for the balance itself. As ζυγός (ὁ), it also meant a rank of soldiers as opposed
to a file (στοῖχος). The problem of maneuvering a rank of soldiers is familiar to anyone
who has had to make a turn as part of a marching band.

23   The main reference here is to *Movement of Animals* 1–7, but Aristotle uses πηδάλιον,
rudder, in the plural for the rudder oars of the nautilus (*History of Animals* IX.37, 622b13), the
springing paddle legs of some insects—these legs bend backward (*History of Animals* IV.7,
532a29)—and in the singular for the tail wings of birds (*Progression of Animals* 10, 710a3).

and from that base in animal motion, to emotional reactions in animals and to embryological development. The principle is also the foundational explanatory trope for differential speeds of heavenly bodies in *On the Heavens* II.

Experience of Mathematical Properties

The ubiquity of the principle and its relation to kinesthetic experience based in the human body provides an occasion to reevaluate the relation of mathematics and physics in Aristotle. The question arises: where did the principle come from? The answer I will give is the following: with the undergoing of mechanical forces and the subsequent reactive utilization of these forces in elementary technique, the circle and its property of movement *were being perceived*. At least in the case of mechanical principles, mathematical objects originate in perception.[24] I will present evidence for this claim as an account of Aristotle's own practice in the construction of parts of his natural philosophy. I am interested in what Aristotle thought and why he thought it. What I present is an interpretation of the details and texture of Aristotle's empiricism.

From one standpoint, it is wholly uncontroversial that, for Aristotle, mathematical objects are perceived. He himself says that mathematical objects and mathematical properties belong to things. His use of a mathematically expressed mechanical principle provides a vantage point from which to evaluate what this means. For the most part, however, mechanics reveals the subject matter of mathematics by means of contrast. For Aristotle, mathematical objects are abstracted not just from body but also from motion. The moving radius principle, however, is a mathematical formulation *of motion*. As such, it is allied with the subject matter of physics more than mathematics. For this reason, though the topic of abstraction is relevant to the mathematical character of mechanics, *aphairesis* will not be my main topic of interest.[25] Indeed, the difficulty in

---

24   Recent philosophy of mathematics relevant to this claim include Philip Kitcher, *Mathematical Knowledge*, and Penelope Maddy, *Realism*. Each develops the position that mathematical objects are perceived. Kitcher calls for a history of mathematics informed by the recognition that "a very limited amount of our mathematical knowledge can be obtained by observations and manipulations of ordinary things. Upon this small basis we erect the powerful general theories of modern mathematics" (92). Husserlian phenomenology has made a strong contribution to understanding how mathematical objects are perceived. See Husserl, *Crisis*, §9a, and Drummond, "Perceptual Roots."

25   On this topic, see in particular Cleary, "Terminology of 'Abstraction.'" Other rele-

seeing that mathematics could figure in Aristotle's thought in some other way than as pure mathematics is one reason the significance of mechanics in his thought has not been noticed. A broader concern of my study, then, is to introduce another way of looking at mathematics in Aristotle.

Interpretation of the relation of mathematics and physics in Aristotle has justifiably focused on his systematic pronouncements on the limits of mathematical explanation in physical science. The settled doctrine became this: although mathematics sometimes gives the reason why (*dioti*) something occurs as it does (circular wounds heal slower than elongated wounds), this "reason why" remains a remote cause insofar as it is not drawn from the principles of physics itself. The mathematical science that explains a physical phenomenon remains subordinated to its mathematical genus—optics is subordinated to geometry—but has principles that are a mixture of mathematics and physical hypothesis, e.g. the visual ray.[26] We need to bear in mind, however, as recent scholarship shows, that the systematic pronouncements of Plato and Aristotle on the status of mathematics were in their own time newly minted and a matter of on-going probing and debate.[27] There is evidence in Aristotle's writings of a very significant understory—both in the sense of growth below the tall trees of philosophical doctrine and in the sense of a second narrative—an understory of mathematical insights and principles being drawn directly into physical accounts. The most obvious example is one treated regularly by scholars, Aristotle's analysis of the continuum in the *Physics*. Aristotle does not abstract the continuum from physical magnitude in *Physics* IV–VI. Indeed, the oft-cited foundational problems in the account arise from this fact. My examination of Aristotle's empiricism about mathematical

---

vant studies include Mueller, "Geometrical Objects," Modrak, "Mathematics," and Lear, "Philosophy of Mathematics." Hussey distinguishes different ways that mathematics appears in Aristotle's writings, one of which is "mathematical investigations into questions which underlie whole fields of natural science" ("Aristotle and Mathematics," 218). He focuses on natural continua, however, and still regards abstraction as central to understanding how mathematics concerns the world (219).

26   See in particular *Posterior Analytics* I.7 and I.13, 78b34–79a16. On the medieval interpretation of these passages that remains influential in interpretation of Aristotle to the present day, see Weisheipl, "Classification of the Sciences," Sylla, "Experience and Demonstration," and Grant, *Natural Philosophy*, 155–170.

27   Though Zhmud and Huffman differ on points of interpretation (e.g., about Archytas as the founder of mechanics), they each present a vivid picture of the relation between physics and mathematics as an intellectual work in progress in the 5th–4th centuries (Zhmud, *Origin*, 61–76, 100–133; Huffman, *Archytas*, 76, 83–89).

objects provides a reason why Aristotle would not have been troubled about this.

In what follows, I shall sometimes have to use the term "mathematical" in a way that reflects modern usage, where mathematical objects and traits are characterized in terms of their separate subject matter. I do this to avoid the continual circumlocution of describing these traits in the way they are perceived—as empirical and physical but with features that, when analyzed, are separable into a distinctive subject matter. If someone were to say that the difficulty of eliminating the term "mathematical" shows mathematics really originates in reason and not the senses, my rejoinder would be that mechanics is incurably concrete at this period of time, because of two things: its involvement with motion and the fact of weight. Motion and weight are not separable as part of the Platonic or Aristotelian subject matter of mathematics, even though they manifest traits identifiable as mathematical. The difficulty of reconciling weight in particular to the emerging fourth century consensus about the nature of mathematics is one reason that mechanics as a science went underground, so to speak, issuing in the narrative natural science of *Physics, On Generation and Corruption,* and *Movement of Animals.* Aristotle believed he was taking into this narrative science many of the lessons learned empirically from the mathematical features of things. That mechanics was recognized as a subject matter by means of traits that could be schematized mathematically does not mean these traits were purely mathematical all along. The traits were mechanical because they were perceived in motion and because they appeared repeatedly the same way in the behavior of weight. Especially in the ancient period, mechanics was not reducible to mathematics.

Experience and *Dunamis*

Unlike continuity and infinite divisibility, the moving radius principle has been overlooked as an example of a mathematical insight appropriated by Aristotle for his natural philosophy. We shall see that Aristotle both (1) makes use in physics of mathematical features of the principle—enhancement of effect in proportion to the distance of the effect from its points of origin—and more profoundly, (2) understands the principle to index natural powers. In relation to power, *dunamis,* scholars have noted the importance in classical philosophy of the idea that action is the index of being, what really exists. What can produce an effect is real.[28] Both Plato and Aristotle used the term *dunamis* for the ability to produce action, including reaction. What produces action is real. It seems clear then that the lever could be both exemplary and instructive with respect to *dunamis*. In its own sphere of mechanical actioh, the lever unveils power. As we shall see, in *Movement of Animals* 1 and 7 and *Generation of Animals* II.1 and 5, Aristotle takes advantage of just this exemplary feature of the lever. *Dunamis* in living systems is linked by Aristotle to the principle of the lever by means of the trope of the rolling cone and the example of *automata*. Taking the principle as instructive, he applies it beyond the mechanics of exerted forces, weights, and locomotion to other natural situations in which the effect exceeds its cause in magnitude and diversity of type.

The question might be raised, though, whether the lever does unveil power or whether it simply, by arrangement, brings about a momentary concentration of force, what is called mechanical advantage, something easily dissipated by breaking up the arrangement and hence not itself real. The *assembly* of a block and tackle, for instance, accounts for its magnification of force. The question here is what Aristotle thought about that. The query calls to mind the ancient debate framed by Aristotle between himself and Democritus. Democritus said that what is real are the atoms, which only appear differently because of arrangement, shape, and size. It would seem that part of Aristotle's response to Democritus is precisely that the atoms cannot bring about the enrichment and enhancement of action typical, not just of living systems, but of mechanical ones too.[29] Natural power is a flagrant irregularity by atomist standards, something that cannot be digested by their explanatory accounts. It is an indication that their principles are too meager. To take the craft example, the atomist has to claim, unconvincingly, that the power of simple machines is only an appearance. This shows that there is a strong natural philosophical

---

28   Compare Plato's *Sophist* 248c5 and Aristotle's *Metaphysics* Θ.1, 1046a11 on power or potency (δύναμις, *dunamis*) as the real (τὸ ὄν). Frede makes the comparison in the course of his argument that the root philosophical meaning of Aristotle's potentiality is its meaning in relation to motion ("Notion of Potentiality," 181). He alludes without elaboration to a "tradition in Greek thought" whereby what can produce an effect in something must be real. Gerson believes this passage in Plato (242d–249d) and the conception of the real it contains are an important link between Plato and Aristotle (*Other Platonists*, 39–41).

29   For relevant passages in Aristotle on Democritus, see *Parts of Animals* I.1, 640b30–641a17 and *On Generation and Corruption* I.2, 315a34–b15.

reason for action, or actuality (*energeia*), to be central to Aristotle's first principles. It is not only a matter of how substance should be conceived metaphysically. Enhanced action is the index of previously latent power. That powers depend on contributing causes only shows that powers are in the world of generation and corruption that depends on such causes. It is only in such a world, also, that there are *dunameis*, because powers are potencies for change.

The atomists' acknowledgment of the need for materials to be configured for more complex entities to exist may be what makes Aristotle say Democritus came close to the real explanatory principle of essence, or actuality. For Aristotle, arrangement is analogous to actuality or form.[30] The argument to be made is that one of Aristotle's routes to principles like form, potentiality, and actuality was by means of the recognition of natural powers empirically grasped. We shall see that this route to principles was guided along the way by a mechanical rule of action expressed variously and applied to a range of phenomena. Sometimes, as in his astronomy, the rule is allied not with powers, since the heavens do not undergo change in the way the sublunary realm does, but with an idea of distribution of force through a rigid body. It will be important, in considering the range of these cases, that experience of natural phenomena, *empeiria*, was not a mass of data but had a mathematical structure already.

This study is relevant to the ongoing assessment of the meaning of *dunamis* in Aristotle's philosophy. My results reinforce the idea that taking the primary sense of Aristotelian *dunamis* in the terms of potentiality (Latin, *potentia, potentialitas*), understood as correlated to substantial form in a metaphysical sense, has for modern readers emptied the concept of content. Frede makes this point on philosophical grounds, analyzing Aristotle's *Metaphysics*. I will make the point in the context of Aristotle's natural philosophy as it extends into *Movement of Animals, Physical Problems,* and *Mechanics*. A criticism of the *dunamis* concept for centuries has been that it is tautologous. The criticism is so common that it is cited over and over in the shorthand of Molière's sleeping draught, which works because of its "dormitive power." Potentiality, or potency, taken in the realm of natural philosophy, is only a name that conveys nothing

---

30   *Metaphysics* H.2, 1043a5. For other references to Democritus as on the right track but falling short, see *Parts of Animals* I.1, 642a24–31, *On Generation and Corruption* I.2, 315a35, *Metaphysics* H.2, 1042b9–1043a7.

more than the very result it was supposed to explain.[31] In fact, there is plentiful evidence that *dunamis* was, for Aristotle, an empirical concept closely linked to a universalizing mathematical rule. It was content-rich physically and explanatory in mathematical terms. The case of Aristotle's appropriation of the moving radius principle, analyzed in repeated instances, also shows that his concept of experience was more sophisticated scientifically than it is usually taken to be. The contrast of experience and experiment still holds in reference to Aristotle. He did not do experiments as we find them in early modern science. Some of the things supposedly only learned from experiment, however, Aristotle gained by judicious analysis of what he called *phainomena*. Most importantly, this case study shows that Aristotle had a philosophy of nature, not just a philosophy of common opinions about nature. He does not simply read physical principles off the surface of things, and his way of analyzing the limitations of received explanations was not primarily to discern their logical inconsistencies. His philosophy of nature is scientific in its method and empirical temper, in a sense of "scientific" usually reserved for early modern and later science.

Powers and Mechanical Philosophy

The action-enhancing features Aristotle observed in both simple machines and living things contributed to his great confidence in deploying the *dunamis* concept widely in his philosophy. Once this connection is suggested and then bolstered by textual evidence, it seems very reasonable. Indeed, my argument is that the very mundane familiarity of experiences of mechanical advantage and disadvantage ensured that phenomena of this sort would play an important role in Aristotle's science. This need not be a contentious point. A philosopher could acknowledge it and perhaps still maintain that it has very little to do with Aristotle's real philosophy, his logic and metaphysics. So, why has the physical base for the *dunamis* concept not been recognized before? One reason is the received historiography of mechanics. Mechanics is the invention of modern science. Before the early modern period, there was only a rudimentary theoretical understanding of simple machines and a few fragmented analyses of the balance in the Middle Ages. This part of the historiography has a certain amount of truth to it, in part because of the poor survival rate

---

31   For a recent statement of the problem and one solution, see Graham, "Prime Matter."

of ancient texts in mechanics and mathematics.[32] The problem has been the alliance of this judgment with another, namely, that the mathematical science of mechanics appropriately issues in a single philosophy of nature, the mechanical philosophy. In the mechanical philosophy of nature, matter is all of the same kind though divided into tiny parts, which are either atomic or infinitely divisible. Differences in things originate from the size, shape, speed, impact, and accidental coherence of atoms. Power is replaced by force, the rigidity of bodies, and motion as causes.

Fortunately, recent scholarship undertaken in a variety of venues is probing the meaning of "mechanism" in the history of science and gives reason to question the inevitability of the alliance of mechanics with mechanical philosophy.[33] Indeed, it has become clear that early modern developments in mechanics were fed by rediscovery of the ancient accounts of simple machines. The mechanical philosophy came later.[34] I shall not belabor the point that, considered both historically and philosophically, principles from mechanics may plausibly foster either a powers model of nature or a matter-in-motion model. What we shall see, however, is that a powers model is closely linked to the practical side of mechanics, because power was first intelligible as a natural source of the effects that emerge in machine arrangements. Interestingly, a mechanical philosophy, such as that of Descartes or Mersenne, is more theoretical—both in the sense of being based on principles conceived in a purely rational way and in the sense of being separated from use and experience—than a powers model.[35] It is important to recognize that in matters of natural philosophy the division between practical and theoretical was not rigid for Aristotle and his school. Aristotle understood that machines work as they do because of underlying natural principles.

---

32   See the Introduction to Laird and Roux, *Mechanics and Natural Philosophy*, for the range of textual sources where mechanics might be found before the seventeenth century.

33   Berryman, *Mechanical Hypothesis*, ch.1, and "Ancient Automata"; Des Chene, *Spirits and Clocks*; Dear, *Intelligibility*, ch.1; Meli, *Thinking*, ch.1 and 5; Machamer, Darden, and Craver, "Thinking About Mechanisms."

34   Meli points to the emergence of theoretical interest in machines in the sixteenth century. It is important that the Aristotelian *Mechanics* was not available in the Middle Ages but was published in Italy for the first time at the end of the fifteenth century. It was later, in the middle of the seventeenth century, that the mechanical philosophy became "a leading player on the intellectual scene" (*Thinking*, 18–19, 135–140).

35   Newton wished to ally his mechanical philosophy with the ancient tradition of machines and make it more methodological. See his Preface to the *Principia* and Dear, *Intelligibility*, 31–38.

Automata in Plato and Aristotle

The idea that the animal or human body is a machine, or works like a machine, is associated with the mechanical philosophy of the early modern period. Though connotations of the machine-model vary with the author, it is basically Democritean: shape, arrangement or disposition, and linkage of parts define the unity of a functioning body.[36] Methodologically, the aim is to reproduce living phenomena by artifice. Simulation proves causation.[37] Both Plato and Aristotle spoke of animals and their parts by alluding to *automata* and linkage of parts, though considerably less often than we find in early modern texts. As might be expected, their aims in citing simple machines were quite different from those of Descartes, for instance. Yet, Aristotle for his part did not simply borrow *automata* to be a model for the powers of natural things. Though I used the term "powers model" in the previous section to make clear an important contrast in philosophy of nature, in the main part of the book I will avoid use of the term "model" in discussing references to *automata* in Plato and Aristotle. This is because their own command of the issues of likeness, illusion, and analogy reached deeper than simply taking man-made self-movers as either imitations or epistemic models.

For understanding the role of machines in ancient philosophical thought, the word "device" is a better translation of the Greek word, μηχανή, than "machine." Device may mean either

a. contrivance, i.e., construal or arrangement of existing things in a way that makes them instrumental to an otherwise unrealizable end, or

b. the instrument made by contrivance.

Plato and Aristotle tend to take the two meanings together. They were quick to see a link between the simplest device, like a wooden simulacrum on a stick, and more complex contrived phenomena, like *automata*.[38] This

---

36 On this aspect of early modern modeling of living things, see Des Chene, *Spirits and Clocks*, 83–88, 125–131.

37 This statement simplifies the matter for the sake of comparison. Descartes' *Traité de l'Homme*, for instance, works on several levels to overcome limitations of the machine model. The salient point, however, is that simulation has a very different import in ancient uses of *automata*.

38 These were artificial figures designed to be capable of a range of movements usually

is a sign that they were not simply trying to explain natural things as machines. Device was a source of enlightenment, a disclosure of reality that was otherwise inaccessible. In device, the distinction between the real as given (*phusis*) and what else can come from the real demands attention. Real and its derived counterpart are separated. From the beginning, device appeared in feats of subterfuge or outwitting another, so that what is real and what can come from the real often merged after their separation. What could be done or accomplished—the overcoming or outwitting—was real. To this extent, device did not have to be taken as artificial or counterfeit, even when used by the illusionist.[39] So, Aristotle says that wonder is banished by knowing the cause (*archê*) of a wondrous phenomenon.[40]

Device makes possible the conception of image and artifice. A puzzling part of Plato's Allegory of the Cave in the *Republic* has always been that the shadows seen by the prisoners are cast not by real living things from the world above but by statues of men and animals being carried along a road.[41] The prisoners see shadows of the objects carried but no shadows of those carrying the objects. The road is bordered by a little wall that Plato likens to the puppeteer's screen (τὸ παράφραγμα) like the bottom frame of a Punch and Judy show. Here the puppets seem of the crudest sort, no more than images held aloft. Their relative simplicity is of value in the story. They are likenesses moving but without principles of movement beyond the humans carrying them.

This introduction of the illusionist's show deepens and complicates the significance of image. The walkers along the road are part of a pageant that lays claim to be something other than it is. The way Plato interweaves reality, image, and ideology makes clear that artifice will not be banished soon from the city or the soul. Life by images is impervious

---

for a theatrical presentation (but see the reference in Homer, *Iliad*, treated in Chapter 3). Hero of Alexandria (AD first century) describes the apparatus for producing these movements as part of an automatic theater conceived as a whole. Whether or not Plato and Aristotle knew the entire automatic theater of Hero's design, they both speak of apparently jointed figures moved by sticks or wires attached to limbs of the figures. Both allude to or address directly the principle behind the mimetic effects. Simple and complex devices were made in accordance with the same few principles.

39   Schiefsky argues against the interpretation of ancient mechanics as trickery and as contrary to nature. See his "Art and Nature," 67–68.

40   *Metaphysics* A.2, 983a12–21, *Mechanics* 1, 848a34–36.

41   *Republic* VII, 514b8–c2.

even to human discourse, which Plato presents as irrelevant to his allegory (some carriers of images speak, some do not). It is not clear that Plato could have made his point as well counting on the idea of image alone. He borrows from the store of theatrical device the idea of re-presentation of the real. Plato would persuade us that this re-presentation is different from what is real. In the *Republic*, the pageant is not to be trusted.

One could note that the allusion to crafted figures here is hardly one to foster belief in an underlying physical reality revealed by theatrical display. Plato says, however, that the figures are made, engineered (εἰργασμένα) in stone, wood, and a variety of materials suitable for working into shapes. So, they have whatever substance contributing materials can give them. His point in the *Republic* is that this is no genuine reality (τὸ ὄν) at all.[42] He uses references to theatrical wonders in a more realistic fashion in other contexts and also uses device as a trope for the working of a discussion.[43] However utilized, what is important is that device is the staging area for philosophical distinctions while remaining itself outside the notional. It escapes the net of conceptualization. This is most clear in the Allegory of the Cave, but Aristotle uses device similarly to make key philosophical distinctions—between power and actuality, for instance. His reference to *automata* in *Movement of Animals* 7 is a prime example of the combination of crude device, a tóy wagon, and complex contrivance to make a single point about the universality of natural powers. In Aristotle, simple machines provide a setting for his own distinctive kind of analogical thinking.[44]

With regard to taking machines as models óf the living, then, the ancients had an advantage over early modern philosophers in the newness of their conceptions of artifice and image. By the early modern period, the machine is itself an image. For Plato and Aristotle, on the other hand, device makes possible the conception of artifice—imitation or contrivance considered straightforwardly as such—but device itself is not reducible

---

42   He says they are φλυαρία, nonsense. See 515c–d.

43   He thus regards a discussion or argument as a scaffolding or contrivance for (usually false) display. See, for instance, *Republic* VII, 533c4. In *Sophist* 235b5, Socrates speaks of a net contrived from instruments of speech that can catch the sophist who is a maker of wonders. Sometimes a discussion becomes an unwieldy contraption, as in *Euthyphro* 15b–c, moving around where we would not wish it to go. Socrates here likens Euthyphro to Daedalus.

44   For a valuable survey of Aristotle's use of machine analogies in *Movement of Animals*, see Bénatouïl, "L'usage des analogies," discussed below in Chapter 5.

to imitation. Philosophically, device is as fundamental as nature (*phusis*) in classical philosophy, but it is not always opposed to nature. To understand the role of simple machines in Aristotle's natural philosophy, then, we must recover at least for a time the spontaneous belief or assent of this original philosophical outlook, where the distinctions among real, natural, artificial, and conceptual were first being made. Device could unveil nature, suggest the limit of nature at supra-natural reality, and disclose nature's principles. Certainly, the scientific attitude that has been delineated as distinctive to mechanics—thinking along with the very behavior of material things—was not foreign to Greek science and the natural philosophy based on it.[45]

---

45   Meli delineates the theme of thinking with objects as a feature of the progress of mechanics in the seventeenth century (*Thinking*, 2–4).

Chapter 2

Expressions of the Moving Radius Principle in the Fourth Century BC

One indication of the significance of the principle examined in this study is that it appears in philosophical and scientific texts of the classical period in different forms and applied to a wide range of natural and craft phenomena. In some cases, it is stated clearly as a mathematical property of the circle. At other times, it is treated as barely separable from the phenomenon it structures. *Mechanics* is the earliest surviving text whose entire topic is mechanics and mechanical effects in simple machines. The treatise is an extended treatment of the moving radius principle both mathematically and in terms of its practical applications. In the text, the moving radius explains the lever, and the lever is then shown to be the root of a host of devices in current use. The writing of *Mechanics* should probably be dated to roughly fifty years after Aristotle's own floruit. Some scholars have placed the text in the circle of Aristotle's own research associates, however, or even made it the work of Aristotle himself.[46] My treatment of *Physical Problems* XVI under the heading of the fourth century assumes what is yet to be established by careful assembly of facts and interpretation in this book, namely that the mechanics in Book XVI can be dated this early. The purpose of the present chapter, however, is simply to display the range of expressions of the principle, and I ask the reader's indulgence with the present classification for that purpose.

---

46   On the question of the text's authenticity, see Krafft, *Betrachtungsweise*, 13–20, Bottecchia-Dehò, *Meccanici*, 27–51, and Schneider, *Technikverständnis*, 234n103.

The Aristotelian *Mechanics*

Famously, *Mechanics* begins with the human response of wonder (θαυμάζεται) both at occurrences in nature and accomplishments of craft. We wonder at natural things whose cause is obscure and at human actions that overcome or rule nature with the aid of craft. Mechanics (μηχανή) is the part of craft by which the lesser rules the greater and things having a small force move great weights (847a22–24). It is important to keep in mind this fairly narrow definition of mechanics, because the same reversal of ordinary relations of force and rule occurs in nature. Wonder is the human reaction to mechanical phenomena in either sphere. Mechanics is associated then with devices of human origin, but it has many points of contact with mathematics and physics (847a27), subject matters the author understands to be theoretical.[47] He says that mechanical problems (i.e., situations where the lesser rules the greater) are not the same as physical problems but are not entirely separate from them either (847a25–26).[48]

Any configuration, contrived or natural, that involves moving a great weight by a small force falls into the genus of the lever (μοχλός).[49] In the final analysis, it is the circle that accounts for the lever's ability to reverse conditions of force and weight:

> What takes place in the balance can be referred to the circle, and what occurs in the lever, to the balance, and nearly all other mechanical motions to the lever. Further, because *none of the points on a line drawn from the center of the same circle are moving at the same speed but the one further from*

---

47   The author salutes Aristotle's doctrine of the relation of mathematics and physics without conforming to it, by saying that the how or because (τὸ ὥς) in mechanics is made plain through mathematics while that to which the mathematical pertains (τὸ περὶ ὅ) is made plain through physics. (Compare *Posterior Analytics* I.13, 79a7–13.) This seems a weaker assertion of the priority of physics over mathematics in giving the "why" (διότι) than Aristotle claims for physics in *Physics* II.2, 193b31–94a7 or *Metaphysics* E.1, 1026a1–18.

48   On the ancient understanding of the natural in relation to simple machines, see Schiefsky, "Art and Nature."

49   Μοχλός, *mochlos*, is an old word. It is listed in *L-S* as a root. It means any bar used for lodging something securely, e.g., bars across a gate, or a bar that moves a weight. One can note the similarity of μοχλός to μόχθος (*mochthos*), toil or hardship, whose root is μόγος (*mogos*), trouble or distress. The lever looses toil. No connection between the words is established, however.

> *the stationary limit always moves faster*, many marvels in the
> movements of circles come about, and these will be evident in
> the following problems.[50] (848a12–19)

The part of the quotation I have italicized states the principle of the lever
in the simplest terms possible considered kinematically. There is only a
line stationary at one extremity and rotating about that stationary point.
A radius is thus revolving, and the points along the radius are moving at
different speeds. We can imagine the line as a rod rotating on a horizontal surface and describing arcs
(**Figure 2.1**). This simplest formulation does not include even
the conception of concentric
circles. It says that the moving
radius generates arcs or circles
but does not mention concentric
circles.[51]

Figure 2.1

Later in *Mechanics*, the principle is formulated in terms of radii lying
opposite one another and receiving the same force. This formulation is
more obviously relevant to practical mechanics. The one force applied
at an end of a lever (a balance of unequal beams) produces larger and
smaller movements (distance covered in the same time) at the longer and
shorter ends of the beam. In the course of *Mechanics* 1, this version is
stated in terms of the lever, the balance, or the circle.

1. A lever moves a weight that cannot be moved without it. The
    weight is displaced quickly and by application of a small force,
    even though the lever contributes additional weight to what is to
    be moved (847b11–15).

2. Larger balances are more accurate than smaller ones (848b3).
    This is because, by application of the same force, the arm of a

---

50   The text used is Bottecchia, *Mechanica*. The translation of this passage is by the
author, using Forster's locution, "referred to," for ἀνάγεται εἰς. I avoid his translation of
τὰ γινόμενα as "phenomena."

51   In *Elements* I, propositions 1–3, Euclid uses the supposition of a rotating line to make
a circle: With center B and distance BC, let the circle BCD be described (prop. 2). For this
construction, he relies on postulate 3 of Book I: To describe a circle with any center and
any distance. He makes additional constructions based on radii to delimit line segments
equal to one another.

longer beam covers in the same time a greater distance than the arm of a shorter beam. A greater distance is more easily perceived (849b28).

3. Subject to the same force, a point more distant from the center of a circle moves faster than one nearer (848b5).

The state of affairs is captured simply in the representation of opposite arcs in **Figure 2.2**. A force acts similarly though in opposite directions at the ends of the beam, but the effect is greater at one end.

This version of the principle is clearly dependent on the simplest one, the single moving radius, but it introduces a notion of force as a single push or impulse capable of initiating movement. Effect manifest in action is central to the cogency of the presentation. Force is measurable in terms of arc-distances covered at either end of the beam. In this way, the circumferences of concentric circles enter within the explanatory frame of the ac-

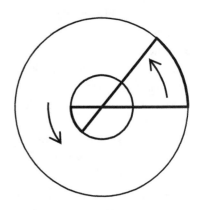

Figure 2.2

count. Since the context is the lever, there is a force exerted at one end of the beam, while a weight is moved at the other end. For force exerted, the author uses the terms, *ischus* and *dunamis*, often without discernible difference in meaning. Weight, *baros*, is often treated as a countervailing force. Whether the author's conceptualization of weight and force carries significance for the history of physics in antiquity or whether his terms are words of ordinary usages employed loosely within an account that is mainly kinematic is a question of interest about the *Mechanics*. For understanding basic expressions of the principle, however, what is important is that this second formulation of the principle shifts attention from a moving radius to arcs lying opposite one another, understanding these as distances covered in the same time. The comparison of arc-lengths closer and further away from a central point links this more practical version of the principle to the formulation in Plato and Aristotle.[52]

52 There are variations of the principle that appear in the course of the author's applica-

Two Versions in Plato and Aristotle

Two ways of expressing the moving radius principle are found in both Plato and Aristotle. The first is that points moving circularly at different distances from a common center are covering different distances in the same time.[53] This is an expression of the moving radius principle that does not suppose the longer and shorter distances are either points on the same radius or opposite one another. Nevertheless, the proportional relation among their speeds means the moving points are somehow linked (**Figure 2.3a and 2.3b**). Placing the arcs on a disk in Figure 2.3b illustrates the linkage, which Aristotle expresses in *On the Heavens* II.8 by saying circles are bound (ἐνδεδεμένων) to a central point (289b35).[54]

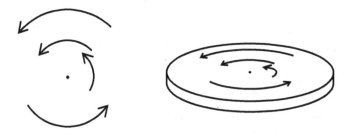

Figures 2.3a & 2.3b

Distances covered by these points scattered about a central point are arc-distances of larger and smaller concentric circles. The points are endpoints of radii, but neither Plato nor Aristotle uses a word for "radius"[55]

---

tion of the moving radius to different devices in *Mechanics*. A few of these will be cited at the end of the chapter, and more are treated in the chapter on *Mechanics*. For the moment, I focus on expressions of the principle most relevant to Aristotle's natural philosophy.

53   Plato, *Laws* X, 893c–d; Aristotle, *On the Heavens* II.8 and *Movement of Animals* 1 and 7, all treated below.

54   It is worth noting the similarity of Figure 2.3a to a time-lapse photograph of the diurnal movements of stars around the celestial pole. Without photography, the Greeks would have noted such movement. The principle may have been regarded as relevant to one of the chief functions of astronomy in the fourth century, the tracking of the risings and settings of the heavenly bodies. Eudoxus' writings on this topic have not survived. Treatises of Autolycus of Pitane, a contemporary of Aristotle, were preserved as part of the Little Astronomy. They are *On the Moving Sphere* and *On Risings and Settings*. (See Autolycus, "La Sphère en mouvement," ed. Aujac.)

55   Διάμετρον (*diametron*), diameter, was used by ancient authors for the radius, chord,

or even the locution of *Mechanics* 1,"line drawn from a center." They speak in terms of the size of circles or distance (*diastêma*) from a central point. The narrower formulation in terms of a single moving radius must have been clear to them, however, because both rely on the correlation by which arc-lengths of concentric circles covered in the same time have the same ratio as the lengths of their distances from a central point:

$$\frac{Arc\,length_A}{Arc\,length_B} \propto \frac{d_A}{d_B}$$

Although this proportion states a property of the circle, it is taken by our authors only in relation to motion.[56] Rotation of a radius adds the dimension of speed, i.e., distance covered in a time. The correlate arc-distances are arcs covered in the same time. A definite time provides the constant that makes the comparison of arcs of different circles meaningful.

To say that points at different distances from a center move faster or slower involves a presumption that a segment of the circumference of the larger concentric circle is a longer curved line than a segment of the smaller circle. Because there was no common measure for the diameter and circumference of a circle and no method for measuring the size of an arc apart from the still unsatisfactory methods for squaring the circle, whenever this principle is used, the conception of relative size of arcs

---

or diameter of a circle as well as for the diagonal of a polygon, especially rectangles. Aristotle uses the word in *Movement of Animals* 3 for a line from the earth to the heavens in the context of criticizing a version of the Atlas myth (699a29).

56   To the modern sensibility, the proportion derives from the relation of circumference and diameter for a circle. This relation for the ancients was bound up with the problems of approximating the value of the number later called π and also with squaring the circle. The problem of squaring the circle was to construct a rectilinear figure with the same area as a given circle. Areas were the issue early on, not measurement of circumference. The Rhind Papyrus (2nd millennium BC) contained an approximation of π expressed in terms of area of a circle. Among predecessors of Plato and Aristotle in the Greek tradition, Thales is said to have shown that the diameter divides the circle in half. Anaxagoras is reported to have devoted attention to the squaring of the circle. We have the most information about Archimedes' work in the approximation of π and squaring the circle, in particular from his treatise *Measurement of the Circle*. In this work, Archimedes derives the ratio between the circumference and diameter of a circle. His methods were in general Eudoxan. He used infinite divisibility and approaching limits to render results for measurement of the circumference and area of the circle. The proposition that circumferences of circles have the same ratio as their diameters was proven by Pappus. Ptolemy offered an approximation of the relation of diameter and circumference of a circle. On these topics, see Heath, *History*, vol. 1, 220–235, Knorr, *Geometric Problems*, 76–86, 153–170, and Dijksterhuis, *Archimedes*, 222–241.

remains vague. Arcs of different circles are not directly comparable, since the curve of the arc of one circle cannot be fitted onto the other (**Figure 2.4a** and **2.4b**). Nor can the two arcs be stretched out alongside one an-

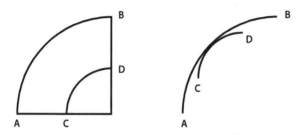

Figures 2.4a &2.4b

other in straight lines, like bits of string. Archimedes' formulation of the ratio of the diameter and circumference of a circle (late third century BC) does involve the construction of a straight line the same length as the circumference,[57] but in the fourth century, straight and curved lines were regarded as incommensurable. They are not superposable and are only comparable by the mediation of ratios. The formulation in terms of the moving radius makes a ratio of arc-lengths knowable by a ratio of radius lengths. The moving radius principle thus enables a finessing strategy: it relates heterogeneous magnitudes that cannot otherwise be made equal or multiple. As such, it allows factors that later in the history of science were treated as separate (e.g., weight and force) to appear as causes of motion in a similar way. Weight, force, and distance are covered by a single broad mathematical principle.

The second formulation of the principle in Plato and Aristotle, closely related to the first, is that revolving concentric circles are traveling at different speeds. This formulation focuses on the path of a point on a circumference of a rotating circle and not on the path of points scattered at different distances from a center. Mathematically, the two formulations are equivalent, and Plato presents them together in *Laws* X, 893c–d:

> And we observe that in this revolution [circles revolving when their common center remains immobile], a motion such that

---

57   See Prop. 1 of *Measurement of the Circle* (Heath, *Archimedes*, 91–98) and Dijksterhuis, *Archimedes*, 222–223.

> it covers the largest and smallest circles in the same time dis-
> tributes itself proportionately[58] to small and large [circles] and
> is correspondingly slower and faster. This is the source of all
> sorts of wonderful phenomena,[59] since there are set in motion
> smaller and larger circles at corresponding slower and faster
> speeds—an effect one might have expected to be impossible.
> (893c7–d5)[60]

Plato speaks both of circles revolving in place and speeds that vary in
relation to distance from a single center. His words show that the moving
radius and revolving concentric circles were closely related characterizations of the principle. Note also that the principle was already considered the root phenomenon of surprises and marvels. When Plato says
that motion distributes itself so as to produce faster and slower speeds,
he brings into play some sort of ordered apportionment of motion among
the circles. He reiterates this point with his reference to faster and slower
speeds agreeing or corresponding (ὁμολογούμενα) (893d4). The revolving circles are connected, like points on a revolving disk (**Figure 2.3b**).

   This is Plato's most explicit reference to the moving radius principle
in astronomy. Plato understood, in both the *Timaeus* and the myth of Er
in the *Republic*,[61] that the outermost heavenly sphere carries the planets
around with it, that there is a zodiacal band within which the planets move
more slowly than the stars, and that the planets are moving with contrary
circular movements that counter the overall cosmic movement. The motion of the outer sphere is the movement of the Same in the *Timaeus*.
The overall movement imparted by the outer sphere to the cosmos is the
movement produced by the Spindle of Necessity in the spectacular vision
of the Myth of Er in *Republic* 616c–d. The spindle (ἄτρακτον) is the axis
of the whole cosmos. In the Myth of Er, Plato understands the spindle as
involved with a whorl (σφόνδυλον) around it, but he keeps to domestic
metaphors of the whorl—spinning an axis with yarns balanced on two
sides and fitting bowls inside one another. He does not use the terms δίνη
or δίνησις for the whirling movement. He maintains an idea of necessity

---

58   ἀνὰ λόγον ἑαυτὴν διανέμει.

59   διὸ δὴ τῶν θαυμαστῶν ἁπάντων πηγὴ γέγονεν.

60   The translation is modified from Saunders' translation in *Complete Works of Plato*,
ed. Cooper.

61   *Timaeus* 36b–d; *Republic* 616b–617c. See also *Epinomis* 987b, where Plato speaks
of an eighth sphere moving in the opposite direction to the other circles and carrying all
things with it.

reigning within the space of the cosmos along with references to it being hollow (616d3–5). So, he would seem to understand the influence on the things within it of a rotating large circumference, but he does not speak in the *Republic* of inner circles moving more slowly with the movement of the whole cosmos while the stars move faster. He does not mention any speeds of heavenly bodies moving with the outer sphere at a speed proportional to their distances from the outer sphere.

In *On the Heavens* II.8, Aristotle presents a formulation more in keeping with Plato's account in the *Laws,* but he develops it to a much greater extent,[62] returning to the topic in chapters 10–12. The context is his argument that it is the circles to which the heavenly bodies are bound that are moving and not the heavenly bodies themselves.[63] He says that it is necessary that the speeds of circles be in proportion (ἀνάλογον ἔχειν) to their size. Larger circles move faster (289b15–18). He repeats the principle later: "It is reasonable that, of circles with the same center, the speed of the larger circle is faster" (289b35). He likens "other cases" (presumably rectilinear movement) to revolution in this respect. In each, the motion proper to the greater body is the faster (290a1–2).[64] Aristotle thus presents the principle at a high level of generality and as widely applicable and known. Like Plato in the *Laws,* he understands speed in terms of distances covered in the same time along circumferences of larger and smaller circles.

Aristotle presents an additional reason for the proportion, however. Of segments of concentric circles cut by the same two radii,[65] the segment of the larger circle is the larger arc and so it is reasonable that the larger circle is moving faster in the same time (290a2–5). Here he presents a geometrical picture involving rays from a central point that cut arcs on different circles. There are then three slightly different formulations of the principle in Plato and Aristotle. It is expressed in terms of

---

62   This contrast may support the idea that Plato knew more about Eudoxus' astronomy by the time he wrote the *Laws* than he had known before. Eudoxus wrote a treatise, *On Speeds,* which is lost. Simplicius preserves a portion of *On Speeds* in his commentary on *On the Heavens* II.10 (*Commentaria in Aristotelem Graeca* [hereafter *CAG*], vol. 7, ed. Heiberg, 492.31–497.8.

63   Aristotle says both that the stars are bound (ἐνδεδεμένα) to the circles, and the circles are bound to a common center (289b32–35).

64   In *Physics* VIII.9, 265b13–14, Aristotle makes it a common feature of circular and rectilinear motion that the further the moving point is from its origin, the faster it moves.

65   τῶν ἀφαιρουμένων ὑπὸ τῶν ἐκ τοῦ κέντρου.

1. the connection between the ratio of radii (distances from a common center) and the ratio of arcs of different circles,

2. the different but related speeds of revolving concentric circles of different sizes, and

3. the relative size of arcs subtended by radii cutting smaller and larger concentric circles.

In *On the Heavens* II.10 and 12, Aristotle expresses the principle in terms of its influence on the separate movements of the different heavenly bodies. Each planet moves on a sphere of its own on an axis that keeps its movements within the band of the zodiac. These circles are meant to account for the fact that the planets do not keep pace with the stars in their daily movement from east to west and for the fact that they move latitudinally with respect to the celestial equator and the background of fixed stars. In *On the Heavens* II.10, he presents the two ideas together:

> The movements of heavenly bodies vary—some faster, others slower—depending on their distances. Since it is established (ὑπόκειται) that the outermost circuit of the heavens is simple and fastest, and the circuits of the others slower and [moved with] more [movements] (for each of them moves on its own circle in a reverse motion to the heavens), it is reasonable that the circle nearest the simple and first circuit takes the greatest time to go through its own circle, the one furthest from [the fastest sphere] takes the least time, and of the others, those nearer always take the greater time and those further a lesser time.[66] (291a32–b6)

In this passage, the speed communicated to interior spheres by the outermost sphere interferes with the circular movement in a contrary direction with which the heavenly body is also moving. One of the things for which this additional contrary circular movement accounted is the speed of planets being slower than would be expected on the basis of the moving radius principle. Viewed from the earth, which is the central point of a three-dimensional system of described arcs, points closer should maintain the same position in relation to points moving on larger arcs further away.[67] The relation of the moving radius to the supposition of influence

---

66   Modified Oxford translation (trans. Stocks, in *Complete Works of Aristotle*, ed. Barnes (hereafter *CWA*), 1, 480).

67   Additional circles also give an account of separations and conjunctions of the plan-

is examined in more detail in Chapter 4. In *On the Heavens* II.8, where he presents the principle alone as accounting for faster and slower speeds of the heavenly circles, he also gives a version of Plato's notion that faster and slower movements are in agreement following the principle. He says that the heavens not breaking apart (διασπᾶσθαι) is due to the principle he has presented and to the fact that the whole is continuous (290a5–7).

The context for Plato's discussion of moving concentric circles in *Laws* X is mobility and immobility. Revolving concentric circles share in both because they move in place. The author of *Mechanics* appeals to the circle as the source of the wonders possible with machines, as Plato does. He formulates the circle's moving in place as one of the ways the circle combines opposites (847b20, 848a7). In the passages we have examined so far, Aristotle treats the principle as the basic reason for heavenly bodies moving at different speeds. The root phenomenon for him is that the outermost sphere of the stars is moving with the fastest speed and so, circles inside that sphere would be expected to be moving more slowly without falling behind. The importance of the principle in Aristotle's celestial mechanics is interesting, since the other chief application of the principle, the lever and the balance of unequal arms, is exceptionally mundane. The differences between the physical principles governing the heavens, corruptible physical nature, and craft were not an impediment to application of the principle in these diverse settings.[68]

The Lever In Aristotle's *Movement of Animals*

Aristotle makes use of the most basic formulation of the principle, the moving radius, in *Movement of Animals* 1–7. In the first chapter of *Movement of Animals*, he presents the movement of an animal limb by means of a simple diagram, in which the joint is a motionless center around which a straight limb bends (**Figure 2.5a–b**). Aristotle specifically mentions the diameter of the circle, DB, and represents the limb in terms of movement of half of the diameter from one position on the

---

ets, sun, and moon. At the beginning of *On the Heavens* II.10, Aristotle gives these two problems—relative speed and relative position—as what are to be explained in astronomy (291a29–32). For more on the aims of fourth century astronomy, see Bowen and Goldstein, "New View," and Mendell, "Eudoxus."

68   This seems true also for Plato. The fact that Plato mentions the principle as the source of wonders shows that he has in mind its effect in bodies. Whatever the wonders are, they are natural or craft phenomena.

circumference to another (698a23). In the course of *Movement of Animals* 1–7, he makes use of two features of this geometrical picture. The first links it quite clearly to the lever: for motion to occur, there must be something stationary against which the animal exerts force (ἀπερειδόμενον)

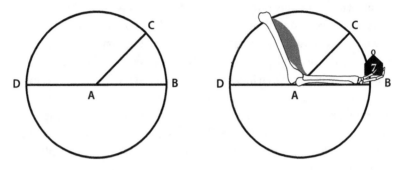

Figures 2.5a & 2.5b

to move. Aristotle is quick to note that the push off point varies depending on which limb is moving. The mathematical center is relative to the situation (698b1). In relation to the arm, it is the shoulder; when only the lower arm moves, it is the elbow. The need for something stationary emphasizes that his model is the lever, which has a fulcrum.

The second feature of the moving radius on which he draws is the greater effect caused by the same force at outlying points around a center. As we shall see, his use of *automata* and the toy wagon in *Movement of Animals* 7 are shorthand references to this feature of the moving radius principle in its application to the lever. The wagon exemplifies the principle most simply and shows what the reference to *automata* means. The toy wagon has unequal wheels on each side, so that pushed by its rider at the larger wheel, it travels inward in a curve. The amplification of effect of the same force at points further along a radius is implicit in his portrayal of the radial movement of limbs in chapter 1, but he makes it very explicit in chapter 7. Furthermore, he applies the model beyond locomotion to alterations like blushing and shivering. These he conceives as large-scale effects at the extremes of the body caused by a small change around the heart (701b28–32). The original cause of the movement around the heart are the small-scale percepts and thoughts that produce anger and fear. In this context, Aristotle compares animal movement to the rudder, which produces great changes because of a slight shift of the tiller (701b26).

That Aristotle moves without comment between different types of levers in *Movement of Animals* 1 and 7 shows his familiarity with the various formulations of the principle and manifestations of its effects. The radial movement of a limb given by Aristotle in his diagram appears at first to be an example of what we would call a second-class lever, in which the fulcrum, the stationary point, is at one end of the lever, and force is exerted at the other end. A wheelbarrow is a second-class lever— its single wheel is the fulcrum. The diagram of *Movement of Animals* 1, by itself, gives no indication of the position of force exerted to produce motion. In fact, as Aristotle proceeds in *Movement of Animals*, when he treats the movement of limbs as a model for other changes in an animate body, he treats the force as exerted somewhere along the beam and not at the end. In the diagram of the movement of the forearm, force is exerted where the muscle is attached (**Figure 2.5b**). This would make the arm in modern terms a third-class lever, where the fulcrum is located at one end of the beam of the lever but force is exerted *between* the fulcrum and the weight to be moved. Aristotle does not speak of muscles in applying the lever principle, but he understands two movements to be at work, a smaller one exerted near a motionless point and a greater effect further away. That Aristotle works conceptually with two movements, one where force is applied and a second correlate to it, will be an important point in my analysis of Aristotle on animal motion in later chapters. Either a first or third class lever serves his purposes.

The rudder, drawn upon by Aristotle in *Movement of Animals* 7, we would call a first-class lever, because the *fulcrum* is positioned between unequal lengths—the longer boat and the shorter rudder. At the end of the rudder opposite the tiller, a longer arc is covered in the same time. The ancient rudder was positioned on the ship three-quarters aft, i.e., near the stern—not at the stern extremity of the boat, as are modern rudders (**Figure 2.6a**), and its shape resembled a large oar (**Figure 2.6b**).[69]

---

69 Interestingly, in *Mechanics* 3, the author speaks of the rudder (πηδάλιον) being located at the end of the ship (ἐπι᾿εσχάτῳ πλοίῳ) (850b28). Use of the word *eschaton* may not be decisive in this usage for locating the rudder *at* the stern. Casson translates *eschaton* in this passage as "rearmost" (*Ships and Seamanship*, 224n2). Our information about the ancient rudder comes from artists' likenesses, where rudders often appear as symmetrical large oars, and from literary references. In visual evidence, there are usually two rudders, one on each side of the ship. Ships with widened and shaped rudders are common in illustrations of both sailing vessels and galleys dating from the first century BC.

 Although there is debate about how many movements the rudder had, it must have at the least pivoted in an arc (slanted slightly away from the horizontal) that reached away

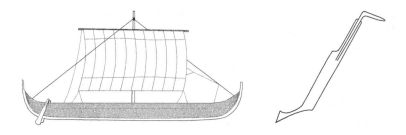

Figures 2.6a & 2.6b

Ancient steering oars did not function any differently from modern rudders though. The stern of the ship moves in the direction that the rudder moves. The bow of the boat moves in a direction opposite to the tiller's movement. With the rudders in the position of **Figure 2.6a**, the portside rudder will make the stern (back) of the ship move to port (left side of the ship) and the bow move to starboard (right side of the ship). A similar situation is portrayed with the rudder at the stern in a modern dory (**Figure 2.6c**). Accordingly, in *Movement of Animals* 7, Aristotle speaks of moving the tiller and producing a disproportionate *change* in the movement of a ship (701b27) (**Figure 2.6c**). The tiller (οἴαξ) is the handle of a rudder. In the case of the rudder, the smaller and larger movements are in opposite directions, and the lesser *speed* of movement of the rudder is correlated to a faster movement of the bow in its longer arc.

The author of *Mechanics* speaks of the sea as a weight against which the helmsman braces his ship (850b37) when he moves the tiller. The sailor does not shift the sea but rather quickly changes the direction of his ship through an arc. This point is worth dwelling upon in order to understand what Aristotle derives conceptually from experiences with leverage phenomena that are all slightly different. The fulcrum plays an essential

from the ship. Casson puts the matter simply:
"The ancient version [of the rudder] consisted of an oversize oar hung in slanting fashion on each quarter in such a manner that it was able to pivot . . . It was operated by a tiller bar socketed into the upper part of the loom [neck of the blade]. . . . Pushing or pulling the tiller bar made the loom pivot within its fastenings, and this put the blade at an angle to the hull and thereby directed the ship" (*Ships and Seamanship*, 224–225).
On large ships, especially sailing vessels, the rudder would have to be fastened in a housing specially designed for it. A thole-pin, or oarlock (σκάλμος) would not have sufficed to control it. Reliefs portray such housings.

role in magnification of a small movement due to exerted force. In the fourth century, the three modes of the lever were not distinguished, and the Aristotelians draw out slightly different implications of enhancement of power from different practical situations.[70] In rowing, for instance, the fulcrum lies between the sailor's grip on the oar and the sea. In *Mechanics* 4, the author queries why rowers in the middle of a ship pull to greater effect than those located more forward or aft. He says that, because the ship is widest in the middle, the rowers in the middle have more oar above the thole-pin. They move the ship more, because their own arc of movement is greater (850b15–17). In general, he says the movement of an oar is such that the oarsman's end of the oar braces against the

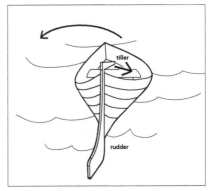

Figure 2.6c

sea as he pulls the oar toward himself. The boat moves in the direction of the oarsman's pull (850b20–24).

Yet the sea against which the oar pushes is not completely unmoved: "Insofar as the oar divides more sea, to this extent the boat is pushed forward more. It divides more to the extent that more of the oar is above the thole-pin" (b26–27). The passage suggests that the author also understands the oar as moving a part of the sea around the oar. This part of the sea Bodnár understands to be both what is moved and also the support against which the oar pushes the boat forward.[71] A question at issue in this case is whether the resistance offered by a stationary object, or a load to be moved, is also a force.[72] Bodnár believes that *Mechanics* observes the distinction between load and force.[73] In general, there are not stationary powers. So, Bodnár seems tentatively to suggest that force and resistance are conceptually different. Schiefsky points out, however,

---

70   The author of *Mechanics* 5 seems almost to treat the rudder as a second-class lever. He says that the lever is the whole rudder and the helmsman is the mover (850b33–34).

71   Bodnár, "Mechanical Principles," 139.

72   Load in Greek is φορτίον. The author of *Mechanics* uses τὸ φορτίον (852a29) for a load carried on rollers.

73   Bodnár, "Mechanical Principles," 142.

that in *Mechanics* weight (*baros*) is responsible for movement in the same way as forces exerted (*ischus, dunamis*). Weight is treated as a force.[74] This is also my understanding of weight and force in *Mechanics*. These interpretations may not be mutually exclusive.

Consideration of the terms in which classic leverage phenomena are conceived is relevant to understanding *Physical Problems* XVI but also to the broader question of whether Aristotle and the Aristotelians believe there is some "common dimension"[75] of power or force across the spectrum of factors brought into proportional relation in applications of the lever principle. The issue of a common dimension implicates different issues as it appears at the scientific level of *Mechanics* and *Movement of Animals* 7 versus at the level of the *dunamis* concept in Aristotle's narrative natural philosophy. I will argue that, reasoning from experience, Aristotle conceives an analogical similarity across different physical situations, which supports a conception of power applicable across subject matters.[76]

Returning to expressions of the moving radius and conceptions of the lever, we see that, when Aristotle draws upon the moving radius to explain the connection between percepts and thoughts (small changes) and reactions of anger and fear (greater changes), the changes are in the same direction, so to speak. Rather than opposite arcs, as in the rudder, we have different magnitudes (and types) of effect of a single cause. He makes clear in the argument of *Movement of Animals* 7 that his interest in explaining animal motion is to correlate two movements in the body, percept and response. He does not himself distinguish first- and third-class levers. The ease with which Aristotle moves back and forth among these conceptions, however, makes it clear he is in command of the underlying principle of these different forms of the lever. Clearly, the need for a stationary point is not the only way in which the lever is important in *Movement of Animals*. There is also the character and magnitude of action produced by a cause. Between chapters 1 and 7 of *Movement of Animals*, Aristotle capitalizes on both features of the moving radius principle.

---

74   Schiefsky, "Structures of Argument," 59–61.

75   This term is Bodnár's, "Mechanical Principles," 143.

76   The argument for this position has to be made in a way that does not confuse "common"—*koinon* in Greek—with proportional relation, the chief scientific tool of ancient authors and the basis for making precise the similarity present in the scientific treatment of phenomena. A notion of power or potency that applies analogically to phenomena from mechanics to biology is not, by virtue of that, a common power.

In chapter 2, he points to the impossibility of moving a boat by exerting force from within it and to the ineffectiveness of wind or other moving air propulsion, like Boreas blowing into the sail of a ship, to move something without outside leverage (698b21–699a12). In chapters 3 and 4, he considers the cosmic applications. Must the heavens too have a mover outside? He does not give an immediate answer to the question but mulls over the interplay of forces in motion within the cosmos. He is sensitive to the foundational requirement that what moves have magnitude. There cannot be a motionless central point within a revolving sphere, for every part of it is moving if the whole is. If the central point in a moving sphere were motionless, the whole would break apart.[77] It is also a misconception that either the poles or the center of the cosmos have power to cause motion, something that can only belong to a magnitude (699a21).

Next in *Movement of Animals* 3, Aristotle presents a version of the myth of Atlas that places the origin of the movement of the heavens inside the cosmos.[78] In this version, the god is not holding up the heavens but is rather responsible for the very movement of the heavens by being himself like a moving radius (ὥσπερ διάμετρον). With his feet planted on the earth, he turns the heavens around the poles. This point of view would be attractive to Aristotle to the extent that the moving radius principle itself accounts for the speed of the heavenly sphere. Atlas is, so to speak, the embodiment of the mathematical account of the quickest motion of the heavens that Aristotle cites in *On the Heavens* II. If Atlas is a radius, though, Aristotle points out, the earth must be stationary and so somehow outside the universe. This is for the reason given already—that every part of a revolving magnitude must be moving if it revolves as a whole. Aristotle rejects the account on this basis, because if the center is a stationary magnitude, Atlas and the earth are then related to one another according to the same principle governing any sort of movement. If the earth remains unmoved, then the force (*ischus*) of the mover and the force

---

77   Διασπᾶσθαι (present mid. inf.), used here, is also the word Aristotle uses in *On the Heavens* II.8 for the breakup of the heavens due to internal forces if the concentric circles principle were not in effect. This is interesting since, in *On the Heavens* II, application of the moving radius to the ratios of speeds in the heavens depends on a motionless point that coincides with the center of the cosmos and the position of the earth. Nussbaum points out that the earth could be a motionless body at the center of the cosmos without being "part of the system that is moved" (*Aristotle's* De Motu, 128).

78   On the background of the Atlas myth, see Nussbaum, *Aristotle's* De Motu, 300–304. She treats the connection of the passage to Aristotle's arguments for a mover outside the universe (127–132). See also, Lefebvre, "Mythe d'Atlas."

of the unmoved must be equal (699a33–35). There is some amount of power by which something remains unmoved as well as by which something moves. He states a rule of equal and opposite forces:

> And there is of necessity a certain proportion, just as of opposite motions, so also of states of rest. And equal forces are unaffected by one another, but they are overcome by an excess of force. (699a35–b1)

Equal forces produce no resultant action. So, if there is a physical principle like Atlas sustaining the heavens, he or it must exert no more force than the earth in its immobility, and the earth's force of immobility is as great as the force of movement of the entire heavens. That the earth exerts so much force of immobility as to counterbalance the entire heavens is something Aristotle believes highly unlikely. So, it must not be the case that the heavens are moved by anything within the universe.

Aristotle's concern in making this argument becomes clearer in *Movement of Animals* 4. If the immobility of the earth is something it is possible to overcome by a certain amount of force however great, then it could possibly be moved from its place and the universe dissolved. This is only impossible if its opposite is necessary, namely that the cause of the movement of the heavens is outside them (699b30). Chapters 3 and 4 are part of his rationale for a first mover outside the universe and, in the case of an animal, a first mover—the soul—that is not a body. What is important for our purposes, however, is the way Aristotle thinks it necessary to analyze the problem if all the sources of motion are within the universe. The lever would be the beginning of analysis, because its principle is applicable wherever motion is an issue. The moving radius, for him, is allied with the notions of equal and opposite reactions and the force needed to overcome rest, understood as a resistance to motion. It is worth noting that, in this discussion, Aristotle ascribes power to movement. Motion has power to overcome rest (699b14). This is a formulation especially suited to the lever, in which a small motion is capable of setting in train a larger motion proceeding in either the same or the opposite direction.

Physical Problems XVI

The next text to be considered as presenting variations on the moving radius is *Physical Problems* XVI, which is extraordinarily rich in material for the early history of mechanics. *Physical Problems* XVI.5 gives a very important alternate formulation of the principle in terms of the contrast of a rolling cone to a rolling cylinder. This contrast will be key to interpreting *Movement of Animals* 7, linking it to the ancient mathematical explanation of *automata*. The issue is that both a cylinder and a cone move in a circular path, but the cylinder describes a straight

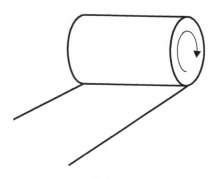

Figure 2.7a

line as its path of movement, while a cone describes a circle, with the apex of the cone as the center of the circle (**Figure 2.7a** and **2.7b**).

In *Physical Problems* XVI.5, the question is raised of why this difference obtains, since both are traveling in a circle (913b37–914a5).[79] It is the fact that in the cone there are *unequal* concentric circles, and the larger circles are borne along more quickly around the common center at the apex of the cone. The author considers the line that extends from apex to base on the surface of the rolling

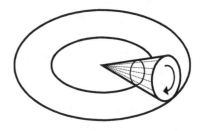

Figure 2.7b

cone and that is in continuous contact with the plane surface (**Figure 2.8**). He makes explicit that the points along this line do not describe cir-

---

79   On *Physical Problems* XVI, see Heath, *Mathematics*, 264–268; Flashar, *Problemata*, 579–588, Louis, *Problèmes* ii, 67–69, and Mayhew, *Problems* 1, 479–499. For a seventeenth century assessment of Book XVI (Biancani), see Berthier, "Les apocryphes mathématiques." The Greek text of *Physical Problems* used in this book is the Ruelle–Knoellinger–Klek edition (Teubner, 1923) as it appears in the Loeb publication, which does not have a full apparatus. I have accordingly consulted Louis' edition of 1991. Flashar translates from the Ruelle edition. I take note of Ross's emendations (cited by Forster in *Works*, ed. Ross, vol. 7). See Chapter 7 below.

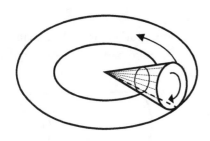

Figure 2.8

cular paths of the same length in the same time (914a8–11) (**Figure 2.8**). Accordingly, he draws on the fact that these points must all be traveling at different speeds to account for the different paths of the cylinder and cone (914a5–6). The principle of the moving radius is at work here in the *paths traced* by unequal concentric circles in the surface of the cone. There are two sets of concentric circles involved in the rolling cone. The circles on the surface of the cone itself take points along the axis as their centers. These are "concentric" in the sense that all their centers are on the axis of the cone. There are genuine concentric circles on the plane surface where the cone rolls. These are traced by the line of contact, and their center is the point where the cone's apex contacts the plane surface. The line of contact is a moving radius for the circular path traced on the plane surface. There is in effect an application to the plane surface of the paths of the unequal circles in the cone. This will prove to be an important point for interpretation of *automata*.

The principle appears in a very different form in *Physical Problems* XVI.3 and 12. We are back with the lever principle in these chapters, with emphasis placed on the correlation of faster and slower movements on opposite arcs. The account is so contextualized, however, that movement and weight, not the circle, become the focus of the account. The problem is why an unbalanced body, when thrown, revolves in a circle in its forward motion. One can imagine throwing an object like a hammer or baseball bat (an oblong shape) or a conch shell (a overall rounded shape), where the weight varies in different parts of the body (**Figure 2.9a**). The author describes the throw of such an object in terms of the force of the thrower being exerted at the lighter end of the object (915b15). That end will move away from the thrower, in accordance with the forward thrust exerted on it, so that the heavier end of the object will turn back toward the thrower. His own example is loaded dice, which are thrown in such a way as to turn back toward the thrower (913a37, 915b10) (**Figure 2.9b**). If the object is compact, like a loaded die, the heavier part will spin back when the player throws the die with the lighter part facing himself (915b10).

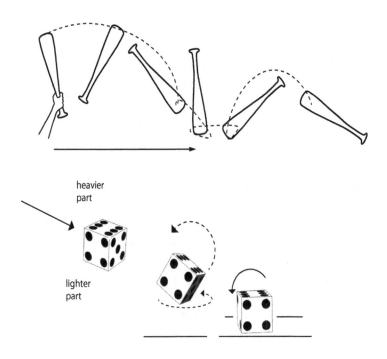

Figures 2.9a & 2.9b

Knucklebones of animals were used as dice in antiquity. A die was made unfair, or "loaded," by drilling a small channel in one of symmetrical parts of the bone and inserting lead, whence the term *memolibdômenoi astragaloi* in *Physical Problems* XVI.3 and 12. The disequilibrium of weight acting as forces within the die causes a rotating motion.[80]

The two chapters give slightly different but complementary reasons for the revolving movement of the unbalanced body. Put briefly, the solution is that the parts of the body tend to move rectilinearly, but being of different weights, they move with different speeds (913b38, 915b13). The only shape, or path described, in which a body can move different speeds at the same time, he says, is a circle. The author specifically mentions that it is points opposite one another in a body that move circularly at different speeds (913b5). He furthermore introduces a stationary middle in the

---

80   A similar phenomenon is known in golf. A "rub of the green" is having to hit a fairway shot when the ball has mud on one side. A golf shot has back spin, but the mud on one side of the ball makes the path of the shot through the air curve in the direction of the lighter side.

body around which outlying points in the body revolve (915b14). These chapters, along with others of *Physical Problems* XVI, will be examined in detail later. Clearly, though, they draw on the elements of the lever or balance of unequal beams—a stationary point and opposite arcs—for explaining how uneven weight affects the trajectory of forward motion. One important aspect of these chapters is their conception of weights being linked to one another and, by their linkage, modifying the motion each would tend to follow on its own. This is a fresh variation on the principle and one of considerable historical importance, when taken in the context of later developments in classical physics. It should also be noted that weight, in *Physical Problems* XVI.3 and 12, is not conceived in terms of the tendency downward of a certain type of body but rather as a cohort of force and of motion as the effect of force. The formulation of the principle in *Physical Problems* XVI.3 and 12 does not include any rule of proportionality.

The rolling cone and the revolving unbalanced body are alternate conceptions of the moving radius principle. It will be argued that they were both fruitful in their ancient context as part of the science of mechanics. Other chapters of *Physical Problems* XVI that draw upon the principle will be considered later. For now, Table 2.0 summarizes the main expressions of the principle that have been found in Plato's *Laws* or the Aristotelian writings.

Table 2.0

1. The moving radius	When one extremity of a line is fixed and the other extremity rotates about the fixed point, the speeds at which the points on the line are moving are all different in proportion to the distance of the points from the unmoved extreme. The points further away from the unmoved point move faster. The revolving line is a radius and the unmoved extremity is the center of the circle generated by the moving line.
2. Revolving concentric circles	Of concentric circles linked as on a revolving disk, the larger circles move faster than the smaller circles. Differences in speed are proportional to the distances of points on the disk from the center. The points do not need to share a radius for the proportional rule to apply.

3. Subtended concentric arcs	Of arcs of concentric circles cut by the same two radii, the arc of the larger circle is a longer arc. For this reason, movement of the radius from one position to the other will be faster for the larger arc.
4. Movement over opposite arcs	Points along a diameter on either side of the center of a circle cover in the same time distances proportional to their distance from the center of the circle. When the opposite arcs are distances covered by a balance of unequal arms or a lever, the same force causes points to move different distances in the same time.
5. Amplification of effect	A small change near the origin of movement brings about a larger change further from the origin.
6. Ease of start-up movement	A push at the periphery of a wheel (or axle) moves a whole.
7. Push-off corollary of the lever (there are equal and opposite forces of motion and rest)	The initiation of movement is impossible without an unmoved point against which the mover pushes to exert force on a moved thing. Corollary: movement is the result of the excess of the power of movement over the force of rest. When the forces of motion and rest are equal, there is no action.
8. Rolling cone	A cone, when it rolls, traces concentric circles on a plane surface. This is because there are, in the surface of the cone, circles of different sizes parallel to one another and at right angles to the axis of the cone.
9. Revolving unbalanced body	An unbalanced body, when it is thrown, moves in a circle as it moves forward, because a circle is the only path in which things moving at different speeds can move together.

Now it might seem tedious to distinguish these different expressions of the principle. Versions 1–4 in particular are very closely related. A reason for noting them is to show, first of all, that they are references to the same principle, and secondly, that the principle was well enough understood, in Aristotle's own time and in the decades after, to receive different formulations without special note. Careful examination of these different versions of the principle will make less conjectural efforts to date the different texts from which they come.

These are certainly not the only, or exclusively definitive, variations of the principle. In *Mechanics* 1, for instance, the author points to the mechanically important feature of circular motion whereby a circle in contact with other circles at their circumferences causes motions in an opposite direction from its own. Though the author does not say so in this context, the speeds of these other circles will be different from the speed of the mover circle in proportion to the sizes of the circles. Another important passage is *Mechanics* 8, where the author distinguishes three kinds of circular motion, based on whether or not the center of the circle moves along with the outer rim. There are

1. movement along with the felloe, where the center also moves, like a wagon wheel,

2. movement around a stationary center, as the sheave of a pulley moves, or

3. motion parallel to a plane when the center is stationary, like the rotation of a potter's wheel.

Though the author distinguishes the three types, he does not treat any one as having an advantage of speed over the others. He is interested in two facts applicable to them all: (1) that resistance, weight, or force is exerted at a single point on the circumference, and (2) that "the circle has come to be from two motions." This last statement seems to have a dual reference. On the one hand, a point poised on the circumference may incline in either direction. There is a potential for contrary motions for a point on a circumference. The tendency of the point is to go in the direction of whatever motion it is presently undergoing. If at rest, it is susceptible to the slightest impulse either way. On the other hand, the impulse a point on the circumference receives, if it is poised and stationary, will be for motion at a tangent to the circle. Its original inclination to move, however, would be motion along its own diameter toward the center: "For the mover will push its motion to the side, but it is itself moved along the diameter" (852a8–12). Circular motion is thus the resultant of separate tendencies to two rectilinear motions (ἐχ δύο φορῶν) (852a8).

The apparent composition of circular motion from rectilinear motion is a distinctive feature of *Mechanics* that seems to place it outside the group of Aristotelian treatises ascribed to Aristotle himself. Both *On the Heavens* and *Physics* include the simplicity of circular motion as a foundation of cosmology. There are two types of simple motion (αἱ κίνησεις ἁπλαῖ), curved and rectilinear.[81] Whether *Mechanics* should be so clearly separated from the rest of the Aristotelian corpus, however, is debatable. The author of *Mechanics* does not say that circular motion comes from two movements as a mixture or composition of them. In that case, there would be really only one simple motion, rectilinear. *Mechanics* uses a locution, common in Aristotle too, that a body following a circular path "is moved with two motions."[82] It remains an open question whether Aristotle acknowledged that circular motion could sometimes be a resultant of two rectilinear motions. It is a question in addition to this whether circular motion as a resultant could for any reason still be described as simple.

A New Proportional Rule

In *Mechanics*, nevertheless, moving with two motions is closely connected with another difference between *Mechanics* and the other Aristotelian expressions of the principle that is quite important. In all the passages presented so far, speeds along circumferences of arcs of differ-

---

81   On this theme, see *Physics* VIII.8, 261b28–32, VIII.9, 265a13–17; and *On the Heavens* I.2, 268b26–269a30. Krafft (*Betrachtungsweise*, 64) sees a similarity between *Physics* VII.2, where Aristotle treats *dinêsis*, a whirling motion, and *Mechanics* 8. Krafft takes this similarity to show that Aristotle composed circular motion from rectilinear motion also. Aristotle refers again to *dinêsis* in *On the Heavens* II.13, 295a10 in reference to the atomists' hypothesis of an original cosmic whorl, which Aristotle understands to be a description of violent or forced motion.

82   For instance, see *Mechanics* 848b24, b34, b35, 849a6. Aristotle has the heavenly bodies moving with more than one circular motion in *On the Heavens* II.10, 292b1. He presents oblique motion as a result of upward and downward tendencies in *Meteorology* I.5, 342a22–28. Hussey understands these combination movements as resultants not compounds. The powers of the components remain in the resultant motion. Even if they are opposed powers, like hot and cold, they may remain in a Heraclitean way like opposite pulls on a string (Hussey, "Mathematical Physics," 221–222).

ent circles are represented as having the same ratio as the radii of their circles respectively. *Mechanics* replaces this direct ratio with a different ratio, which involves *two* rectilinear elements from each circle, not just the one straight line, the radius taken from each circle. The argument proceeds like this:

> For any segment of a radius measured from a point on the circumference (**BK**), drop a perpendicular from another location of the same circumference to the termination point of that radius segment (**KG**). Take this to be a distance covered when **B** is subjected to a force. (**Figure 2.10**)
>
> For any other circle with the same center, O, if the similar rectilinear elements of that circle, e.g., **XF** and **FH**, have the same ratio as **BK:KG**, then the arcs subtended by those elements on the respective circles are arcs covered in the same time when **B** and **X** are subject to the same force.
>
> So, arcs covered in the same time are those that have the same ratio of particular rectilinear elements drawn from within the circles taken respectively. In particular, $\frac{BK}{KG} \propto \frac{XF}{FH}$ picks out arcs covered in the same time.

This ratio of rectilinear elements for each circle is a sort of "finder" proportion. It identifies arcs covered in the same time for a system with a common center.

The author of *Mechanics* takes the lines *BK* and *XF* to represent the motion of the point along its diameter that contributes to the resultant curved motion. In *Mechanics* 1, this is understood as constraint (*ekkrousis*) operating in the direction of the center of the circle. Lines *KG* and *FH* represent the force (*ischus*) exerted at the circumference to move the body. This force operates at a tangent to the circle. For example,

> BK = measure and direction of constraint (*ekkrousis*)
> KG = measure and direction of force exerted (*ischus*) or weight (*baros*) acting to produce motion.

He calls the movement by force exerted at the circumference natural motion (*kata phusin*) and the movement toward the center brought about by constraint motion contrary to nature (*para phusin*). As will become clear later, although the author gives these rectilinear motions dynamic (causal) names, the reason for choosing these particular rectilinear elements is kinematic and depends on the geometry of the circle. Importantly, this proportion of *Mechanics* 1, which involves rectilinear elements of the circle besides radii, is not explicitly cited by Plato or Aristotle. It would appear to be a more sophisticated statement of the moving radius principle and may, for that reason, indicate that *Mechanics* is later than the other versions of the principle treated so far. It has

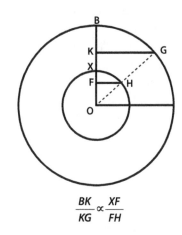

$$\frac{BK}{KG} \propto \frac{XF}{FH}$$

Figure 2.10

the advantage of making the selection of arcs covered in the same time more independent of the movement of a single radius, and so also makes more natural the comparison of movements with different centers of rotation. These advantages were present embryonically in Plato's formulation but are clearer in *Mechanics* 1.

Two more items about the proportion of *Mechanics* 1 should be noted in this brief account. The first is that the ratio of elements as determined above for movement along an arc has a different value for every point along the circumference of a single circle. The ratio itself continually changes as a point moves along an arc. As B moves along its circumference toward G, $\frac{BK}{KG}$ will continually change in numerical value. The author contrasts this fact to the parallelogram of movements for rectilinear movement that he also presents in *Mechanics* 1. A rectilinear movement, placed as the diagonal of

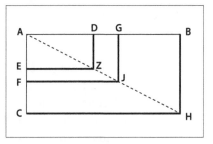

Figure 2.11

a parallelogram, can always be characterized in terms of the very same ratio, which is the ratio of sides of the quadrilateral constructed around it (**Figure 2.11**). As Z moves along the straight line AH, $\frac{DZ}{EZ}$ remains the same ratio. So, $\frac{DZ}{EZ} \propto \frac{GJ}{FJ} \propto \frac{BH}{CH}$. That the ratio of contributing rectilinear elements in rectilinear motion is the same while in curved motion that ratio is continually changing, is the foundational contrast between straight and curved motion. The relation between the proportion for the parallelogram of movements and movement over concentric arcs is presented in more detail later.

Second, the characteristic proportion that picks out arcs covered in the same time may, by alternation of proportionals, be converted to a proportion of linear elements from the two different circles involved in the proportion. That is, by alternation of proportionals:

$$\frac{BK}{KG} \propto \frac{XF}{FH} \ \Rightarrow \ \frac{BK}{XF} \propto \frac{KG}{FH} \ .$$

The author presents this alternation in the context of insisting that the ratio of natural rectilinear elements for each circle ($\frac{KG}{FH}$) is the same as the ratio of rectilinear elements representing constraint for each circle ($\frac{BK}{XF}$) (849b5). He does not say the two proportions (original and alternated) are the same proportion, i.e., are equal in the same terms.[83] This point will be drawn upon later in interpretation of *Mechanics* 1.

Classification of Expressions by Texts

I have now presented the basic elements of mechanics taken by fourth century authors to follow from the moving radius principle. I have presented these elements simply and without much discussion of their implications in particular cases. This will come later. Let me indicate what I take to be the salient grouping of the texts and their historical relation to one another. There are:

1. References to the principle in natural philosophical works of the Aristotelian corpus generally taken to be Aristotle's own writing or lectures and dating in essentials from his lifetime. These include *On the Heavens* II.8–12, *Movement of Animals* 1–7, and *Generation of Animals* II.1. Passages from *Physics* III, IV, VII, and VIII are not to be excluded from this group but do represent a more attenuated application of the basic principle.

---

83   A simple numerical example will illustrate the point. Six has the same ratio to eight as 18 has to 24 ($\frac{6}{8} \propto \frac{18}{24}$). By alternation of proportionals, it is also the case that $\frac{6}{18} \propto \frac{18}{24}$. In the first proportion, the sameness of ratio is $\frac{3}{4}$. In the alternated proportion, the sameness of ratio is $\frac{1}{3}$.

2. Expressions of the principle in *Physical Problems* XVI.3–6, 9–12.

3. Iterations of the principle in the single extended treatise on mechanics, *Mechanics*, and in particular chapter 1 of that treatise.

4. References in literary texts involving bodily experience and everyday arts that are even more basic than the lever and balance. This group is potentially much larger than the few texts to be considered here.

Considering the first three groups, which are philosophical and scientific texts, I will argue that the evidence supports the view that *Physical Problems* XVI is early enough to be the product of Aristotle's own school. Louis, Flashar, and Huffman have concluded that passages or chapters in Book XVI are close in time to Aristotle.[84] They make this judgment on the basis of the language of Book XVI. I will add to their views an analysis of the content of Book XVI and evidence of connections between it and the texts from group (1), the writings taken to represent Aristotle's own thought. The concepts and reasoning of *Physical Problems* XVI are consistent with, and so could have been made contemporaneous with, concepts and insights in the attested texts of Aristotle.

Mechanics is a different matter, however. It is less likely that its concepts and inferences are as close to Aristotle chronologically as those of *Physical Problems* XVI. The point has already been made that its mathematical argument goes into more detail kinematically. Chapter 1 contains something like a geometrical demonstration of the moving radius principle and adds to that demonstration new dynamical notions like constraint, on the one hand, and force operating at a tangent to the circle, on the other. Curved motion is the result of a point on a circumference moving with two rectilinear motions. In fact, both constraint and the idea of curved motion resulting from rectilinear tendencies of force figure quite significantly in several chapters of *Physical Problems* XVI (3, 4, 11, 12). There is, however, nothing like the elaboration of that idea in the kinematic detail of *Mechanics* 1. This first surviving text in mechanics, then, is either later than Aristotle, and departing to some extent from the influence of his natural philosophy, or if part of his school, perhaps represents the influence of a different ancient source, where mechanics had begun to be developed as a mathematical discipline.

---

84   Louis, *Problèmes*, 69; Huffman, *Archytas*, 517; Flashar, *Problemata*, 347–356, 579–588.

In connection with the second possibility, that *Mechanics* draws on another ancient source, it will be worthwhile to consider the intriguing but incomplete reference in *Physical Problems* XVI.9 to Archytas' explanation of the circular growth of non-specialized parts of both plants and animals. This passage, taken in its context as part of *Physical Problems* XVI, is a clue that the characteristic proportion apparently so new to the moving radius principle in *Mechanics* 1 might have been involved in a mechanical explanation earlier. Certainly, we must bear in mind that Aristotle himself would not have been inimical to the incorporation of Archytan elements in his own explanations in natural philosophy. Indeed, on many topics, he prefers Archytas' approach to that of Plato. For instance, he seems to acknowledge Archytas' influence on his own idea of definition by matter and form.[85]

The next chapter begins with a few representatives from Group (4) of the mechanical principle at issue. This is important for developing the theme that the mechanical property of the moving radius was something perceived and that it was assimilated into ancient science as part of experience. The philosophical significance of the principle will begin to be seen, insofar as it bears upon a correct understanding of Aristotle's own analysis of *empeiria*.

---

85 *Metaphysics* H.2, 1043a14–26. On this passage and Archytan definition in Aristotle, see Huffman, *Archytas*, 489–507.

Chapter 3

Kinesthetic Awareness, Experience and *Phainomena*

The absence of experimentation has been cited as a characteristic of early science. Experiment, the hallmark of modern Western science, is usually described as the contrivance, for the purpose of discovering underlying principles, of empirical states of affairs not encountered in the natural course of events. Experiment is defined over against experience, a term of art among historians of science that refers to a collection of empirical encounters with the natural world. Experience may mean more or less detailed observation of physical phenomena, anatomical inspection, astronomical data collecting, or any kind of induction from one or many cases. Experience is often taken to involve a strong component of conventional wisdom and shared cultural presuppositions. It is usually associated with what is called qualitative science, while experiment is thought to go hand-in-hand with applying mathematical principles to nature.[86] There is a significant equivocation to be flagged in this view, however. The reliance on experience that is attributed retrospectively to Aristotle is a conception broader and less precise than Aristotle's own concept of experience, *empeiria*. It is important to distinguish the historian's conception of experience and Aristotle's. The latter will be my main topic of investigation. The hope is that this investigation will enrich the conception of experience applied in the history of early science. In the final analysis, it will become clear that many of the things thought only to be obtainable through experimentation were available to the ancients by

---

86   These themes are well-stated in Peter Dear's *Discipline and Experience.*

51

perspicuous investigation drawn from experience as Aristotle conceived it. In particular, the unusual or unexpected played a greater role in gaining new knowledge in ancient science than has been realized.

It is certainly true that the Greeks did not do experiments in the sense of much twenty-first century experimentation. This difference in scientific practice has legitimized a collective gloss of ancient "experience" that hides the complexity of ancient empiricism. My primary aim in this and the next chapters is to present two levels of Greek empiricism. The first is illustrated by the most ancient testimonies of mechanical knowledge among the Greeks and also in the later appropriation of mechanical knowledge by Aristotle and his school. This knowledge is contextualized and concrete, sometimes relevant to craft but sometimes explanatory of natural phenomena, whether ordinary or wondrous. I will give some examples of mechanical knowledge in kinesthetic perceptual awareness, examples whose philosophical significance will be fleshed out later in this chapter and in chapters to follow.

The second level of empiricism comes to the fore when we understand that what are experienced and observed are *phainomena*. The relation of *empeiria* and *phainomena* has been much discussed by scholars of ancient philosophy. I will argue that Aristotle sometimes means by *phainomena* what comes to us through the senses, not common opinions. Also, perceptual *phainomena* are structured. They have a simple organization. They are not what is called Baconian data but are articulated. Articulated here means structured or of parts, like an articulated lorry (a semi-trailer truck). It does not mean spoken in words. Even though articulated, *phainomena* are not cognized first as propositions. They are forerunners of propositional knowledge. A *phainomenon* in this sense corresponds in cognition to a vague grasp of some necessity or natural compulsion belonging to a state of affairs.

The second type of empiricism comes out of the first, as the following example shows. A novice sailor in rough surf is capsized in her small boat. Her awareness might be made sense of in a quick realization: "Here I go—I cannot stop my boat from turning over!" This is an exclamation of unavoidable mild calamity. The calamity is overtly verbalized in my example for the sake of illustration. One would probably have the awareness of being unable to stop the event, without saying or thinking this expression. The vocalization at the time might be, "Oh-h-h, n-o-o!" Such an awareness—let us call it a cognition of what cannot be otherwise in a particular situation—can come from a single instance of undergoing or seeing. To constitute *empeiria*, there must be a re-recognition, the work of a universal of some sort. For example, "Why am I out here? Over again!" One might experience the consternation of having once more not avoided capsizing but without speaking or thinking the universal. The consternation nevertheless registers the awareness of something experienced before. A *logos* is present in memory or experience. We should bear in mind that Aristotle believes a universal (*to katholou*) is the object only of intellect. Some animals with memory may have a *logos*, but no animal without intellect has access to universals.

An experience is still of a *phainomenon,* if one knows that a particular trait in the state of affairs, which has an effect on her or is seen by her, is always present in the state of affairs *and* that the property belongs to *something.* For example, "Waves dashing upon the gunwale straight on—trouble!" At this stage, the property of the state of affairs bringing about capsizing has been recognized, waves exerting force on the side of the boat. The experiencer even associates particular symptoms with the property, e.g., a hard, slapping sound on the gunwale. The knower is aware of the capsizing having to be in some subject in the state of affairs. Once back on shore but wishing to venture out again, a physical problem could be formulated. For example, "Waves hitting my boat sideways capsize it—when *what* is the case?" The suitable resolution in knowledge (*gnôsis*) of this problem statement may well be a mathematical formulation of subject and attribute, not a proposition in words. Experiential knowledge is the basis for truth claims made at a later stage of knowing but also for mathematical knowledge of sensible subjects, which may not incorporate a truth claim as such, at least not in the way a proposition does.

Finally, there is the stage of holding in thought or speech that "It is the case that property X belongs to exactly Y." The subject, Y, would be the boat, but the boat in a particular position when waves are above a certain height. For example, "Capsizing [belongs to] my boat parallel to and in the trough of waves above four feet." This stage of articulation involves a claim of the truth of a proposition, which is expressed linguistically and separated into subject and predicate. The state of affairs is clarified with respect to its parts.[87] Aristotle recognizes this sort of assertion as involved

---

87   The possibility of error always needs an accounting when one gives a description of experience. Van Fraassen goes too far, though, in citing a "major historical confusion" that conflates events that happen to us with judgments involved in awareness of what happens

in stating propositions (*On Interpretation* 2). The sailor would probably not bother to state the proposition in this way, because she would be better served by another, which is more action oriented: "My boat capsizes when I do not shift the helm *into the waves* when they are this high." Capsizing is now avoidable. We could say that this is a proposition, since it involves a claim, "Capsizing [belongs to] my boat in a position other than directed into the swell." As a whole, though, the expression is more like a rule or instruction—"Helm (steer) into the waves."

It should be noted that the example of the boat capsizing, even when propositionalized, does not yet constitute scientific knowledge (*epistêmê*). The cause of capsizing in waves this height and not lower, when adrift in the swell, still needs to be found. Considered in ancient terms, the reason might well involve the size of the arc and the speed of points along the circular path of the cylinder-like wave.[88]

The two levels of empiricism I have distinguished—the barely conceptualized handling of mechanical phenomena by means of action and reaction, and the grasp of a sense percept as a property belonging to a subject—will be shown to be related to one another. I will begin with some early Greek formulations of mechanical phenomena in order to make precise the notion of perceptual kinesthetic experience.[89]

---

to us (*Empirical Stance*, 134). He gives the example of mistaking a garden hose for a snake. Stepping on the hose and judging the hose to be a snake are by no means the same thing, he says. This much is true. Even in this happening, however, there are properties that figure prominently in the mistake. The hose is round like a snake and sits in the grass in a curved position. If water is coursing through the hose, it might well exhibit seemingly autonomous motion when stepped upon, heightening its snake-like properties. It is unlikely that someone would mistake stepping in a bucket for stepping on a snake. The happening of stepping on a hose has traits that make it not a judgment but an experience in the sense explicated here.

88   For the wave as a cylinder, see Apollonius of Rhodes, *Argonautica* II, 594.

89   My aim is not to account for all the features of experiential knowledge in relation to Aristotle's theory of science but to substantiate by historical example and analysis that there is experiential knowledge of the sort I describe involved in Aristotle's natural philosophy. The moving radius principle is treated in the Aristotelian literature as a causal account. I do not, however, attempt to give any rule or logical sieve that will always distinguish *kath'hauto* traits that are part of essence from *kath'hauto* traits that are always present but outside of essence. See *Posterior Analytics* I.4 for this distinction. There is a large scholarly literature concerning essence and what follows from essence that also involves the interpretation of *Posterior Analytics* II.1–2 and 8–10. See for instance Gomez-Lobo, "Question of Existence," Bolton, "Essentialism," Landor, "Demonstrating Essence," and Charles, *Meaning and Essence*.

The Moving Radius in Kinesthetic Awareness

In the *Iliad*, Homer recounts the advice of Nestor to his son Antilochus concerning how to drive the upcoming chariot race at Patroclus' funeral.[90] The assumption is that Antilochus' horses are slowest among the competition, but this does not rule out victory in the race. The key is horsemanship, especially rounding the post, the turn at the halfway point of the race. The course is smooth on either side of the turn, Nestor says, a space broadened into a mound by human intervention at some time in the past (330–333). The advice he gives for making the turn is a model of contextualized, non-abstracted knowledge of the moving radius principle:

> And you must hug it close
> as you haul your team and chariot round, but you
> in your tight-strung car, you lean to the left yourself,
> just a bit as you whip you right-hand horse, hard,
> shout him on, slacken your grip and give him rein
> But make your left horse hug that post so close
> the hub of your well-turned wheel will almost seem to scrape
> the rock—just careful not to graze it! . . .
> Trail the field out but pass them all at the post,
> no one can catch you then or overtake you with a surge
> . . . . (335–345)[91]

Antilochus is to take the turn on the inside of the other chariots. By doing so, the shorter distance covered compensates for the slower speed of his horses. The strategy is especially suited to the course this day, which has a wide, rounded curve. How he handles his own two horses is important. His outside steed will need a lighter rein so that he will run faster, while the horse on the inside must be held back. So, even of his own pair, one runs faster than the other, depending on its distance from the center of the turning curve. The driver's own bodily attitude is important, too. He must lean into the curve, so that the chariot travels mainly on the shorter inside circle. As Homer describes the actual race, its outcome depends more on the condition of the ground and the recklessness of Antilochus than this point of charioteer skill. Nevertheless, Homer gives a formulation of the mechanical principle with which we are concerned in terms of economy

---

90   *Iliad* XXIII.304–350.

91   Translation is by Robert Fagles, *Iliad* 23, lines 375–392 in the English text.

of distance and speed. He describes how exertion of force by the charioteer is related to these. He further understands the execution of the set of
actions and attentiveness involved in making the turn to be a feature of
skill or cunning (μῆτις, κέρδος):

> The average driver, leaving all to team and car,
> recklessly makes his turn, veering left and right,
> his pair swerving over the course—he cannot control them.
> But the cunning driver, even handling slower horses,
> always watches the post, turns it close, never loses
> the first chance to relax his reins and stretch his pair
> but he holds them tight till then, eyes on the leader.
> (319–325)

Already in Homer, then, the handling of mechanical forces has been externalized in a set of instructions. The involvement of skill is the reason
Plato quotes in his *Ion* these details Homer gives for making the turn.[92]
Plato makes his familiar point that the one who knows his subject matter
better and knows what to do in any given circumstances is the one who
is expert in that area. He asks Ion if he remembers what Nestor's advice
is. Ion first replies, "Lean (Κλινθῆναι)"—lean to the left. What is most
vivid in the advice is what pertains to the bodily awareness of the charioteer himself.

This example provides a baseline for the meaning of the term "kinesthetic awareness." It is human awareness, held consciously or uncon-
sciously, of how to leverage mechanical forces by means of one's own
body. The awareness is "kinesthetic" because it is action taken in response to movement underway. Inevitably, exertion of muscular force is
involved.

There is an instance where Homer draws upon his auditors' knowledge by kinesthetic awareness to make plausible a particular battlefield
death scene. Experience of leveraging forces with one's own body is, I
believe, deeply embedded in this image. The passage is Homer's description of the death of Thestor at the hands of Patroclus. From the ground,
Patroclus has risen alongside Thestor who, in his chariot, has lost the
reins and huddles in panic.[93] Homer likens the deadly moment to the landing of a fish. Patroclus' spear lodges firmly in Thestor's right jaw. The

---

92   *Ion* 537a–d.

93   It is not clear if the chariot is in motion or not, but Thestor has lost control of it. The
entire passage is at *Iliad* XVI.402–410.

spear being hooked in the jaw is the conceit by which it is imaginatively plausible that force could be exerted in such a way as to drag Thestor first upward then down toward the ground. Since Knox singled out the passage as near the limit of plausibility of Homer's battle scenes,[94] it is interesting to consider the mechanical kinesthesia underlying the vivid picture and its imaginative plausibility. Homer says:

> He dragged him with the spear, lifting him over the chariot-
> rail, just as a man
> taking his seat on a jutting rock hales some fish
> out of the sea with line and glittering bronze hook.
> So Patroclus dragged him gaping off his car with the bright
> spear, ... [95] (16.403–409)

Most visually striking in this scene is its culmination, the dying Thestor gaping like a hooked fish. Thestor being lifted out of the chariot, however, is a surprising route to his ignominious end. The reference to the fisherman's seat on a jutting rock draws attention to the unmoved point in the physical situation that makes Patroclus' action imaginable, evoking for the hearer the recollection of how force is applied in such a situation (**Figure 3.1**). The fisherman analogy seems in some ways remote from this action, however. The quick lift and transfer of weight seems like a pitchfork movement, where the fulcrum of action would lie between ends of the spear. Along the spear the force of the blow is magnified sufficiently to hoist another human being out of a chariot in an upward arc movement. Homer's fisherman image is more elegant,

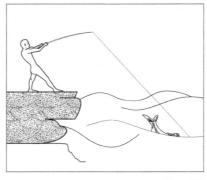

Figure 3.1

perhaps serving an aesthetic of the nobility of the victorious warrior amidst all the carnage. Mair, translator of Oppian's *Halieutica* (*Fishing*) (AD second century) cites this passage in Homer as an example of line fishing, but

---

94   See Knox's Introduction to *The Iliad*, trans. Fagles, 28.

95   The lines in Fagles's English translation are *Iliad* 16.477–489. I have altered this translation from Fagles's version. The word I translate "hales" is ἕλκω, "drag" or "draw up." Compare Mair's translation of Oppian in the quote immediately following, also *L-S* ad loc, II.4, 5, 8.

Oppian himself in *Cynegetica* (*The Chase*) gives an account of rod-fishing[96] that parallels Homer's passage:

> The angler sits on the rocks beside the sea and with curving
> rods and deadly hooks he catches at his ease, the fish of varied
> sheen; and joy is his when he strikes home[97] with barbs of
> bronze and sweeps through the air the writhing dancer of the
> sea, leaping high above the deeps.[98] (*The Chase*, I.56–61)

We see, in Oppian's picture, the smaller movement of the rod lifting the
fish a much greater distance (**Figure 3.2**). The fish is not a dead weight,
and so the fisherman is adept at transferring some of the fish's convulsive
movement (ἀσπαίροντα) into the upward movement. Homer himself
gives an example of rod fishing (περιμήκεϊ ῥάβδῳ) in similar terms in
Odyssey XII.251, also mentioning the fisherman being on a promontory

---

96   Oppian gives four modes of fishing: (1) with line and hook, either by hand or with
a rod, (2) with nets of various kinds, (3) with weels, i.e., traps or baskets, and (4) with
tridents. See Oppian, *Fishing* (*Halieutica*) III.72–91. Homer does not mention fish traps
(though Plato famously does, *Timaeus* 78b4), perhaps for the reason Oppian gives—fishing by traps requires little labor (*Fishing* III. 87), and Homer for the most part deals in
descriptions of forces and action with his fishing similes. In *Sophist* 220b–d, Plato divides fishing methods into those utilizing enclosure (ἕρκος) versus strike (πληγή). Both
baskets and nets enclose. Hooks (ἄγκιστρα), as well as tridents or spears (τριόδοντες),
work by strike. Plato distinguishes night fishing with tridents from day fishing with a
three-pronged spear, which he calls "hooking." The latter involves strike from below the
fish. The difference in the two types of spearing likely has to do with the light bringing
the fish closer to the surface at night. Plato sets apart from spearfishing the use of rods
or reeds (ῥάβδοις καὶ καλάμοις) with hooked line, associating this method particularly
with striking only in the area of fish's head and mouth (*Sophist* 221a). He mentions pulling the fish upward from below with this method (ἀνασπώμενον) (221a3).
Fishing with artificial flies is first described by Aelian (AD second century) as practiced on a Macedonian river. The passage from Aelian's *Natural History* is quoted and
discussed by Radcliffe (*From Earliest Times*, 187–190). The focus of the passage is the
artificial fly and not the method of casting. It is not clear if Aelian conceives fly-fishing
along with the modern gentle netting of the prey. This contrast between modern fly-fishing and the other methods that appear in Homer, Plato, and Oppian lends insight on the
conception of fishing in these ancient texts. Apart from weels, the methods do seem to
involve an idea of exertion of force on the part of the fisherman, which perhaps makes
the decision between hand versus rod fishing for the *Iliad* passage less important. In
Fishing, Oppian heightens the interest of fishing by insisting that the fisherman has the
hardest task among all hunters, since he can never see his prey but must depend on his
array of devices—bronze hooks, reeds, and nets (*Fishing* I.50–56).

97   τορήσας.

98   ὕψι μάλα θρώσκοντα βυθῶν ὕπερ ἀσπαίροντα εἰνάλιον φορέῃσι δι'ἠέρος
ὀρχηστῆρα.

(ἐπὶ προβόλῳ). In this passage, the writhing fish is hurled upon a rocky ledge[99] (XII. 254–255). The fish are sailors seized by Skylla. In the passage we are examining in the *Iliad*, Homer does not mention the fisherman's rod except as it might be Patroclus' spear. The forces involved

make clear that, if he describes line fishing, he still has in mind a powerful, quick movement by the fisherman of raising his catch above the sea from his stable position on the jutting rock.[100] The line becomes a flexible radius originating with the angler's quick movement. In Thestor's displacement, the involvement of bodily weight in the leverage movement might be more the source of the image's intelligibil-

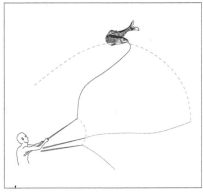

Figure 3.2

ity than the flying arcs of the fishline. Yet, Oppian too includes a firm situation of the fisherman on rocks, which is important to exerting the quick force on the line that can fling the fish out of the sea (**Figure 3.2**). The connection Homer makes to fishing drives home the familiarity of the experiences of force kinesthetically. This is not first a grotesquery unique to the battlefield but something anyone might have experienced in landing a large fish. It seems unlikely that the event described by Homer could really happen.[101] This does not detract, however, from the value

99 ἀσπαίροντα δ᾽ ἔπειτα λαβὼν ἔρριψε θύραζε, ὡς οἵ γ᾽ ἀσπαίροντες ἀείροντο προτὶ πέτρας.

100 Radcliffe analyzes Homer's eight references to fishing in *From Earliest Times*, ch. 2. He thinks the simile offered for Thestor's death could have been a reference to rod fishing (77–79). One reason is the adjective, ἱερός, whose usual meaning is "sacred" or "hallowed" to describe the fish. In this context, it may retain its older meaning of "strong" and indicates that the fish is large. Modern fishermen, according to Radcliffe, say the rod is more valuable the larger the fish (77).

101 Thestor's jaw would break before the subsequent movement had occurred. As the incident is described, the motive force of Patroclus' initial thrust adds force to the mechanical advantage latent in the relative positions of Patroclus and Thestor (404–405), and this could possibly provide the force to move the weight of a human being in a flattened arc-movement from one place to another. Patroclus "pushed him (ἕωσε) down face-first" (478). Knox gives another reason the described movement might take place: that the wounded man's head would follow the motion of withdrawal of the spear. The simile to the angler emphasizes, in painfully familiar terms, the loss of dignity of the victim and the

of the passage as an example of empirical knowledge of application of forces in curved motion.

Homer's hyperbolic imaginative use of a mechanical phenomenon in this instance bears comparison to another reference of his to mechanical skill. This reference does not involve the moving radius principle but is worth noting for its invocation of the term *automatos* for a moving device. Homer describes the room in the palace of Hephaestus, where the craftsman god has hot cauldrons at the ready to roll on golden wheels to wherever the gods are meeting. Thetis finds Hephaestus thus:

> . . . sweating, wheeling round his bellows,
> pressing the work on twenty three-legged cauldrons,
> an array to ring the walls inside his mansion.
> He'd bolted golden wheels to the legs of each
> so all on their own speed (*hoi automatoi*), at a nod from him,
> they could roll to halls where the gods convene
> then roll right home again—a marvel to behold.[102]

This image must be inspired by examples of movement by steam or heated air exhaust propulsion. The image is hyperbolic in the ease and completeness of the machines' execution, not to mention Hephaestus' control of them by what could be as slight as a raise of his eyebrows.[103] What is important is to note the use already by Homer of the term *automatoi* for self-movers working by some sort of machine principles.

Let us now consider a simpler case of the moving radius, one more immediate in bodily awareness. This example is drawn from a text closer to Aristotle's own time and context of thought. In *Physical Problems* XVI.4, the Aristotelian author mentions an experience that must also have been common in battle. This is the fact that a person struck from behind on his legs falls not forward in the direction of the blow but backward and down (913b19–22) (**Figure 3.3**). In *Physical Problems* XVI.4, this case is included in an analysis of the principles governing the rebound of

---

superiority of the killer. See Knox' Introduction to *Iliad*, trans. Fagles, 28.

102 *Iliad* XVIII. 373–377 (Fagles, *Iliad* 18.434–40).

103 This passage is noted in particular by Schneider for the wheeled self-movement and the description of the movement as a wonder. He interprets the passage to mean that the freedom from work possible from the god's skill is not available to men (*Technikverständnis*, 23).

objects when striking a surface. Falling due to a blow from behind is presented to reinforce the phenomenon of a rectangular solid falling backward when striking an oblique surface. When formulated simply in terms of the direction of the blow on the legs, however, the falling backward is not what one would expect. Yet, as observed or experienced, it becomes part of the kinesthetic awareness by which a person learns to manage the weight of his own body. Gymnasts are experts at the leverage of body weight in motion. The backward arc of the person hit from behind is a basic gymnastic move undertaken intentionally. Everyone manages body weight more or less unthinkingly, however, sometimes with unrecognized skill. A person about to slip on icy pavement undertakes immediate unpremeditated coping action.

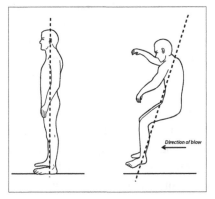

Figure 3.3

Considered in terms of the reason for loss of balance, the fall backward of *Physical Problems* XVI.4 is akin to the charioteer's gaining a lead by leaning into the curve. Although Nestor pedantically makes the strategy along the inside at the post a matter of instruction, in fact both the compensation for a blow from behind at the knees and leaning into a curve at high speed are actions undertaken thoughtlessly, i.e., as reflexes at the level of rudimentary skill performed during the course of action itself. Action counteracts action. Kinesthetic awareness does not exclude the intellectual resources of the person but is built on reactions of the sensory-motor system, which prioritizes experiences even below the level of consciousness and modifies empirical understanding over time. One point I argue is that Aristotle understood *empeiria* to *include* kinesthetic awareness of this type and that he also had a notion of this awareness as bodily "knowledge" whose outlines were, to some extent and for a while, submerged to intellectual awareness. To make this point, it will be necessary to give examples of Aristotle's utilization of such awareness in his natural philosophy but also to examine what he says about experience. The first task, showing how Aristotle uses leverage phenomena, is the subject of Chapters 4 through 6. I will begin, in this chapter, with the second task, the consideration of Aristotle's concepts of *empeiria* and *phainomena*.

Three points are important to note at the outset. These will be developed in the rest of this chapter. The first point is that kinesthetic awareness is not inductive knowledge, as induction is usually conceived. It is both a more immediate cognition than the formation of a universal from many particulars and too little conceptualized to qualify as induction. Kinesthetic awareness issues immediately in action. Insofar as an appropriate kinesthetic response—avoiding falling on an icy sidewalk—comes out of a previous occurrence under similar conditions, success in parrying a bad outcome could be considered a result of induction, but the notion of induction would have to be broader, suited to non-intellectualized knowledge and possibly appropriate to memory in animals as well. The second point, then, is that kinesthetic awareness, though understanding of a state of affairs and not grasp of an object, is non-propositional knowing. This non-propositional understanding may be vague by the standards of clear propositional expression—that is to say, hard even to put into a cogent proposition. It may not yet be fully realized in consciousness. In spite of that, kinesthetic response is usually highly effective, even efficiently targeted. Thirdly, this knowledge is important, in spite of its initial vagueness, because it is perception of what is later clarified as a necessary property of some subject. Subject and property are not separated in kinesthetic awareness, but a particular kinesthetic response takes the form it does, because it includes a grasp of a necessary attribute as part of a state of affairs. For example, someone who learns to parry a blow from behind does so, in good gymnastic style, by moving with the blow and enhancing his movement in a backward arc. The completion of that action would be a stable landing on his feet. In this move, there is implicit understanding that the head covers a shorter distance than the longer arc of a point along the legs where the blow lands. The next stage is to recognize a subject/property relation—the human body as extended (subject) and the arc-paths it covers (property) when subject to force in a distinctive way. This level of knowledge might belong to the special forces operative, the old-fashioned Hollywood stunt man, or the computer graphics artist who, like a present-day Homer, engineers hyperbolic stunts for action movies. Eventually, we give falling backward and passing at the post a propositional formulation in order to say they are experiences and to analyze the underlying reason for the action, but their core experiential character is not propositional. Indeed, an intermediate stage between kinesthetic awareness and propositional knowledge would be the issuing of commands about how to deal with unavoidable forces showing themselves in motion:

> "Lean toward the left and pull the horse's rein in that direction."
>
> "Move your diaphragm and thorax quickly upward, while springing off the ground to a position with your knees near your chest."

These commands are not disguised propositions but serve a different action-oriented function while still organizing mechanical knowledge possessed by the instructor and the student. The view of Aristotelian *empeiria* to be developed here, then, understands experience as based in sense perception, concerned with necessary traits, and not mediated in the first instance by linguistic formulations.

Empeiria and Universals

It is reasonable that human undergoing of mechanical forces and our consequent managing of such forces would be an instance of the kind of thing Aristotle calls *empeiria*, experience. There are, however, crucial scholarly issues that need to be brought into relation to this claim. These issues are (1) how *empeiria* involves perception and memory, and (2) whether universals—understood as traits that come to be expressed in *kath'hauto* predications—are present in experience. These issues are of great moment in the interpretation of Aristotle's philosophy in general, for they impinge on whether Aristotle is an empiricist, as his own statements about the source of knowledge would indicate, or a rationalist, as he is sometimes interpreted by contemporary philosophers. Key texts for this investigation are *Posterior Analytics* II.19, *Metaphysics* A.1, and *Prior Analytics* I.30.

Posterior Analytics II.19 begins by seeking the faculty that knows first principles. These presumably would be propositions, since the scientific syllogism is composed of propositions. This faculty, it will turn out, is *nous*. Yet, the route Aristotle chooses to the delineation of *nous* as a faculty for knowing first principles is to describe the origin of universals in the psychology of concept-formation. In *Posterior Analytics* II.19,

63

experience is one of the faculties that support formation of the concepts of knowledge (*epistêmê*). It is one of the itemized capacities (*dunameis*) that distinguish the human being from non-rational animals. Among human capacities, experience comes between memory and craft. It involves the coalescence of many memories into recollection of a single thing— no mean achievement among the traits of cognition, since many animals cannot do it.[104] Accordingly, some single cognition, a one standing in for many, is present in experience (100a3–9). In the dichotomous sieve by which Aristotle winnows cognitive soul-functions in *Posterior Analytics* II.19, some animals may have memory but not experience. It appears, however, that experience is the transitional capacity between the human soul and other animals, for experience is more closely linked to craft and science (*epistêmê*) than is memory. This is the implication of Aristotle's emphasis on the "one" of experience rather than the "many" of memory as providing the basis for the next capacity, craft (a6–9).[105] Nevertheless, Aristotle's formulation keeps experience close to the powers of perception. As Aristotle expands upon the theme in *Metaphysics* A.1, a few animals with memory and perception have a little experience (980b27), but in human beings, the payoff of experience is grand, leading as it does to craft (*technê*) and calculation (*logismois*).[106] This seems to make these latter capacities conceptual and intellectual in a way experience is not. In *Metaphysics* A.1, Aristotle makes clear that the craftsman may have some grasp of the causes of things but not the man of experience (981a28).

Nevertheless, Aristotle has such regard for experience that he does not make it merely an aspect of perception and memory. He notes that craft without experience can lead to practice actually inferior to the practice of the person with experience only (981a13–15). This is because doing—the aim of craft—involves particulars, just what experience knows.

---

104 There is a difference between treating memories of the same thing or kind as one experience and recognizing the difference itself between many memories and the one experience of them. Possibly this difference is what distinguishes the limited experience of animals (*Metaphysics* A.1, 980b27) from that of humans, who actually distinguish memory and experience. On this point, see Sorabji, "Rationality," 314–318.

105 On this point, see also *Metaphysics* A.1, 981a1–7.

106 The use of λογισμός in the plural, coupled as it is with τέχνη, craft, may indicate that Aristotle has in mind the Archytan designation for the range of practical versions of arithmetic. See Archytas' fragment B3 in Diels and Kranz, *Die Fragmente der Vorsokratiker* (hereafter Diels–Kranz) 1, and Zhmud's discussion in *Origin of the History of Science*, 61–62. Mueller treats the plural use of the term by Plato in the context of the origin of the quadrivium ("Mathematics and Education," 88–93).

He uses the example of Callias or Socrates, a particular person, being ill (981a8). Doctoring without experience can lead to the wrong therapy being administered (a23). Aristotle's father was a doctor, and it may be that this perspective leads him to reduce the distance between experience and craft. He goes on to divide craftsmen into directors or architects (ἀρχιτέκτονες) and manual craftsmen (χειροτέχναι). The former are wiser and have knowledge of what to do that is more to be honored because it is knowledge of causes, which the artisan laborer does not have. A key difference between craft and experience, which must lead us to say craft is "more science" than experience is that craft is teachable, while experience is not (981b8–10). The non-teachability of experience is sometimes taken to show its limitation to the realm of perception and to inarticulate awareness that is by itself useless.[107] Given the superiority of the practice of the man of experience in some cases, the non-teachability of experience could just as likely indicate that an extensive and valuable sort of knowledge is attained in some other way than by reasoning to or from principles or by copying understanding from one mind to another.

A problem in developing an interpretation of *empeiria* as extensive and useful knowledge is its relation to memory and universals.

---

107   It would not be accurate to say, on the basis of *Metaphysics* A.1, that Aristotle associates experience with the manual laborer. The chapter includes a passage that has been very influential in the Aristotelian tradition but is quite possibly not by Aristotle at all. In these lines (981b2–5), the *ethos* of the manual worker is compared to the nature (*phusis*) of inanimate things that act without knowledge in the way fire burns. The passage makes a human cognitive activity even more necessitated than any animal behavior. The passage is enclosed in double brackets in Burnet's Oxford edition but is generally not flagged as of doubtful origin in translations of the *Metaphysics*. The thought expressed does not seem to be part of the even-handed assessment of experience that has just preceded it. Different in content and tone from what surrounds it, the lines interrupt a development of thought that is otherwise quite consistent in terminology concerning who we think is wiser and more to be honored in knowledge and why. The passage is omitted in the text of one recension, A^b, where it has been added marginally in another hand. Alexander does not include the passage in his commentary (*CAG* 1, *In metaphysica*, ed. Hayduck, 6). Concerning this passage, see Steel, ed., *Metaphysics* A, which includes a new critical edition of *Metaphysics* I by Oliver Primavesi. In his Introduction to the edition, Primavesi understands the manuscript A^b to be a version of a β family of manuscripts that follow Alexander's commentary on the *Metaphysics*. Nevertheless, he acknowledges the presence of passages in the α family of manuscripts, which seem to be supplements, "passages which are extant in α, absent in β, and not paraphrased or commented upon by Alexander" (Steel, *Metaphysics* A, 439). Primavesi treats 981b–5 in this group (452–454). He does not reject it outright as part of the text but notes the difficulties of its placement in the text, saying "The supplement is acceptable if and only if it does not tear asunder the treatment of the master-workers, but follows it, . . ." (453).

In *Posterior Analytics* II.19, experience is characterized in terms of a "one experience" formed from many memories of the same occurrence (100a3–6).[108] Out of this one experience, not the many memories, comes craft and science. Since this one that came from perception and memory is applicable to many, it is universal in a weak sense. Aristotle calls it a *logos* (100a2). Aristotle's privileging of experience in relation to craft knowledge in *Metaphysics* A.1 makes it seem that the *logos* of memory utilized in experience is consciously held in a context of reasoning. The untrained but practiced midwife, for instance, does not act by rote or instinct but knows what she is doing and chooses among alternative actions, even if she cannot explain the "why" of complications in childbirth as a doctor could. It has been common in scholarship, however, to say the *logos* known in experience must remain at the level of particulars. It is the connection to particulars, after all, that makes experience occasionally superior to craft. Frede goes so far as to deny that there can be a grasp of universals except through first principles.[109] A grasp of the relation of significant attributes of things involves concepts. The features involved in concepts must be truly relevant to whatness and relation, and cognition at this level is thinking. Either experience is composed of true concepts, in which case it dissolves into craft and science, or else it is inarticulate, numb holding of a one that has emerged out of many perceptions and represents them. LaBarge presents the problem with the latter option, which I have just addressed in the example of the midwife:

> Any person who has the ability to sort particulars and recognize connections in the way that a person with *empeiria* does must be aware at some level of the existence of those sortal categories too, at least in a rough and inarticulate way, and is able thereby to ask what ultimately distinguishes those categories and makes them what they are.[110]

---

108 The problem arises in part from the ambiguity of the text itself in *Posterior Analytics* II.19, 100a3–b5. See 100a16–17 and b1, where the one experience making a stand out of many memories is described as a universal. Here, Aristotle says that even perception is of the universal "man" and not of the particular man Callias. Compare that to 100b2, where the word *kathalou* is used of genera like animal, the grasp of which may come later in the refinement of concepts (ἕως ζῷον). For treatments of the problem, see Ross, *Analytics*, 677, and LaBarge, "Empeiria," 27.

109 Frede, "Rationalism," 163.

110 LaBarge, "Empeiria," 36–37.

How can the person of experience do the things with which Aristotle credits him without being aware of the common property he holds and without knowing the property to be persistent enough in cases of this kind to justify taking action of a particular sort?

LaBarge's solution is that experience is cognition of a universal but not a conscious grasp of articulated essence. It is fitting to call experience "knowledge," in Aristotle's general sense of *gnôsis*. What distinguishes types of *gnôsis* are their proper objects, LaBarge says. Perception and experience address themselves to particulars, while the next faculty up the cognitive ladder, craft, already treats universals. For this difference in objects to be in effect, however, does not mean a given faculty has nothing to do with the other objects. Perception and experience are both mentioned by Aristotle as being cognition of universals.[111] For this view of experience to be helpful, the universals of experience must be relevant in the way Frede says belongs only to thinking. That is, much of experience must be "on target" in the sense of being primitive universal knowledge of what will be known later in terms of essence or whatness. Following Ackrill, LaBarge connects experience to the *hoti–dioti* framework of the *Posterior Analytics*, making experiential knowledge *hoti* knowledge of the unity shared by some subjects because of a feature they possess. The *hoti* grasp of a fact is not just of a unity cognized perceptually, however, but is a grasp of a unity that is scientifically explicable.[112] Accordingly, experiential knowledge contains natural kind features waiting for appropriate clarification.

This solution to the problem of the universal in experience focuses on pre-demonstrative knowledge in propositional form.[113] There is, however, a problem with this view. It leaves unaddressed how the knower distinguishes accidental or merely apparent unities from unities that are scientifically explicable. It is still left to thinking to perform this task. If there is work done by the faculty of experience in distinguishing traits

---

111 LaBarge, "Empeiria," 39. For perception in relation to universals, see *Posterior Analytics* II.19, 100a17. See also *Posterior Analytics* I.31, where Aristotle contrasts knowledge of the universal, as cause, to perception of the particular. Here he is not concerned with cognitive faculties, but his aim is to deny that we ever perceive a cause as cause. Grasp of a cause takes intellect, *nous*.

112 LaBarge, "Empeiria," 35–36.

113 This interpretation of pre-demonstrative propositional knowledge as precursor is endorsed by many interpreters and is not disputed by the account offered here. See in particular Pritzl, "Opinions," 44–49, and Lennox, "Data and Demonstration," 41–46.

that simply are in effect in a state of affairs from traits that cannot be otherwise, it is not clear what the work is. That experience is a weak contributor to knowledge is the view of Frede, who says knowledge of essences and reasoning to connections among things has no part even in the day-to-day reasoning of ordinary life. Accordingly, he says Aristotle's insistence that all knowledge begins in sense experience is puzzling, for Aristotle himself is a rationalist: "it turns out that nothing that could be said to be known by experience could possibly constitute the explanation of something."[114]

Awareness of mechanical forces presents a different perspective on the knowledge gap between experience and thought. The moving radius principle is perceived vaguely in kinesthetic experience as a particular kind of irresistibility of the force of motion. The pattern of compelling movements is registered in cognition, because the one undergoing the forces reacts. The experience that makes one able to avoid a fall on ice or lean into a curve to pass an outlying charioteer or racer is grasping a property of circular motion without having separated subject and attribute. The first, avoiding a fall, is the ability of the sensory motor system to respond to what we call torque. Leaning into a curve, on the other hand, involves a level of awareness of how the weight of one's body will affect motion and its direction. Nestor's instructions to his son do not rise to the level of craft—perhaps for everyone in earshot he seemed to state the obvious. Plato nevertheless uses Nestor's advice to explicate a crisp notion of expertise for philosophical purposes.[115] By the time of Plato and Aristotle, however, the property at work in leaning at high speed or landing a fish with a pole or reed is formulated as a remarkable feature of circular motion. There is a *kath'hauto* relation of the subject—i.e., the circle—and its property. Experience of forces of motion provides a way of understanding how experience is a *logos*. Aristotle uses this term because an experience is articulated; a property is noticed as distinctive and as the means of re-identifying an experience.[116]

---

114 Frede, "Rationalism," 160, also 165–166.

115 *Ion* 537c. See also *Gorgias* 448c, where Plato makes *empeiria* what leads to craft.

116 Cambiano suggests that the problem of experience being "of the same thing" yet not universal knowledge might be resolved by the sameness being "an identity among relations" (Cambiano, "Desire to Know," 18). Unfortunately, he then goes on to characterize experience as a conjunction of similar propositions about the past, so that what is distinctive about human experience is the ability to form propositions. While I would endorse Cambiano's suggestion to consider experience as general knowledge of relations, I under-

There are three stages discernible in the articulation of experience. First, there is recognized as belonging to a state of affairs either (*a*) a natural coercion, or (*b*) a natural requirement for the success of an action undertaken. In terms of the examples of the capsizing boat and the charioteer, this stage would be the following:

> (1*a*) the coercion of capsizing in a choppy sea,
> (1*b*) the requirement to pull to the inside at the post if you want to pass the others.

Then, there is the rough first separation, by the one undergoing the experience, of the state of affairs into subject and predicate:

> (2*a*) the boat capsizing when slapped by waves parallel to it,
> (2*b*) a circular shape being the route that allows slower horses on the inside to pass faster horses.

Finally, there is a recognition of the universality of the phenomenon together with a resolution of its coerciveness:

> (3*a*) steer into the waves when it is windy and the wave are this high,
> (3*b*) get to the inside of the track, lean to the inside, and rein the inside horse harder than the one outside.

These are all cases of *empeiria*, but only the first could be said to be without conscious acknowledgment of a necessity at work at the time of its occurrence. Stages (2) and (3) do involve acknowledgment of the coercion or requirement as something compelling. Essential to that acknowledgment is some level of articulation in cognition. Stages (2) and (3) do not qualify as craft or science, because they only separate subject

---

stand the knowledge (*gnôsis*) to be pre-propositional, because relational attributes exert themselves in perception and experience. Alexander of Aphrodias refers to experience as *gnôsis*: "How experience comes out of memory he says clearly. For experience is already a kind of rational knowledge (*tis logikê gnôsis*). Experience falls short of craft in that experience is a sort of universalizable (*katholikê*) knowledge of what is remembered frequently, which itself is the particular; while craft is knowledge not only of this but also of every [particular] similar to this *as one*. So, as experience is in relation to memory, which is of a particular thing or relation (*logos*) one in number, in this way craft and science are in relation to experience" (*in Metaphysica* 4.20–28).

and predicate in a situation identified as involving necessities. The third stage incorporates an element of control of the necessities, which depend on a cause that remains submerged to understanding. This most articulate level of experience is best expressed by commands, because the requirement or coercion of the situation has been fully acknowledged in a way that involves parrying action. The command form of statement parallels *empeiria*'s limitation to particulars.

A passage in Aristotle supporting this threefold division of *empeiria*, including its involvement of something like commands, is *Nichomachean Ethics* VI.1–2. Aristotle says that faculties of the soul sharing in reason deal either with what cannot be otherwise (*to epistêmonikon*, the faculty for science or knowledge) or with what can possibly be different than it is (*to logistikon*, the faculty for calculation) (1139a3–9). Calculating is the same as deliberating or planning (*to bouleuesthai*) to attain a desired end (a12–13). Just as in reasoning there is affirmation and denial, so also in desire there is pursuit and avoidance (1139a21–22). Experience is the domain of calculation and involves a level of awareness appropriate to pursuit and avoidance. Thus, its reasoning and awareness, if verbalized, would be articulated in the way appropriate to commands.[117]

How might the identification of these levels of experience aid in resolving the outstanding problems attendant to Aristotle's idea of *nous*? For a long time, the challenge in interpreting Aristotle's insistence that *nous* grasps first principles of science was to overcome the idea that *nous* is simply rational intuition, an immediate (quick and unmediated) grasp of sophisticated starting points of deduction. Another problem has been to separate it from induction, which is more recognizable as a psychological process—generalizing from many cases—than is *nous*, which seems to be the outcome of induction. Understanding *nous* as the *faculty* of knowing principles or starting points of deductive science has helped to dissociate *nous* both from induction and from a serendipitous talent for dis-

---

117   To stave off a possible confusion, I will note that, on my account, experience concerns natural necessities expressed through coping action and simple machines. The fourth type of *kath'hauto* in *Posterior Analytics* I.4, the *di'auto* (73b13–16), may sometimes fit the type of necessity with which experience deals. In Galileo's treatise on demonstration (appropriated from Carbone and Vallius), the author says that many propositions in the fourth mode of *per se* are contingent. The example Galileo gives is that a hot thing heats (Galileo, *Treatises*, 164). This could be said either of fire or of a heated piece of iron. The latter is only contingently hot. Aristotle's too succinct example is that an animal, being slaughtered, dies.

covery.[118] First principles are grasped by a distinctive faculty because the connection between subject and predicate, in their case, follows directly from essence. This is reflected, in logical discourse, in premises that are not mediated by any other terms.[119] As recent scholarship shows, the natural precedent to *nous* in the psychology of knowing may not always be induction but may be a pre-demonstrative stage of reasoned discourse about the connections that will figure in first principles. As Frede's interpretation also makes clear, however, it has remained difficult to say how the action of *nous* as a faculty differs from rational intuition.

The interpretive solution coming out of the view of *empeiria* that I have developed would be as follows. We must take Aristotle at his word, in *Posterior Analytics* II.19 when he answers the question of the source of first principles so decisively as being perception (99b35). The percepts of natural necessity may receive an immediate response, a sign of an assertive and genuine coercion. This is the first stage of experience, because a property has been noticed as distinctive to the undergoing. The property in its state of affairs is what remains (99b36) as a percept (e.g., stage 1a: choppy waves/over I go) and becomes a memory for those animals capable of memory. *Nous* is not involved in this stage.

Nous plays a role in the second and third levels of experience. Intellectual cognition makes incursions into experience, so to speak, solidifying the connection noticed between, e.g., the position of the boat relative to the waves and its capsizing (stage 2a). Solidifying the connection means an intellectual cognition of the commonality noticed in experience but cognized now as something that, locally at least and in this situation, cannot be otherwise. So, intellectual cognition, in its incursion into experience, thinks the commonality (the *logos* of experience) as what needs to be addressed in action: Do this, do that (3a, 3b).

The *logos* of experience is already a bit of organized knowledge, though, before *nous* begins to intellectualize it. The subject and the property are distinguished in a *logos*. For example, the boat being parallel to the waves ($B_{parallel}$) is the subject, and capsizing (X) is the property; so

---

118   Aristotle recognizes such a talent but calls it ἀγχίνοια, quickness of wit in discerning first principles (*Posterior Analytics* I.34).

119   Aristotle distinguishes demonstration in the strict sense as having not only a cause as the middle term but a cause that *qua* itself (ᾗ αὐτό, *hê auto*) accounts for its predicate (*Posterior Analytics* I.4, 73b27, I.13, 78b13–23). This is called commensurate universality. The middle term is not a remote cause, in the way that life could be said to be the remote cause of breathing.

71

$\Phi(B_{parallel})$.[120] *Nous* as a faculty cognizes what is predicated insofar as it is always present in the subject. There is necessity, but it may turn out to be the necessity of a mediated conclusion. As we might say colloquially, there is an unmediated necessary connection in there somewhere. So, *nous* is rough-and-ready enough to be a faculty at work in everyday life.

It seems clear, though, that in *Posterior Analytics* II.19 Aristotle means for *nous* to grasp foundational premises for a true science. In this its core role in knowledge, a good term for *nous* is "secured knowledge." Secured knowledge is knowledge so reliably descriptive of what cannot be otherwise that it is capable of translation into other situations as constituting their explanatory cause. This is just the method of *Mechanics*, where the author shows that the faster and slower speeds of moving concentric arcs explain the working of a host of simple machines. In its scientific role, *nous* concerns knowledge that can be propositionalized, but as *Mechanics* shows, propositional formulation is not always necessary to science if a mathematical formulation better expresses the cause. A feature separating *nous* from other faculties is its proper object. The predicate in a propositional formulation known by *nous* is a trait related to the subject either as descriptive of its essence or as a property always present in the subject without being part of essence. This is why it is explanatory.[121] As Aristotle says, "the unit in deduction is the unmediated premise, but the unit in demonstration and science is *nous*."[122]

I have distinguished two functions of *nous*—(*a*) its reinforcement of a subject/property *logos* formed in experience, and (*b*) its resting in a trait being predicated of a subject where the predicate follows from the subject as what cannot be otherwise and without any intermediate term. The two different functions of *nous* have their parallel in the different kinds

---

120   To be more precise, the boat being parallel to the waves is itself a state of affairs, $\Pi(b)$. This state of affairs is linked to the boat capsizing (X). So, if $\Pi(b)$, then $X(b)$. In thought, $X(b)$ is a deduced property of b. Once we are aiming at precision, the wind velocity or height of the waves should also be included, etc.

121   These are the first two kinds of *kath'hauto* in *Posterior Analytics* I.4. There is a debate extending through the historical Aristotelian tradition as to whether the second kind of *kath'hauto*—what follows from essence without being part of essence—appears in premises or only in conclusions. This debate involves how different the fourth kind of *kath'hauto*, the "through itself" (*di'auto*), might be from the first and second. For a treatment of the underlying problem in Aristotle, see J. E. Tiles, "Triangle." For a sense of the issues in the tradition of commentary on *Posterior Analytics*, see Wallace, *Discovery and Proof*, 179–181, and *Galileo's Logical Treatises*, D2.8–2.10 (158–167) and commentary.

122   *Posterior Analytics* II.23, 84b39–85a1.

of demonstration given by Aristotle in *Posterior Analytics* I.13. Even in demonstrations that take the *dioti* form—i.e., demonstrations where the premises are prior in the order of nature to the conclusion—there is a demonstration he calls *hoti*, a demonstration *that* something is the case rather than *why* it is the case. This is because some demonstrations in which premises are prior in themselves to the conclusion still do not state the cause that is most immediately the cause of the predicate. So, even though the premises are necessary in the requisite sense and also prior, they are not proper to the conclusion.[123] Giving life as the cause of breathing is giving a remote cause rather than a proper cause, since some living things do not breathe but absorb oxygen in another way. *Nous* in its incursions into experience often reinforces the kind of reliable necessity—what breathes also lives—that needs further analysis. We realize this when, having learned some rudimentary boatsmanship, we want to know more precisely why the boat sometimes rocks gently when parallel to the waves and sometimes is capsized in that configuration.

I have argued that Aristotle believes knowledge of necessity (ἀνάγκη) and of what cannot be otherwise (ἀδύνατον ἄλλως ἔχειν or μὴ ἐνδέχεσθαι ἄλλως ἔχειν) has its beginning in the coercion and requirements laid upon us by nature in the midst of actions we take. These are known in experience, *empeiria*. Aristotle makes clear, however, that the chief faculties concerned with what cannot be otherwise are *epistêmê* and *nous*.[124] If he meant for *empeiria* to be concerned with the same topic, why did he not say so? One answer to this question is that he did say so, with the sequence of faculties that he gives in *Posterior Analytics* II.19 and *Metaphysics* A.1 but that it is difficult for modern readers to see this answer as sufficient. We assume the vantage point of theoretical science. For a philosopher with Aristotle's sensibilities as a naturalist, the novelty about the emerging idea of science (*epistêmê*) in the fourth century BC is not that it depends on familiarity with the requirements of craft and *praxis* but rather that there could be a single proper cause from which a set of *phainomena* are related by deduction. The term, *to katholou*, for the universal is for him an honorific term, its primary sense being, as also for *nous*, its connection to disinterested knowledge of what always holds the same way. The sequence of faculties given in *Posterior Analytics* II.19 is not a sparse account but one bursting with occasions for comparison to

---

123 *Posterior Analytics* I.13, 78a22–26, 78b13–21.

124 *Posterior Analytics* I.2, 71b9–17; *Nicomachean Ethics* VI. 4 and 6.

the behavior of animals and the manners of articulation of human beings. The sequence tells us not just that these faculties in this order function in the formation of scientific concepts but also that these faculties form a continuum of awareness and understanding. We can only take his point if we understand that first principles come out of our perception of all the ways the world "hems us in" in physical terms. Natural necessities are perceived, but we do not yet call them natural necessities when they are perceived.

Considering the origin of knowledge about torque and mechanical advantage provides a reason—and a textual basis—for expanding into a more detailed spectrum Aristotle's range of facultative knowledge at the levels of perception, experience, and craft. Experience is wide enough to include experiential knowledge either closer to perception or closer to craft and science. Since reactive knowledge can be present in a way that is submerged to intellectual cognition, experience of this sort is close to perception. This proximity to perception does not rule out grasp of an attribute—the effect of leaning in circular motion—being universal knowledge that is intellectually respectable, because mechanical forces are experienced in the body in repeated instances as what cannot be otherwise.[125]

My consideration of the ways the principle of the lever was expressed in pre-scientific discourse provides an example of how *kath'hauto* traits were known in experience. What we will see in subsequent chapters is that Aristotle himself drew upon the experience of lever phenomena as he forged key concepts of his natural philosophy. His remarks on perception, experience, and craft are consistent with his own cognitive process and methodology, as well as with the practices and technique he saw around him.

There are some impediments in scholarly expectation to accepting that necessities are noticed in perception. One is the widely accepted view, argued by G. E. L. Owen and Martha Nussbaum, that the method of Aristotelian science is dialectic and its subject matter is τὰ λεγόμενα, things said. This makes natural philosophy not essentially different

---

125 Frede seems to acknowledge something like this origin of knowledge in saying that reason is "acquired" in a natural process ("Rationalism," 171). He says, however, that first principles are only causally based on perception, whereas what is important is their epistemic base, and this is why Aristotle is still an "extreme rationalist" (171). Frede makes a great deal depend on a distinction (tenuous as applied to Aristotle) between causal and epistemic foundations of knowledge.

from ethics or logical analysis in either its subject matter or method. Perceptions must be the subject of science as statements, propositions. Another scholarly impediment is the tendency of some to ground all the important concepts of Aristotle's natural philosophy in metaphysics rather than in nature. In either the dialectical or metaphysical interpretation, philosophy of nature is derivative, lacking a method corresponding originally to its own subject matter, changeable and perceptible things. A brief treatment of the limitations of both the dialectical and metaphysical approaches to natural philosophy will highlight the more general philosophical import of finding mechanical necessities in perception. I will begin with the metaphysical approach to natural philosophy.

Experience and Natural Philosophy

One scholar who held the view that universals are items of perception is Joseph Owens.[126] A brief consideration of Owens' argument will show what is at stake in universals being part of experience or not. Owens analyzes *Physics* I.1, a fundamental text concerning Aristotle's way of making progress (μέθοδος) in natural science. In this passage, Aristotle describes the progress of knowledge from what is closer to perception and more easily grasped (γνωριμώτερα ἡμῖν, more knowable to us) to the knowing of the same things in terms of first principles. Aristotle's example is moving from the vague notion of roundness to the formulation of a circle in terms of its principles. In this passage, Aristotle says that the earlier vague knowledge, more knowable to us, is a universal (τὸ καθόλου) and that the later knowledge of principles is a distinguishing into particulars (καθ'ἕκαστα) (184a25–b3). This apparent inversion of the terms involved in the progress of knowledge—from universal to particular—led Ross to conclude that, in *Physics* I.1, *katholou* "is not used in its usual Aristotelian meaning."[127] Owens insists that Aristotle means by *katholou* the same thing that he meant in all other context, namely "said of many." Aristotle does not have in mind either a determinate nature (as Philoponus thought) or a generic nature (Ross's interpretation) with his reference to the wholes more knowable in experience. Aristotle does have

---

126   Joseph Owens, "Universality," 61–69. (Note that G. E. L. Owen and Joseph Owens are different scholars of ancient philosophy writing during the same period of time in the twentieth century.)

127   Ross, *Physics*, 457.

in mind a different meaning for καθ'ἕκαστα. The particulars at issue in the passage are parts of the correct definition of the original whole.

Owens carries his interpretation so far as to say that the original perceptual universal remains a genuine universal, because it is always something predicable of many. In this, he differs from interpreters of *Physics* I.1 like Bolton, who relate the passage to *Posterior Analytics* II.8–10. Bolton sees the original universal superseded by a scientifically articulated replacement.[128] Again, the original predication is taken in a *hoti–dioti* framework of scientific understanding. Owens's insistence that perceptual universals remain and are not cognitively mutable, so to speak, stems from his commitment to there being a distinctive philosophical method different from any scientific method. Starting with the sensible in general, it takes a difficult process of reasoning and judgment to attain the distinction between material and immaterial being and the concepts common to both realms. These concepts common to both realms include concepts of principles—potentiality and actuality, matter and form. Such distinctions are not offered to the human mind by the sensible. For Owens, the universal in perception is barred by the noetic structure of metaphysical knowledge from yielding principles. Importantly for our purposes, perception is incapable of knowing of natural necessities *that they are necessary*.[129] All varieties of necessity treated by metaphysics, like essence or property, are grasped by the special method of metaphysics being applied to the original most vague grasp of the sensible thing.

Owens's characterization of perceptual universals moves too quickly from a primitive sensible universal to the elaboration of sophisticated principles in terms of their immaterial character and metaphysical features. Philosophy of nature, he says, treats these principles insofar as changeable being has them. This approach emphasizes the deductive structure of Aristotelian philosophy, but raises the question of where metaphysics gets its necessities, potencies, and forms on which its distinctive method operates. Were none of these present in sensible things until metaphysics found them? The metaphysician can say either that, from his standpoint,

---

128   Bolton, "Method," 10–13.

129   Knowing of something that cannot hold otherwise that it has this feature of necessity is one of the criteria Aristotle gives for scientific knowing in *Posterior Analytics* I.4. Owens says, "The first confused notion for human cognition is that of 'something sensible.' This functions as a universal in the Aristotelian noetic for all further cognition. . . . It does not allow any notion that extends beyond the sensible to be seen immediately in the objects directly presented to human cognition" ("Universality," 72).

it does not matter how they were present in sensible things, or simply that they were not there without metaphysical method. Owens's answer is to emphasize the sensible universal as the starting point of cognition as well. This answer repeats the original problem at the level of philosophical psychology. The assumption is that our understanding of things is actually satisfied by conceiving of form in terms of visual properties like shape. A zebra is what it looks like. The unity of a thing is the unity noticed in its first sensible appearance. Owens embraces this implication:

> In the philosophy of nature, any form of a thing is conceived in the manner of the shape or figure that will make the wood in one case into a table, in another into a chair. That is the model on which the notion is developed when used in that branch of philosophy. Now, in the primary philosophy, the explanation has to be given in terms of being. The concept will be of exactly the same object, but will be framed in metaphysical fashion. It will aim at making manifest the kind of being that the form involves. It will be meant therefore to express in strictly metaphysical language the way the form is always the basic type of being for the matter and the composite.[130]

This interpretation of philosophy of nature makes the conception of form in nature quite limited. Any conception of potency derived from this contrast of natural philosophy and metaphysics would be similarly narrow and understandable only from the viewpoint of metaphysics. To be fair, Owens's main concern is to delineate the subject matter of metaphysics, but philosophy of nature is a casualty of the process. In fact, between the sensible universal and the being of form, there is much that philosophy of nature must clarify.

Philosophy of nature is the first manner of reflection on the experience of necessity. Its focus on changeable things makes it the theater for the disclosure of properties, because natural philosophical analysis identifies properties as recurrent powers for change. As we have already begun to see, the contrast of subject and property emerges in this theater of reflection. Philosophy of nature also explicates, by the content of real cases, the difference between essence and property. It can also shed light on what forms and potencies are or how they are manifest in the natural world.

---

130   Owens, *Gradations,* 109.

I have addressed the view of Joseph Owens, because he expresses in an especially clear way some tendencies present in much contemporary Aristotelian analysis.[131] First, there is the assumption that Aristotle never got far beyond a conception of form as what is most immediately intuitable about a thing. Form may not be conceived solely in visual terms, but a whole known by sensible traits alone always suffices as a placeholder for analysis of form in first philosophy.[132]

This assumption goes along with another—that Aristotelian science, even in its pre-demonstrative stage, is a science of concepts expressed in words. It is not mathematical in conception or content. In contrast to this point of view, I would identify two key aspects of form: (1) it is the source of unity in a thing or in a change, and (2) it requires a distinguishing of subject (τὸ ὑποκείμενον, the underlying) and what is essential to a subject (καθ'αὑτό). These two aspects of form are manifest in some mathematical relations and in attributes of mathematical objects. There is no bar to forms being conceived in terms incorporating mathematical understanding if the conception manifests these form-features. One reason to dwell upon the gradations of experience and intellectual knowledge of the moving radius principle is to show concretely how mathematical properties of a subject, a material body subject to forces, come to be understood as necessary and thus become candidates for the *kath'hauto*.[133] Aristotle's natural philosophy—i.e., a philosophy about natural things— makes a crucial contribution to the meaning of form and potency respec-

---

131 Frede more or less reiterates Owens's view of how little in the way of actual knowledge can be part of a universal in perception. See the quote above from his "Rationalism," 160, and footnote 125 in this chapter.

132 In contrast, Sokolowski has argued for an understanding of form that hinges on the distinction of property and accident as these are revealed in progressively more sophisticated forms of ordinary knowledge (*Phenomenology*, 103–135). He further notes that a property is a potentiality, or power: "Any time we use a word to designate a feature of a thing, we surreptitiously invoke the distinction between potentiality and actuality" (119–120). This is a useful point in relation to the meaning of *dunamis* addressed in Chapters 5–6.

133 These traits would appear in the category of relation, for Aristotle, not quantity. Additionally, in speaking of mathematics in this ancient context, we should note the difference between form (εἶδος) and the modern notion, "formal." Although there are elements of structure and relation in Aristotle's appropriation of the moving radius principle in natural philosophy, it is not empty of content in physical terms, as modern mathematical formalism is sometimes understood to be. We must also bear in mind that this mathematical principle incorporates motion from the very beginning of its being reflected upon by Plato and Aristotle. To this extent, it was never a candidate for interpretation in terms that are strictly mathematical. Aristotle followed Plato in making mathematical objects immovable. Mechanics as incorporating mathematical traits is treated in a later chapter.

tively. It misrepresents Aristotle's natural philosophy, and perhaps also form, to move directly from sensible form, as shape, color, and texture, to metaphysical subjects.

To fill out the meaning of *empeiria* in Aristotle's science and to understand better the range of the concept of form, we need to see some instance of knowledge of mathematical features of motion that is continuous with experience but treated by Aristotle at the level of natural science. We also need to see how Aristotle understands these instances in relation to perception. At this point, we come up against the limitation of the dialectical interpretation of Aristotle's science, argued originally by G. E. L. Owen.[134] On this view, Aristotle's science develops dialectically on a base of conventional wisdom expressed propositionally. Briefly put, this view weakens the sense and importance of perceptual cognitions, because *phainomena* are accessible to knowledge only as what people say.[135] An examination of what Aristotle means by *phainomenon* and *ta phainomena* as he discusses the scientific import of particular instances is thus crucial. These Greek terms are singular and plural respectively of the present participle for φαίνεται, a verb in the middle voice meaning "to become plain or to be evident." The singular is often translated as "appearance." The meaning of the plural, translated as "observed facts" by Ross, became the subject of revision as *phainomena* became a subsidiary player in a debate about the role of *endoxa*, common opinions, in the discourse that establishes knowledge.

Owen argued that Aristotle's treatment of place in *Physics* IV is dialectical and starts with commonly held opinions about nature. In developing his view, Owen presented *Prior Analytics* I.30 and *Nichomachean Ethics* I.2 together but distinguished the senses of *phainomena* in the two passages. In *Nichomachean Ethics* I.2, *phainomena* are details of human ethical behavior that vindicate *endoxa*, commonly accepted facts about human behavior. In *Prior Analytics* I.30, astronomical experience provided the principles for astronomical science, "for when the *phainomena* were sufficiently grasped, in this way astronomical demonstrations were found" (a19–21).[136] This sentence has always been read to mean that a

---

134 See *"Tithenai ta phainomena,"* in *Collected Essays,* ed. Nussbaum.

135 Bolton gives a thorough treatment of the problem in taking perception seriously after Owen in "Aristotle's *Posterior Analytics* and *Generation of Animals.*"

136 The word for astronomy here is ἀστρολογική from ἀστρολογία, the term he uses for mathematical astronomy in *Physics* II.2.

critical quantity of observational data is required for induction of first principles in a science. The example is taken to yield, as G. E. L. Owen puts it, "a Baconian picture."[137] Astronomical *phainomena* are parallel to evidence from human social experience but more strictly "data of observation."[138]

Nussbaum disputed Owen's Baconian interpretation of *phainomena* in *Prior Analytics* I.30. She replaced it with a conception of *phainomena* as being the product of human critical faculties but also as laden with communal belief.[139] She did not develop this interpretation in relation to *Prior Analytics* I.30, however, because she was most interested in *phainomena* in human social and ethical behavior. Nussbaum understood *endoxa* to be themselves subject to revision. Nussbaum claims there is no need for two different conceptions of *phainomena*, one for science and one for ethics.[140] *Phainomena* and *endoxa* are thus roughly the same—opinions (statements) subject to logical analysis. That both *endoxa* and *phainomena* need to earn their credentials as reliable knowledge came to be itself a received opinion.[141] For Nussbaum, this idea is connected to the "internal realism" she ascribes to Aristotle. Every person finds truth only inside a circle of appearances, inside of our own language and lived experience.[142]

That some *phainomena* are perceptual without being also common opinions is sometimes noted in the scholarship on *endoxa*,[143] but

---

137 Owen, *"Tithenai,"* 239. Shute gives a similar rendering of *Prior Analytics* I.30 (*Writings*, 5). Although the Baconian exaggeration has been tempered by other scholarship, the assimilation of *phainomena* to opinions as the starting points of science remains common. *Endoxa* and *phainomena* are both appearances (Nussbaum, *Fragility*, 245; Burnyeat, "Repute," 11–12; Wians, "Appearances," 146).

138 Owen, *"Tithenai,"* 241.

139 Nussbaum, *Fragility*, 244. See also her "Saving Aristotle's Appearances."

140 Nussbaum, *Fragility*, 244–245 and ch. 8n11. She distinguishes a scientific account from practical deliberation to the extent that a single account of place or the cosmos might emerge from analyzing physical *endoxa* while no single account of the good would emerge from ethical *endoxa* (192).

141 The view is explained by Barnes, "Method of Ethics," 490–491. Pritzl argues against it, making *endoxa* statements of what is the case rendered in such a way that they can be given a reason or cause ("Opinions," 45).

142 Nussbaum, *Fragility*, 257–268. The position she ascribes to Aristotle is given both a philosophical and textual critique by Cooper, "Authority."

143 Pritzl distinguishes perceptual *phainomena* from *phainomena* that are *endoxa* ("Opinions," 45). Irwin similarly recognizes a subset of *phainomena* that are more purely

the weight of Owen's groundbreaking article and subsequent scholarly commentary was to make perceptual *phainomena* of small import when taken outside of statements of commonly held opinions about nature. Aristotelian natural science was propositional and had its sources in conventional opinion about nature. Scholars who remained focused on the robust empiricism of Aristotle's science apart from the endoxic method include G. E. R. Lloyd, James Lennox, D. M. Balme, and Allan Gotthelf. In many quarters, however, it became accepted that there is no essential difference between logical analysis and natural philosophical analysis in Aristotle.[144]

The interpretation of Aristotle's science as endoxic in origin and method makes Aristotle's natural philosophy a subsidiary of logic, as Joseph Owens's view makes it a subsidiary of metaphysics. Natural philosophy is an enterprise lacking a method of its own arising from and suited to its own subject matter, changeable things. The endoxic interpretation is certainly an impediment to understanding how mathematical traits might be perceived and grasped in perception as necessary. This is because no knowledge even enters the frame of reference of the scientist or philosopher until it is expressed propositionally. Indeed, scientific knowledge so conceived is oddly detached from perception and experience, because it is statements that are analyzed, not occurrences or properties. While Aristotle gained a great deal from analysis of what others had said in the area of natural philosophy, his regard for opinions of the physicists was not, I contend, the main thrust of his scientific interest. Let us then begin to flesh out an alternate view of Aristotle's empiricism, by considering *Prior Analytics* I.30 apart from the logical and ethical context of dialectical reasoning, taking it instead in connection with the meaning of *phainomena* in astronomy.

---

perceptual and not opinions but sees problems for Aristotle in how these can be identified so as to be utilized in investigation (*Principles*, 30–31).

144 For Aristotle's empiricism, see, in particular, the essays in Lloyd's *Explorations*. Lennox understands *phainomena* in astronomy as data but focuses on the phase of critical pre-demonstrative investigation, *historia*, as what finds candidates for *kath'hauto* predication that figure in premises of demonstration ("Data and Demonstration," 43). See other essays in Lennox's *Aristotle's Philosophy of Biology*. For a comprehensive evaluation of Aristotle's achievement in biology, see Gotthelf's *Teleology, First Principles, and Scientific Method*. See also Grant's balanced assessment of empiricism and rational methods in Aristotle (*Natural Philosophy*, 33–51). For a recent statement of the endoxic and dialectical character of all Aristotelian discourse but in terms of the possibility of this method serving articulation of the real, see Haskins, "Epistemological Optimism." Salmieri argues against dialectic as a mode of ethical inquiry for Aristotle in "Aristotle's Non-'Dialectical' Methodology."

Chapter 4

Phainomena in Aristotle's Astronomy

That ancient astronomical *phainomena* have been understood in Aristotle's astronomy to be Baconian facts is due in part to the influence of twentieth century interpretation of the Greek phrase, σώζειν τὰ φαινόμενα—saving the appearances. Pierre Duhem articulated a view of the models of ancient astronomy as mathematical fictions aimed at rendering celestial movements accessible to calculation. Physical theory, in his view, did not enter into Greek astronomy.[145] If Duhem is right and a mathematical model is the substance of astronomical theory, then there needs to be a body of non-theoretical observations for which the exclusively mathematical model is meant to account—hence, the alliance of mathematics and data in the philosophical interpretation of Greek astronomy. G. E. R. Lloyd, among others, showed that the opposition of physical and mathematical theories in ancient science is not supported by the texts to the extent that Duhem claims.[146] Furthermore, it has become clear that "saving the appearances" as closely approximating the daily movements of the heavenly bodies by mathematical theory alone was never really a candidate for the meaning of *sôzein ta phainomena* in 5th–4th century Greek astronomy.[147] On this basis and for the sake of simplicity, I omit consideration of Duhem's thesis in assessing the meaning

---

145   Duhem, "*ΣΩZEIN*," (*To Save the Phenomena*, trans. by Doland and Maschler).

146   Lloyd, "Saving the Appearances." Lloyd does not think that even the famous passage from Geminus, quoted by Simplicius, fits Duhem's thesis (212–214).

147   For the re-centering of early Greek astronomy in terms of the issues proper to it and not to later Ptolemaic astronomy, see Bowen and Goldstein, "New View." See also Mendell, "Eudoxus," 86, and Goldstein, "Appearances."

of *phainomena* as Aristotle uses the term in relation to the structure of the heavens.[148] We shall need to be concerned, however, with whether or not *phainomena* in astronomy were conceived in the fourth century BC as a collection of data.

Phainomena and Propositional Knowledge

In *Prior Analytics* I.30, Aristotle connects *empeiria* to the notion of *phainomena*, in particular to astronomical phenomena. He says "it belongs to experience to deliver (παραδοῦναι) the principles for each [area]" (46a18). The larger passage reads as follows:

> In each science, principles special (ἴδιαι) to the science are the most numerous. Thus, it belongs to experience to give the principles of each science. I mean, for example, for astronomical experience to give the principles of astronomical science. (For when the *phainomena* were sufficiently grasped, astronomical demonstrations were found)—similarly too with any other art or science; so that if the facts (τὰ ὑπάρχοντα) concerning each thing are grasped, it is for us readily to make plain (ἐμφανίζειν) the demonstrations. For if none of the attributes truly belonging to things have been left out by investigation (κατὰ τὴν ἱστορίαν), we should find and give a demonstration of everything of which there is demonstration, and of what cannot be demonstrated, make this evident.[149] (46a17–27)

Note first that the passage associates experience with the particular subject matters of the sciences. Principles appropriate to different sciences come from the experience special to that subject matter. Experience thus corresponds to the skilled but untutored familiarity with a given area that is mentioned in *Metaphysics* A.1, which sometimes outperforms learned skill. Aristotle here glosses *phainomena* as τὰ ὑπάρχοντα from ὑπάρχειν, a verb that carries a connotation of existing, holding, or being in effect. With the dative, it signifies what holds of a subject. There are two instances of τὰ ὑπάρχοντα in the passage quoted. In the first, there is no accompanying dative, allowing translation of the term as "facts" (46a23).

---

148   For a comprehensive assessment of Duhem's interpretations of early science, see Murdoch, "Pierre Duhem."

149   Modifed Oxford translation (Jenkinson, *CWA* 1, 73).

The second occurrence (a25) includes "to things," allowing translation as "attributes of things."[150] Aristotle also uses *historia* for investigation, a term which connotes in his biological works pre-demonstrative empirical investigation.[151] So, we have some indication of what experience is: detailed familiarity with the traits belonging to things, which is gained through some sort of reflective investigation. *Phainomena,* as the content of experience, carries a connotation in this passage of reliability or correctness: when the *phainomena* were sufficiently grasped,[152] scientific astronomy was possible.

The astronomical example would suggest that these traits are known by perception. In *On the Heavens* III.7, Aristotle makes clear the priority of perception for knowledge of principles. He argues scathingly against a theory that he attributes to the followers of Empedocles and Democritus that the elements arose by separating out of what already exists[153] (305b3). His grounds for the rejection of the view are that the *phainomena* of perception do not agree with what they say and that they base their accounts on preconceived notions. Perceptible things must be explained from principles drawn from that realm (306a5–10). They argue not to explain facts but like those defending a position in argument (a9–13). The end of natural science is "the *phainomena* always and properly given by perception" (a17).[154] Here, Aristotle emphasizes the importance of principles being suited to what they are meant to explain. There are *phainomena* that are distinctively perceptual. To begin with, at least, it seems clear that Aristotle distinguishes perceptual *phainomena* from statements and claims of the atomists about them. He also distinguishes, conceptually, perception from *phainomena* of perception.[155]

This passage from *On the Heavens* III.7 can be taken, however, to reinforce the view that Aristotle's use of perceptual data was inductive in a simplistic way. The atomists show how science needs bold hypotheses,

---

150 Irwin translates both occurrences as "facts" (*Principles*, 29–30). Jenkinson (*CWA* 1, 73) and Lennox ("Data and Demonstration," 43) translate both as attributes or predicates.

151 On *historia*, see Lennox, "Between Data and Demonstration," 43–46.

152 ληφέντων ἱκανῶς.

153 ἐνυπάρχον ἕκαστον ἐκκρίνεσθαι.

154 Oxford translation of Stocks (*CWA* 1, 500). The Greek of the concluding phrase reads: τὸ φαινόμενον ἀεὶ κυρίως κατὰ τὴν αἴσθησιν.

155 For a valuable textual analysis of *phainomena* and discourse that is *logikôs, eulogon, kata logon* in *On the Heavens*, see Bolton "Two Standards of Enquiry."

and Aristotle is obtuse not to acknowledge this. Indeed, *Prior Analytics* I.30 seems to say clearly that, *before* there can be demonstrations, *phainomena*—multiple appearances—must be in hand. There has been little doubt among scholars that this means a body of data for inductive generalization. In astronomy, the *phainomena* would be measurements of positions of heavenly bodies at given times and their conjunctions and separations—ephemeris data. Astronomical *phainomena* would be expressed in numerical or geometrical notation. There must be a considerable number of such measurements to be meaningful for fitting to a theory. Note, however, that Aristotle says, in *Prior Analytics* I.30, that the *phainomena* are "traits belonging to things" (46a25). This is a formulation he uses in *Posterior Analytics* I.4 for attributes that are essential (*kath'hauta*) either as parts of essence or as necessary properties dependent on essence (73a34–40). Accordingly, multiple appearances in *Prior Analytics* I.30, *ta phainomena*, are attributes proper to particular heavenly bodies, attributes the investigator is confident enough to have settled upon as significant for investigation. In this context, *phainomena* are not the accumulation of daily astronomical sightings, recorded by mapping or position. They are pre-demonstrative knowledge, not raw data but rather attributes that will figure later in a *hoti–dioti* framework of predication. This places them at the perceptual end of a spectrum of knowledge, *gnôsis*.

One problem regarding *phainomena* as perceived has been to know how they should be characterized apart from propositional knowledge. Irwin thinks there are *phainomena* that are more or less purely perceptual for Aristotle, but authoritative percepts are mute, so to speak. Aristotle has a problem in how they can be identified as veridical before investigation.[156] In general, it seems even perceptual *phainomena* must be articulated. If we take them as attributes perceived as significant, and therefore as candidates for the *kath'hauto*, are they perceived as belonging to a subject? If so, are not they already articulated propositionally?

The alternative to propositional knowledge is *nous*, the grasp of whatness associated by Aristotle with knowledge of causes. The forerunner to *nous* in perception is sensible form. Aristotle's remarks on reception of form without the matter are so general that it is difficult to know how to take them into a philosophy of science.[157] In his psychology of

---

156 Irwin, *Principles*, 30–31.

157 *On the Soul* II.12, 424a19.

perception in *On the Soul* II, there is a gap between reception of form without the matter and the holding of causal knowledge by *nous*. This gap is filled by the sequence of cognitive faculties that we have examined in *Posterior Analytics* II.19, and particularly by *empeiria* among those faculties. Aristotle tells us here in *Prior Analytics* I.30 that *phainomena*, as the content of *empeiria*, are ordered to some extent already in a given subject matter. If *phainomena* are perceptual forerunners of *kath'hauto* traits, then they could be regarded as the "parts" of sensible form. Still, what can we say about these attributes when they are percepts and before their proper subjects of attribution have been clarified? If perceptual knowledge has not been formulated propositionally, how is it not something like data? If it has been articulated into subject and significant attribute, why is it not then "something said," and therefore grist for the dialectical mill? To address these questions, let us consider perceptual *phainomena* in relation to Aristotle's own use of the astronomical knowledge gained from the Babylonians.

Percepts and Intelligibility

In *Prior Analytics* I.30, Aristotle's reference to *phainomena* leading to demonstration is closely targeted. He is commenting on the fact that the collection of Babylonian observations on the heavens—the supposed Baconian data—had come into Greek hands relatively late, possibly at the time of Archytas and Plato.[158] He does not actually say what the usefulness of that knowledge is for getting demonstrations. It is our assumption that the very quantity of data provided a base for theorizing. Aristotle does occasionally refer to the longevity of human observation of the heavens supporting some general claim, e.g., that there have been no changes in the heavens.[159] In *On the Heavens* II.12, however, he gives an example of what Babylonian observations added to investigation. *On the Heavens* II.12 begins in the following way:

---

158   On the transfer of Babylonian astronomical knowledge to Greece, see Burkert, *Lore and Science*, ch. 4. He argues for the Greek origin of the important features of the Greek conception of the universe.

159   *On the Heavens* I.3, 270b13–16 reads, "For in the whole range of time past, so far as our inherited records reach (κατὰ τὴν παραδεδομένην ἀλλήλοις μνήμην), no change appears to have taken place either in the whole scheme of the outermost heaven or in any of its proper parts" (Stocks's translation, *CWA* 1, 451).

> There are two difficulties (ἀπορίαιν), which may very
> reasonably here be raised, of which we must now at-
> tempt (πειρατέον) to state what seems to be the case (τὸ
> φαινόμενον), for we regard the zeal (προθυμίαν) of one
> whose thirst for philosophy leads him to accept even slight in-
> dications (μικρὰς εὐπορίας) where the difficulties are great,
> as a proof of modesty rather than over-confidence (αἰδοῦς . .
> . μᾶλλον θράσους).[160]

Here, *to phainomenon*, the singular, means a fact or state of affairs trust-
worthily established as true. The verbal adjective for trying, *peirateon*,
indicates that it may be difficult to establish facts. So, *phainomenon* in
this context, though something empirical, is not obvious but something to
be determined or established, even if it is an outcome mediate to a larger
aim. It is not a datum with which one begins.

Aristotle mentions two puzzles concerning which we try to state the
phainomenon. The first is the question why the heavenly bodies of intermediate distance between the center of the universe and the outermost
sphere, namely the planets, show the greatest variety of movements. One
would expect that those nearest the "first body," the outermost sphere,
would depart least from the movement of that outermost sphere and then
inferior bodies would wander more because of their distance from the
outermost sphere, whose influence diminishes with distance. As it is, the
opposite happens, he says. The sun and moon exhibit fewer movements
than some of the wandering stars, the planets (291b28–292a3). Aristotle
presents this fact as amazing (θαυμαστόν).[161]

The second puzzle is why the uncountable myriad stars of the outermost sphere have an order in common in all their movements, while
the lone planets do not have even two or three movements in common
(292a10–14). These are the puzzles, but what is the fact or state of affairs,

---

160   Oxford translation of Stocks (*CWA* 1, 480). Stocks's translation places emphasis
on the virtue of the researcher. Aristotle, I believe, places emphasis on the combination
of great problems with a limited prospect of resolving the problems. The one thirsting for
knowledge takes an approach commensurate to the context. A translation following more
closely the structure of Aristotle's sentence would conclude thus: "believing it a proof
of modest respect rather than rashness, if someone, because of his thirst for philosophy,
cherishes even small solutions concerning things of which the puzzles are great." The chief
obstacle to astronomical knowledge is our inability to observe the subject matter in close
proximity.

161   This problem is treated at 291b35–292a9 and 292b25–293a14.

to phainomenon, that we must try to state in relation to them? It is the *true ?* fact that the planets are indeed closer to the outermost sphere. There is a cosmic structure under threat from the planets wandering. This structure is grounded in the principle we already know well.[162] Let us consider how Aristotle involves the moving radius principle in the astronomy of the fourth century, beginning with the framework of observational astronomy and then summarizing the basic principles of a mathematical accounting of those observations.

In simple observational astronomy, each heavenly body other than the sphere of fixed stars has three fundamental movements as manifest to unaided sight—diurnal motion, motion within the band of the zodiac, and synodic movements. The last are conjunctions and changing separations between planets, sun, and moon, not to mention apparent changes in speed. Diurnal motion is the change of place of the heavenly body in the sky over the course of a full day. Every heavenly body, starting with the sphere of fixed stars, completes a circuit from east to west each day, but the planetary stars are less regular in their diurnal courses on successive days than are the fixed stars. Both Plato (in the *Timaeus*) and Aristotle speak of the movement of the planets, sun, and moon along a zodiacal circle. They understood the zodiac to have an axis inclined from the axis of the sphere of fixed stars. All the planets identified as moving along the zodiac move slower in their own diurnal circuits from east to west than the outermost sphere.

These three types of apparent movements (combined as motion projected upon a sort of two-dimensional canvas of the dark sky) are accounted for, in the astronomy of Eudoxus, Callippus and Aristotle, by slightly different three-dimensional movements. All three endorse the diurnal movement of all the heavens together. This movement is the one Aristotle understands to follow the requirements of the moving radius principle drawn upon also in earth-bound mechanics. In *On the Heavens* II.8, he says that, far from being impossible, it is in fact necessary that

---

162 In a rich article (Mendel, "Eudoxus") that distinguishes Aristotle's astronomy from that of Eudoxus and Callippus, Mendel repeatedly questions what are the *phainomena* that each sought to explain. He does not think their concerns are Simplicius' concern with preserving appearances, even though Simplicius is one of our main sources of information on their theories. Another is Aristotle himself. See Mendel's §2–4 of "Eudoxus" (62–83). Aristotle can be seen to distinguish his aims, at least in essentials, from the astronomer-mathematicians, but he took their work as offering supporting evidence for his basic picture of the cosmos. I develop this suggestion further below. On the astronomy of this period, see also the sources listed in footnote 147 in this chapter.

speeds of the planets are proportional to the sizes of their spheres. If the heavenly bodies exchanged spheres, then the body would move with the speed appropriate to the size of its new sphere, and vice versa (289b15–21). Later in the same chapter, he says it is reasonable that the speed of the larger circle is faster, since the circles are all bound to the same center (289b35), and he gives an account of the matter in terms of radii from the same center cutting arcs of larger and smaller circles covered in the same time (290a1–5).[163] By itself, however, this diurnal movement of the cosmic sphere would, to the human gaze, maintain each planet in its same place in relation to the stars. The planets would not appear to be moving slower than the stars, even though they would be. The movement of each planet along the zodiac, however, and their variations in separation with respect to one another changes on a daily basis the position of these non-planetary stars against the background of fixed stars.

The planets' changes of position in relation to one another Aristotle takes up in *On the Heavens* II.10. He credits the astronomers with giving accounts of the changing separations of the planets in accordance with those planets' faster and slower speeds *along circles of their own* (291a29–b4). Eudoxus and Callippus associated conjunctions and separations with a planet's completing a revolution along a great circle of the sphere responsible just for that motion. Each planet had a different year, or period of revolution, along the zodiac, because it had a faster or slower motion of its own.

In *On the Heavens* II.10, Aristotle addresses the effect of the first spherical motion, the diurnal revolution, on the backward movement of each planet along the zodiac. The outermost sphere has a single motion, which is fastest of all in the heavens, but each planet, by its own movement, moves against (ἀντιφέρεται) that heavenly movement (291a34–b3). The planet shares in this fastest movement, we know already, at a pace slower than the outermost sphere, in the proportion of its own radius to the radius of the outermost sphere. Aristotle says that it is reasonable that the body nearest the simple and primary circuit (the outermost sphere) takes the most time to complete its own circle, because of its being ruled more (μάλιστα κρατεῖται) by the speed of the outermost

---

163   On this basis, in *On the Heavens* II.4 and 6, Aristotle presupposes the outermost sphere of the heavens moves fastest among all the heavenly spheres. In *On the Heavens* II.10, he includes the proportionality of speeds to length of radii. He says that inner spheres are influenced by the quickest motion belonging to the outermost sphere in proportion to their distances (291a33, b9).

sphere, the sphere of fixed stars (291b7). This is the movement whose speeds are distributed by the moving radius principle. So, a planet close to the outermost sphere of fixed stars, like Jupiter, has its own movement contrary to the constant east to west movement of the stars, but Jupiter will take longer to complete a full circuit on its own circle. Its own movement is dissipated to a greater extent than would be the movement of a nearer planet, like Venus, which is farther from the outermost sphere. Venus has, to begin with, a slower movement imparted by the diurnal rotation of the cosmos than Jupiter has. Its movement being slower in the direction of the fixed stars, its proper motion in the opposite direction will have a greater effect. It would be less ruled by the rule of proportional speeds given by the moving radius principle.

In his own reflection on these movements, Aristotle is less concerned with the details of the planets' movements on their own spheres and more concerned with the two foundational problems mentioned above: (1) why the intermediate planets show the greatest variety of movements, and (2) why the wanderers, the planets, seem to have none of their secondary movements in common. Let us consider how Aristotle treats the first puzzle. Aristotle characterizes the moving radius effect in astronomy both kinematically and dynamically. Here, kinematic means an account given in terms of geometrical features of movement and dynamic means a causal account or one making use of a concept of force:

> *Kinematic formulation*: The outermost sphere of the stars moves fastest because it is most distant from the earth. Spheres of the planets, sun, and moon within the outermost sphere move more slowly in concert with the outermost sphere in proportion to their distance from the outermost sphere.

This principle presents the speeds of the heavenly bodies as related proportionately with reference to a motionless center and an outermost fastest circular speed. The planets move like interior points on a rotating disk. Aristotle adds an additional formulation, however:

> *Dynamic formulation*: The speeds of heavenly bodies are ruled by the fastest motion of the outermost sphere of the heavens in proportion to the distance of the heavenly body from the outermost sphere.[164]

---

164 *On the Heavens* II.12, 291b3–6.

This formulation says that the shared movement of larger and smaller concentric circles interferes with the motion proper to each planet. Ruling as a causal notion is weakly causal. The idea is that the outermost sphere is moved first like the rim of a wheel or a windlass that is spun when force is applied. As with a bicycle wheel, this force moves whatever is inside the rim.[165] This means force is distributed through the rotating body. If points within are on interior wheels that are also moving but in the *opposite* direction to the rim, the movements of those points in their own opposite direction will be affected less by the movement of the whole if their movement along with the rim was at a slower pace to begin with. Interior points further from the rim do move slower in the common forward movement than those closer to the rim, and so their movements in the opposite direction are interfered with to a lesser extent—i.e., they have a smaller component of the common forward movement. We could say the cancelling effect on the secondary movement is less. This is what is meant by being ruled more or ruled less (291b7). The dynamic formulation falls back upon the kinematic account for its meaning.

One thing of importance in noting the connection between the two formulations is that Aristotle's mechanics of the heavens is not a physical conception overlaid on a mathematical astronomical model but begins just as a mechanical model of the kinematic type. The *phainomenon* Aristotle has in mind as what we must try to state is that the planets are indeed intermediate between the stars and the sun and moon, a fact that should be supported by their speeds being intermediate too. This is what seems not to be the case, and so it must be substantiated by some particularly convincing evidence.

The *phainomenon* of the middle position of the planets is substantiated by a carefully chosen and remarkable observation. Aristotle goes on to present evidence from seeing (τῇ ὄψει) that the planets are more distant than the sun and moon. He says that "we have seen" the moon, at half phase, pass below Ares (Mars). The perfect tense and first person plural of the verb (ἑωράκαμεν) indicate that he reports a contemporary observation.[166] Possibly, he himself was one of the observers. Mars was hidden for a time behind the dark part of the moon until the planet emerged on

---

165 For a treatment of the winch or windlass in these terms, see *Mechanics* 13.

166 Kepler dated this occultation of Mars by the moon to April 4, 357 BC. More recent computation dates it to May 4 of the same year. See Stephenson, "A Lunar Occultation of Mars Observed by Aristotle."

the moon's bright side (292a2–6) (**Figure 4.1**). It is to support this striking observation that Aristotle turns to the Egyptians and Babylonians,
whom he characterizes as οἱ πάλαι, the men of old or those who have
gone before. They have similar observations concerning other stars tak-
en over many years. From them, we have many proofs (πολλὰς πίστεις) concerning each of the planets.[167]

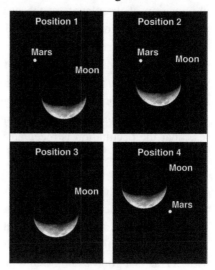

Figure 4.1

In this case, the additional observations of the Babylonians are not of interest as a large empirical base for induction or con-
struction of models but serve more narrowly to support a crucial test of an already accepted cosmic structure. The observa-
tion of the moon's occultation of Mars is a crucial test in the sense that it establishes that those heavenly bodies moving with the greatest variety of motions are
indeed the intermediate ones. This being the case, though, the observa-
tion of the planets' movements lagging behind the sun and moon at such
different rates and their wanderings in other respects becomes an urgent
matter, since it is, on the face of it, a falsification of the kinematic principle of heavenly motion derived from the moving radius. There is conflicting evidence, but the observation of Mars passing behind the moon
makes the central explanatory trope, the moving radius principle, secure.

---

167 Aristotle uses the term ἀστήρ, star, and τὰ ἄστρα in his discussion of Mars. The
planets and the brightest stars, like Sirius, are often similarly designated by ἀστήρ. In his
last reference, I take it that he is referring to similar occurrences involving Mars or another
planet. The point is that occultation of the planets by the moon is not that rare. The word
πίστεις means warrants or assurances, reasons for belief, or convictions. In his earlier
reference to inherited astronomical knowledge (270b11–13), Aristotle involves πίστις.
He says that if the heavenly bodies are ungenerable and impassible, the heavens are rightly
associated with the divine. He says that to infer from the apparent immutability of the ungenerable substance of the heavens to the aether's being the first substance above others is
"well said." The evidence of perception is sufficient to believe this, at least with the degree
of conviction (*pistis*) possible for human conviction (συμβαίνει δὲ τοῦτο καὶ διὰ τῆς
αἰσθήσεως ἱκανῶς, ὥς γε πρὸς ἀνθρωπίνην εἰπεῖν πίστιν).

In Aristotle's use of Babylonian observation in this passage, there is a sort of bare perceptible, the observation of the disappearance of Mars at a particular time. But this observation is not what Aristotle calls the *phainomenon*, which is rather the intelligible fact of the intermediate position of the planets in the heavens. This instance shows that, in a *phainomenon*, an observation is taken as intelligible within a context. While we can separate the percept strictly speaking, it is noticed because of its further meaning. There is merit, then, to Nussbaum's general idea about *phainomena* that their notice or formulation involves critical faculties. Aristotle incorporates the occultation of Mars into a scientific evaluation of the cosmic picture of the relative distances of the heavenly bodies. That the occultation is received into a framework of understanding does not, however, color or corrupt it as a piece of evidence. Mars disappearing behind the dark part of the moon, which is itself barely visible by earthshine, is a very striking visual percept. It loses nothing of its value as an arbiter of the order of the planets because its intelligibility comes from the expectation that Mars is further away than the moon. Indeed, its meaning for us is the same as for Aristotle in that regard: Mars is further away. This is a good example of a percept taken experientially, because it is immediately interpreted as a *phainomenon*—the relative distances of Mars and the moon. Furthermore, the visual percept is itself a state of affairs, articulated first into objects (Mars and the moon), on the one hand, and their nearness to one another and visibility over time, on the other. The objects and their attributes in the *perceived* state of affairs are a vaguely conceived version of the clarified *phainomenon*. Yet, the perceived state of affairs stands on its own as a significant observation that promises to be related to some natural necessity. That the visual percept comes to be flagged as promising a natural necessity has something to do with its being a relatively unusual observation. It is possible to see from these considerations how closely situated the perception of necessary attributes might be to the activity of *nous*.

It may seem that what I have presented supports the view that *phainomena* are opinions, since the *phainomenon* follows upon perception and involves Aristotle's preconceived notion about the order of the heavenly bodies. There would be two parts to this objection. The first is that the *phainomenon* is articulated in thought or speech and so is propositional. The second, to which I will return later, is that the intelligibility of the *phainomenon* depends on culturally conditioned preconceived no-

94

tions. Concerning the first point, the example makes quite clear that it is not the propositions stating *phainomena* that are being examined but the facts. The case shows the limitation of understanding Aristotelian science *yes* as analysis of *endoxa*. In endoxic science, an appearance, which is a percept, becomes the opinion that states the appearance. The observation loses its separate cognitive status and comes to be treated as a logical puzzle. Thus, Mars passing behind the moon is simply the claim to be considered that "Mars passed behind the moon [at a particular time on a particular day]." Aristotle's problem in *On the Heavens* II.8–12 would be fitting a theoretical hypothesis, the intermediate position of the planets, to a claim of "what we have seen." In this endeavor, the observational claim is as much subject to evaluation as the hypothesis on which it impinges. This means too that science is boxed into a propositional and syllogistic form, when another form, say that of geometry or logistic, might better disclose the basis of appearances.[168]

In fact, Aristotle treats the occultation of Mars as an observation that is telling. It does not lose its perceptual veridicality when propositionalized. A propositional form of expression is incidental to its scientific import. Also, as we shall see momentarily, he did think that another form of knowledge than the proposition best disclosed the reality in this case. If we wish to understand Aristotle's science, the gradations and kinds of perceptual awareness are important, not just for evaluation of evidence that Aristotle brings to bear on a question but also in the formation of the cosmic picture that lends intelligibility to the evidence. This leads to the second part of the objection that *phainomena* really are conventional opinions. What about Aristotle's preconceived notions concerning the structure of the cosmos, the geocentric universe? This question is the subject of the next section. Before proceeding to that question, let me offer two more points. The first is that Aristotle does not rely entirely on the phenomenon of occultations for evidence supporting the order of the heavenly bodies.

Aristotle thinks that, besides observations like the occultation of Mars, there are other warrants for knowing the ordering of heavenly bodies as a fact. In *On the Heavens* II.12, he says that "the mathematicians" have shown that the planets move with speeds intermediate between that of the outermost sphere and what lies closer (291b8–10). If the astronomers are the mathematicians, presumably he is not referring to *observa-*

---

168 On logistic, see Huffman, *Archytas*, 68–76, 232–244.

tions that prove the planets move at intermediate speeds. Mathematical astronomers are those able to separate the wandering movements of the planets into two, three, or more movements, one of which is the moving radius as a kinematic principle in astronomy. The planets move along with the movement of the outermost sphere. The model making of the astronomers reinforces the set of principles to which Aristotle subscribes. He does not mean to compete with Eudoxus and Callippus in their mathematical modeling but is interested in how their models reinforce the foundational principles to which he is committed.

The second point to make tells against the idea that Aristotle could have understood astronomical *phainomena* as a mass of observational data for theorizing. In the passage from *On the Heavens* II.12 where Aristotle states his two problems that need addressing, he begins with enthusiasm about the prudential virtues of the investigator. We seek to establish what is the case but to do so with the virtue of decency (αἰδώς), which would mean in this case respect for the limitations of gaining experience of the heavens and respect for oneself as a researcher in such circumstances (291b24–27). Αἰδώς is a characteristic of good judgment and proportionate response. The difficulty to be parried with αἰδώς is making judgments about things so far away. He mentions explicitly the paucity of starting points (ἀφορμαί) (292a14–17). He is upbeat about the possibility of a reasoned treatment of the problem nonetheless (a17–18). In a companion passage in *Parts of Animals* I.5, Aristotle addresses the study of living things, taking note of the wealth of evidence (τὰ φανερά) available concerning them. His remarks here track his comments in *On the Heavens* II.12, because he contrasts the study of perishable things to study of the other natural beings, heavenly bodies, for which the evidence of the senses is altogether paltry (644b27). He uses the same word for finding solutions, εὐπορῶμεν (εὐπορία in *On the Heavens* II.12) in reference to the study of living things. Where the evidences are abundant, we are well-placed to proceed toward knowledge, especially since we live alongside other perishable things[169] (644b28–30). He mentions again the joy of even partial solutions concerning the heavens (644b35) but uses that as a foil to query why we would withhold study of what we could come to know so thoroughly. He uses the word *phainomenon* in this context—what appears to us—to refer to what he has established about the things beyond us (645a4–5).[170]

---

169 διὰ τὸ σύντροφον.

170 τὴν περὶ τὰ θεῖα φιλοσοφίαν. Compare Plato in the *Epinomis* on the character

It is hard to see why Aristotle would make this contrast, if he looked upon the knowledge from the Babylonians as having provided a rich harvest of raw data.[171] While we might think the accumulation of observations of the heavens from the Babylonians would make astronomy the ancient science with the largest evidential base, Aristotle regards the situation of astronomy to be just the opposite. We are hampered by paucity of sensory data. In this subject matter, he will use a few significant observations targeted to prove particular points. Let us now consider the wider cosmic picture to which the observation of Mars is relevant.

Experience and Concentric Circles in the Heavens

The moving radius principle in its kinematic formulation as setting the speeds of east to west diurnal movements and in its dynamic formulation as affecting the west to east movements proper to each planet occupies pride of place in Aristotle's account of heavenly movements in *On the Heavens* II.4–12.[172] It is interesting that the moving radius principle, which in the case of the balance and lever seems indelibly linked to the earth-bound forces of bodies and weight, should be taken by Aristotle as an organizing principle of the movement of heavenly bodies, which have no weight. Without weight, it seems, neither should the heavenly bodies be subject to forces. The way Aristotle applies the principle to the heavens shows that he recognized mechanical phenomena quite apart from weight conceived as a downward pull toward the center of the universe. In *On*

of astronomy as giving us venerable objects for contemplation of the divine (986a–988e). Heath believes that Plato here presents a view opposite to that of the *Timaeus*, rejecting that the movement of the stars carries the other heavenly bodies along with it (Heath, *Astronomy*, 62n1).

171 Bowen and Goldstein say the Babylonian contribution came to be regarded in this light, as data, in the second century BC with Hipparchus ("New View," 339).

172 Since interior spheres are in contact, any movement belonging to an outer planet would be communicated to interior planets. Aristotle adds additional spheres for each planet, unwinders, to neutralize alien communicated movements leaving only the influence of the outermost sphere for the next inferior planet. This is one factor raising the number of spheres in the heavens to somewhere around fifty. See *Metaphysics* Λ.8, 1074a1–14, Heath, *Astronomy*, xlviii–xlix, and Mendel, "Eudoxus," §4.4. Thus, contact between adjacent spheres is a fateful, and by Heath's account, unfortunate commitment of Aristotle's. Nevertheless, contact would seem necessary to preserve the continuity of the heavens and thereby provide a reason why all heavenly bodies share overall the east to west movement of the stars. The moving radius, or rotating disk, principle explains this and also provides for an even distribution of force that keeps the heavens, so gigantic, from breaking apart. See below.

the Heavens II.8, when presenting the moving radius principle as part of astronomy, Aristotle says the fact that the heavens do not break apart (διασπᾶσθα) is due to this principle (290a5–6). He makes this point in the context of arguing that it is the circles of the heavenly bodies that are moving and not the bodies themselves:

> Since, then we cannot reasonably suppose either that both are in motion or that the star alone moves, it remains that the circles should move while the stars are at rest and move with the circles to which they are attached. Only on this supposition are we involved in no absurd consequence. For, in the first place, the quicker movement of the larger circle is reasonable when all the circles are attached to the same centre. Whenever bodies are moving with their proper motion, the larger moves quicker. It is the same here with the revolving bodies; for the arc intercepted by two radii will be larger in the larger circle, and hence it is reasonable that the revolution of the larger circle should take the same time as that of the smaller. And secondly, the fact that the heavens do nòt break in pieces follows not only from this but also from the proof already given of the continuity of the whole. (289b30–290a7)

The mechanical principle governing speeds is here placed in the context of possible sources of force in the heavens. The great size of the universe, the rigid expanse of the moving crystalline aether spheres, and the speed of them all ought to place strain on components of the system. The moving radius principle explains why this does not happen. Interestingly, the expression of the principle in celestial motion depends for Aristotle on the heavens being a continuous whole (290a6–7). The moving radius principle, considered in the effect of movement it describes, is about an equal distribution of force through a rigid body. This is perhaps one reason for the heavenly spheres being solids. The plenum of the heavens is treated as a system of movement in which force is continually distributed through a rigid body.

It is often said that Aristotle's astronomy is to be contrasted to the astronomy of Eudoxus and Callippus by Aristotle's concerns being mechanical and physical. This is taken to mean he wants to make the mathematical account fit a system of communication of movement by contact of spheres with one another. Seeing how he used the moving radius principle casts the meaning of "mechanical" in a new light. There is communication of force by contact, but Aristotle also considered influences affecting local motion that are a function of the size of bodies in motion and the distribution of bulk or density within them. The movement of the whole heavens he treats as movement of a continuous body. Even in the heavens, there could be latent forces of both constraint and separation that come into play when bodies are in motion.

Aristotle treats the theme of physical effects of the great size of the universe also in refuting the idea that the heavenly bodies make harmonious sounds in their rotation. He notes that the sound of thunder can shiver massive objects and crack rocks,[173] so that if the heavenly bodies were making noise as they move, the effect would be many times greater. It would not be discountable as unnoticed background noise, as the Pythagoreans say. The very difficulty that leads them to suppose the heavenly bodies make noise reinforces, he says, the truth that it is the circles to which heavenly bodies are bound that move, not the stars and planets themselves. A part of a ship makes no noise of its own in moving nor a ship borne along in a flowing river.[174] The other prior reason to think the planets and stars are attached to their circles is that there is no rationale for the heavenly bodies alone moving in accordance with their distance from an immobile center, but there is a reason, indeed it is necessary (ἀναγκαῖον), that the circles themselves would move at different paces.[175] We see here how thoroughly Aristotle's use of the moving radius principle conditions details of the rest of his astronomy.

In his treatment of *On the Heavens* II.12 and other passages where Aristotle draws upon astronomical observations, G. E. R. Lloyd does not separate the moving radius principle from the "concentric circles theory" of Eudoxus.[176] In general, scholars understand Aristotle to be adopting Eudoxus' system in all its complexity for his own cosmological purposes. In this context, Lloyd takes Aristotle to task for not confronting the limitations of the Eudoxan model. For example, from a purely observational standpoint, he should have noted the variation in brightness of the plan-

---

173 Οἱ γὰρ ὑπερβάλλοντες ψόφοι διακναίουσι καὶ τῶν ἀψύχων σωμάτων τοὺς ὄγκους, οἷον ὁ τῆς βροντῆς διίστησι λίθους καὶ τὰ καρτερώτατα τῶν σωμάτων (290b34–35).

174 *On the Heavens* II.9, 290b34–291a13.

175 *On the Heavens* II.8, 289b15–17.

176 Lloyd, *Explorations*, 168.

ets, which would need to be explained in the system. From a theoretical standpoint, he should have given some account of why the planets move at speeds different from the distant stars. The first problem Aristotle mentions not at all, and on the second, Lloyd says, he simply "adopts the usual view" that the motion of the outermost sphere is fastest.[177] Lloyd has not noticed, however, that Aristotle explains the differential speeds of the heavenly bodies by the moving radius principle and that he treats the principle as independent of the astronomers' accounts. Contrary to his contention, Aristotle does have an explanation of that general observation.

I have noted Aristotle's use of the work of the mathematical astronomers to support his own main concern in the mechanics of the heavens. Aristotle's reference to the mathematicians in *On the Heavens* II.10, Lloyd calls "just a matter of hand-waving," but the limitations he cites were problems for all of early astronomy. The particular charge Lloyd makes against Aristotle is that he uses astronomical information too loosely. In fact, Aristotle used the work of the mathematicians crisply in support of the intermediate position of the planets. The mathematicians are able to separate the planets' wandering into two or more movements, one of which is movement in conformity with the moving radius principle. They too take the kinematic version of the moving radius principle as part of their astronomy. With his reference to the mathematicians, Aristotle knits together his own mechanics of the heavens with current developing research in mathematical astronomy. The mathematicians assume the basic explanation of slower interior speeds of intermediate objects in coming up with a more precise account of the movement of planets. This is the logic of Aristotle's appeal to their work and a normal strategy for the growth of knowledge in an emergent science.

Lloyd says that, in the end, Aristotle's deference to the expertise of the mathematicians is "pure eyewash," because he takes refuge in teleology to make up for his failure to master the technical detail of Eudoxus' system.[178] Lloyd refers to Aristotle's likening of the heavenly bodies to living things in *On the Heavens* II.12. This is the second place in *On the Heavens* II.12, after his mention of the occultation of Mars, where Aristotle addresses the first puzzle mentioned at the beginning of his chapter 12, why the intermediate heavenly bodies exhibit the most variability in motion and not the ones nearest the earth. As in the case of his

---

177 Lloyd, *Explorations*, 170–172.

178 Lloyd, *Explorations*, 171, 173.

citing of the occultation of Mars, however, Aristotle offers his animate model for the heavens as a point narrowly focused. The problem is still the variety of movements that the planets display, and the roadblock to knowledge is the lack of starting points for astronomy and the paucity of direct experience. This does not make the problem anything insoluble, he says (292a17).

He offers his comparison to living things as a novel alternative to how we would ordinarily think of them (292a18–20). The point is that heavenly bodies have a *range of movements* more like that shown by a living thing, and so we ought not to think of the planets as bodies having the order of simple monads (292a19). The mathematical reference is significant, because he believes the order of the planets is mathematically governed but in accordance with a more subtle and remarkable principle than the order of succession.

Aristotle then discusses the relation of an end to some immediate action of a body in terms of the number of actions that must be involved for a distant end to be achieved (292a30–b10). In his discussion, nearness to the divine has rational value for organizing stronger and weaker imitations of the outer sphere's movements. The outermost sphere naturally shares more in the divine than things nearer the center. The earth, most distant, moves not at all. Things near the earth, like the moon, move with the least movements, because of being almost as little influenced as the earth (292b20). Aristotle is giving a rationale based on the moving radius principle for why additional movements enter most into the behavior of the intermediate bodies. Teleology plays only a supporting role in his likening of the heavenly bodies to animate things. As we shall see in *Movement of Animals* 1–7, Aristotle applies the moving radius principle to animate movement also. His reference to the intermediate heavenly bodies being possibly alive is not a fallback position, a rote invoking of extra-scientific principles, but a point at which heavenly and sublunary *phainomena* may manifest a single principle. Aristotle does not make as decisive a division between non-living and living as we in the modern age do, but this does not mean that he thoughtlessly ensouls the non-living by imposing on inert matter principles that do not pertain to it.

This examination of the structure of Aristotle's heavens was begun in order to evaluate the context that makes the occultation of Mars by the moon intelligible and meaningful. In reference to this observation, the case was made that Aristotle's *phainomena* in astronomy are not bare perceptual data or the orderly numerical locative data of ephemeris entries. A *phainomenon* begins with perception, where a version of a *kath'hauto* trait makes its appearance early in the cognitive process, sometimes not yet separated from its subject. A *phainomenon* as an observed fact, however, is something intelligible, the perceived trait made meaningful because of being placed in its true physical context. It was at this point that it seemed, since Aristotle's cosmos is the physical context for the observation of Mars, even natural *phainomena* must be regarded as saturated with cultural presuppositions, in this case the geocentric universe. Seeing the role of a mechanical principle, the moving radius, in Aristotle's conception of the heavens, should change our conception of the source of Aristotle's cosmic picture.

It is significant that Aristotle is so cognizant of the limitations of human experience in deciding what principles govern the heavens. In this situation, he takes as his reference the most fundamental mechanical principle available that is clearly verified in perception. The bodily reaction to mechanical forces seemingly created by motion is the inevitable point of departure for the analysis of any sort of circular motion, even in the heavens. The moving radius, though a wonder, is not a kinematic oddity. It is a principle of wide applicability grounded in experience. The faster and slower curved movement of outlying points bound to a central point was a *logos* of perception before it became an articulated universal. Indeed, by the time it was applied to the heavens, it had assumed iconic status as the principle of distribution of forces of motion.[179] Aristotle draws upon this feature of the principle in explaining why the heavens do not break apart.

Accordingly, the context into which the observation of Mars is taken is itself saturated by perceptual knowledge, namely, the understanding of mechanical forces in rotational movement. Perceptual knowledge is not the same as cultural presupposition. This is so even though the experience giving intelligibility to the observation was already ancient in the time of Plato and Aristotle. Nor is Aristotle's framework of interpretation experience of the immobility of the earth, as is sometimes claimed—the earth does not seem to be moving. It is critically evaluated kinesthetic awareness of how things behave. As its relevance to the lever and other simple

---

179 "Iconic" here means being a fundamental exemplar of distribution of force. The role of the moving radius in this regard is explored further in the analysis of *Physical Problems* XVI in Chapter 7 below. Use of the term seems already to be justified by Plato's manner of drawing attention to the principle in *Laws* X.

devices shows, the moving radius principle concerns action. It is relevant to what happens in the natural realm as well, where action is unassisted by human contrivance.

Mechanical Properties as Perceived

At the beginning of Chapter 3, two levels of empiricism were distinguished as relevant to showing how a mechanical property of the mathematical sort is something perceived. The first level includes both sensory-motor and conscious awareness of mechanical forces. In relation to this level of empiricism, it was important to show how the key mechanical principle (the circle and its property) is first perceived as a property in a state of affairs. In this perceptual knowledge, there is awareness of something as what cannot be otherwise, but it is not formulated intellectually.

The second level of empiricism concerns observed facts as treated by a faculty called *to logistikon*, the faculty for calculating. In relation to this level of empiricism, it was important to see how intelligibility is grounded in perception even when some framework of interpretation makes a perception meaningful. This has been the topic of Chapter 4. In developing the second level of empiricism, which is usually taken as *empeiria*, a distinction had to be made to understand how *phainomena* are genuinely perceptual and not automatically opinions and therefore propositional knowledge. The occultation of Mars belongs to a class of singularly striking visual percepts that have a bearing on massive facts like the relative distance of heavenly bodies. It is an observation that qualifies as evidence in a context. This class of observation is one kind of perceptual knowledge that is not propositional in the first instance.

The other kind is the framework that makes the observation meaningful. This framework is the moving radius principle as a sort of covering rule of action. The rule would not function so, however, if it did not indeed "cover" a wide range of experiences. It was in fact derived from experience, as our investigation of mechanical phenomena at the first level of empiricism has shown, and then applied to a subject matter where first-hand experience is so lacking, astronomy. This framework derives its authority from the experience of forces sketched at the beginning of Chapter 3, experience very close to perception. It comes to be expressed as a property of the circle, first in a mathematical formulation and later as a proposition that is a candidate for being a first principle.

103

This second kind of perceptual knowledge—the refined framework—has in general not been recognized as coming from perception. In the case of astronomy, it has been shunted into theoretical astronomy as part of the detail of combined circular motions. Articulated propositionally, the rule is easy to treat as part of theory. Aristotle distinguishes the principle manifest in the moving radius as more fundamental than the accounts that explain the wandering of the planets, however. Furthermore, he makes it the explanation of why the same force issues in different speeds, as if maintaining a sort of equilibrium in motion. In the next chapter, we shall see how widely Aristotle applies the kinematic formulation of the power of the lever. I will end this chapter with consideration of a passage where Aristotle himself characterizes *phainomena* in the terms I have laid out.

Theôrein Ta Phainomena

There is a passage in *Parts of Animals* I.1 where Aristotle characterizes the method of the mathematicians in astronomy. He says:

> Ought the student of nature to follow the plan adopted by the mathematicians in their astronomical demonstrations, and after considering the phenomena presented by animals, and their several parts, proceed subsequently to treat of the causes and the reason why; or ought he to follow some other method?[180] (639b7–10)

The crucial phrase in this passage is "after considering the phenomena presented by animals, and their several parts" (τὰ φαινόμενα πρῶτον τὰ περὶ τὰ ζῷα θεωρήσαντα καὶ τὰ μέρη τὰ περὶ ἔκαστον). Lennox translates τὰ φαινόμενα . . . θεωρήσαντα as "survey the appearances." The astronomer first surveys the appearances. Lennox interprets *Prior Analytics* I.30 and this parallel passage in *Parts of Animals* I.1 in standard inductivist fashion. Demonstrations in astronomy were gotten only after principles were obtained from observations. A survey one might expect to be a continuous action undertaken or completed in the past, signaled by either a present or perfect participle. The verb here is, however, an aorist participle (θεωρήσαντα) indicating by its verb aspect a single action taken—so "seeing" rather than "surveying." *Theôrein* (θεωρεῖν) has a root meaning of going someplace as a spectator—to a festival or games—and

---

180   Translation is by Ogle (*CWA* 1, 995).

a (historically) later connotation of grasping something as it is.[181] In this passage, as in others of his scientific works, Aristotle uses the term in his own somewhat elevated sense of the scientist's seeing and understanding at the same time.

In *Parts of Animals* I.5, the passage we considered before in relation to *On the Heavens* II.12, he uses the substantive *theôria* in contrast to sense perception to explain how the study of animals repugnant to ordinary sensibility can nevertheless be a joy to the practicing scientist:

> For if some [animals] have no graces to charm the sense, yet nature, which fashioned them, gives amazing pleasure in their study (κατὰ τὴν θεωρίαν) to all who can trace links of causation, and are inclined to philosophy. (645a8–11)

Theôria is here associated with the road to causes. *Philosophia* is linked, as in *On the Heavens* II.12, to the pleasure of discovering even partial solutions. In these three passages—*Parts of Animals* I.1, I.5, and *On the Heavens* II.12—there is a pattern of *theôria* taken in conjunction with *phainomena* to mean seeing things as they truly are. In *Parts of Animals* I.1, this grasp of the basic intelligibility of a natural situation precedes knowing causes. In *On the Heavens* III.5, Aristotle uses the verb, *theôrein*, in a refutation of the atomic hypothesis, saying that it is not possible for those wishing to hold to an indivisible primary body to make it work in physical terms. It is not possible for them to see (*theôrein*) the matter physically in the way they wish it to be (304a25).[182] The reason Aristotle gives is built on the principle of infinite divisibility of body and combines rational and empirical considerations. It includes perception of the relative quantities of air and water to make a sophisticated point derived from reasoning about quantity and ratio.[183] Aristotle's overall point, though,

---

181   *L-S ad loc* III.

182   The Oxford translation of the sentence reads, "And further the theory is inconsistent with a regard for the facts of nature" (*CWA* 1, 497).

183   Aristotle makes the empirical observation that there is more air than water in the universe. If the quantities of these two elements can be compared, so can the sizes of the individual particles of these elements. He enunciates a general principle: the lesser quantity is contained in the greater. The air-element must be divisible as is the water-element. So, if the size (μέγεθος) of the cosmic mass of water is contained in the quantity of air, then the water-element particles, when divided the same number of times in their respective masses, must be smaller and represent a part of an air-element particle. The same is true of all elements for which there is relativity of fineness. Fire would have to be divisible, and

is that there will be no seeing (*theôrein*) of what truly is the case in nature on the atomist hypothesis, because the hypothesis does not work in combining rational and empirical considerations. In the terms of *On the Heavens* II.12, we can contrast seeing (ὁρᾶν or ὄψις) to seeing/understanding (θεωρεῖν). One sees (ὁρᾶται, βλέπει) Mars pass behind the moon, but one sees (θεωρεῖ) what is the case (τὸ φαινόμενον) because of it—namely, that the planet lies in distance *between* the stars, on the one hand, and the sun and moon, on the other.[184]

---

its parts would no longer be pyramidal, if that is the fire shape.

184 In *Parts of Animals* I.1, Aristotle does make clear that the seeing (θεωρήσαντα) comes before the statement of causes. But to claim that a particular subject/property relation is necessary to the subject is a stage of pre-demonstrative science already quite close to demonstration. There are a number of stages of cognitive recognition that involve understanding some traits to be associated with some subjects necessarily. My position is not so different from that of Lennox but my concern is to fill out details of how traits are ever taken as candidates for properties or essence in the first place.

Chapter 5

Dunamis and Automata in Aristotle's Movement of Animals

Prospectus

The last two chapters have sketched out the sense in which there is mechanical knowledge at the perceptual kinesthetic level and how it was expressed in the management of mechanical phenomena in the fourth century BC and earlier. If we look at the instances of ordinary life in which circular motion figures, it is clear that management of mechanical forces is something one "has to do." The element of necessity in these phenomena was prominent from the beginning of awareness of them. We have seen that Aristotle drew upon this knowledge as he developed important ideas of his astronomy. This mechanical knowledge of the Greeks had much to do with the physics of circular motion.

My aim in the next two chapters is to show how the moving radius principle—and its chief mechanical manifestation, the lever—were taken by Aristotle into parts of his natural philosophy that are generally thought to depend on empirical considerations only crudely or in very general ways. For instance, it has been said that the main thing Aristotle seeks to explain in his embryology is why offspring are of the same species as parents.[185] While this is an important part of any embryology, Aristotle has in *Generation of Animals* II a sophisticated argument concerning why embryological development continues, once begun. Embryological development is a prime case of self-regulation in growth, a key thing to be

---

185   See Cooper citing Furth ("Metaphysics," 176–177).

explained in the biology of any age or time. Aristotle does not say what many assume he says: that the sperm carries and imparts the form of the organism to the female, who contributes blood and other materials to the embryo.[186] He gives a detailed argument about continuous embryological development precisely because inspection shows that the sperm apparently perishes early on in the process. Indeed, a great part of his argument concerns how motion proceeds without unmoved movers complete with the form of the whole clearly in evidence. In approaching such a difficult problem, Aristotle the empiricist has recourse to the lever as an analogy for the enhancement of effect in life processes. His treatment of this topic is the subject of Chapter 6.

In the present chapter, I will first show in detail how the principle of the lever figures in Aristotle's analysis of animal movement in *Movement of Animals* and then show how it adds content and intelligibility to the idea of soul as the form of the body. My concern is with Aristotle's account of the *faculties* of soul. In *On the Soul* II.2, Aristotle gives a provisional definition of soul in terms of these faculties: "At present, we must confine ourselves to saying that soul is the source (*archê*) of these phenomena and is characterized (ὥρισται) by them, viz., by the powers of self-nutrition, sensation, thinking and movement" (413b12). The concern, then, is with what soul does, what are its powers. In *Movement of Animals* 7, Aristotle gives an extended analogy between the action and power of a lever and natural powers of growth, alteration, and sensation in the animal body. The analogy conveys that latent *dunameis* are the sources for the actualities (*energeiai*)[187] of soul faculties. Through the analogy, mathematical features of the lever are transposed to structural features of soul's enactments.

In *Movement of Animals* 8–9, Aristotle gives a quite detailed account of the relation of extremities of an animal body that are moved to an unmoved portion of the limb, usually the other end, like the elbow or shoulder (702a22–b12). He points out that in this regard there is little difference between an inanimate thing like a stick and a limb of the body. He goes on to say, however, that the wrist that moves the hand

---

186   This point has been argued convincingly on a textual basis by Mayhew, *Female*.

187   A good word for *energeia*, activity or actuality, in this context might be "enactment," to connote both the element of execution of the function or end (*telos*) of a soul-faculty and the need for that execution to use bodily components (en-) so as to serve accomplishment of the end.

is itself moved by something higher (ἐν τῷ ἀνωτέρω) and that neither is the origin there at the next higher level (702b10). Of the continuous whole, then—namely, the living body—the origin is in the middle (*meson*) (b16), for this is the limit of the respective extremes of a continuous body. Aristotle uses the locution "origin of the moving soul" (τὴν ἀρχὴν τῆς ψυχῆς τῆς κινούσης) and associates this origin with a place (*topos*) in the body (b22). He says, however, that this mover in place in the body must be sometimes both mover of some extremity and itself the moved thing for another movement. Accordingly, it cannot be this middle that is the genuine unmoved mover for the body, for if moved it will be a magnitude (702b24–31). Even points in the sense of unmoved extremities would be like two people bracing their backs against one another and so would not be unmoved at all. So, what is unmoved with respect to both movements cannot be some magnitude in the middle location but instead something else. "This something is the soul, being distinct from (ἕτερον) the magnitude just described and yet located therein" (703a2–3).[188] This line of reasoning would seem to make the soul as first mover something incorporeal.

It would be easy to think that this is the end of mechanics as a model for soul's action. Further explanation will fall back on metaphysical notions. Finding this limit, however, does *not* launch all further explanation of animal movement on a completely different course from the foregoing informative analogy.[189] Aristotle is an empiricist seeking the sort of structural necessities that can explain the wholeness of a living organism. Mathematical properties are something either a material body or an incorporeal entity (e.g., numbers, triangle or circle as such) may possess. To this extent, such properties may appear in either venue. Furthermore, a mathematical principle already has the aspect of unity that is sought as a defining feature of soul. In a mathematical formulation of properties necessary and immediate to a subject, subject and attribute or parts of a

---

188 Forster's translation (*CWA* 1, 1094).

189 As he makes clear in *Movement of Animals* 10, souls *ensoul* bodies (703a6). Aristotle goes on to speak of the connate pneuma (πνεῦμα σύμφυτον) as what has power (*dunamis*) and force (*ischus*) locally. The connate pneuma is itself a moved thing with respect to the unmoved soul. The relation is like that of a point (soul) to the flexion based at the point (the changing pneuma) (703a11–14). The organ of movement must be able to expand and contract. Finally, he likens the soul to the principle of a well-governed city. Each organ fulfills its role, and soul is not a micro-manager active constantly in each part (703a30–703b1). Aristotle regards the soul as a principle of an organic body as a whole. See the sequence of definitions of soul, in *On the Soul* II.2, as the actuality (*entelecheia*) of an organic body.

whole participate in a relational syntax distinctive to that mathematical rule. One grasps subject and property together in a whole. Thus, once we reach a principle that is not a magnitude, it makes sense for a mathematical principle to be in some way the model for soul as form of the body. This need not be a mysterious Pythagoreanism.[190]

In this chapter, I return to a distinction made in my Chapter 1 between device (*mêchanê*) as an object and device as contrivance. It is important to separate these senses of device, because the idea of contrivance allows for exploration of the parameters of design taken generally. Contrivance is the field or horizon within which actuality meets the conditions for the fulfillment of actuality. As mentioned before, in his Allegory of the Cave, Plato makes clear that the contrivance of produced actualities can be missed, so that the product is taken for reality. In Plato's political world, the contrivance remains mostly hidden: you can fool most of the people all the time. Aristotle's awareness of *mêchanê* as contrivance directs him more along the lines of Heraclitus' aphorism that "nature loves to hide." *Dunamis* is the nature revealed in contrivance, whether natural or engineered. While contrivance can mean torturing nature to reveal its principles, a broader notion of contrivance will be maintained here. Contrivance induces latent power to be active power. Any designed object discloses reality, but the underlying power is more than is evident in any single mode of disclosure.

What is *Movement of Animals* About?

At the beginning of *Movement of Animals*, Aristotle announces an investigation of the common cause of moving with any movement whatsoever (698a3–7). This beginning recalls the stated aims of both *Physics* II and III, where all natural motion is the subject, whether with respect to an investigation of causes of motion (*Physics* II.1) or the conditions for and the structure of motion (*Physics* III.1). In *Movement of Animals*, Aristotle aims at a general account of animal motion in particular. He immediately refers to an earlier discussion of the possibility of eternal motion, in which it was ascertained that, for movements that are not eternal, there

---

190 The mathematical principle under consideration incorporates motion and is therefore distinctive to a subject matter of its own, mechanics. So, it is not numerological. It should be noted that I do not make an argument for the immateriality of soul in *Movement of Animals*. I advocate taking a mathematical model as a fresh approach to the idea of the soul's providing the *ethos* of the body (703a34).

must be some first mover that is itself unmoved (*Physics* VIII.5–6). This topic will also be an important theme of *Movement of Animals*, because he says that it is necessary to provide an account of the unmoved mover not just in general terms but in the case of particulars and things perceptible (698a12–15). Accordingly, although his manner of argumentation differs considerably from that of the *Physics*, his plan of explanation is nearly as broad.

Nussbaum understands Aristotle's stated aim to be a test by particular cases of the general account of the first mover in *Physics* VIII. Aristotle himself says elsewhere that a general account is lacking in value if it is the particular account of nothing.[191] Bénatouïl believes Aristotle is offering a comparison of eternal movement and animal movement with respect to the necessity of a first mover but to an even greater extent, Aristotle is extending to animal movement a conclusion demonstrated elsewhere.[192] Both interpreters highlight the cosmological character of *Movement of Animals*. Aristotle speaks of the first mover of the heavens. He makes animals the movers of inanimate things, on the one hand, and locates a non-bodily mover resident in the animal (soul) and *telê* that move the animal from the outside.[193] From this interpretive standpoint, traditional issues of ontology are prominent. Bénatouïl says Aristotle establishes analogies between moved and unmoved parts of the body for animals, stars, and the universe as a whole. The main point is always to establish that there is a mover that remains itself immobile.[194] Nussbaum highlights cosmic teleology and, in this context, the final cause of the animal body.

Focus on the cosmological aspect of *Movement of Animals* has obscured another important theme of the treatise—movements bringing about other movements and the relation of this pattern to *dunamis*. Aristotle's references to movement of the heavens or the whole universe in *Movement of Animals* do not present a cosmic first mover as the final term in a sequence starting with animal motion but rather present the cos-

---

191 Nussbaum, *De Motu*, 116, 273–275. She quotes *On the Soul* 414b22.

192 Bénatouïl, "L'usage des analogies," 84. Nussbaum affirms the analogical interpretation to some extent (*De Motu*, 120).

193 For inanimate things, see *Movement of Animals* 6, 700b12; for *telê* outside the animal, chapters 6 and 7. He alludes to the first mover's moving of the material universe in the context of animals' causing movement of inanimate things (700b6–7), not as part of his account of *telê* outside the animal.

194 Bénatouïl, "L'usage des analogies," 90, 94.

mos as a case parallel to the animal.[195] The connection to the eternal he makes is one of similarity where important differences remain (700b29–701a1). I would suggest that Aristotle's manner of introducing the first mover manifests a strategy of appeal to consilience in Whewell's sense.[196] Principles established in one area of science gain greater claim to conviction by being linked to phenomena and principles in a different investigative area. Aristotle himself places emphasis in *Movement of Animals* on movement within the animal body and on the animal's immediate surroundings that harbor mover causes. The cosmology of *Movement of Animals* is not explicitly hierarchical.[197]

Cosmological themes come into play because the lever, which the very movement of limbs makes relevant to animal motion, involves an unmoved position located within a body. Given his arguments for a first mover in *Physics* VII, this is too great an opportunity for consilience for Aristotle to neglect. He will bring it to bear on the question of the unmoved mover in general. In its own terms, though, the argument for the immobility of soul explores the physical meaning of being stationary in relation to the lever principle, which has a mathematical form. The ambiguous status of points as being in bodies but without magnitude is unstable ground conceptually in the treatise, and this shows up in the analysis of *Movement of Animals* 8–9. The problem becomes part of the argument for soul not being a magnitude or point extremities.

For understanding the treatise, it is important that the moving radius as manifest both naturally and artificially is a theme running all through *Movement of Animals* 1–7.[198] The radius of *Movement of Animals* 1 that

---

195 *Movement of Animals* 4 comes closest to giving a sequence of movers with animals in the middle, because of its reference to animals as movers of inanimate things (700a18). Aristotle does not, in this context or later in *Movement of Animals*, treat the goods moving a soul to desire as hierarchical goods, however.

196 Whewell, *Novum Organon Renovatum*, Book 2, 88–90.

197 Bodnár's judgment on this matter is similar ("Mechanical Principles," 145–146). His understanding of Aristotle's use of the lever and balance in *Movement of Animals* differs from mine insofar as he understands it as entailing "that the motions effected are forced motions of the parts of the animals" (146). While my interpretation does not rule this out for individual movements undertaken by the animal, I see Aristotle as incorporating the import of the moving radius at the level of the central principles of his natural philosophy. Bodnár views biomechanics as a separate realm of explanation from Aristotle's other causal principles (137, 146).

198 See the sequence of appearances of the lever principle in *Movement of Animals* as laid out in Chapter 2 above.

is transposed from one position to another in portraying the movement of a limb is one configuration of the lever. For Aristotle, the moving radius as a mechanical principle concerned with bodies finally lends itself to a causal solution on a very different plane, the first mover of the living body. The mechanical root of the central explanatory trope of the treatise thus needs to be addressed. My concern is to shift attention at least temporarily away from the unmoved mover to the other equally important theme in *Movement of Animals*. As we shall see, Aristotle is concerned with the inner dynamic of movement itself—in particular, how small changes bring about larger changes.

To begin, I will show how the examples central to the argument of *Movement of Animals* 7 are grounded in a dextrous and nuanced appeal to the principle we have been investigating. With this mechanical citation of Aristotle's own, it is possible to read Aristotle's references to *dunamis* in *Movement of Animals* 7 in relation to the physical content revealed by leverage phenomena. He understands *dunamis* to be latent power for change but for change in ways proper to the entity under examination or the materials that make it up. The generality Aristotle claims for his investigation of animal motion at the beginning of *Movement of Animals* bears fruit in his own generalization upon the lever as he delineates a physical conception of *dunamis*.

The Rolling Cone in *Movement of Animals 7*

In *Movement of Animals* 7, Aristotle uses the example of a small wagon with unequal wheels as a cohort to *automata* in explaining how a small change produced in the organ of sense by something perceived can result in a variety of movements of much greater magnitude in an animal body. A word overheard makes someone redden with anger, or a feeling of cold produces shivering all over. Aristotle says:

> The movements of animals may be compared with those of automatic puppets, which are set going on the occasion of a tiny movement (the strings are released, and the pegs strike one another); or with the toy wagon (for the child mounts on it and moves it straight forward, and yet it is moved in a

circle owing to its wheels being of unequal diameter—the
smaller acts like a center on the same principle as the cylinders).[199] (701b2–7)

Aristotle's reference to automatic puppets has been taken by modern
readers to connote a series of movements caused one after another by a
sort of domino effect—pegs striking other pegs and causing movements
one after another. An *automaton* would be a type of mechanism—material parts arranged so as to propagate a series of movements—that
yields an overall appearance of animation or self-movement. Nussbaum
understands this to be the import of *automata* and the small wagon (*to
hamaxion*) taken together. She attributes the sustained movement to "the
nature of the mechanism itself." She adds that the difference between
the two examples "seems to be primarily one of emphasis: the puppet
example underlines the generation of a whole series of motions from a
single initial motion, the cart example the change in character of a motion
because of the nature of the functioning mechanism."[200] Furley takes the
examples a little differently. They are meant to show "that one small and
simple movement can by purely automatic means bring about a complex
series of *different* movements."[201] The emphasis is on the ramification of
effect into different species of motion. Combining elements of both these
accounts, Berryman says, "The presence of internal complexity in these
devices allows that, unlike projectile motion, they do not merely continue
a motion they are given, but transform one input into an output of a different kind."[202] These scholars focus on the construction of the *automaton*
and the series of material parts in contact as transferring motion. This
analysis fits better the puppetry example than the wagon, however, since
the latter has a minimum of intervening connective causes. What is the
wagon doing in this account, then, and what does it add?

I will argue that neither example is meant to convey primarily a sense
of a mechanical series of the sort we have come to expect in the case
of clocks or mechanical robots. The connection between the wagon and

---

199   The text of *Movement of Animals* used is Nussbaum, *De Motu*. Translations of the
Greek are taken from the modified translation in *CWA* 1. When I have altered translations
or translated the text myself, this is noted.

200   Nussbaum, *De Motu*, 347.

201   Furley, *Greek Atomists*, 216.

202   Berryman, "Ancient Automata," 359. See also Matthen, "Four Causes," 176–177.

automatic puppets is the moving radius principle that explains each. The expression of the principle in terms of the rolling cone is at work in this passage. We saw, in Chapter 2, that the rolling cone is a formulation of the moving radius found in *Physical Problems* XVI.5. Aristotle's evocation of the rolling cone both dates *automata* similar to those of Hero's description to the fourth century BC and provides reason to place *Physical Problems* XVI.5 near in time of composition to Aristotle himself.

In *Physical Problems* XVI.5, as we saw in Chapter 2, a contrast is made between a rolling cylinder and a rolling cone. Both are traveling in a circle, but the cylinder describes straight lines on the plane on which it rolls while the cone describes a circle. The difference is due, the author says, to the cone having unequal concentric circles in its surface. The larger circles in the cone, those nearer its base, are carried more quickly around the common center at the apex of the cone. All these circles described by the cone on the plane are described by the same straight line (914a9). The author thus conceives a rotating line of contact between the cone and the plane surface (**Figure 5.1**). This single straight line is, of course, a moving radius for the circles described on the plane surface. The rolling cone, as an expression of the moving radius, incorporates mechanical information not present in the basic principle, however. For one thing, it includes the translation of movement from one plane to another. The upright circles in the cone make concentric circles on the plane surface. This translation to another plane is an important element in the construction of complex machines. The rolling cone expresses *iteration* of the lever principle by translation to another axis. Secondly, by being a stiff surface, the cone exemplifies the distribution of a single force through a body so as to produce even but unequal speeds.[203] This is the feature of rotational movement to which Aristotle alludes in his remark about why the heavens do not break apart. Conceiving rotating circles in the rigid

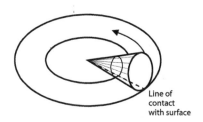

Line of contact with surface

Figure 5.1

---

203 Both these elements of the rolling cone, reiteration of the basic principle and even distribution of force, appear in Hero of Alexandria's *Automatopoiêtica* (AD first century). See below in this chapter.

surface of the cone gives a fully mechanical expression to this mathematical feature of bodies. The simplicity of the mechanical expression by means of a mathematical solid, the cone, is a mark of a certain degree of refinement of the basic principle as part of mechanics at the time of composition of *Physical Problems* XVI.5. Aristotle's description of the little wagon is similar to the formulation of *Physical Problems* XVI.5. The wagon travels in a circle, though pushed straight ahead by its rider. It travels in a circle because of having wheels that are unequal (701b4–6) (**Figure 5.2**). Aristotle goes on to say that the smaller wheel on the wagon works like the center of a circle (ὥσπερ

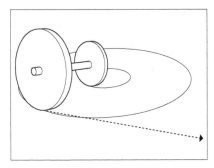

Figure 5.2

κέντρον), just as in the case of cylinders (καθάπερ ἐν τοῖς κυλίνδροις) (b6). It has not been clear to scholars what is intended by the reference to cylinders.[204] In *Physical Problems* XVI, it is said that all the circles of a cylinder move about the same center (914a13), though in fact what they share is an axis. When cylinders are turned by an axle or spindle, the axle is like a center but moves. (See the wheel and axle assembly of **Figure 5.3**.)

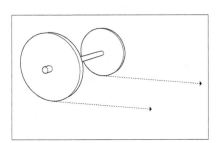

Figure 5.3

---

204   Louis suggests that καθάπερ ἐν τοῖς κυλίνδροις refers to conical rollers (*rouleaux tronconiques*), not a true cylinder (*Marché des animaux,* 167). This interpretation is not adopted here for several reasons. The passage from *Physical Problems* XVI understands the term as referring to the geometrical cylinder, and what is remarkable about the rolling cone is still clearest in contrast to the rolling of a true cylinder. Furthermore, there is reason to think Aristotle means to invoke with this allusion the axle of a rolling cylinder as a kind of moving center, one cylinder within another. As for other meanings of the word, Galen (in *Opera Omnia* [ed. K. G. Kühn], 18.1, 462) refers to a child's rolling toy by the word κύλινδρος, distinguishing it from a cylinder that is pillar-shaped. He says a part of the body is ἰσόρροπον, equally balanced, when it is most like a true cylinder. Apollonius of Rhodes describes a ship in a storm, running along a huge wave like a cylinder; see Apollonius' *Argonautica* II, 594 (Seaton, 142). This latter reference suggests that the looser meaning of *kulindros* is the shape of free movement along a curved path, which is the type of movement common to the rolling cone and rolling cylinder.

Viewed in cross-section, the cylinder and its axle are two concentric circles. Similarly, the smaller wheel on the toy wagon describes a small circle, functioning like a moving center. The rolling cylinder would travel in a straight line, as would two wheels of equal size at the ends of an axle. When likening the movement of the linked unequal wheels to cylinders, Aristotle perhaps highlights that the motions of both the wagon of unequal wheels and a cylinder on an axle depend on the movement of unequal concentric circles. This would be consistent with Aristotle's insistence in *Movement of Animals* 3 that no part in a moving circle that is a physical magnitude could itself be stationary. In any case, placing the wagon in the context of the contrast of cone and cylinder in *Physical Problems* XVI.5 reinforces the judgment of Louis, Farquharson, and Nussbaum that this is a cart with a small wheel or wheels on one side and a larger wheel or wheels on the other.[205] There is an implied though not explicit contrast to the rectilinear movement of the rolling cylinder in Aristotle's reference to the rider of the cart pushing straight ahead but going in a circle (701b4). This passage in fact illustrates in a concrete case the difference between cone and cylinder stated in *Physical Problems* XVI.[206]

Aristotle's interest in the example of the wagon is the way the movement of the smaller wheel is coupled with a greater distance covered in the movement of the larger wheel. This is the feature of circular motion

---

205   The diminuitive form, τὸ ἀμάξιον, is taken by scholars to indicate that the wagon is a child's toy, though Preus points out the uncertainty of this on textual grounds alone (Preus, *Movement and Progression*, 86) (The rider is simply ὁ ὀχούμενος). By most accounts, the wagon has only two wheels, one smaller than the other. Preus, however, claims two unequal wheels would make an unstable vehicle, and so Aristotle could not have had that in mind. A two-wheeled cart might nevertheless make an interesting toy with the challenge of keeping one's balance. Farquharson (*De Motu, De Incessu*, in *Works* 5) believes it is a toy but a four-wheeled cart, with two small wheels on one side and two larger wheels on the other. He attests to having seen such a toy on the streets of London. Taking the view the cart has four wheels, Preus suggests an interpretation very much like a modern skateboard in which circular motion is produced, on four *equal* wheels, by shifting of weight alone. Preus's model seems generally consistent with the interpretation presented here, because the shift of weight causes a smaller arc of movement to be described on one side of the skateboard than the other.

206   For the sake of completeness, it should be noted that circles on the cone cannot be perpendicular both to the axis of the cone and to the surface on which the cone rolls. If the circles of the cone are rendered as wheels on a cart, then the weight of the rider likely makes the wheels more vertical and so seated at a slight angle on their axis. The assembly would need to be adjustable or fitted loosely or with bearings, and unavoidably the wheels would wear unevenly. Modern skateboards, which have wheels the same size, achieve turnings arcs of different sizes by means of the "truck" underneath the board, which is a pivoting axle assembly cushioned by bushings.

that figures most prominently in both the references from *Laws* and *On the Heavens,* as well as in *Mechanics,* and Aristotle seeks to liken the case of animal motion to it. Generalizing as he applies the principle to animal movement, he says:

> And it is not hard to see that a small change occurring at the center makes great and numerous changes at the circumference, just as by shifting the rudder a hair's breadth you get a wide deviation at the prow.[207] (701b24–27)

Aristotle's reference to the rudder (more precisely, the tiller or handle of the rudder, οἴαξ) connects the cart and the rolling cone to a chief example of the lever, which is specifically cited in *Mechanics* 4 as an illustration of the moving radius principle. He goes on to liken the movement of animals to this case of the wagon with unequal wheels, applying the principle to the way hot and cold, and even imagination, produce shivering and trembling throughout the body from an initial slight alteration around the heart (701b16–32).

Aristotle's evocation of the principle of the moving radius and the amplification of effect involved in leverage seems clear in *Movement of Animals* 7. Indeed, it seems that the toy wagon is invoked precisely to bring into play the trope of the rolling cone. The simplicity of the wagon argues against its being meant to illustrate, along with *automata,* that animation is a result merely of the complexity of arrangement of a succession of causes in contact. Aristotle makes it clear, nevertheless, that he means for the wagon and the *automata* to illustrate the same thing in living things. Accordingly, let us consider how the rolling cone sheds light on his understanding of the automatic puppets.

An initial problem is to know to what type of *automata* Aristotle was referring. He says their activity begins with a small movement (701b2–4), and is carried on with cables being released and pegs striking one another.[208] Looking at texts from Plato to Michael of Ephesus, Nussbaum

---

207 ὅτι δὲ μικρὰ μεταβολὴ γινομένη ἐν ἀρχῇ μεγάλας καὶ πολλὰς ποιεῖ διαφορὰς ἄποθεν, οὐκ ἄδηλον· οἷον τοῦ οἴακος ἀκαριαῖόν τι μεθισταμένου πολλὴ ἡ πρώρας γίνεται μετάστασις.

208 There are different interpretations of the pegs (ξύλα, *xula*) and what they strike, depending on the reading of the text. See Farquharson, *De Motu / De Incessu,* in *Works* 5, 701b3n4, and Nussbaum, *De Motu,* apparatus for this line and her article, "Text of *De Motu,*" 150–151. Hero mentions pegs (πασσαλίσκους) as regulating the release of the cord moving the figures (*Automatopoietica, Opera* I, 344.13).

divided ancient puppetry into two types: (1) figures moved only by their parts *via* cables attached to limbs, or (2) figures moved as wholes by a mechanism below a platform. Based on texts from Galen and Michael of Ephesus' commentary on *Generation of Animals,* she interprets the puppets as being of the first type. Even if this is right, however, Aristotle's reference to pegs makes clear there is some sort of drive mechanism, and Nussbaum seems to be aware of this. The pegs are involved in transmission of effect. Thus, the puppets are not plain marionettes. Nussbaum considers the moving figures in Hero's full-scale automatic theater of *Automatopoietica* to present a very different picture of *automata.*[209] Momentarily, I will present some evidence from Hero's text for thinking Aristotle did mean to refer to the sort of drive mechanism of Hero's theater. Even if Aristotle is referring to marionette puppets, though, and not to figures (whether jointed or rigid) moving above a platform, he would be invoking the moving radius principle. Cords attached to limbs lift those parts in a way similar to the description of radial motion Aristotle gives at the beginning of *Movement of Animals*, where he says that animals use their joints like a center (698a21–24). The multiplication of effect from origin to extremity that is radial motion is an example of a lever also.

Hero of Alexandria (AD first century) makes a very explicit connection, however, between *automata* and the principle of unequal speeds along concentric circles in his work devoted to the mechanical theater, *Automatopoietica.*[210] Despite Hero's late date in relation to Aristotle and the Aristotelian *Mechanics*, his account bears careful consideration in relation to *Movement of Animals*. Not only does he explain *automata* in terms of different size circles in rolling cones, he also links these contrivances to puppeteering effects already known to "the ancients" (342.3). His account provides a link between Aristotle's two examples in *Movement of Animals* 7.

Hero describes apparatus situated beneath a base or plane that produces the different movements of figures mounted above the base. The components of the apparatus are wheels of different sizes, axles on which the wheels are mounted, cables wrapped around the axles, and a drive wheel or lead weight (344.9–48.23).[211] The *archê* of each type of move-

---

209 Nussbaum, "Text of *De Motu*," 147–150.

210 Hero, *Automatopoietica* VII–VIII (Schmidt, ed., 362–365).

211 One indication that Aristotle had in mind moving *automata* like Hero's is that along with pegs Aristotle mentions iron parts, which he likens to bones (701b7–10). Hero insists

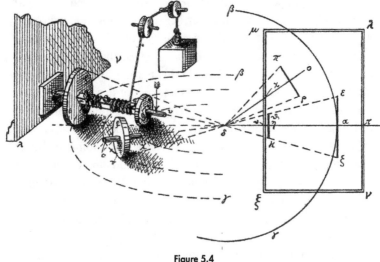

Figure 5.4

ment is the tension in a cable wound around an axle. In the case of the gravity-driven power train, the cable unwinds by gradual descent of a weight. The cables drawn by the weight move at equal speeds, he says, but the movements produced are not equally fast but vary according to the larger or smaller circles of the wheels attached to the axles (348.5–9) and also according to the manner in which the cord is wrapped on the wheels. **Figure 5.4** from Hero's *Automatopoietica* illustrates the essential mechanical and geometrical features of a diagram to which Hero refers.[212] He goes on to decribe how rectilinear and circular movements of the figures are brought about.

---

that the turning parts of the apparatus in the automatic theater be made of smooth hard material, like iron or bronze, to facilitate movement (342.24–344.6). The hardness of the material is important because of the stress on parts moved by tension on a cord and linked to other parts. Plato also mentions metal parts, both iron and gold, in an account that has figures jerked and pulled by cords (*Laws* I, 645a). This suggests Plato and Aristotle were acquainted with jointed figures moved by a complex sort of mechanism as in Hero's theater.

212   This imaginative and functionally meticulous diagram is Figure 87 drawn for the 1899 Teubner edition of Hero's works. It was drawn on the basis of the German translation of the text and a manuscript diagram. See Schmidt's remarks in his recension of the text (*Opera* I, LI and 363n). Illustrating essential elements in a small space, the artist places the descending weight above the working mechanism. He portrays what Hero describes: the movement of two different-sized wheels directly linked in a single cone but the movement also of a third on a different axis. In the frame to the right, he projects the dimensions of the cones into two dimensions. The horizontal platform below the figures sits vertically on the left in the diagram.

Circular motion is achieved along the paths described by wheels of different sizes that are either fixed to the axle or are, by cables, moved with the same motion as the axle.[213] Hero explains the possibility of circular motion of different diameters and speeds in terms of a cone rolling about its stationary apex. He says that if a cone is rolled along a plane, its base describes a circle whose distance from the center is equal to a side of the cone. The cone's apex is the motionless center of the circle (364.8–11). He says a cone rolling on its side is equally balanced (*isorrhopos*) within itself (364.17). One aspect of the meaning of this statement is that, when stationary, the cone is subject to the slightest force exerted in either direction.[214] It also means that all points on the cone are subject to the same force exerted anywhere along it, so that it rolls smoothly and evenly. He says the cone is cut in half by a plane at right angles through the side of the cone in contact with the surface. He has in mind a plane containing the axis of the cone and dividing the different-sized circles within the cone into half-circles. He continues:

> Whenever [the cone] is pushed by an outside force (ἑτέρᾳ δυνάμει) and rolls, each of the semi-circles on the same side [of the cone] by an equal force pushes the other semi-circle in its own circle, and in this way it moves. (364.19–22)

The force applied in one half of the cone forces the other half over, translating the different sized circles on the cone's surface to the horizontal. The point of dividing the cone in half is to show that motion requires a magnitude to be moved. He imagines semi-circles along the cone all the way up to the apex in order to explain that the apex does not move because it has no extension on which the moving force can act (364.23–29).[215] The way he explains the circular motion of his figures is that the same force moves arcs of larger and smaller circles on the cone in the same time. He thus understands the cone as a three-dimensional version of the moving radius principle. The two-dimensional version applies directly to the path

---

213 Transmission of circular motion by contact of circumferences is a fundamental principle presented early in *Mechanics* 1. Hero more commonly transmits motion with cables (e.g., *Automatopoietica* II and IX).

214 Compare *Mechanics* 8, 851b27–35.

215 Aristotle made a similar point in *Movement of Animals* about the poles of the heavens and about the origin-point of motion in the joint (*Movement of Animals* 3, 699a20).

traced by the cone on a plane surface (364.15). The larger and smaller circles of the cone are wheels (τροχοί) of different sizes (362.15) that share an axle. He includes in the same account, however, a second cone having the same center as the first but a different axis (362.13) (**Figure 5.5**). He thus extends the principle of faster and slower speeds of concentric circles beyond even the opposite arcs that figure in the account of the lever (364.3–4, 12).

Figure 5.5

This feature of Hero's account capitalizes on the rolling cone's iteration of the moving radius. The unexpected character of the effects in his theater is due, not only to differences in speed throughout the cone but also to changes in the direction of movement. Arc-motion in a vertical plane becomes arc-motion in a horizontal plane. Circular movement can be translated a number of times by means of different sized wheels in contact and can also be transferred a considerable distance by axles. Accordingly, variations on this feature of the rolling cone and additions to it generate the wide range of lifelike movements he claims for his figures.

Thinking back to Aristotle's examples, it is interesting that Hero specifically refers to larger and smaller wheels that share an axle (ἐξελίκτρα), which the unwinding cord turns (348.5–9). This is the same general picture as the wagon with different size wheels. Hero's account gives a reason why Aristotle would present *automata* together with the *hamaxion*, the toy wagon. Some movements of automatic puppets depend on the principle behind the toy's functioning, and even quite specifically, on the manifestation of that principle in the rolling cone. Hero's treatment also shows why the principle would be best expressed by a rolling cone. The cone being a stiff surface, all the points on the cone are subject to the same force. The import of the cone is "different speeds / same force" for arcs being described by the rolling cone. (Hero in fact belabors the connection to force, when he speaks of semi-circles on one side of the cone pushing over their cohorts on the other side, making the cone roll.) In Aristotle's toy wagon, the force is applied at a point on one circle[216] and is distributed by the axle. The cone illustrates the linkage of one effect (dis-

---

216 ὁ γὰρ ὀχούμενος αὐτὸ κινεῖ εἰς εὐθύ.

tance covered) to the other. It is important for understanding Aristotle's reference that this linkage does not necessarily implicate a series of intervening causes. The reason behind the linkage of effects is rather that all points are subject to the same force. This is why Aristotle would refer to the wagon along with the puppets. The wagon is a simpler illustration of the principle itself but incorporates the translation of effect into another plane that is crucial to the novelty of the puppet's movement.

It is interesting that, even at Hero's relatively late date, he appeals to the expression of the moving radius principle in the rolling cone. This is an indication of what the ancient tradition took to be both marvelous about *automata* and capable of explaining them. Important elements of the rolling cone formulation are:

1. the linkage of smaller and larger effects,

2. the idea of a single force applied distributively, and

3. the translatability of motion to different planes and axes.

Movement of *automata* is not explained by arrangement and a series of contacts but by a rule that governs a whole phenomenon.

For modern authors, the series of movements taking place in train has made the account relevant to classic issues of mechanism, especially as applied to human action.[217] The interest is determinism. Nevertheless, the evidence I have presented shows that the series or train of movers is not the key to the picture for Aristotle. What he seeks is the *principle* behind the movement in train, and he is most interested in the principle as an account of the *connection between an initial smaller change and a larger correlative change.* This interpretation is borne out by the context of his reference to the automata in *Movement of Animals* 7. He seeks to explain how perception and desire, changes in the soul associated with minor alterations in a sense organ, produce greater changes in the body in response (701a32–35, b24–26).

In relation to the issue of determinism, it is interesting that Chrysippus much later uses the difference between the movements of cylinder and

217 See Furley, *Greek Atomists*, 210–226. In *Laws* I (644a–45b), Plato uses the puppets in a straightforward causal analogy. Reason and the passions both act on the human being like cords and strings that pull and tug. But he also says these are to be aided or resisted, implying the pulls and tugs do not necessitate absolutely.

cone to deflect an argument for determinism in relation to human action.[218] Just as the cylinder and cone roll differently, people respond differently to what happens to them, because of their natures and dispositions. To this extent, actions originate within the person and are under one's control. The example was for Chrysippus a trope pointing to principles and natures, not to what we now understand as mechanism.

Dunamis, Leverage, and Form

Having brought the moving radius so decisively into his account of animal motion, what does it mean to Aristotle and how does he make use of it? The context in which Aristotle presents his examples of the toy wagon and *automata* in *Movement of Animals* 7 is the question of how objects of desire exert force (ὁρμῶσι) on animals so that they act (701a34). The mechanical principle of the moving radius explains how a small change in the body, reception of a percept, brings about in an animal a large-scale coordinated response in the pursuit of an object of desire. Thus, Aristotle's topic is sensing and the action consequent upon sensing.

The mechanical principle accounts for the amplification of effect between sensing and action, and by analogy to the reiterative effect of the cone, the transformation from an alteration to a locomotive change. The rolling cone also highlights the feature of orderly distribution of the force of motion across a distance within a continuous body. These properties applied to the case of sensing an object and acting upon that sensation implement features of the moving radius principle itself. It must be noticed that, if a mathematical idea is central to his treatment of sensing and the action it produces, then how the effect from small to large is *transmitted* will not be considered the central problem. There is some sort of continuity that links the movements of different magnitude, but any sort of commotion from part to part in the animal body serves as a placeholder for the distribution of effect in accordance with the rule.[219] This last is an important point, because it suggests that recourse to materials and hypo-

---

218   H. Van Arnim, ed., *Fragmenta*, vol. 2, 974. On the Stoic description of human action in terms of the cone and cylinder, see D. Frede, "Stoic Determinism," 192–196.

219   I will discuss the issue of transmission of effect, or more properly continuance of movement, in Chapter 6 in the context of Aristotle's embryology.

thetical substances is not Aristotle's default position for explanation.[220] It also means that the mechanical principle plays a role in the conceptualization of the sensitive faculty at a level higher than the level of material constituents of sensing. So, we can hope to find in Aristotle's use of the analogy to mechanical action some insight on his conception of the faculty of sensation or perception in general.[221]

In the passage following introduction of the two examples and their principle of motion, Aristotle likens parts of the body to parts of the *automaton*. Bones are like the wooden pegs or the iron in the device; nerves are like the cables (701b8–9). Release of these initiates movement. Aristotle immediately points out, however, that animal movement involves alteration and other species of movement while the mechanical devices translate locomotion only (b11). He makes this point using the language of capability:

> In an animal the same part has the power (δύναται) of becoming now larger and now smaller, and changing shapes, as the parts increase by warmth and again contract by cold and are altered. Imagination, sensations and ideas all bring about alteration. Sensations are obviously a form of alteration, and imagination and thinking have the power of their objects (τὴν τῶν πραγμάτων δύναμιν). For in some measure, the form being conceived be it of the pleasant or fearful thing is like each of the objects.[222] (701b13–19)

Both inanimate and animate things are subject to amplification of movement after its first initiation. From this standpoint, the greater variety and mutual translatability of the changes utilized in living things, e.g., growth to increase, is the difference between living and non-living. Aristotle immediately returns to the significance of the moving radius in explicating

---

220 On this point, see Chapter 9 below.

221 Aristotle does not distinguish *aisthêsis* with respect to what we would call passive sensing, on the one hand, and cognition or active perceiving of a whole, on the other. Since he does not distinguish stages of sensing and perceiving in his conception of *aisthêsis* or in his terminology, I shall use the two terms "sensation" and "perception" as meaning roughly the same thing.

222 I have altered slightly Farquharson's translation (*CWA* 1, 1092). One reason is that I follow Nussbaum's text. The other is to render faithfully Aristotle's remarks on alteration in particular.

capability and received form. Sensing is an undergoing (*pathos*) registered in a faculty, and an alteration (b23). This alteration brings about greater and lesser effects in the body (b23–24). He refers to the different kinds of movement brought about as he generalizes the principle involved: "a small change occurring at the origin makes great and numerous change further away, just as by shifting of the tiller slightly, there is a great change of position in the prow of a ship" (b24–27, passage quoted above).

What the moving radius principle contributes to this account in *Movement of Animals* 7 is a particular structural similarity among capacities for action, a similarity that lends itself to refinement and greater detail. This structural similarity is the crucial link between sensing and action. The first structural similarity is the correlation of slight and great changes. Aristotle's reference in *Movement of Animals* 7 to the tiller rather than the rudder itself emphasizes the contrast in magnitude of the *correlated movements*. The parallel structures are as follows:

Chart 5.1

slight change due to force exerted	*great change—effect of the same force*
shift of tiller by hand	movement of the ship's prow
percept causing a small movement around the heart	coordinated bodily movement toward an object of desire

Although this correlation may seem simple at first, it is informative both with respect to craft and to Aristotle's implementation of the mathematical principle more widely.

In the chart, *dunamis* is neither pole of the relation but is what makes possible the connection between the two movements according to a proportion like the one given with the moving radius principle. If we think in terms of perception, *dunamis* is the capability, latent but consistent in its manifestation, by which a single actor, the percept, produces both a change small in magnitude and at the same time a greater change of whatever type of change is at stake. The moving radius principle, then, is a *tropon* in the sense of being the canonical mode of appearing of *dunamis*.[223] It is a more

---

223 A *tropon* (accusative case) is a way of acting, a recognized fashion or habit of acting

precise universal expression of *dunamis* as a capability. The mathematical principle is the "how" of the many appearances of a latent necessity-within-a-range. In the contrast of device as object or as contrivance, *dunamis* is neither but is the underlying nature shown through modes of contrivance instantiated in objects.

It is important to keep in mind a distinction between *tropon,* the "how," and the content or real-world range of a given *dunamis.* The present discussion concerns not so much the content of *dunameis* in different contexts as the way *dunameis* in general are to be understood, and the analogy to leverage is at that level. In any given case of *dunamis,* its appearances with the expected properties attendant on these appearances, cluster around some version of the moving radius principle as their root *tropon.* In the comparison Aristotle makes to the rudder in *Movement of Animals* 7, *dunamis* is a latent property being particularized or narrowly channeled by the rudder so that *dunamis* issues in a particular instance of action. I propose to follow the case of the rudder quite closely so as to capture the elusive *dunamis* at work in the analogy between the rudder and reception of the percept that brings about action.

To begin with, the rudder brings into actuality a particular magnitude of motion, i.e., a distance covered. The rudder's outermost edge describes an arc in the water and the stern of the ship follows it. To this extent, the rudder is instrumental, because it serves the redirection of the bow. Even though the rudder is an instrument, its actuality (the rudder's steering effect) is as fitted to its purpose (a new direction and speed) as is the actuality of the new direction and speed—just in a different way. This leads me to suggest that the instrumental form of the rudder and the *telos* form (in this case, purposive form) are actualizations of the same *dunamis,* because the tool is dependent on the end for its intelligibility. The rudder depends on other *dunameis* as well. It has to be made a particular shape and from materials strong enough to steer the boat but flexible enough to bear the strain of resistance of the sea. Instrumental form, then, is form by virtue of its functionality.[224] The correlation of small and large changes

---

or being. "Canonical" implies somewhat more definition and precision than *tropon* usually entails. On "canonicality," see Mazur, "Equality," 11.

224   That the activity of the tool and its movements is one kind of actualization of the potentiality for the end is consistent with Aristotle's definition of motion as the actualization of potentiality *qua* potentiality (*Physics* III.1, 201a11). Motion is the actualization of the potency for the end but not as the end. Instrumental ends figure at the level of movement taking place. Aristotle's references to nested or hierarchical ends may add detail in support

across cases thus involves three moments, not just two. In **Chart 5.2**, the middle column is new:

Chart 5.2

slight change due to force exerted	instrumental form—link between changes	great change—effect of the same force
shift of tiller by hand	rudder	movement of the ship's bow
percept causing small movement around heart	likeness of an object registered in cognition as an object of desire	coordinated bodily movement toward an object of desire

In the case of perceiving an object, the rudder is comparable to a particular sensible likeness.[225] In perceiving, the hungry lion receives a likeness

---

of the idea that the potentiality for an instrument is a version of the potentiality for the end the instrument serves. In this connection, see *Nicomachean Ethics* I.1 and *Physics* II.2, 194b1–9. A subordinate end must have a potency for supporting or sharing in the end it serves. This does not mean that the instrumental end does not have more proximate potencies that figure in the realization of its own form but that the potency for the final end presupposes the potencies of subordinate ends.

225 Since *Movement of Animals* 7 concerns things identified as objects of desire, my analysis must concern not only the proper objects of perception, like colors and sounds but also the perception of a whole—what Aristotle treats only tangentially in *On the Soul* II as the incidental object of sensing. I use the term "sensible likeness" for the perceived likeness of a whole. I call it a likeness rather than a sensible form so as to treat what is common to animal and human perception and to allow for the possibility that accidental traits may contribute to a likeness.

"Sensible form" is a term sometimes used by students of Aristotle's psychology to describe the sum of what is actually received in perception. Lear, for instance, says that there is a sensible form of a tree that is perceptual awareness of the tree, not intellectual knowledge of what a tree is, and that this sensible form is in the tree (*Desire to Understand*, 103, 109–110). My term "sensible likeness" does not extend this far. It can be understood in the terms of *On Interpretation* 1 as the likenesses (ὁμοιώματα) impressed upon the soul (so παθήματα) by things (πράγματα) (16a7). In the case of objects of desire, the sensible likeness will fit some *logos* already held in memory, and possibly also in intellect.

The issue of perceiving something as a whole is not unproblematic. Aristotle says that the sense faculty receives the form of the object without the matter (*On the Soul* II.12), but the senses receive only their proper objects. So, not even human beings perceive *what* something is by perception (*On the Soul* II.3). There is not another sense organ for putting together what or who something is. There is a faculty, the common sense, working through individual senses, that perceives common sensibles like magnitude and motion and that also is aware of the act of perceiving (*On the Soul* III.1). Aristotle does not say the common

of the zebra standing on the plain in front of him. In this case, *dunamis* is the cognitive ability of the soul (ἡ αἰσθητική, τὸ αἰσθητικόν), something specific only to a given faculty of sense rather than specific either to a particular object of sense—black rather than brown for vision—or to a specific sensible whole, e.g., a zebra.[226] This ability is narrowed and made definite by reception of some likeness, e.g., brown or black, a stage of particularization that appears in **Chart 5.2** in the bottom of the central panel. Once again, *dunamis* as cognitive ability is not itself in the chart.

Considering the analogy more intently, it becomes clear that, from the standpoint of the second aspect of contrivance I elucidated early on—design taken generally—the rudder has two aspects that follow the two senses of device as an object and device as contrivance. Perception (αἴσθησις) similarly has two aspects:

Chart 5.3

Instrumental form *(1) Rudder (πηδάλιον)* *(2) Faculty of perception (ἡ αἰσθητική)*	
(a) device as object	*(b) device as contrivance*
(1a) rudder as a made object	*(1b)* rudder as a design for implementing power
(2a) sensible likeness registered as a percept	*(2b)* organ of perception as capable of receiving sensible likenesses

Separating these aspects of instrumentality reinforces both that the rudder actualizes in some way the potentiality for the end and that *this* rudder is one design among others that may channel the *dunamis*. The rudder as a design for implementing power (*1b*) includes the understanding that

---

sense perceives a sensible form of a whole. For a detailed analysis of the issue of the common sense, see Modrak, *Power of Perception*, ch. 3. My analysis herein does not replace a fuller development of other aspects of Aristotle's psychology. It is not a stimulus-response model of sensing but an account of the powers of animate things as powers.

226 The specificity of power or potentiality to a kind of perceiving rather than to a particular sensible object, like brown, or a particular sensible whole, like the zebra is expressed by Aristotle directly: Δυνάμεις δ'εἴπομεν θρεπτικόν, αἰσθητικόν, ὀρεκτικόν, κινητικὸν κατὰ τόπον, διανοητικόν—"Powers we call [capable of] nutrition, sensing, desiring, moving from place to place, discursive reasoning" (*On the Soul* II.3, 414a30–32).

there are other designs akin to this rudder because of underlying principles that allow implementation of power similarly. *Dunamis* is the more generalized level of "parameters of design for steering devices" of which a ship's rudder is one particularization. Aristotle himself, at the end of *Physics* II.2, points to this difference in aspects of instrumentality in the disclosure of *dunamis*, when he refers to two levels of craft activity, that of the carpenter and that of the supervising designer (194b1–7). He even uses the example of the rudder. The carpenter makes a rudder for a particular task, but the supervising designer understands more generally how it should be made and why. We might expect the supervising craftsman to have some grasp of the moving radius principle, or at least to know that the rudder is a lever propped against the sea, like many other levers he designs that push against something relatively unmoved.

Just as with the rudder, there is both the general and the particular level in the case of the faculty of perception. A sensible likeness is specialized to cognition of a *particular* thing, like the rudder taken as an object. The question is how *dunamis* as latency of form should be distinguished from instrumental form in this case. Any of the faculties of perception is a power for receiving all sensible forms that qualify as its proper object, e.g., vision receives colors. If a likeness-perceived is something specified and concrete like a rudder of particular design, and the faculty of perception is underlying *dunamis*, what is comparable to the level of instrumental form as contrivance, the kinship of designs based on underlying principles of the *dunamis* in question? It is the organ of perception (τὸ αἰσθητήριον) as one of a possible range of bodily organs suited to perceiving (*2b* in **Chart 5.3**). The eye can receive many different sensible likenesses of the kind suited to the underlying power for sight. The eye's design is for receiving a range of color. Furthermore, different animals have different object-organs for perceiving light and light-enabled phenomena, which are suited to the lives of those animals—a light-sensitive spot or strip, an eye that perceives only shades from white to gray to black.

Indeed, the distinction of two levels of instrumental form provides a reason why Aristotle distinguishes a faculty of perception (τὸ αἰσθητικόν) from the organ of perception (τὸ αἰσθητήριον). This distinction is not made to provide a physical location—the organ of perception—for an immaterial activity—the exercise of the faculty. This would be a crude way of understanding the relation of cognition to sense organs. A better approach is to consider the sense organ as possessing the intelligibility proper to instrumentality for its specific but still relatively generalized range of perceptibles, e.g., all colors and visible light (again **2b** in **Chart 5.3**). At this level, instrumental form is related by common intelligibility to the form of the end to be achieved. The eye is one of a number of contraptions for the perception of color and light found in different organisms. These natural contraptions share the intelligibility of design for vision in the broad sense. To this extent, a sense organ itself has built-in intelligibility *oriented toward the object to be perceived*. The intelligibility of the objects to be perceived is already present remotely in sensing, due to the way an instrument has a form.

The eye is also, however, a specific contrived tool for vision, and at this level, the object perceived is directly involved. As design in the broad sense, the eye must share in the nature of what is to be captured by perceiving. This is the rule of instrumentality we have been uncovering in the common potency of instrument and end. So also for perceiving something in particular, the nature of the sense organ cannot be entirely distinct from the nature of its object. We might say that just as an instrument serves the end of vision, so must it also serve the origin of vision, the sensible object. For Aristotle, the eye must be composed of watery, transparent, material for it to see.[227] This is material capable of having color not in the way the object seen has color but in a way that can be instrumental to vision. Then, in the perceiving of yellow, for instance, the water in the eye is *yellow-y*. That is, the substratum organ of perception is qualified, not changed as to what it is but nevertheless altered. Perception involves the contrived object, eye, being qualified in a specific way suited to its narrow range.

So, we have an object perceived, which acts as an agent but which could never without the appropriate receptor produce seeing in that on which it acts. There is the organ of sensing, which has two aspects: that

---

227 Transparency, which is present in a number of naturally occurring bodies is a key part of the eye's instrumentality. Aristotle understands transparency as an attribute of some substances, like air and water. A luminous object in a transparent medium actualizes the trait of transparency, allowing for light to be present throughout the medium, a condition facilitating the transmission of colors from object to eye. If transparency is an attribute and light is an actualization of that attribute, it is not the case that two bodies are in the same place at the same time, when light "fills a space." Relevant texts on this topic in Aristotle include *On the Soul* II.7 and *De Sensu* 6. The sense organ incorporates a transparent medium in its structure, and the actualization of light shares some of the characteristics of the sense faculty as a "second actuality" (*On the Soul* II.5). On this topic, see De Groot, *Aristotle and Philoponus*, ch. 3–4.

of a general design for perceiving and a particular material constitution that renders it an object like the object perceived. In addition, there is the founder of the entire process, the faculty of perception, the *dunamis,* The faculty of perception is not altered in any sense of alteration that corresponds to change or development.[228] The perceiving faculty can in some sense *be what it perceives,* because of the instrumental features of the organ of perception.

We are now in a position to place *dunamis* and the *aisthêtikon* (*aisthêtikê*) in relation to the other functional distinctions made so far. *Dunamis* can be brought into relation to the two kinds of instrumental form of Chart 5.3 in the following way:

Chart 5.4

Latent form	Instrumental form	
dunamis	*device as contrivance*	*device as object*
(1a) power of leverage	*(2a)* rudder as a design for implementing force	*(3a)* rudder as a made object
(1b) sensitive soul: faculty of, e.g., vision	*(2b)* organ of perception: e.g., eye, light-sensitive spot	*(3b)* sensible likeness registered in the organ of perception: e.g., seeing a tree

In **Chart 5.4**, *dunamis* comes first, because it is prior to either actualization of instrumental form based on it. Device as contrivance is placed next in order after *dunamis*, because contrivance implies greater generality than either the rudder or sensible form received. Contrivance is the possible range of designs, based on the *dunamis* in either case.[229] Contrivance is structure that capitalizes on latent form to produce an object or register a percept. A sensible likeness makes determinate that design for the reception of forms, limiting it to a particular percept instrumental to further

---

228 *On the Soul* II.5, 417b12–21.

229 Contrivance in this meaning itself has two aspects. There is the range of designs possible at all for reception of light and color, and there is the design actualized in a particular case (eye or light spot) but taken just as one design in nature. This last meaning of contrivance is the actualization or selection of one design from the whole range.

action on a larger scale. In the case of the rudder, the object constructed in accordance with the general design principle of a-small-movement-pro-ducing-a-large-movement is a tool capable of turning a boat against the sea. The rudder is specialized. A particular sensible likeness is similarly specialized. It is an *end* of the *design for* vision or hearing, for example. Yet, it produces a small movement in the body undergoing the percept and that small movement generates a very great result. The reception of a sensible form is an origin (*archê*) of movement or activity.

One thing shown by teasing out of the difference senses of instru-mentality and form is that device is operating on a more fundamental level in Aristotle's thought than the more limited concept of artifice. Aristotle's *Physics* II begins with a contrast of nature and artifice (τὸ ἀπὸ τέχνης) and ends with an assertion of their kinship based on art using the principles of nature.[230] If we take into consideration that artifice depends on device, this change from contrast to comparison does not have to be contradiction, carelessness, or a circuitous expression of a hidden truth. The statements are different because of what he is talking about in the parts of *Physics* II. Aristotle knows that device to some extent hides the natural (hides *a* nature or *natures*) but not because it changes the nature.[231] By using a nature, device reveals nature in the actuality of what has been devised. Transparent liquid can be (part of) an eye.

It is important to notice how close to one another latent power and contrivance are. Should the peculiarities of the moving radius be regarded as a property of natural things or as a principle governing human con-trivance? Once we formulate a mathematical principle of motion out of sensory-motor reactions and hard-won experience, is it then ours, part of intellect and not nature? Furthermore, in the parallel that can be drawn from *Movement of Animals* 7, the sense organ is a natural contrivance, but is the sensible faculty also contrived?

I would say "no," but perhaps relevant to this last question is Aristotle's statement, in *On the Soul* II.1 that if the eye were an animal, vision would be its soul (412b18–19). The faculty of perception is the driver of the sense organ's form and function. If the contriver can be con-trivance, then perhaps the sense faculty can also. In general, the foregoing

---

230   *Physics* II.1, 192b13–23, and II.8, 199b26–33.

231   On this point, see Aristotle's notice of the fact that artificial objects have an in-born principle of change to the extent that they are made out of something (*Physics* II.1, 192b19–20 and 193a12–17).

analysis allows for a perspective on the intertwining of nature with our understanding of what nature is. To be aware of the difficulty of separating these is a kind of enlightenment. In the service of this enlightenment, Plato with his Cave Allegory shows that contrivance (the parade of puppeteers behind the wall as screen) went unnoticed by the prisoners as being contrivance, in the initial stage of the prisoners' understanding. As his contrasting citations of the relation of nature and craft in *Physics* II show, Aristotle reflected upon this intertwining of nature and device, and he sought not so much to disentangle them but to bring into relief the rules of nature amidst the contrivance. *Dunamis* is Aristotle's separation, within our craft-based understanding of nature, of an element that is not identical with contrivance but is manifest by it. Some forms made manifest are so basic as to define all actualities that cluster around a given nature (a *dunamis*), and the moving radius is such a form.

If sensitive soul is a capacity structured for the production of large changes out of small ones, then there is "depth" in form—a background generative *dunamis* and a foreground actuality produced. Instrumental form is midwife to the actuality produced. Form itself is dual even without artifice, because *dunamis* is manifest through naturally occurring instrumental forms.

The dual aspect of form is an important distinction to make, because without it, the duality will appear in philosophical discussion as a pernicious vagueness afflicting attempts to make precise what form, unaided by the artificial, could be. The duality is continually on display in *Mechanics*, whose chapters reiterate the presence of a natural form in device. To take just one example, the potter's wheel is a human contrivance. It has an instrumental form, but its very utility closely mirrors the root *tropon* of the moving radius. In *Physical Problems* XVI, the same duality can be seen in analysis of natural phenomena that accord with the principle.

The two aspects of form were distinguished by understanding powers in natural change in accordance with the most accessible mathematical feature to be found in nature. We might say that the moving radius principle for Aristotle is at the level of the most general principles of all design. It is not easy to give a description of a fundamental latent property in the way that it is latent—in its non-appearance or absence. This is what Aristotle accomplishes by giving to latency a structure modeled on a natural phenomenon describable mathematically. The universal mathematical regularity gives physical content to the process through which sensation moves an animal body by desire. The *dunamis* concept is revealed by the analogy to be neither of the conceptions empty of physical content that it is often taken to be: *dunamis* is neither a very generalized placeholder for any capacity to change (e.g., qualified non-being only) nor an over-determined antecedent of familiar outcomes that is too specific to be of scientific interest (dormitive power). This analysis of the relation of *dunamis* and *mêchanê* has been made in terms of perception, Aristotle's interest in *Movement of Animals* 7. It could be repeated for other functions of living things. In Chapter 6, it will figure in an analysis of the powers of the nutritive soul.[232]

Dunamis as Active Receptivity

A question naturally arises as to whether *dunamis* conceived with the help of this mathematical rule is an active or a passive power. *Dunamis* has always been understood as a kind of invisible characteristic belonging to something already fully actual on another level. For example, water is clear and liquid, but it has the power to nourish living things. Usually, *dunamis* is a passivity that supports additional action or essence, upon the reception of a form—in an appropriate time, place, and way—from something other than the *dunamis*. For instance, blood and bone become a vertebrate body. On this conception, only what acts on *dunamis* has the form that the potentiality comes to possess when actualized. Other causes besides *dunamis* are determinative of what *dunamis* becomes. *Dunamis*, then, is passive power. *Dunamis* conceived on the model of the lever does not fit this characterization. With the lever, the power itself is exerted or activated and is manifest in action. *Dunamis* in the case of the lever does not receive form but rather a push or initiating impulse, and the latency immediately issues in action of a distinctive sort. At the same time, this

---

232 For Aristotle, living things all function—either grow or flourish—in accordance with final cause. This is his teleology. The introduction of a mechanical model into perception does not alter the teleological import of his natural philosophy, but it does introduce a new route toward analysis of it. The concept of *dunamis* partly concerns the range of physical feasibility, because potentiality is an issue only where the presence of an end depends on matter and change. The present analysis also brings into focus the issue of the design of designs. The divisions of instrumental form with which Aristotle is working are similar to divisions in contemporary discussions about whether there are universal features of design in computer science and engineering—whether there are general design principles for making designs. On this topic, see Brooks, *Design*.

activity comes out of a receptivity harbored in an arrangement and structure of materials. The power of the lever is power in both a receptive and active sense.

Traditionally in Aristotelian scholarship, it has been thought that capacities are either active or passive. This assumption is closely linked with another, namely, that capacities are either for motion or for being something. Both these divisions are given in *Metaphysics* Θ.1, it is said.[233] In regard to active and passive powers, *dunamis* is defined in *Metaphysics* Θ.1 as "a principle (*archê*) of change in another or [in the thing itself] *qua* another" (1046a11). Aristotle immediately explicates this definition in terms of change of the second sort residing in what undergoes change (τῷ πάσχοντι) (a13). So, here is passive potency (as opposed to active), the ability to receive action and be changed. As for the division between potencies for change or for being, Aristotle says in *Metaphysics* Θ.1 that, although the prior meaning of *dunamis* is in reference to motion, it is not the most useful for his present purposes (1045b36). This has been taken to signal his greater interest in potencies for being. The development of Book Θ, though perhaps not the first five chapters, in general bears out this interpretation. The two contrasts have a textual basis, then. Nevertheless, both dichotomies—between active and passive potencies and between potency for motion or being—have been under revision in recent scholarship.

Frede addressed the two oppositions together, as he sought to re-center the meaning of *dunamis* as defined by action, whether the capacity is for change or for being.[234] Frede believes the division between active and passive potencies, as well as the discernment of potentiality (*potentialitas*) as "a kind of item in the ontology, a distinct, somewhat mysterious kind of possibility," are both accretions of centuries of commentary on Aristotle in changing philosophical contexts. Neither common interpretation of *dunamis* is a compelling reading of the original text. He believes

---

233 Ross, *Metaphysics*, 240–241. Frede criticizes the interpretations of both Ross and Bonitz in "Notion of Potentiality," 179.

234 See Frede, "Notion of Potentiality." Most other treatments of *dunamis* in *Metaphysics* Θ.1 focus on potencies for movement as a springboard to potential being, which lacks sense without reference to its prior actuality (*energeia*). See, for instance, Kosman, "*Energeia*," Menn, "Concept of 'Ενέργεια," and Witt, *Ways of Being*. Freeland concentrates on *dunamis* as capacity and gives definitions of the kinds of *dunamis* ("Capacities"). Beere takes Aristotle's treatment of the capacity for movement in *Metaphysics* Θ as the beginning of a strategy to make being-in-*energeia* a way of resolving the battle of Gods and Giants in the *Sophist* (*Doing and Being*, 11–12, 23–25).

being-capacities get their meaning from change-capacities. Capacities are real but within a much more pedestrian ontology than the one developed within the Aristotelian tradition. Frede says: "Aristotle thinks that there are truths of the form 'A possibly is F,' in some special sense of 'possibly,' which cannot be reduced to truths of the form 'A is actually G.'" The physical world just is characterized by this fact, that there are *dunameis* as well as *energeiai* or *entelecheiai*, actualities.[235] In this context, Frede points out the artificiality of separating potencies for change or for being. Without existing, a thing can no more *be changed* than it can change something else. So, potencies are not merely conceivable possibilities but exist. Let us consider a particular example that can illustrate Frede's point about *dunamis* and also be an example of the relation of small and large changes.

Aristotle's treatment of "oily" (*to liparon*) as a passive power illustrates the close relation of receptivity and action for *dunamis*. Something oily is what can burn (1046a24). As able to burn, oiliness is a power that requires some agent in order for the power to act. So, "oily" is a receptivity. Yet, oil's flammability shows that even a capacity conceived as passive is an active power when it shows itself under the prompting of some external agency. A warehouse fire started from a match dropped in oil is destructive in multiple ways, threatening even to take calamitous control of all the surroundings. More oil burns and the warehouse is set ablaze. It is hard to say that the passive *dunamis*, in the way it exists in this case, simply follows along behind the power that acts on it, as a weaker double. The match is not "more" than the fire it caused. The flammability of the oil is the more powerful active power of the two contributors, agent cause and capacity.

Someone might counter that there is a clear transition from passive power to active exercise in this case, since the flammability turns into actual burning. Furthermore, the match is actuality and to that extent "more," being already alight before it hits the oil. In contrast, I would point out that it is by the burning power of the oil that the oil burns. Combustion spreads through the body of the oil by the oil's own power. Oil has the power to burn, which is something active. In this case, so-called passive power and active power are very closely allied. Passive

---

235   Frede, "Notion of Potentiality," 173. For another statement of capacity as real because of its relation to change, see Makin, *Book Θ*, 18. Makin treats the puzzles of correlating passive and active powers in his commentary on *Metaphysics Θ*.1 (*Book Θ*, 29–34).

power might be better called something's "*receptivity* to exertion of its own active power." Indeed, the present analysis supports Frede's suggestion that passive and active powers should not be separated into two.

In many Aristotelian contexts, "passive" is a poor English translation for the Greek, *pathêtikos*, which has a connotation of "undergoing." In *Nichomachean Ethics* II.5, *pathê* is often translated as "emotions," but *pathê* are really the non-rational side of our responses to things that happen to us, i.e., responses to our "undergoings." The undergoing of a trial or bad experience is also the expression of anger or sadness coming from the experience. *Pathê* are "emotions" that are expressed because they are evoked. We have *dunameis* for *pathê* (1105b25). It is by virtue of *dunameis* that we are said to be *pathêtikos* (b26). The ethical virtues and vices are not *dunameis* but states (*hexeis*) we are in relative to *pathê*, when our responses have been formed to the stable and predictable by choice and repetition. *Dunamis* needs a translation that connotes both receptivity and response. The word "reactivity" for *pathêtikos* has too much of a connotation of stimulus-response or action due to irritability in the subject. The neologism "ractive," so ugly that it will be used even by me only now, at least illustrates the seamless combination of receptivity and activity most appropriate to *dunamis* as Aristotle develops its meaning for animal motion in *Movement of Animals* 1–7.

Someone wishing to resist this syncretism of passive and active *dunamis* might, at this point, turn to action theory and distinguish the case of the burning oil into an *energeia*–activity, the burning of the oil due to its flammability, and a *kinêsis*–activity, the oil burning up the warehouse. What is an actuality from one standpoint (the exercise of the flammable quality of the oil) is a motion from another standpoint (the warehouse being burned down because of the oil in it). The paradigm case of this distinction is the difference between the activity of building (which is the exercise of the builder's skill, itself a form expressed in activity) and the process of housebuilding (which must be supervised by a knowledgeable contractor but takes place in the materials). This difference allows a capacity to be conceived as passive in one sense (the flammability is activated by an agent) and active in another (the oil burns the warehouse). Adding this distinction makes clear that my discussion of this example concerns an *energeia*–activity—the oil just burns—but it does not change the basic point that the power to be acted upon is a receptivity to the altered state of exerting active power—burning up.[236] Making the distinction of types of action does raise the question as to whether a similar analysis can be applied to a *kinêsis*–activity—that is, if receptivity and active power are also closely allied in motion. This question will be addressed in a particular case of animal movement in the next chapter.

Comparison to the case of flammability shows some of the other information yielded about *dunameis* by involvement of the mechanical principle in explanation. Note that the warehouse fire simply grows as long as there is something to burn. Animal powers, on the other hand, are closely targeted to an action or accomplished end. Aristotle makes this point himself in *On the Soul* II.4:

> By some the element of fire is held to be the cause of nutrition and growth, for it alone of the bodies or elements is observed to feed and increase itself. . . . A concurrent cause (συναίτιον) in a sense it certainly is, but not the principal cause; that is rather the soul for while the growth of fire goes on without limit so long as there is a supply of fuel, in the case of all complex wholes formed in the course of nature there is a limit or ratio (πέρας καὶ λόγος) which determines their size and increase, and the limit and ratio are marks of soul but not of fire, and belong to the side of account rather than that of matter. (416a11–18)

Aristotle, somewhat mysteriously it has been thought, often portrays the unfolding of animal powers as dependent on a proportion of materials utilized in growth or soul functions and a proportioned orderliness of movements involved in the powers becoming active.[237] His appeal to proportionality makes more sense in the context of the mathematical trope he applies to animal motion. Powers taken in particular proportions (and thus also the bodies that have the powers) are suited to certain resulting actions. Aristotle's appeal to *logos* initiates a scientific research program for finding the context and proportions that foster the fruitfulness of powers. Animal movements are better fitted to the finite limits of the lever arrangement and its proportions than to the profligacy of the raging fire,

---

236 For Aristotle's use of the language of alteration to describe the transition from capacity to active exercise, see *On the Soul* II.5.

237 Other passages where Aristotle cites a proportion (*logos*) as definitive of the actions of soul powers include *Parts of Animals* I.1, 642a20 and *On the Soul* II.12, 424a27. For other citations, see below Chapter 6.

139

but the power of change or action in animals is an active power nonetheless. Also, if the exercise of a capacity implicates movements (as the nutritive faculty in particular does), the *logos* as a ratio of powers, materials, timing, and context will include that those movements have connections among themselves, like the different movements transpiring for points along the moving radius. To develop this idea further, it will be helpful to place these active latent powers in relation to efficient and formal causes. This is a topic of the next chapter.

For the moment, some assertions may be allowed to stand on the basis of the evidence presented. First, actualization of animal capacities does not fit the limited terms of an interpretation of *dunameis* as divided into (*a*) shaping agents, or (*b*) recipients, the latter passively hospitable to active agents that impose their forms on others, as the signet ring acts on wax.[238] In *Movement of Animals* 7, Aristotle is dealing with resident capacities that have actualizations with character, so to speak—like oil's flammability. Secondly, as we shall see further in Chapter 6, the lever provides an inner physical dimension—a vision of physical process—that it is often claimed is missing in Aristotle's science. Thirdly, exploration of the analogy between the operation of lever devices and natural processes opens a space where *dunamis* and contrivance can show themselves as two sides of natural form. It is not necessary to contrive a separation of nature and human design to distinguish *dunamis* and device.

---

238   Aristotle uses this comparison in *On the Soul* II.12, 424a20.

Chapter 6
Dunamis in Aristotle's Embryology

In this chapter, receptivity and acting are explored further as aspects of a single *dunamis*, in a case where it is clearly movement that results from actualizing *dunamis*. The movements under consideration are the many small movements coming in a sequence that constitute an embryological development. In this case, as Aristotle treats it in *Generation of Animals* II.1–5, the salient capacities are those of the nutritive soul, not the sensitive soul. Aristotle used the *automaton* analogy to explore powers of sensitive soul in *Movement of Animals* 7. In *Generation of Animals* II.1–5, the analogy serves understanding of how the nutritive soul is capable of movements that produce a completed animal offspring. This suggests that Aristotle did not think of the correlation of small and large actions in *Movement of Animals* 7 merely as a single illustration of one function of animal soul, the response to a percept. Correspondingly, the field on which we may consider the connotations of the *automaton* analogy is considerably expanded, for now both the two broad capacities defining animal life, nutritive as well as sensitive soul, are involved.

Several issues will be significant in developing an understanding of the powers of nutritive soul. One is the role of the male seed as the cause of the continuing development of the embryo. An important distinction to make in reference to this issue is sperm *imparting form* versus *bringing about movement*. Aristotle understands the male seed to do the latter in the process of development.[239] A second issue concerns Aristotle's

---

239 In what follows, the emphasis is on the male and female contributions to embryological development. These are separated from the soul principle of the embryo itself only in

own statements in *Generation of Animals* I.1–5 that movement produces movement. These assertions seem to fall outside the standard understanding of causation in Aristotle, so much so that they have become orphans in scholarly interpretation. They seem to lead nowhere. A third issue is to understand the powers of the nutritive soul as active powers. I will begin with the role of the agent or efficient cause in sexual reproduction.

Causes and Motion in Embryology

In *Generation of Animals* II.1–5, Aristotle gives an account of why there are two sexes in most animals. The account is very detailed and rich, and it would be difficult to treat it in its entirety. For present purposes, I will focus on the relation of *dunamis* in the female to the male contribution of efficient cause and the principle of soul. In his account, Aristotle spends a great deal of time discussing what I shall call the micro-structure of motion. By "micro-structure," I mean descriptive details of the many small movements between the beginning and end of a development, and also their sequencing. In his discussion of the micro-structure of embryological development, Aristotle tracks the self-organizing progress of the embryo in much the same way a contemporary cell geneticist or embryologist might do.[240] Throughout his account, Aristotle insists that the *agent cause* of each interstitial process of an embryo's development does not have the form of the whole organism.[241] He mentions in particular the male seed in this regard. The immediate active cause of an interstitial process is in contact with the materials undergoing development. The original efficient cause, the parent, has the form more completely than these immediate active causes. This contrast of original and immediate causes is central to Aristotle's epigenetic picture of the embryo's different movements. Also central is that movements in the developing embryo are themselves productive of other movements.

---

order to understand how they are contributors to the embryo's formation. The movements described are not separated from one another but succeed one another by contact. They are unified by the *dunamis* of the embryo.

240 The descriptive character of Aristotle's detailed account, identifying causes in minimalistic terms, comes through more clearly in the Greek than in translations. The Greek terms will be noted in what follows.

241 See, for instance, *Generation of Animals* II.1, 734a25–734b4 and 734b17–19, II.4, 740b26–27.

Aristotle says this explicitly several times.[242]

Recent discussion of Aristotle's embryology has focused on two issues, one very general and somewhat contentious—the supposed passivity, in Aristotle's embryology, of the female contribution to reproduction; and the other of special interest to Aristotle scholars—what the embryology has to tell us about the metaphysical dimension of Aristotle's concepts of form and potentiality. The textual analyses of Robert Mayhew and John Cooper support a few broad tenets of Aristotle's embryology where these two important topics converge.[243] First of all, the female contribution to the generation of an animal, the matter, is neither inert as a kind of formless substrate nor is it passive in the sense of being without characteristics making up the organism. Mayhew shows that the word σπέρμα is used by Aristotle to mean seed, not just sperm, and that the sperm and the menses are each an excess or residue (περίττωμα) described by Aristotle as seed. When Aristotle's discussion becomes more detailed and precise, "seed" is used more properly for the male contribution, because it is essential to actual formation of the offspring as an animal. The male seed has sensitive soul in actuality.[244] Yet, seed is a term descriptive of materials along a spectrum of generative capacity, and male and female contributions to the offspring are closely related even in their own material composition.[245]

---

242 *Generation of Animals* II.1, 734b16–17, II.1, 735a1–2, II.5, 740b25–27, 741b7–9. At 734b30–36, Aristotle includes reference to a *logos*, a ratio or proportion according to which elemental qualities, like hot and cold, make (ποιεῖν) qualities of living things, like softness or brittleness. Movement according to a *logos* is repeated at 740b25–34: "[F]or in these [heat and cold, the tools of the soul] is the movement of the soul and each comes into being in accordance with a certain formula." (Platt translation, *CWA* 1, 1149).

243 Mayhew, *Female*, 30–47; Cooper, "Metaphysics."

244 *Generation of Animals* II.5, 741a27–28. To avoid equivocation, it may be helpful to distinguish the sperm as a distinct residue of the male parent, having the form of the parent in actuality and the sperm as an active power contributing the principle of soul to the offspring. As the principle of soul, the sperm can be said to "impart form," because the frame of reference is the embryo's form. In this framework, the female's contribution is receptive, not active, because the female does not contribute this principle of the offspring. The material of the female is active to the extent that it must genuinely partake of movement and not just be pushed around in contributing to the embryo's own development. The female contribution has this capability due to being alive, having nutritive soul. To focus on the movements, however, allows us to avoid misleading connotations of the imparting or carrying of form by the sperm.

245 Aristotle discusses the character of sperm as an efficient cause in *Generation of Animals* I.18, 724a35–b19 and I.21, 729b1–21. At one point, he uses the term σπέρμα, for the combination of male and female contributions to generation (724b4–6), reserving the

Secondly, what male and female have contributed to the developing offspring are certain movements in the materials, which are typical of the species and the individual. By assuming to a progressively greater extent the actualities of its parent, an offspring becomes what it is. As we shall see, this development in actuality is largely the work of the nutritive soul of the embryo.[246] In developing this part of Aristotle's account, Cooper emphasizes that materials contributed by the female must be of a narrowly specific kind in order for the male to impart to it motions that "carry" the form of the human being. Even when the male seed produces a female or an offspring in some other way resembling the female, it is not because parallel movements of the female take over the process but rather because the male itself imposes the properties of the female. A formative principle is always required that acts on materials.[247] Yet, male and female jointly imprint characteristic actualities in offspring because of the movements of nutritive soul from the female.

These points help clear the ground on two other important issues. First, in his embryology, Aristotle uses the terms "active" (*poêtikon*) and "passive" (*pathêtikon*) as elements of his technical vocabulary of change, not as indicating the intrinsic nature of what receives either adjective. Aristotle himself tells us this in *Generation of Animals* II.4:

> [Differentiation of parts occurs because] agent and patient, whenever they are in contact, in the way that one is agent and the other is patient (I mean by 'in the way' (τὸν δὲ τρόπον) the how and the where and the when), straightway the one acts and the other undergoes. (740b21–24)

Something undergoes change because its own nature and current disposition make it suitable for a highly specific sort of actualization, once it is in

---

term γονή for the semen. When σπέρμα refers to the male seed, it is an active principle or power (724b6, 729b6), taking on the designation of form (ὡς εἶδός τι καὶ ποῖον, 724b6) as opposed to the matter of the female. The male seed is not properly speaking a part (μέρος) of the body, since it is homeomerous tissue (724b28–30).

246   In this context, Aristotle says that the embryo's moving power (ἡ ποιοῦσα δύναμις), a term for nutritive soul (740b29), is the same at the very beginning of an animal's development as further along in the process (*Generation of Animals* II.4, 740b34–36). It is just a greater power later on. I will return to this passage in my interpretation.

247   Cooper, "Metaphysics," 176–181. Cooper uses the language of carrying. Sperm or motions in the embryo carry the form, 176. I believe this language is misleading, but see below in this chapter.

contact with something that can bring about the change. It is not because the undergoer's nature is to be passive. It is interesting to consider the different words, "passive," "receptive," and "undergoing," as translations of *pathêtikos*. "Passive" has a connotation of innate inactivity with respect to an outcome under consideration. The passive has no formal qualities of the outcome without an agent that supplies them. This is the sense (as it is usually taken) of the materials as wax receiving the imprint of a signet ring. "Receptive" can mean the same as "passive," but it can also be compatible with a sense of the recipient of agent-action as itself responsive, i.e., productive of actions of its own when acted upon. This sense of receptivity better describes what Aristotle understands to be the meaning of *dunamis* as soul capacity. Receptivity in this sense is even better described by understanding *pathêtikos* as undergoing. If one were to use the term "undergoer" for the one receiving, it would be easier to conceive of receptivity as one with productivity. Receptivity is responsiveness. It is the origin of what the undergoer does in response to agent-action. What is *pathêtikos* itself changes in the direction in which a particular agent is suited to initiate action. The agent is suited to initiate action but is not suited to bringing to completion the action it initiates.

This understanding of *pathêtikos* works in tandem with another exegetical claim. Insofar as they belong to a particular female body, the materials contributed by the female have the form of the species, just as does the active seed, the sperm, coming as it does from a particular male body. The soul that makes something a kind of living thing is not divisible. There is, however, an additional difference in the way the περίττωμα of the female has the form of the animal for the purposes of generation. Aristotle says that the materials contributed by the female have all the parts of the offspring potentially but none actually.[248] Furthermore, the female must possess the form potentially in order for her offspring to be the same species as herself and the father. Aristotle does not say this of the sperm as it initiates change in the female material, though he does say it later of the seminal fluid as material of the parent's body. What each of the parts of the body is actually, such is the semen potentially.[249]

---

248 *Generation of Animals* II.3, 737a23–24.

249 726b15–24. The parts are not yet distinguished in the seminal fluid. For embryological development, it is necessary to conceive of possessing a form potentially as something more than being receptive like wax, but also as something more than showing properties of the materials taken just as materials. For the debate on whether materials have different actualities when contributing to the form of a living thing or whether they exert the

The important point for present purposes is that the *dunamis* belonging to materials in the female truly is one way form is present, namely as a readiness to move in a narrowly defined direction toward an actuality of a particular sort, the end which fully manifests the form in question. To explain how this is the case, let us begin with the agent cause and see how Aristotle's invoking of the *automata* contributes to his account of the agent in embryological development.

Dunamis and Matter

In *Generation of Animals* II.1, Aristotle considers alternative accounts of what keeps an embryological development going, asking what is the agent of the development—not "that from which" (ἐξ οὗ) but "that by which" (ὑφ' οὗ) all the parts come into existence (733b32–33). He says it cannot be something external but must be in the embryo (734a2). Furthermore, it must be something that is contributed by the sperm but then becomes part of the organism (a13–15). So how does this agent make the other parts, since those parts appear in succession? He articulates a general principle: whatever makes another must have something of the character of that other (734a30). This is the principle of *Physics* III.2 (202a11), that what exists potentially is brought into being by what exists actually, and he makes it explicit as a principle later (734b21). Yet he denies that any part of the developed organism exists beforehand in the agent seed (734b1–3).[250]

Accordingly, he modifies his initial view that the cause of the organism is not an external agent. An external agent is one of the causes, but it is not a cause sufficient to bring into being the whole organism:

> It is possible, then, that A should move B, and B move C; that, in fact, the case should be the same as with the automatic puppets (τὰ αὐτόματα τῶν θαυμάτων). For the parts of such puppets while at rest have a sort of potentiality of mo-

---

same properties they have as materials, see Mayhew, *Female*, 48–49. Balme presents one resolution of the relation of tendencies of materials to ends they serve in "Teleology and Necessity," 281–185. Other valuable studies of Aristotle's embryology include Mohan Matthen, "Four Causes," Preus, *Biological Works*, 64–72, and Carteron, *Notion de force*, 77–94. Bolton tracks Aristotle's account of the role of the male seed in relation to the issue of explanation in "Aristotle's *Posterior Analytics* and *Generation of Animals*," §8–9.

250 Οὐκ ἄρα ἔχει τὸ ποιοῦν τὰ μόρια εν αυτῷ (734b3).

tion in them (ἔχοντα γάρ πως ὑπάρχει δύναμιν τὰ μόρια ἠρεμοῦντα), and when any external force (τι τῶν ἔξωθεν) puts the first of them in motion, immediately the next is moved in actuality. As, then, in these automatic puppets the external force moves the parts in a certain sense (not by touching any part at the moment, but by having touched one previously), in like manner also that from which the semen comes, or in other words that which made the semen, sets up the movement (κινεῖ) in the embryo and makes the parts of it by having first touched something though not continuing to touch it. In a way it is the innate motion (ἡ ἐνοῦσα κίνησις) that does this, as the act of building builds the house. Plainly, then, while there is something which makes the parts, this does not exist as a definite object, nor does it exist in the semen at the first as a complete part (ὡς τετελεσμένον).[251] (734b9–19)

In this passage, the problem is that an immediate agent cause does not have the form of the entire organism being generated. The continuing effect of the parent is explained by the analogy to the movement of *automata*. One must think of a first cause moving another, which in turn moves another (734b9). One feature of puppetry Aristotle draws upon here is indeed the one to which scholars have drawn attention: the succession of order-ly effects sustained apparently without contact with the initial formative agent. Yet, the succession of causes is presented as part of the *explanation* of development, containing in some way a kernel of justification for one part of the embryo being capable of producing what is so much more than the part itself. Preus says that the role of each successive part is to serve as a "moved mover" that brings the next into actuality.[252] Aristotle's general theory of causation thus applies to the parts of the *automaton*. There is a problem, however. How is each part "unmoved" if it does not have the form of the parent?

Aristotle is aware of the problem, emphasizing the primacy of the ini-tial mover, the parent, in the puzzle of embryological change. This initial mover is part of the comparison between *automaton* and embryo. Since in the case of the *automaton* the agent is the initial mover, he says, so for the embryo, the sperm or what makes the sperm is the agent of the embryo's development. So, the important feature of the automatic is that it moves

---

251   Oxford translation by Platt, *CWA* 1, 1140.

252   Preus, *Biological Works*, 70.

not by touching anything now but by having been in contact once (οὐχ ἁπτόμενον νῦν οὐθενός, ἁψάμενον μέντοι) (734b14). The contrast of present and aorist participles for ἅτπω, touch, tells the story: the secondary agent is not presently in contact with its mover but was once. The same is true of the agent of embryological development (734b14–16). The sperm is capable of initiating the series of internal movements in place of the external mover.

How does the remoteness of the first mover suffice to bring about the form of the offspring, though? Aristotle says two things: (1) what the agent accomplishes depends on potentiality in the situation, and (2) in a way the innate movement makes the parts. I will consider the first point in this and the following section. The second will be considered in the later section about the micro-structure of movement.

In the passage quoted, Aristotle's justification for ascribing motive power to the male seed is presented in terms of *automata*: "For the parts of such puppets while at rest have a sort of potentiality of motion in them ..." (734b10–13). *Dunamis* in the parts accounts for there being a succession of effects, once the agent acts. Without the principle we have been investigating, this reference to potentiality might seem to be routine, i.e., a standard application of concepts developed by Aristotle elsewhere. In the present context, we might say, Aristotle resorts to potentiality to explain what cannot be reduced to materials or agents. From this standpoint, *dunamis* is a name projected to fill a gap in explanation. Viewed from the standpoint of the practical mechanics lying behind *automata*, however, what he says in this passage is that, within a system of embryological development, parts being at rest are parts in readiness to produce great changes, to amplify or redirect an effect they receive. What this means is that the movement of one part can bring about much greater or more consequential movements in other parts. As we have seen in the case of the puppets, power is present through the arrangment of parts *because of* the properties of circular motion coming into play. By his reference to potentiality, Aristotle means to say there is a similar principle in biological change. It was noted in Chapter 5 that *dunamis* becomes manifest through being narrowly channeled by some instrumental form. The rudder is such an instrumental form. In *Generation of Animals* II.1, the *automata* evokes this same channeling of latent form into actuality. The *automaton* is an instrumental form, a collection of levers arranged so as to mimic animal activity. The channeling of *dunamis* by instrumental form limits *dunamis*, which as underlying or background potency retains wider possibilities for development. This will be an important point to keep in mind in the consideration of the nutritive soul.

In *Generation of Animals* II.5, Aristotle reiterates the connection between the puppets and power present in the material situation of the embryo. He uses the puppets to make explicit that *dunamis* is responsible for the continual developmental change in the embryo. He says:

> Now the parts of the embryo already exist potentially in the material, and so when once the principle of movement has been imparted to them they develop in a chain one after another (συνείρεται τὸ ἐφεξῆς) as in the case of the automatic puppets. When some of the natural philosophers say that like is brought to like, this must be understood, not in the sense that the parts are moved as changing place, but that they stay where they are and the movement is a change of quality (such as softess, hardness, colour, and the other differences of the homogeneous parts); thus they become in actuality what they previously were in potentiality. (741b7–15)

In this passage, Aristotle shifts to the language of potential existence, saying the parts of the organism exist potentially in the matter.[253] It is clear that the analogy to *automata* is not meant to make every change into a change of place. Locomotion he uses as a foil against which to contrast the transformation of the embryo by means of other species of change. Everything depends on the potentiality in the situation: "thus they become in actuality what they previously were in potentiality" (b15). This is the point Aristotle made also in *Movement of Animals* 7 (701b13–16). It is interesting that Aristotle in the passage quoted above interprets the like-like causal theory of the pluralists and Democritus as capable of being assimilated to his own *dunamis* account. Growth by like accruing to like means more activity of the same genus—alteration or increase— contributing to the type of activity appropriate to the species developing. This is his understanding of the action of nutritive soul at *Generation of Animals* II.4, 740b34–36. It is the same activity on a larger scale later in the process.

---

253 ἐνυπαρχόντων δ' ἐν τῇ ὕλῃ δυνάμει τῶν μορίων (741b7).

From the standpoint of modern interpretation, this reconciliation with the pluralists or atomists might seem odd. After all, the pluralists' accounts by chance and necessity seem akin to early modern mechanism. It is something quite distant from Aristotle's potentiality, actuality, and teleology. Aristotle, however, thought that the like-like principle only needed the right kind of enrichment to be reconcilable to his own *dunamis*. *Dunamis* is power capable of accruing additional power. While Aristotle's trustworthiness as a historian of philosophy is often questioned, and the modern interpretation of *dunamis* would make Aristotle's slipstreaming behind the pluralists a mere rhetorical ploy based on a superficial similarity, the evidence from mechanics presented here shows Aristotle's comparison of himself and the pluralists is not superficial. It is hard to render his history in this case null and void.

The *automata* example brings into play both the correlation of small and large movements within a system and the channeling of *dunamis* by instrumental form, a channeling found both in nature and in craft. Aristotle finds evidence of similarity of principle between the lever and the *dunamis* that is soul as he hones an explanatory scheme to make plausible his rejection of a pre-formationist embryology. He has denied both that one part of the embryo contains the essence of the organism as a whole and also that one part, e.g., the heart, can be responsible for generating another part, e.g., the liver. At the same time, he believes that the developed organism is something different from its materials and has its own nature. A necessary part of his answer to the question of the source of the whole, then, is to locate a causal factor in the power of the materials. These materials, the female contribution to development, have the ability—taken together, in the right arrangement, and given the proper external agent—to become something other than themselves. This account is justified by the manifest enhancement of movement beyond the power of the original mover that is possible both in the embryo and in mechanical devices. His example serves a powers model of change.

It is the case that, after the sperm's initial push to development, some local agent or a series of local agents should sustain the process being fueled by the powers present in the proportion and disposition of materials. Aristotle assigns to one organ, the heart, the role of being the source of the continuing influence (741b15). He contrasts his powers model to another, the organization of the embryo like the knitting together of a net (734a20). He rejects this model on empirical grounds (τῇ αἰσθήσει ἐστί φανερόν) and with appeal to observable detail:

> [F]or some of the parts are clearly visible as already existing in the embryo while others are not; that it is not because of their being too small that they are not visible is clear, for the lung is of greater size than the heart, and yet appears later than the heart in the original development. (734a21–25)

Parts cannot be knit together that are not yet present. That parts come into existence earlier and later in development highlights the dynamism of the process. The upshot of Aristotle's line of thought is that the empirical evidence calls for a forceful cause, in addition to the male seed, that contributes to forming parts in sequence out of latency.

The Sensitive Soul and the Nutritive Soul

This cause is in the female contribution to generation and is the nutritive soul.[254] We have seen Aristotle insist upon the sperm *not* being in miniature already the organism coming into existence. Indeed, given other statements Aristotle makes, which we will examine, about the agent in relation to potentiality and substratum, it would make sense to say form is in the substratum and is brought to actuality by the agent. But how consistent is this view with the great importance Aristotle attaches to the role of the male as the agent of the parent's form?

Aristotle himself raises the problem at the beginning of *Generation of Animals* II.5. He asks why, if the female contribution to the new organ-

---

254 Mayhew, Cooper, Freeland, and Balme all highlight the female contribution to formal properties of the developed organism but differ in interpretation of exactly how it contributes. Freeland sees blood playing a central role, since blood is the same at earlier or later stages of development ("Bodies, Matter, and Potentiality," 401). Balme thinks the female contributes "a secondary formal influence" ("Essentialist," 292–293). Cooper emphasizes the responsibility of the male even for traits of offspring lying "well below the level of its specific identity" ("Metaphysics," 198). Mayhew tends toward Balme's view, since he does not think Cooper's interpretation accounts well enough for wind eggs (*Female*, 49). Whether the form of the developing individual should be conceived universally or is an individual form of the parent becomes an issue. Balme opts for individual forms in "Essentialist," 293. Cooper argues against species-forms as an interpretation of Aristotle's account in *Generation of Animals* II but holds that Aristotle's embryology is underdetermined with respect to whether Aristotelian forms are universal or individual entities (202–203).

ism has "the same soul," the female cannot generate a complete offspring by herself (741a6–9). Indeed, the fact that female birds lay unfertilized eggs shows they can generate on their own up to a point (a15). The female animal cannot produce offspring by herself, because animals differ from plants by having sensation, he says (741a9). The logic of this answer would seem to be that sensitive soul only comes along with the male contribution and therefore the male puts form in the matter. Aristotle does not drive this point home, however. He talks about the female contribution instead. He says that those body parts that serve sensation, like the face, hand, or flesh, cannot be generated without there being sensitive soul, either actually or potentially, either in some way or *simpliciter* (πῇ ἤ ἁπλῶς) (a10–12). I believe that Aristotle means for all these ways that sensitive soul can be present to point to the male seed, but let us consider what he says.

Certainly, the male seed is either actual or potential sensitive soul (presumably the sensitive soul *simpliciter* that he mentions). Is the female contribution sensitive soul potentially or in some way? Aristotle does not say it is sensitive soul. In *Generation of Animals* II.1, Aristotle says the male seed both has soul and is soul potentially (735a8–11). His reference to the sleeping geometer in this context suggests that, with his reference to being soul potentially, he has in mind his definition of soul as the first actuality of a natural body with organic parts.[255] A first actuality may be unactualized in the fullest sense of active exercise of its ability, and so be potential to that extent.[256]

How does the female contribution have sensitive soul, then? After introducing the importance of the right body parts for sensation, Aristotle says that they are not enough for sensitive soul to be present. Without soul, the parts that serve sensitive soul would be just like a dead body (741a13–14). The female contribution goes beyond dead body parts, though. This is why he cites the example of wind-eggs, unfertilized eggs that develop like a fertilized egg up to a point. He asks about the wind-eggs, "Are they alive?" His reply is that they are not just like wooden eggs. The fact that they can corrupt shows that they share in life, and so

---

255   *On the Soul* II.1, 412b5.

256   *Generation of Animals* II.1 is an interesting passage for the definition of soul, because in it Aristotle allows for degrees of actualization between simply having a faculty or ability and exercising it. Indeed, he multiplies stages within a development by saying no single part is the cause of the embryo's generation but rather the first external mover (735a12–13).

they have soul potentially (741a23). Corruption is a sign, though contrariwise, of the generative power of soul. He asserts quite clearly that this potential soul is nutritive soul (741a24–25). A particular sort of matter with nutritive soul has the ability to diversify into the appropriate sensitive soul (e.g., bird versus frog), when the materials and circumstances are right and also when they make contact with sensitive soul in actuality. So, the male generator has species-specific sensitive soul, whether potentially or actually. It is the initiating agent for the differentiation of sensitive soul from the nutritive soul, which in a particular case is capable of producing parts appropriate to the species.

The female residue contributing to the generation of an animal does not have sensitive soul potentially, except as an extention of the female parent's soul. The female contribution is nutritive soul. Nevertheless, this nutritive soul is the source of the actual *movements* that produce the organism. To see how this is the case, let us see how Aristotle regards motion as in some way causal.

The Micro-Structure of Movement

In *Generation of Animals* II.1 where Aristotle uses the analogy to *automata*, he says that in one way (τρόπον μέν τινα) the parent or sperm is the cause of the continuing movement, but in another way the movement present in the materials is the cause (τρόπον δέ τινα ἡ ἐνοῦσα κίνησις). This second way he compares to the process of housebuilding (734b17). Matter is never agent but in one way the movement in the matter pushes the change ahead without there being a completed first mover in residence. In *Generation of Animals* II.5, he reinforces this statement by referring to the initial external cause as a cause of movement (ἀρχὴ κινήσεως), not of the thing.

It is not just languid expression on Aristotle's part that it is movement that effects the change in matter. In *Generation of Animals* II.4, he says artifacts are produced by the movement of tools, not by the tools themselves:

> The female, then, provides matter, the male the principle of
> motion. And as the products of art are made by means of the
> tools of the artist, or to put it more truly by means of their
> movement and this is the activity (*energeia*) of the art, and the

153

> art is the form (*morphê*) of what is made in something else, so
> is it with the power of the nutritive soul. (740b25–30)

Most properly speaking, things are made by the movements that are taken to make them. Something-being-made by craft *is* the actuality of craft, and the craft is the form of what is made. Aristotle here renders equivalencies that give form to motion:

motion ≈ actuality of art ≈ form of art
kinêsis ≈ energeia technês ≈ morphê technês

The art (*technê*) is form, and the craft's form is the form of what is being made and so too is the form of the movement that makes it. The power of the nutritive soul (ἡ τῆς θρεπτικῆς ψυχῆς δύναμις) uses things like heat and cold as tools (οἷον ὀργάνοις). The motion of soul is in these and in a certain proportion (740b32–34). Movements of development and their principle (origin) are nearly indistinguishable in the case of nutritive soul. Nutritive soul is *dunamis*, which issues immediately in action.

Bear in mind that these are all comments about the power of nutritive soul, not sensitive soul. It is significant that, in *Generation of Animals* II.5, Aristotle does not use the word *dunamis* for sensitive soul as productive agent but rather *to poiêtikon*, that which is capable of producing or making (741a13). Yet, he describes nutritive soul as the acting power (ἡ ποιοῦσα δύναμις) whose effect is greater at later stages of the process (740b36). In this context, he says nutritive soul is the generating soul and the indwelling nature in both plants and animals (740b37–a3).

The difference in whether the *dunamis* term is used or not as descriptive of soul seems to be the involvement of movement. He uses *dunamis* in conjunction with agency words when he fills out details of what movements are immediately brought about by nutritive soul. Untangling the terminology and meaning in these passages is aided by noting Aristotle's overall strategy. He keeps pushing back the first effect of the agent's sensitive soul, *to poiêtikon*. It is not the heart that makes the liver, but neither is it the sperm that uses hot and cold as tools. It is the nutritive soul-power moving (740b29, 32–34), when the parent, an external agent, starts the process. In place of what we might think should be a singular action of the agent, he substitutes particular movements that, once activitated, do the work of development for the agent. These statements do not make sense within the sole explanatory frame of relatively unmoved movers. They do make sense within the explanatory frame of smaller movements bringing about larger movements because of a latent form-capacity.

Aristotle's treatment of movement as causative is not limited to *Generation of Animals* II.4–5. He emphasizes motion as what effects natures in *Parts of Animals* I.1, where there is also a reference to the difference between the living and the dead. He speaks of the difference between his idea of the definition of a living thing and that of Democritus. Democritus "at any rate says it is evident to all what sort of form (*morphê*) is a man, since he is knowable by his shape and color" (640a34). To take this as defining a living thing is like a sculptor thinking he had made a living hand because he carved the shape in a lifelike color, Aristotle says. No sculpted or painted hand would be able to perform the function (δυνήσεται ποιεῖν τὸ ἔργον) of the hand (641a1). Though he has just downgraded the ability of the artist to produce functional types of the living simply by reproducing shape and color, he nevertheless immediately draws on artists' technique to exemplify a type of account better than that of Democritus and the physiologists. The question Aristotle proposes as the thing sought is this: "by what powers (*dunameis*) is a living thing made?" The artist would answer this question with an account of *how* he produces an object:

> For it is not enough for him to say that by the stroke (ἐμπεσόντος) of his tool this part was formed into a concavity, that into a flat surface; but he must state the reasons why (*dioti*) he struck his blow in such a way as to effect this (διότι τὴν πληγὴν ἐποιήσατο τοιαύτην), and for the sake of what he did so; namely, that the piece of wood should develop eventually into this or that shape.[257] (641a11–14)

In this passage, Aristotle interprets the powers sought as actions. He contrasts the mere fall of a hammer with the particular character of the blow. Interestingly, he keeps the word he used for Democritus' form of man, *morphê,* for the artist's product. Form, even as shape, depends on action of a particular productive type for natural generation.[258] Aristotle does not

---

257 Translation by Ogle, *CWA* 1, 997.

258 Shape, which seems to be due to mere configuration or relative position, in material things is not shape produced at will like an imagined circle or lines that by themselves make a bare triangle. Even shape has to come into being. There must be a reason a natural

pursue his point about actions and ends in this context but returns to the relation of parts and end (641a15–18). The quoted passage makes clear, however, that generative actions too must be specific to ends served. Particularities of different motions can be distinguished as to their suitability to produce a given end.

Aristotle's account of the "between processes," especially in *Generation of Animals* II but also in *Parts of Animals* I.1, to some extent makes movement responsible for outcomes. In scholarship of recent years, emphasis has been placed on the fact that causes are relatively unmoved movers for Aristotle. That is, nothing moves another by virtue of being in motion itself but only by virtue of already being something or other. This is made explicit in *Physics* III.1–2 and is reiterated in *Physics* VIII, where it must be possible to separate a moved and unmoved part within an apparently self-moving object. That soul is an unmoved mover figures quite explicitly in *Movement of Animals* 1 and 8.[259] The emphasis on these passages philosophically has meant that passages where Aristotle gives the character and type of action as crucial to outcome have been orphaned in scholarly interpretation of causation. That causes are unmoved, however, should not be allowed to obscure the things Aristotle says about causal activity within a process. It is meaningful to say motion is causative *in some way* in a context where there is *dunamis*. This is because *dunamis* is not just a collection of materials with actual properties but powers for action latent in materials. The powers become manifest in small movements; this is why Aristotle speaks of *dunameis*. There are multiple, specifically targeted movements. It is crucial to the fruitfulness of this conception of *dunamis* that movements are not "one off." In animal motion, movements are related. They are triggers or hinges linking smaller and larger effects. We can speak of movement as in some way causative, because Aristotle is treating the micro-structure of change. His strategy is to maintain the greatest truthfulness to nature by pushing back the sequence of causes to the real causal first mover, in generation the parent.

His examination of the micro-structure of change in *Generation of Animals* II.4–5 is not unique to that treatise but is consistent with his treat-

---

thing has the shape it does. Its materials must be capable of holding the shape and it must grow into that shape.

259   For discussion of the issues involved, see Lang, *Order of Nature*, and Wardy, *Chain of Change*.

ment of the continuity of change in *Physics* VI. There is no first moment of changing, because change, following magnitude, is infinitely divisible. For every time in which a motion is taking place, there is always an earlier time in which it was taking place. The implication is that one will not "find" the agent with its form at any beginning point in the process, because at whatever point one chooses during the process, the process has always already begun. Consonant with this position, Aristotle would not understand the sperm itself as the bearer of a form being worked into the materials of the embryo. The parent who originates the process has the form the developing animal is coming to possess. Yet, he also says in *Physics* VI that, of every motion, some part has always already been completed. It is not necessary for motion to have ceased to say the thing undergoing motion "has changed" (VI.4, 234b20). Aristotle uses the perfect tense, in its aspectual import, to convey this point. Whatever has changed must be in that into which it has changed (VI.5, 235b27). The perfect tense signifies action completed in the past whose effect continues into the present. At any time during a process, a thing always both "is changing" and "has changed."[260] It is changing (present tense), because it has not achieved its end. It has changed (perfect tense) in relation to a period of the process that precedes the point at which one is using the perfect tense. The applicability of the perfect tense identifies a partial completion of the process. Aristotle gives the example of finishing the foundation of a house within the total process of housebuilding. One has built (the foundation) while in process of building the house (VI.6, 237b13). One would not be able to use the perfect tense in relation to housebuilding if one had built, say, the road in front of the lot. The road is not part of the house in the way the foundation is.

Physics VI.6 seems to be more about signs of final cause within a process than about efficient cause, the topic of *Generation of Animals* II. 4–5. In both treatises, however, he introduces causal structure within motion and does so by using the language of verbs (*Physics* VI) or familiar tropes of dynamism and action (*Generation of Animals* II). This shows that, although natural substances may be the beginning and end of natural movements for Aristotle, he does not make stability of substance the sole explanation of movement. Process is not a blank causally.

The micro-structure of process, as we see in *Generation of Animals* II.1–5, is a world of sometimes short-lived distinct movements unfolding

---

260 μεταβάλλει καὶ μεταβέβληκεν.

along a trajectory because of underlying power. Successive stages may appear very unlike one another. Aristotle likens the original formation of the embryo to the setting of milk by rennet. Earthy parts solidify with a membrane around them. The embryo, like a plant at first, produces its equivalent to a root, to gain nourishment. The real increase and development begin with the establishment of the heart as the first principle intrinsic to the animal. Blood vessels and the umbilicus follow upon the heart's assuming the directing of development.[261] The male seed has long since become one with the developing materials of the female, to which it has imparted its own movements.[262] Aristotle says repeatedly that the agent possessing the form of the animal is outside the embryonic development. At the end of *Generation of Animals* II.1, he says:

> "[A living thing] is produced, then, by something else of the same name, as e.g. man is produced by man, but it is increased by means of itself. There is, then, something which increases it. If this is a single part, this must come into being first." (735a20–23)

The sperm as agent of the parent's form is a material thing imparting to other materials *its own movements*. This produces the great effect it does because of the nature of the materials, which have the form potentially.

What the productive power of nutritive soul shows is that, besides the doctrine of unmoved movers, action as the measure of power is also an important part of Aristotle's natural philosophy. When he treats the structure of movement, the immobility of cause is de-emphasized by Aristotle himself. In *Generation of Animals* II. 4–5, we look in vain for the location of "a whole form" as unmoved mover apart from the actions transpiring. He pushes back to the very beginning of movement the agent cause that actually possesses the form emerging in motion. This does not mean, however, that he has nothing to say about causes within process. He locates and identifies descriptively the sequence of actions and the local proxies of the first agent that keep the unitary process going.

---

261   *Generation of Animals* II.4, 739b20–740b2.

262   *Generation of Animals* II.3, 737a18–25. This is one of the passages where Aristotle says that all the parts of the animal are in the female περίτωμμα potentially but none actually.

Dunamis, Soul, and Efficient Cause

The understanding of power and agency that has been given here is consistent with what Arisotle says about potential being in *Metaphysics* H.6. In this chapter, Aristotle asks what accounts for "what is potentially" (τὸ δυνάμει ὄν) existing actually (1045a30–31). In the case of things subject to generation, there is no other cause beyond the agent. This is because of how matter and form make up a unity, he says. They are the same thing, the one (matter) potentially, and the other (form) actually (1045a23, b18). This view makes the form present later in the condition of actuality something that belongs to the matter as well. Furthermore, it makes most agents (those after the first) more like an initiating force imparting directionality to movement than a bearer of final causality. Aristotle describes the relation of agent and nutritive soul in this way in *Generation of Animals* II.4:

> The differentiation of parts occurs . . . because the superfluity of the female is potentially what the animal is by nature, and the parts exist in it potentially but none actually. For this reason, each of them is generated, and also because the agent and what undergoes, whenever they are in contact in the way that the one is active and the other capable of being acted upon (I mean in the right way, in the right place, and at the right time), straightway the one acts and the other undergoes. (740b12–24)

This passage gives in biological terms the account of the relation of potential and actual being in *Metaphysics* H.6. Both matter and its corresponding actuality have the form. The nutritive soul of the female contribution to generation has the form of the animal that is coming into existence.

There is an implication of this account that is perhaps unsettling in considering the meaning of efficient causality. This is that efficient causes posterior to the parent, even the sperm, possess much narrower active power and formal nature than does the parent itself. The sperm has soul, but this is because it is part of the parent's body and becomes part of the embryo, not because it is a messenger in the sense of being the bearer of the parent's form. In the course of arguing against the idea that the sperm is an agent that passes away after having its effect, Aristotle says something he himself believes about soul: "If, of soul, there is nothing which is not in some part of the body, also this part [the sperm] would be straightaway ensouled" (734a14–15). Soul is itself neither whole nor part but a principle. What he seems to say here is that the soul is in all body parts, including the male seed. So, the male seed shares in the soul of the true agent cause, the parent. But the sperm is not something separate from the embryo that perishes after passing on form. He believes something about the sperm is assimilated into the new being (734a13–14). What is assimilated is not a whole form. Rather, the sperm's material and movement comes to share in the form of the developing embryo and are, from that point on, indistinguishable from the embryo.

Aristotle emphasizes the partialness and narrow function of this secondary agent by his insistence upon addressing the structure of the movements and the order of development in the embryo itself as what accounts for embryological development. In terms of what the developing embryo becomes, it is fitting to say the sperm is partial with respect to form. This does not mean that it signals the presence of only part of form. This would be nonsense. Rather, it signifies that there is required both male and female contributions to effect a form in actuality. So, the substantial form of the developing embryo, the form it will have when development is completed, depends on a condominium of the *dunamis* in matter and the resident active agent. To this extent, the narrowing of the role of efficient cause actually serves a more sophisticated understanding of embryological development than the idea of an efficient cause carrying or bearing form.

This interpretation might seem to be at variance with other statements of Aristotle, particularly at the end of *Physics* III.2 where he says that the mover will always bear the form that is the principle of motion (202a10).[263] So, the efficient cause not only has the form but somehow carries it to the moved thing and conveys it by contact. On the face of it, this statement from *Physics* III.2 is not even consistent with what Aristotle says in *Metaphysics* H.6. How should efficient cause be properly interpreted then? It may help to focus upon the fact that, among the four causes, efficient cause is the agent "by which" a thing comes into existence. So, efficient cause is involved with *the duration in existence of an intelligible whole*. It is the cause of coming into existence. For a living thing, this cause is a parent acting in an entire context capable of incorporating its agency into a real outcome.

---

263   εἶδος δὲ ἀεὶ οἴσεταί τι τὸ κινοῦν.

Considering the question more generally, efficient cause is clearly not the cause of the form as such in any particular case, since form *qua* form is ungenerable and eternal.[264] Sometimes, efficient cause is obviously a cause of something coming to possess a form (one object heating another, for instance) but other times it is not. What removes an impediment to natural motion does not have the form of the moving element, e.g., the snow leopard on the mountain-side that dislodges a log from beneath a boulder, which then falls.

It is often thought, however, that the "by which" is so closely related to formal cause in physical things that it is the cause of this thing having this form, e.g., an animal being the particular animal that it is. As *Physics* III.2 states, the mover bears the form. My contention is that, in the interstices of movement, i.e., in motion examined as process underway and continuing due to an agent, the immediate agents of the embryo's development do not bear the embryo's form in this way but have it actually (either as movement or finished actuality) only in concert with the substratum, which is potentially that thing. The agent in an embryological development is not a cause as *indirectly* as the snow leopard dislodging the boulder. The sequence of agents beginning with the sperm serves the end of the movement (i.e., are for the sake of the end), which has a certain form. But none of the sequence of *agents* has the form of that end, except insofar as they are ensouled and thereby share in the form of the parent or of the offspring as a part contributing to its life.

There is one final point to consider for now in placing the natural philosophical meaning of *dunamis* conceptually. It might be objected that understanding there to be natural powers is really just "getting something for nothing" in natural subject matters outside mechanics. If Aristotle really bases a more expansive concept of *dunamis* on the lever, he is mistaken to do so. The lever is understandable just because it is decomposable into forces, distances, and motions. One could even say that this shows the wisdom of beginning a treatment of capacities from a metaphysical standpoint. There is no need to examine too closely the physical basis for capacities, which could only be treated reductively. This defeatist approach to *dunamis* in natural philosophy is unlikely to have occurred to Aristotle. One reason is that he regarded the relation of forces, distances, and motions to have a mathematical form. Mathematical intelligibility is not nothing.

---

264 See *Metaphysics* Z.8, 1033b5–19.

The "getting something for nothing" cricitism of *dunamis* does presuppose the Greek commitment, thought to have been part of pre-Socratic philosophy, that every thing comes from something pre-existent. Aristotle seems to hold to this maxim in his natural philosophy and to take seriously Parmenides' objections to something coming from nothing (*Physics* I.8). Within this context, however, his recourse to the lever and its underlying principle capitalizes on the labor-saving aspect of simple machines. The ancient interpretation of the lever is that it helps us get something for next to nothing or at least for less than we expected.[265] In *Generation of Animals* II, Aristotle highlights empirically and in detail how natural processes are all the time getting something, not from absolutely nothing, but from very little. The very little is the subject, *to hupokeimenon*. He even gives a mathematical *dioti* explanation of getting something from very little, the moving radius principle on which simple machines are based.

Importantly, though, he believes that we do not really get something for nothing with the lever. As he says in *Metaphysics* A.2, knowing the cause (*aitia*) of *automata* banishes the wonder of them (983a17). This point is repeated in *Mechanics* 1 (848a34–36) in terms of the salient mathematical feature of the circle. As he puts it in more general terms in *Physics* I.8, that out of which something comes, is not nothing (191a33–b10). Change comes out of the non-accidental, he says, but the same argument can be made in terms of *dunamis* (191b28). The connections in Aristotle's text that I have been developing show what this latter statement might have meant to him. Standing Democritus on his head, Aristotle holds that the "very little" from which much comes is only apparently very little. In the very little as substratum, there inheres an active power, which is also a capacity to be acted upon.[266] With this explication of *dunamis* in the philosophy of nature, we have a scientific template suitable for filling out the structure of natural movements and the character of *dunamis*-forms in particular cases.

---

265 See *Mechanics* 1, 847a16–b15. For other passages and the ancient context, see Schiefsky, "Art and Nature."

266 See *Physics* II.1, 192b34, where Aristotle says that nature is always in a subject (*hupokeimenon*). He means by subject in this context identifiable natural substances.

Chapter 7

Leverage and Balance in
Physical Problems XVI

The last two chapters have delineated Aristotle's understanding of *dunamis* as active receptivity, an understanding of natural powers that he believed was substantiated and underwritten by mechanical phenomena. I leave that topic in the present chapter in order to present further evidence from the literature of Aristotle's school that the lever principle was recognized in the fourth century BC in terms of a panoply of its properties and furthermore that it was analyzed within the parameters of kinesthetic awareness and ordinary experience. I will treat Book XVI of the Aristotelian text, *Physical Problems*. My claim up to now has been that mechanical phenomena had a strong influence in shaping Aristotle's understanding of *dunamis* in natural philosophy. This chapter provides a basis for regarding the mechanical phenomena presented in *Physical Problems* XVI as sample discussions from Aristotle's own circle. To make a plausible case for Book XVI as contemporary to Aristotle provides more textual evidence for the claim that mechanical phenomena underlay his scientific thinking more generally.[267] It also extends the

---

267 The reader should recall that Aristotle wrote or commissioned the writing within his immediate circle of a *Physical Problems*, which we do not possess. He called it simply *Problems*. The text edited by Andronicus of Rhodes as *Physical Problems* was an enlarged version of the earlier Aristotelian text, Louis believes (*Problèmes* I, "Introduction," xxxi). Ancient authors universally ascribed this text to Aristotle. This version was consulted by Cicero, Seneca, and others. Another larger version of the *Problems*, closer to the one we possess, gradually came to supplant Andronicus' version but it includes the text consulted by ancient authors (Louis, xxxiii, l). Louis believes a combination of analysis of language, phraseology, and ancient references can, to some extent, establish the state of the text at

range of scientific literature to be taken into consideration in evaluating the import of Aristotle's principles of natural philosophy.

We have already seen one connection between Aristotle's *Movement of Animals* and *Generation of Animals* and the Aristotelian *Physical Problems*. This is the contrast of rolling cone and rolling cylinder found in *Physical Problems* XVI.5. We have seen the connection of this text both to the understanding and production of *automata* and to the moving radius principle. Aristotle himself clearly knew of the contrast of cylinder and cone and its meaning in mechanics. This case is given a clearer mathematical formulation than most of the other cases in Book XVI. In the other cases, leverage and balance are made relevant to a wide variety of natural phenomena and are so familiar to the author(s) as to enter into analysis of both regular and unusual phenomena very flexibly and sometimes without appeal to the moving radius principle itself or to its cohort, the movement of concentric circles. The analysis of chapters 3 and 12, for example, involves a notion of different weights linked by a rod and constraining the motion of one another. I will explore the shades of difference in the presentation of the lever and balance in Book XVI. My investigation will reinforce the judgments of Flashar, Huffman, and Louis, made on the basis of the language of the chapters, on the early dating of Book XVI.[268] The connection between the mechanics of Book XVI and a puzzling reference to Archytas contained within the discussion also points to the scientific ideas of *Physical Problems* XVI being closer to Archytas than has been noticed before. This gives reason to consider whether those ideas were part of discussions surrounding Aristotle himself.

A very interesting aspect of these chapters is their reliance on the composition of circular motion from rectilinear movements constrained from their normal courses. This approach to curved motion is combined with an understanding of circular motion as a form of motion having priority in nature. Circular motion is something like a natural default setting for resolution of the interplay of weights in motion but subject to constraints. Also, the treatment of physical problems like the revolution in motion of an unbalanced body highlights the idea of *movements under constraint*, not interplay of forces as such. Expressed in the terminol-

---

different epochs (xxv). I will present reasons for thinking Book XVI was part of the original *Problems* or at least quite close to Aristotle in time.

268   See note 79, Chapter 2.

ogy of later mechanics, the approach is more kinematic than dynamic. Weight is analyzed in relation to magnitude and is not conceived as the downward pull toward the center of the universe. All these points have relevance to our recognizing an Aristotelian mathematical physics that conceives a substructure of movements in tension as underlying stable phenomena. We shall see in *Physical Problems* XVI a more strictly mechanical version of the influence of movements on other movements that we saw also in *Movement of Animals* 7 and *Generation of Animals* II.1.

In beginning a study of *Physical Problems* XVI, however, it is worthwhile to take note of the literary form of the text we will examine. This will show what were the philosophical expectations concerning the subject of *problêmata*—namely, persistent or especially revealing properties of natural subjects. These were observed traits that, it was expected, would finally take their places as necessary properties in a natural scientific subject matter appropriate to them.

Scientific Problems in the Aristotelian School Literature

There have survived in the manuscript tradition two collections of problem literature in natural science ascribed to Aristotle's school, *Physical Problems,* in 38 books, and *Mechanics*, usually called *Mechanical Problems*, divided into 35 chapters. Aristotle is known to have written or authorized the writing within his school of a *Physical Problems*, but this collection has not survived. The *Physical Problems* we possess is a later compilation by Theophrastus or Strato. Some of its *problêmata*, however, appear also in the standard Aristotelian corpus, so that parts of the surviving *Physical Problems* may mimic Aristotle's own collection. Given Aristotle's involvement in the original project, it is thought that *Physical Problems* was compiled to use in school discussions of principles in natural science.[269] The problems provide a broad base of experiential detail linked to experiences of a similar kind or, more rarely, to a confident assertion of a cause. The topics of *Physical Problems* vary widely within the realm of nature from animate to inanimate phenomena. Shadows, bubbles, wind,

---

269 On the issue of authorship of different parts of *Physical Problems* and references in Aristotle to his own book of natural problems, see Forster, "Pseudo-Aristotelian Problems," Flashar, *Problemata,* 303–316, and Louis's "Introduction," especially xxv, in *Problèmes.* For the continuation of the tradition of problem literature by Theophrastus, see Mansfeld, "*Physika doxai* and *Problêmata physika.*"

sweating, drunkenness, fear and courage are a few of the topics treated.[270]

Mechanics has been thought by some to be Aristotle's own work, and this was the belief in the Renaissance when the text first came into currency. It was not part of the medieval manuscript tradition.[271] Most scholars now believe that *Mechanics* was written 50–100 years after Aristotle's *floruit* but that it is strongly Aristotelian in its point of view and its overall approach to locomotion.[272] In contrast to *Physical Problems*, *Mechanics* focuses sharply on a host of simple but familiar crafted items involved in navigation or weighing. The point of the collection is to show that the lever principle, treated in the first chapter in the terms of a mathematical demonstration of properties of the circle, is the causal principle behind all the other devices. Accordingly, while *Physical Problems* is a compilation without a unifying narrative, the chapters of *Mechanics* make the same point over and over.[273]

Despite their differences, within the two treatises the literary form of inquiry is the same. A *problêma* begins with the "why" question, *dia ti*, for which in Aristotle's conception of science the appropriate answer states a cause. In *Posterior Analytics* II.1–2, Aristotle gives the four types of things sought: (1) that something is, (2) the "why," (3) if something is, and (4) what it is (89b24–25). The first two questions concern an attribute or characteristic, whether it belongs to a subject and why it belongs—e.g., whether the sun is in eclipse or not. In traditional interpretation, the sec-

---

270 Though I present in this section the expectations concerning how to resolve problems coming out of Aristotle's philosophy of science, the range of topics of *Physical Problems* strains interpretation of the whole text as sober pre-demonstrative investigation. Blair touches on other uses of the ancient problem literature ("Natural Philosophical Genre," 172–178), which often included phenomena that were bizarre and odd. Her statement that "Aristotelian *problêmata* are not designed to generate new 'scientific' or certain knowledge—they produce neither new principles nor new observations" (175) is too sweeping, however. The analysis of Book XVI elaborates on the moving radius principle in a way that fosters new applications. The collection of problems in *Physical Problems* appears to be a compilation of materials of varying dates.

271 For the Renaissance history of *Mechanics*, see Rose and Drake, "*QM* in Renaissance Culture."

272 On authorship of *Mechanics*, see Krafft, *Betrachtungsweise*, 13–20, Bottecchia Dehò, *Problemi meccanici*, 27–51, and Bodnár, "Pseudo-Aristotelian *Mechanics*." The last article deals particularly with attribution of *Problems* to Strato, which Bodnár does not endorse.

273 Chapters 31–34 of *Mechanics* depart slightly from this plan, treating the issue of inertial motion for objects thrown or pushed. Bodnár briefly compares *Mechanics* 33–34 to Aristotle's account of projectile motion in *Physics* VIII.10 and *On the Heavens* III.2 ("Pseudo-Aristotelian *Mechanics*," 446–448).

ond two questions concern a subject itself, whether it exists and what it is—e.g., the existence of centaur or a unit in mathematics. For Aristotle, *dia ti,* or *dioti,* is the scientific question *par excellence,* because its answer states a cause through which something necessary holds. This cause would assume the place of the middle term in a demonstration. Scientific knowledge (*epistêmê*) is thus demonstrative knowledge for Aristotle. Accordingly, the *problêma* form in the two surviving problem sets of Aristotle's school addresses a scientific question, "why." *Problêmata* seek, with the degree of necessity possible in the natural realm, what is responsible for some state of affairs holding in the way it does.[274]

That *dioti* is the question is important, because some problems are conceived dialectically, not scientifically, even when their topic concerns nature. Aristotle discusses dialectical problems in *Topics* I.11. A dialectical problem "contributes either to choice or avoidance, or to truth and knowledge, and does that either by itself, or as a help to the solution of some other such problem" (104b1–2). He gives an example of a dialectical problem undertaken for the sake of knowledge alone, namely whether the universe is eternal or not. The key to a dialectical problem as conceived in the *Topics,* is its involvement with opinions held. It may also be invoked when there are conflicts in deduction. Dialectical problems concern *logos,* speech or argument. Indeed, Aristotle says all dialectical problems have come to be considered theses, because they tend to be about paradoxical claims. Really, though, *problêmata* are a wider class than theses (104b29–105a1). In *Topics* I.11, he says this is because some problems "are such that we have no opinion about them either way" (104b30).[275]

In *Prior Analytics,* Aristotle uses the word *problêma* to refer to a statement of what is to be proved through one of the syllogistic figures.[276] The connotation of the term includes the propositional character of the

---

274   In *Parts of Animals* I.2, Aristotle specifies that scientific knowledge, *epistêmê,* concerns what cannot hold otherwise. Nevertheless, he makes clear, in *Physics* II.8, that necessity in natural things is subject to natural impediments and corruptibility and so holds *epi to polu,* for the most part (199b24).

275   On the codification early in the Aristotelian tradition, of these differences in types of inquiry, see Mansfeld, "*Doxai* and *Problêmata.*" He notes Alexander's observation that investigation of a dialectical question about nature might precede and lead into a scientific question on the same topic (Mansfeld, "*Physikai doxai* and *Problêmata physika,*" 71n34).

276   See, for instance, *Prior Analytics* I.26, 42b29 and 43a18, I.28, 44a37, and II.14, 63b18.

statement, but even more important is its character as something to be resolved or shown (δείχνυται). In *Posterior Analytics* I.12, Aristotle discusses what he calls a scientific question (ἐρώτημα ἐπιστημονικόν), which is a question appropriate to a given subject matter from which a scientific deduction may follow (77a36–40). Such a question is a principle, because it is one of a pair of contradictory statements to which assent must be given for the deduction to proceed. He does not discuss in this context *problêmata*, which the *Prior Analytics* passages identified as conclusions. He does use the term *problêma* in *Posterior Analytics* II.15 in the sense of a scientific conclusion, saying that problems are sometimes the same by having the same middle term (98a24). So again, the connection between *problêmata* and knowing a cause is clear. He discusses sameness of genus for the middle term of *problêmata* or subordination of one middle term to another for related *problêmata*. In chapter 16, he points to the universality of *problêmata*, since they are explained through a cause, which is a kind of whole. The cause is universal even when it is applicable to different species. The cause and that of which it is the cause must convert (98b32–36), so both are universal. The example of a *problêma* in this passage is "why do trees shed their leaves?"

What can be seen from these passages is that *problêmata* were conclusions, understood as what is to be explained or proven. In its origin, the problem form was not for speculations on the strange or serendipitous but on the evident and recurrent that also has a significant relation to other phenomena.[277] Sometimes, what is evident is also remarkable. Though in dialectic *problêmata* could be taken mainly as opinions, in Aristotle's science they were conclusions of demonstrations. The problems of *Mechanics*—and also *Physical Problems* XVI—are, in Aristotle's terms, scientific not dialectical problems, because they concern what Aristotle considered questions of necessary traits of natural subjects. *Problêmata* seek resolution in universals as explanatory. They are *scientific* problems, both in the modern sense of being concerned with natural phenomena and in the Aristotelian sense of being subject to explanation by a cause that holds for all instances.

---

277 George of Trebizond, a Renaissance Greek, criticized Theodore Gaza's translation of the *Problems* saying that he did not even know the difference between a *questio* and a problem. A problem is an *inquisitio rationis rei sensu patentis*, he says, "the investigation of a reason for a thing that is plain to the senses" (Monfasani, "George of Trebizond's Critique," 279).

From this vantage point, it is interesting how different even *Physical Problems* XVI is from *Mechanics*. *Mechanics* has one universal as cause, the lever understood in terms of its underlying mathematical principle of motion, the moving radius that covers longer and shorter arcs on different sized circles in the same time. Explanation proceeds from a statement of what a device accomplishes to its underlying configuration as a lever. The lever itself is given a geometrical account in *Mechanics* 1, a demonstration of the moving radius principle. *Physical Problems* XVI, on the other hand, introduces the principle governing circular motion in a variety of ways that embed it in the physical situation without a clear separation of the geometrical from the physical.

As a final note, it is important to be cognizant of the limitations of the text of *Physical Problems* and make explicit the strategy for dealing with these limitations. In the introduction to his translation and commentary on *Physical Problems*, Flashar notes that this text has been the least studied of all works attributed to Aristotle. This has to do with the fact that many passages are difficult to render with complete intelligibility. The problem of translation is exacerbated by the text being likely corrupt in some places.[278] Difficulty in rendering the text is a problem for my study mainly with respect to chapter 4 of Book XVI. A cogent interpretation is nevertheless attempted for that chapter. Although these limitations must be kept in mind in interpreting Book XVI, they do not prevent the text from yielding a great deal of information about the level of mechanical knowledge current in Aristotle's school.

---

278 Flashar, *Problemata*, 295–296. For the most recent comments on text and translations, see Mayhew's Preface and Introduction to his Loeb translation (*Problems* 1, 2011), which replaces Hett's translation.

Recent research discounts Theodore Gaza's contribution to correcting the text. See Monfasani, "George of Trebizond's Critique," and "Pseudo-Aristotelian *Problemata* and Aristotle's *De Animalibus*." Hett, the Loeb translator of *Physical Problems* before Mayhew, held to the value of the Latin translation of Theodore Gaza. He believed Gaza had a number of manuscripts of the text (*Problems*, vii). Louis points out that Theodore offered mostly paraphrases of the text. Monfasani makes plausible Trebizond's claim that Gaza created a new Greek text in the guise of a Latin translation ("George of Trebizond's Critique," 290, and "Pseudo-Aristotelian *Problemata* and Aristotle's *De Animalibus*," 206–211).

I have consulted the most recent edition of the text by Louis. Textual modifications made by Ross and adopted by Forster in his Oxford translation (*Works*, ed. Ross, vol. 7) are noted when adopted or relevant to interpretation. Flashar did not edit the text. Marenghi, who has edited a number of books of the *Problems*, has not re-edited or translated Book XVI. The standard text before Louis's edition is the Ruelle-Knoellinger-Klek edition in the Teubner series. This is the text on which I have for the most part relied. (I am grateful to Robert Mayhew for leading me to the recent history of textual study of the work now being called simply *Problems*.)

The Related Topics of Book XVI

Physical Problems XVI, which bears a title "Concerning Unsouled Things," follows upon a Book that treats problems connected with straight lines, especially in relation to the appearance of the sun and moon. In *Physical Problems* XV, the way straight lines figure in the geometry of circles and spheres has already been brought to bear on natural phenomena. Book XVI concerns more mundane issues but introduces geometrical principles into the analysis of natural movements that are in some way irregular or unbalanced. Book XVI, despite its heading, includes one geometrical problem, chapter 9, about living things.[279] The sequence of topics is as follows:

1. why the bases of bubbles on the surface of water are white and do not cast a shadow

2. why bubbles are hemispheric

3. why a body whose weight is distributed unevenly revolves when thrown

4. why falling bodies rebound from the ground at equal angles to their angle of impact

5. why a rolling cylinder describes straight lines on a plane surface while a cone travels in a circle

6. why, when a book is cut straight and parallel to the edge, it will be straight when unrolled, but cut at an angle and unrolled, the cut edge is jagged

7. why magnitudes when divided appear to be smaller than the whole

8. why air in the ball of a water clock, when the ball is immersed in water sideways, does not prevent water from entering even with its tube plugged

9. why the parts of plants and animals that are not organs are all circular, e.g., stalks of plants, and limbs of animals

10. why objects are rounded at the edges

---

279   As Flashar points out, there is nothing systematic about the designation "unsouled," and the expectation of an exhaustive contrast of "souled–unsouled" for the topics of the chapter is by no means fulfilled (Flashar, *Problemata*, 579).

11. why a circular object that is thrown first describes a straight line and then, as it ceases motion, a spiral

12. why bodies of uneven weight move in a circle

13. why moving bodies rebound from an obstacle in the opposite direction and at equal angles.

Among these chapters, the only ones that do not deal with the circle and diameter in some way are chapters 7, 8, and 13, though chapter 8 on the *klepsydra*, does include references to balance, wedging, and exertion of force.

The chapters of *Physical Problems* XVI that I will treat are listed in **Table 7.0** along with the issue by which the circle becomes involved in their analysis of motion:

Table 7.0

Chapter	*Topic*
3 and 12	Motion of a body unbalanced in weight when the body is thrown
4 and 11	Rebound at equal angles of round or oblong objects impacting a surface at an angle other than right; curved trajectory of fall of a body in projectile motion
5 and 6	Paths of cylinder and cone rolling on a plane surface; shape of an edge of a scroll cut at an angle
9	Growth in a circular pattern
10	Rounding of edges of oblong shells buffeted by waves (compare *Mechanics* 15)

The topics of these chapters are related by their concern with curved motion as arising from constraints operating on a body in motion. Book XVI may be a compilation, but the chapters treat their related topics in a similar way. The moving radius principle is explicitly cited only in the contrast of the movement of cylinder and cone in chapter 5. This fact makes all the more interesting the way the principle is shadowed in other

171

chapters. In these other chapters, circular or curved motion, or a circular shape of a body, comes about

a. due to mutual constraint of linked weights (3 and 12),

b. due to a continuous body moving along a line that is not the axis of equal balance within the body (4) or not the line of equal balance in its ambient medium (11),

3. due to the mutual interference of movements arising from forces of growth acting together (9) or iterative impacts that may be either simultaneous or successive (10).

A presumption appearing often in these chapters is that movement proceeds naturally along a rectilinear path (913b9) but that a circular path is itself a natural outcome of disparate rectilinear tendencies in situations where balance cannot prevail (913b3–5, 915a29–30). Weight always comes with magnitude (3, 4, and 12), and this means that there is always some middle (*meson*) that, whether it is treated as motionless or not (913b17), is a center of balance for faster and slower movements of parts of the body (915b12–15). The disparity of speeds within the body has its effect on the path taken by the body as a whole.

In the sections to follow, I will examine slight differences in the presentations of the principle of leverage, on the one hand, and of properties of the circle associated with curved motion, on the other. There are two reasons for making such a detailed examination. The first is to establish in *Physical Problems* XVI the familiarity with the principle and the diverse formulations of it that we have already seen in the texts of Aristotle from *On the Heavens*, *Movement of Animals*, and *Generation of Animals*. The second is to allow *Physical Problems* XVI to testify to a nuanced and logically connected knowledge of leverage phenomena in the fourth century BC. The analyses given in the chapters of *Physical Problems* XVI are like links of a chain. Each has its own phenomenon and analysis, but there is something connecting the chapter to another phenomenon and analysis. The connection may be different from link to link. Putting together the links among the chapters is what makes for a plausible case that the knowledge in *Physical Problems* XVI stands historically between Archytas and *Mechanics* and that it is the same knowledge that Aristotle possessed.

Constraint and Curved Motion

Chapters 3 and 12 of *Physical Problems* XVI begin with the same question posed in the same language. The two passages in chapters 3 and 12 are identical for roughly 5 Bekker lines (913a34–b1 and 915b7–12) and then diverge giving complementary accounts of the phenomenon. The problem is this:

> Why is it that in magnitudes having unequal weight, if one moves the lighter part, what is thrown revolves in a circle (κύκλῳ περιφέρεται), as happens with loaded dice, if one throws with the lighter part turned toward oneself?[280] (913a35–38)

This *problêma*, as is typical, states an observation and asks for a cause of the occurrence observed. It is something experienced through the senses, which in Aristotle's model of science should finally figure as the conclusion of a demonstration. As stated, however, there is already coherence to the observation. A connection has been made between uneven distribution of weight and a tumbling motion of the body, which occurs along with its overall forward trajectory.[281] The phenomenon is given an initial formulation in terms of a ubiquitous crafted object. The particular manner of throwing loaded dice so as to obtain a favorable outcome depends on each die being weighted unevenly. Chapter 12 makes more explicit the connection to projectile movement. A body's moving in a forward trajectory while at the same time revolving is something that occurs when a continuous body (*megethos*) has greater weight (*baros*) in one part of its extension than another. Most bodies are unbalanced in this way. The author mentions loaded dice, but one can also think of tossing a hammer (the baseball bat of chapter 2) or heaving a large, misshapen boulder (**Figure 7.1a** and **b**). Things whose weight is evenly distributed are often crafted for balance, like a scale, a tabletop, or fair dice.

The object of inquiry is why bodies of uneven distribution of weight share this characteristic tumbling motion. One might expect that natural bodies of all different sizes and distributions of weight would move in

---

280 This translation is by Mayhew (*Problems* 1, 483).

281 The tumbling motion of this sort of body is an example of an empirically cognized property identified as significant (a candidate for a *kath'hauto* trait) and as inhering in some subject (body with weight but of uneven distribution).

completely dissimilar ways. The answers given in the two chapters read as follows:

Chapter 3	Chapter 12
Is it because the heavier part cannot move at a pace equal (ἰσοδρομεῖν) to that of the lighter, when cast with the same strength (ἰσχύος)? And since the whole thing must move, but cannot do so at an equal pace, traveling at the same speed it would be moved in the same line; but with one part traveling more rapidly it must travel in a circle, since it is only in this shape that these points that are always opposite can pass along unequal lines in the same time. (913a38–b5)	Is it because the heavier part cannot move at a pace equal to that of the lighter, when cast with the same strength? Now since it must necessarily move, but cannot do so in an equal pace and so in a straight line, when it travels, it must travel in an inward direction and in a circle; just as if, owing to the weight in the middle, part of it had been entirely motionless, the part next to the thrower would have moved forward, but the other side toward the thrower. But when the whole moves, and holds the weight in the center as it travels, it must do the same thing.[282] (915b10–18)

The first sentence of both answers is this: "Is it because the heavier part cannot travel at the same pace as the lighter, when thrown with the same strength (or force)?" (913a39 and 915b11). This question may state a basic principle or assumption: Bodies of different weight move at different speeds when subjected to the same force. It has often been assumed in modern scholarship that Aristotle takes this erroneous claim as an axiom of motion. Drabkin lists the passages, especially in *On the Heavens*, where Aristotle says that the velocity of a body varies with its weight, whether acted upon by a force or in free fall.[283] The statement may be of somewhat less universal import than an axiom, however, originating

---

282   The Loeb translation of Mayhew with "shape" (for σχῆμα) substituted for "form" in chapter 3 (left column). I have also translated "do the same thing" for ταὐτὸ τοῦτο ποιεῖν at the end of the chapter 12 passage. "Do the same thing" means "act the same way" in this context. These slight changes reflect the interpretation of the passages given below.

283   Cohen and Drabkin, *Source Book*, 207–209. For some scholarly responses to the formulation of Aristotle's error of speed being a function of weight, see Hussey, "Mathematical Physics," 217–218.

rather with cases known empirically where different weights are linked.[284] This is certainly the context of the *problêma* in *Physical Problems* XVI.3 and 12. Linkage was also the condition Plato and Aristotle made prominent in their conceptions of the moving radius principle in *Laws* X and *On the Heavens* II.

Both chapters of *Physical Problems* XVI speak of the necessity that the entire body move as one, though its parts would tend to move at different speeds. If the whole body moves at the same speed, its parts will follow the same (straight) path (τὴν αὐτὴν οἰσθήσεται γραμμήν) (913b2). Since one part is moving faster than the other, the body must be borne in a circle, "since it is only in this shape that these points (σημεῖα) which are always opposite can pass along unequal lines in the same time" (913b3–5).[285] This is stated in chapter 3 as an inevitability given the disequilibrium of the body. This part of the account of chapter 3 is not in chapter 12, but an enlightening supplement is added there. In chapter 12, the supposition that the author invokes (". . . just as if . . .") takes the different weights of different parts of the body as opposites with a middle. It is as if, he says,

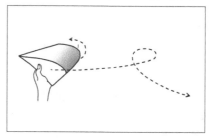

Figure 7.1a

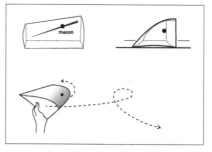

Figure 7.1b

the middle were motionless. His picture suggests a line of balance passing through the middle of the body, which is a center for rotation. The point

---

284 Hussey's suggestion, in defusing Aristotle's supposed befuddlement in mechanics, is that "it is the starting speeds *on the balance* that Aristotle has in mind, when he says that the heavier weight is that which 'moves downward faster'" ("Mathematical Physics," 225). Hussey calls his suggestion a "hypothesis."

285 Reading ταὐτά with Louis, following the oldest manuscript, Yᵃ. Ruelle's edition reads ταῦτα (these). Forster accepts a suggestion from Ross to change ταῦτα to τά (*Problemata* in *Works* 7, ad loc 913b4n3 [Edition is without page numbers other than Bekker numbers.]). This leads him to translate σημεῖα, points, as parts. Forster's Oxford translation reads: "[F]or it is only in this manner that the parts which are always opposite one another can follow unequal paths in the same time."

of the passages taken together is that just as a body of unequal weight might rotate about a stationary middle point of some sort, so also a body in motion has such a middle, which is in movement with the body but stationary relative to the movement of its extremities. The author does not use the word fulcrum, ὑπομόχλιον, for the middle. He calls it a weight in the middle. The *meson* recalls what we would call a center of gravity.[286]

The point of the chapters is to explain rotation of an unbalanced body rather than to find the middle. Accordingly, the strength of the comparison of stationary and moving unbalanced bodies is that they behave the same way or do the same thing (ταὐτὸ τοῦτο ποιεῖν). They both revolve.

The reference to a motionless middle is striking, however, since Aristotle insists in *Movement of Animals* 3 that no part of a moving body with magnitude can be motionless. This disclaimer seems also to play a role in his comparison of the toy wagon to rolling cylinders, one an axle. The author of *Physical Problems* XVI.12 treats the immobility of the middle as hypothetical, however. His language marks this passage as providing something like a model based on the lever.[287] Since there is some weight all along the magnitude of the projectile, it is as if (οἷον εἰ) (915b13) some part of the body is motionless while points further along toward the opposite end from the thrower are carried back in the direction opposite to the forward motion. Yet, the author says a part is motionless, because of (διά) weight in the middle. So, the weight fixes a relatively motionless part as a center for rotation (see **Figure 7.1b**). The author makes it explicit that the unbalanced body cannot move evenly and in a straight line[288] and so moves circularly and inward (εἰς τὸ ἐντὸς φερόμενον κύκλῳ φέρεσθαι) (915b13). The inward revolution of the movement he explains in terms of the thrower's force being exerted on only part of the continuous body, namely, where the thrower has a hold of it:

---

286 For the ancient treatment of centers of gravity, see Archimedes' *On the Equilibrium of Planes* and Pappus' barycentric theory of *Collectio*, Book VIII. Dijksterhuis says that Archimedes writes as if centers of gravity were "a perfectly familiar thing" and had been developed by earlier students of mechanics to a certain extent (*Archimedes*, 295–296). *Physical Problems* XVI perhaps provides evidence of those earlier students' thinking. The presentation to follow in *Physical Problems* XVI.4 is also suggestive with regard to the question of centers of gravity.

287 The form of the statement at 915b13–14 concerning motionless weight at the center is an unfulfilled condition. I take the lack of fulfillment to refer to the immobility of the central weight, not the movements of the extremities.

288 ἐξ ἴσου δὲ καὶ ἐπ᾽εὐθείας.

just as if, owing to the weight in the middle, part of it had
been entirely motionless, the part next to the thrower would
have moved forward, but the other side toward the thrower.
(915b14–16)

Force is exerted at an extremity of the body (incidentally, in the same way
as Aristotle's rider of the toy wagon in *Movement of Animals* 7 pushes
off on the larger wheel). The body tumbles in its forward motion around
a hypothetical motionless middle.

This seems to be the basic physical picture, but a question remains
concerning interpretation of the weight in the middle. There are two references to it in chapter 12. After the initial reference already cited to the
immobility of the weight that happens to be in the middle of an unbalanced body, he adds:

But when the whole moves, and holds the weight in the center
as it travels, it must move in the same way. (915b14–18)

The Greek text reads:

ἐπεὶ δὲ κινεῖται μὲν τὸ πᾶν, ἔχει δὲ ἐν μέσῳ τὸ βάρος
φερόμενον, ἀνάγκη ταὐτὸ τοῦτο ποιεῖν.

The passage allows different interpretations in translation. The question
is whether the sentence carries a meaning adversative to the case of the
unbalanced body: when the whole moves but its entire weight is kept at
the center, the body will move "in the same way" (*tauto touto poiein*).[289]
Moving in the same way would mean every part moving with the same
speed (and so in the same straight line). The problem with a translation
interpreted this way is that it makes the middle ἔχει clause convey a very
sophisticated notion of concentrating the force or effect of weight in a
point or at least in one location.[290] The sentence in Greek is, however,

---

289 Hett's translation allows this reading: "But when the whole moves and keeps the
weight in the center as it travels, it must move in the same way." The Oxford translation
by Forster reads: "But when the whole object moves and, as it travels, has a weight in the
middle, it must necessarily behave in the same manner" (*Problemata* 915b18 in *Works* 7).
Flashar translates: "Da er sich nun aber ganz und gar bewegt und bei der Bewegung in der
Mitte ein Gewicht hat, macht er notwendigerweise eben das (was oben beschrieben ist)
(Flashar, *Problemata*, 149).

290 Hett's reading could be maintained and this problem mitigated if we attribute to the

open to other interpretations. One other would take the ἐπεί clause as key: "when the whole is moved," and the particle δέ, as "and," rendering "since the whole moves and there is weight moving in the middle." Since the parts of the body move together, even the weight in the center, hypothetically motionless with respect to circular motion, moves with the forward motion of the body as a whole. In this case, ἀνάγκη ταὐτὸ τοῦτο ποιεῖν still means the body moves in the same way,[291] but the reference is to the revolving *forward* motion of the entire body. The ἔχει clause means that the weight in the middle of the body, which has just been described as motionless, also moves forward along with the whole body. So, the author means that the body still moves in a forward path traceable as rectilinear overall.

This interpretation is consistent with the author's interest in the path traced by extreme parts of the body. Opposite points cover unequal lines or paths (ἀνίσους διέρχεται γραμμάς) (913b5). The translation of γράμμα—line, trace, or path—is worth pondering, since the solution offered to the puzzle is that only in circular motion do points opposite one another cover *unequal lines*. Given the solution, we expect these unequal lines to be arcs. Rectilinear motion is constrained, and the unequal lines are arcs of different-sized circles. But might these unequal lines be rectilinear distances covered along the forward trajectory of the object? Let us consider the physical situation more carefully. The author believes that a weight differential within a body introduces dual movements. The body as a unitary projectile still has forward motion, however.[292] The au-

---

author a simpler notion—the weight of the body is equally distributed. This is also contrary to the main case under consideration in the passage. In this interpretation, the sentence then means that there is weight also in the middle between the extremes, and this provides for a situation of balance arising within the body. Presumably this body would not tumble, as long as it was thrown so as to preserve the equal balance within the body. In that case, moving in the same way would mean all the parts of the body moving forward together at the same speed.

291   The use of the verb ποιεῖν, rather than φέρεσθαι or κινεῖσθαι, makes the passage more obscure. The author may have in mind that the moving body is making a circular figure (σχῆμα), as he says in chapter 4 that a moving body makes equal angles (913b7). Compare Flashar's translation, "macht er notwendigerweise eben das (was oben beschrieben ist)" (Flashar, *Problemata*, 149). Flashar does not comment on possible meanings for the sentence. His translation is consistent with taking the "moving in the same way" to be the tumbling motion being explained, not a hypothetical rectilinear motion as Hett's translation suggests.

292   Since points of a magnitude lie apart, it would be more precise to say parts of the body are inclined to move along parallel straight lines. This would assume no differential

thor surely has in mind that revolution of the body makes it possible for different parts to move in a net *forward* motion at different speeds. If we followed a single point in the unevenly weighted body, what we would see is a spiraling forward motion (**Figure 7.1b**).[293] The conception seems to be that parts of the body tend to move at their own speed and in fact do move at different speeds by describing curvilinear forward motion. Their motion is not impeded and dissipated by the rest of the body but simply constrained and directed in another path.

Whether the author keeps the forward trajectory in mind in what he says is a relatively minor point, and the alternate interpretation I have given is not that of either Forster or Louis. Forster interprets the movement "in the same way" to be revolving motion.[294] Forster takes weight in the middle to be a real part of the body ("a weight"). Thus, there is weight in the center as well as at the extremes. This, it seems to me, is the important point in interpreting the passage. Furthermore, however the *meson* is understood in the passage, what is significant is that the author mentions it, since the middle holds the place of the fulcrum for the opposite extremities where the differences in speed show up. Equally important is the maxim given, in the companion chapter 3, of why the unbalanced body moves in a circle: because this is the only shape in which points lying opposite one another cover unequal lines in the same time (913b4–5). This statement represents circular motion as in some way a resultant motion but still a natural motion. Rectilinear paths are constrained to a circular shape as they maintain a consistent forward motion.

Let us consider what sort of account the author has given. The movement of the body falls into revolution because the circle has the property of allowing or incorporating different speeds in the same body. This is a kinematic point: curved or circular is the locus of motion when different weights are linked. A stronger interpretation of the mutual constraint of rectilinear motions would be that circular motion results because the

---

in force applied because of the thrower grasping the unbalanced body in one part rather than another. Even a balanced body, like a baseball, revolves when thrown because of differences in how the force of the throw is applied—hence, the curveball in baseball.

293 *Physical Problems* XVI.11 says the motion of a projectile is a spiral as it loses speed. See below in this chapter.

294 *Problemata* 915b18n4 (*Works* 7). Louis understands the movement described by the ποιεῖν passage to be the emergent revolution of the body: "Mais comme l'objet est tout entier en mouvement et qu'au course de sa trajectoire il a le pois au milieu, il faut nécessairement qu'il fasse exactement le mouvement en question."

movements of parts not only constrain but also modify or change one another. This would be mixture of motions in a physicalistic sense. There is no evidence that the author of *Physical Problems* has this stronger physicalistic conception of mixture of movements. Indeed, it would seem that the kinematic meaning of the statement is a genuinely mechanical notion, because it understands a mathematical formulation taken as a whole as accounting for the relation of different weights at different distances to the trajectory of a body. In this connection, it is quite important conceptually that the author includes in his application of the moving radius principle the idea of weight present in the middle of the body as well as at the extremes. In principle, he recognizes that there is weight all along the body.

This account of the motion of an unbalanced projectile has a number of interesting features. First, its explanation in terms of the properties of circular motion is only obliquely expressed. Nevertheless, the principle seems well known to the author, because he understands how it would show itself in this instance. It is invoked to explain a familiar experience, i.e., what happens in throwing an unbalanced object from one end of it. Secondly, the author presumes the distribution of the force of a throw throughout the body. That a continuous rigid body is subjected to the same force throughout in revolution is, as we have seen, part of the mathematical account of leverage phenomena in its first express formulations in Plato and Aristotle. Thirdly, although the language of geometry is used, abstraction does not play a role in the account. Weight is everywhere in the body, at least in the center as well at the extremities, and the center of the body is not a point. Finally and quite remarkably, weight is not a tendency downward toward the center of the earth. Rather, weight figures as a force of impulse and constraint in shaping the trajectory of forward motion of a projectile.

Constraint plays a major role, in these chapters, in rectilinear tendencies issuing in circular motion. Yet, the issue of constraint is not explicitly addressed. *Physical Problems* XVI.4 does speak of constraint in language that figures importantly later in *Mechanics*. The properties of circular motion make a fleeting appearance in chapter 4, but the idea of balance associated with circular motion is very prominent.

The Rebound of Objects from a Surface, Falling, and the Descent of Airborne Objects

In chapter 4, the author focuses on the balance of objects in motion, whether the objects are curved or straight-edged. He conceives these objects as each having a diameter that divides the object equally (913b13). When an object strikes a surface perpendicularly, it rebounds along the line of impact and so rebounds at equal angles (**Figure 7.2a**). When any object strikes a surface other than perpendicularly, the angle of incidence formed with the rebounding surface is always acute (913b35) (**Figure 7.2b**). An object striking a surface at any acute angle will strike, not at the perpendicular and diameter within the body, like the object falling straight down, but at a point "higher than" the perpendicular (913b13–15). The meaning of this last statement is one point of reference for interpreting the passage. It is clear the author understands the diameter in the body to be a line of equal balance for an object in movement (913b22). In Figures 7.2–7.4, this line of balance is labeled "A." The diameter indexes balance of weight in motion. There is only one such diameter per body for a line of motion, though we can conceive of a new perpendicular formed after rebound at an acute angle (913b29–33). What is to be explained is that the object rebounds at equal angles, though acute angles, even when it hits a surface at an oblique angle—i.e.,

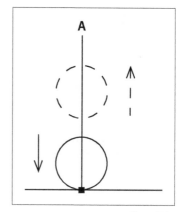

Figure 7.2a

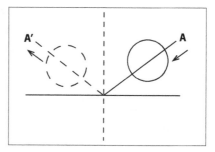

Figure 7.2b

hits the surface off balance. The case of perpendicular impact makes the other cases understandable because the perpendicular remains the point of division (ὅρος) of opposite angles of rebound (b36).

The author distinguishes three cases: (1) rebound perpendicularly along the line of balance within the body, (2) rebound of round objects (τὰ στρογγύλα) at an acute angle, and (3) rebound of equilateral objects (τὰ εὐθύγραμμα) at an acute angle. In the second case, he speaks

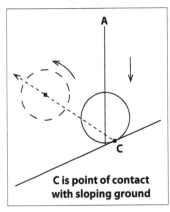

of a falling object hitting a surface εἰς τὰ πλάγια, to the side. This can mean either that the path of the object is sideways—producing a glancing blow on a level surface (**Figure 7.2b**)—or that the ground it hits, when a body is dropped, is situated obliquely to the level (**Figure 7.3a**).[295] Given the terms of the problem posed (913b5–9), it would seem that an object hitting a plane surface obliquely and rebounding at an equal oblique angle is what is under consideration. This geometric picture seems not to be the author's concern, however. What

C is point of contact with sloping ground

Figure 7.3a

he addresses is the shift of movement on rebound away from symmetry around the body's axis or plane of balance.[296] He says that "bodies falling obliquely, striking the spot not at the perpendicular but at a point above the perpendicular, are thrown back from the place of impact and move

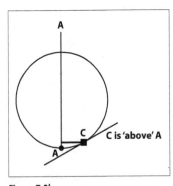

in the opposite direction" (913b13–15). An interpretation of hitting the surface above the perpendicular is illustrated in **Figure 7.3b**. In the case of a round object striking an oblique surface, the rising ground meets the object at some point to the side of and above the perpendicular of balance. So, this seems to be the case to which the author points. The case for oblique impact on a level surface is clearly the same in the geo-

C is 'above' A

Figure 7.3b

---

295 The case of hitting an oblique surface obliquely is omitted because it would not differ from the other two cases treated.

296 The author uses both κάθετον, perpendicular or tangent, and διάμετρον, diagonal, for the axis of balance in the body hitting the surface. He uses *katheton* most frequently since he is interested in departures from the model case, in which the line of balance of rebound coincides with the line of balance in the body.

metric terms of equal balance the author considers (**Figure 7.4a–b**). In either case, intersecting lines of balance on impact and rebound make equal angles around a point slightly above the surface.

Introducing the issue of a diameter of balance of weight complicates the geometrical answer as to why bodies rebound at equal acute angles when hitting a surface obliquely. Equal angles appear in the diagrams not at the place of impact at the surface but at a point further along the path of the body after rebound. The equal angles are equal opposite angles of intersecting lines of balance at different positions (**Figures 7.3b** and **7.4b**). Since the author's concern is how balance is involved in rebound at equal angles, it would seem that the opposite equal angles around a fulcrum or center of concentric circles are relevant. We are dealing with a situation of a body losing and then regaining its balance. This takes place in accordance with the equal angles around the point of intersection of successive lines of balance. The passage does not pursue this logic of development, however.

With respect to the issue of loss and regain of balance, after oblique impact the round body will be revolving in motion, and

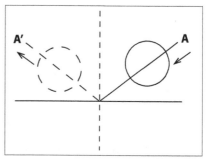

Figure 7.4a

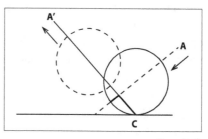

Figure 7.4b

the author gives the revolution, due presumably to impact off balance, as a reason the object rebounds in a direction opposite to its direction upon impact: "This in the case of round objects is due to the fact that, striking against it in their course, they revolve in an opposite direction to that in which they are thrust back, whether their central point is at rest or changes its position" (913b15–18).[297] The revolving body regains its balance and proceeds in the opposite direction. We are left to speculate as to why the angle of rebound is *equal* to the angle of impact. His interest is in showing the angles are acute. He assumes the equality of the acute

---

297   The translation is by Forster (*Works*, ed. Ross, 7).

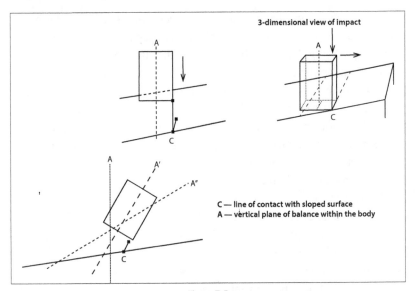

Figure 7.5

angles as following from the equality of angles at rectilinear impact on a level surface.[298] The most important point would seem to be that the body rebounds from a point that is not on its axis of balance, and this is the reason rebound is oblique. Revolution accounts for its path being in the opposite direction. This is explainable in terms of lines drawn from the point of impact to the axis of balance (**Figure 7.3a** and **7.4b**).

The chapter considers the cases of rebound of curved and straight-edged objects one after the other. In the case of an equilateral solid (**Figure 7.5**), the object's diameter, or internal perpendicular of balance (b18), will be thrust forward on impact and then backward.[299] The object will thus be forced to deviate off its course (ἐκκρούεσθαι).[300] While we

---

298 Why bodies rebound at opposite and equal angles is a topic resumed in *Physical Problems* XVI.13. The author says that the body retains the motion (φορά) imparted by the thrower and so makes an angle of apex at the reflecting surface. Both the angle and the motion are reversed, and so the angles of impact and return are similar (915b32–36). Proving the equality of angles of rebound could perhaps involve the way Euclid uses *Elements* I.32 to prove that exterior angles of a triangle are equal to the two interior and opposite angles. The proof involves creating a parallel to one side of a triangle, thereby forming with the opposite side an apex of three angles. Heath describes this proposition as discovered at an early stage of Greek geometry and speculates that it was known first for isosceles triangles. *Elements* I.5 would also be relevant to an application to movement.

299 Reading προσενεχθεῖσαν with Forster and Louis.

300 The word, ἐκκρούεσθαι, is used in *Mechanics* for the action of force directed to-

might first think an object would always be forced forward when glancing off a sloping surface, the author thinks the reverse takes place. He illustrates this case by means of a comparison to a person who falls backward when hit on the legs or when the scrotum is pulled downward:

> All such fall is in the opposite direction and backwards, because the perpendicular giving things balance is both raised and forced forward. For it is evident that the opposite portion of [the perpendicular][301] will go both backward and down, and what is borne downward is heavier. So, what is a fall to these people is change of place in things rebounding.[302] (913b21–26)

This passage describes a perpendicular that is an axis of upright stance in a human being. The upright stance is disturbed by a blow from behind on the lower legs, so that the perpendicular is dislocated in the direction of the blow upward at the point of impact but in an opposite direction at the head and torso (**Figure 7.6**). The passage describes two movements at *each end* of the perpendicular—(*a*) in the direction of the blow and upward, and (*b*) in the direction opposite to the force of the blow and downward. A fall results for the person because the upper body goes in the direction opposite the blow and downward. Similarly, it would

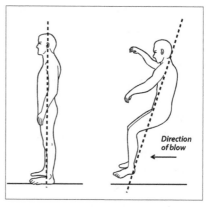

Direction of blow

Figure 7.6

ward the center of a circle, the fulcrum of a balance. This forcing toward the center interferes with the motion at a tangent that would be the natural motion of a weight subject to a force without the beam of the balance keeping its motion turning inward. The only thing in common with this passage is using the same word for forcing or constraining.

301 τὰ γὰρ ἐναντία δῆλον ὅτι αὐτῆς.

302 Flashar is right that ἰσάζειν αὐτά should not be omitted from the passage as Ross emends (Flashar, *Problemata*, 581), so Forster's translation, which follows Ross, is not as reliable as usual in this case (*Problemata* 913b24 n1 in *Works* 7). Flashar understands the displacement described to pertain to the object or person struck, not the perpendicular. My translation is closer to that of Louis, *Problèmes*, which is not subject to Flashar's criticism of Hett. The displacement backward of the imaginary perpendicular of a standing figure is what is described.

seem, the rectangular solid striking an inclined plane undergoes along its lower edge C a force of impact tending toward the direction of incline but also falls backward due to weight above the edge. Insight into the working of a lever seems to lie behind the analysis of this observation.

The author's treatment is similar to the unbalanced projectile motion of chapters 3 and 12 in resolving an actual movement into two rectilinear components. The impact on the lower legs sets up movement in opposite directions, like the movement of unequal balance beams. The axis of balance would shift backward, and the object would travel in something like a flattened arc, because it would remain out of balance. The author does not address whether such backward falling could ever regain equilibrium to produce rebound at an acute angle. Experience shows that a compact and heavy rectilinear solid does rebound backward, but it then falls on the sloped surface and slides down it. Without considering the matter further, the author returns to the question of angle of rebound. His main concern in later lines of the chapter (913b30–37) is simply to show, by the fact that there cannot be more than one perpendicular to an object at a given point in its movement, that objects rebounding obliquely cannot rebound at right angles and so must rebound at an angle other than right. Since it cannot travel at right angles, the angle it makes on either side of the point at which it strikes is acute (913b29–37).

The cases in **Figures 7.3** and **7.5** finally do not account for why the acute angles are *equal* in rebound from an oblique surface.[303] The cases highlight the shift from balance to imbalance that is due to the body's weight being in motion at oblique impact. In both chapter 3 and 4, disturbance of balance is the occasion for resolution of a body's movement into rectilinear components. Chapter 4 does not speak directly of circular motion as the condition for balance in the relation of rectilinear elements, as chapter 3 does. It seems clear, however, that leverage phenomena are drawn upon to find an underlying structure accounting for unbalanced motion. The comparison to the human experience of falling backward draws directly on the idea of the sharing of force throughout the body as if it were a balance beam moving forward and backward at the same time.

We should not leave *Physical Problems* XVI.4 without considering chapter 11, which applies the axis of balance within a body, the theme of chapter 4, to projectile motion. The question is why a circular object, when thrown, first describes a straight line, and then as it ceases moving,

---

303 For this, see chapter 13 of *Physical Problems* XVI.

describes a rounded shape (ἕλικα) until it falls (915a37–38). The answer involves the much derided Aristotelian appeal to the role of the air in projectile motion[304] but uses that causal factor to give an aeronautical account of the phenomenon. The thrown circular object describes a straight line at first, because the air guides it straight (ἀπορθοῖ), supporting the body similarly on either side. When the force (*rhopê*) exerted by the air is equal on either side, the projectile's path must be a straight line that divides the place on either side equally: "But when it is weighed down on one side owing to the unevenness (δι' ἀνωμαλίαν) of the surrounding air, the inside and outside parts of the body no longer describe an equal line but it must necessarily be rounded (περιφερῆ)" (915a38–b6).[305] The reference to inner and outer parts must refer to the portions along the edges that, in dissipation of motion, describe a curve, so that the part describing the longer curve is on the outside of the path of the whole body.[306]

This answer makes use both of natural variations in the ability of air to exert force and the idea of a balance of forces of air exerted on edges of the body. The motion is rectilinear as long as forces are equal. Note the use of the term *rhopê*, a word for force used with some regularity in *Mechanics* but appearing here for the only time in *Physical Problems* XVI. In *Mechanics*, *ischus* and *dunamis* are used fairly indiscriminately to mean the exertion of a force at a point, therefore a simple push. *Rhopê* has been thought to have a more robust connotation of the force capable of making a change in the state of motion or rest of a body. This meaning fits its use in this passage, where *rhopê* can be "equal on either side." There are forces but neither overmasters the other. What is very interesting from a modern standpoint is that decrease in *rhopê* exerted by air on one edge of a body produces a change in the trajectory of the body. The author applies the idea to the spherical object's lowering rounded path and its eventual ceasing motion (915b38).[307] In *Progression of Animals*,

---

304 See *Physics* VIII.10, 266b27–267a20.

305 Translation is by Mayhew (*Problems* 1, 499).

306 I concur in Forster's interpretation where he translates *meros* as edge (*Problemata* 915b5, in *Works* 7).

307 There is no reference, in this account of airborne movement, to the need for a support against which the moving object, even one thrown, can push off (ἀπερειδόμενον) to keep going. This support, which is essential to movement in both *Movement of Animals* and *Progression of Animals* (*Movement of Animals* 2, 699a2–6), is perhaps taken for granted in *Physical Problems* XVI.11, insofar as parts of air serve as unmoved movers until their impetus for filling this role can no longer exert itself. See again *Physics* VIII.10, 266b27–267a20.

Aristotle says all things progress because "what being beneath them as it were gives way up to a point" (*Progression of Animals* 10, 709b27–29).[308] This is a reason why wings need to beat, and why there is an origin (*archê*) of the wing's movement at its base. Wings push off the air. The projectile of *Physical Problems* XVI.11 ceases movement because of imbalance in the force of air. The air below it gives way to the greater force of air pushing from the other side.

This account has points of interest in relation to Bernoulli's principle of fluid dynamics, according to which it can be explained why airborne objects stay aloft.[309] In *Physical Problems* XVI.11, the force of air holds the place of pressure exerted by a gas. In the chapter, the force of air is equal or unequal on different edges of a body. The object divides the space (*topon*) equally when the forces are equal. But when one edge gets heavy (βρίση) due to unevenness in the exertion of air, the inside and outside parts no longer describe the same path.[310] Instead, the whole object describes a rounded path. Lying in the background of this account is the overall conception of leverage phenomena as a system. The system maintains the sort of equality manifest in a proportion among weight, force exerted, movement, and distance covered.

The Cone, the Cylinder, and the Scroll

The next topic of *Physical Problems* XVI is the one that we have already seen was understood by Aristotle and utilized by him in *Movement of Animals* 7. In chapter 5, the question is why a cylinder when rolled moves in a straight line and describes straight lines with its circular ends, while a cone whose apex remains in place travels in a circle and describes a circle with its base (913b37–914a1) (**Figures 2.7a–b**).

---

308 Translation of this passage from *Progression of Animals* is by Farquharson in *CWA* 1. The Greek reads ἅπαντα γὰρ εἰς τὸ ὑποκείμενον μέχρι τινὸς οἷον εἰς ὑπεῖκον προέρχεται. To move, any animal pushes off against something, which can be yielding to some extent but not without any resistance at all. Aristotle has been talking about the flight of birds.

309 This topic is treated in Chapter 9. Anderson and Eberhardt criticize the "principle of equal transit time" (Bernoulli's principle) as inadequate to explain flight in their *Understanding Flight*, xv–xvii. They also discuss the misapplication of the principle to giving an account of the curveball in baseball (279–281). They give what they believe is a more adequate account of flight in terms of Newton's first and third laws.

310 *Physical Problems* 915b3. This is stated as a general conditional, in contrast to the unfulfilled or unreal conditional of chapter 12's *meson*.

The relation of the two solids, and the reason the question would arise, is that both travel in a circle (914a2). The reason for the different paths described by the cylinder and cone, the author says, is that there are unequal circles in the cone and the larger circles moving around the same center always move faster (a5). So:

> When all of the circles in the cone move at the same time with unequal speed (ἀνίσως), it happens that the outermost circles cover the greatest space (τόπον) in the same time and the longest line. Thus they travel in a circle.[311] (914a5–8)

He adds a γάρ clause to the effect that all the lines traced by the rolling cone are being described by the same straight line—meaning a line of contact between the cone and the plane surface (**Figures 2.8** and **5.1**). When a straight line moves in a circle, not all its points can describe equal lines in the same time. This only occurs when the points move in a straight line (a8–12). So far, the author explains the phenomenon from two directions. First, he brings into relief the circles that are in the three-dimensional surfaces of the cylinder and cone and makes a straightforward appeal to the property of the circle whereby arcs of larger circles cover a greater distance, and hence move faster, than arcs of smaller concentric circles. The cone has larger and smaller circles in its surface; the cylinder does not. From the standpoint of the circles in its surface,[312] the cone is a variation on, or a species of, the cylinder.[313] Second, he points to the line of contact between the surface and the cone. The fact that this straight line has a fixed point at the apex of the cone means that it moves in a circle, and so, in accordance with the principle of unequal distances covered by the unequal circles, its points are all moving at different speeds. Presumably, this second approach could be taken without incorporating in the account the circles in the surfaces of the cylinder and cone respectively. The two

---

311 Translation is by the author.

312 The chapter does not make more precise what it means for the circles to be in a surface. The minimal expression φερομένων δὲ ἀνίσως πάντων ἅμα τῶν ἐν τῷ κώνῳ κύκλων is used. It is not asserted that the cone and cylinder are composed from circles, nor is there any suggestion that there is an infinite number of circles in them.

313 Κύλινδρος did not have a solely mathematical meaning and was used in ordinary discourse for shapes of bodies other than a true cylinder. See note 204 of Chapter 5 of this book.

approaches can be seen as related, however, since the different-sized circles in the cone are, so to speak, laying down points on the surface with the line of contact between the cone and the flat surface.

The author presents the cylinder in this way in what he says next. All the circles in the cylinder are equal and move about the same center, he says. Actually, they share an axis, but he does not use this word. He presents a less than rigorous but clear enough picture of the revolution of corresponding points on the circles along the cylinder. These points contact a plane surface together (ἅμα) (914a12–17). The circles in cylinders move at the same speed, "because the cylinders are equal" (a15). Accordingly, points on different circles return to the surface at the same time, describing "equal lines" (a18). The lines are equal, because (γάρ) they were described by contact of circles that are equal and moving with the same speed. Interestingly, he evokes a picture of the line of contact between the cylinder and the surface itself necessarily moving in a straight line (a19–20). In this respect, it makes no difference whether the cylinder is dragged or rolled. The line of contact is what counts in judging the cylinder itself to move in a straight line. So, we encounter in the passage a notion of displacement of a line, as well as the describing (γράφειν) of a line by contact between a solid and a surface.

We have already noted the mechanical features portrayed by the rolling cone. The cone represents a refinement of mechanical conception in its mathematical portrayal of linkage of weights in different locations and distribution of force through a rigid body. In *Physical Problems* XVI.5, the author almost belabors the connection between the cone and cylinder, the point being to emphasize the slight separation between them in principle, despite the very different trajectories of their movements.

Chapter 6 continues the theme of parallel and equal circles in the surface of a cylinder in its consideration of a scroll cut in two different ways. If the roll is cut parallel to its rolled straight edge, i.e., a base of its cylinder, then when it is unrolled, the parts will be straight, as the whole would have been when unrolled. If the cut is made at a slant across the roll, however, the edges of the cut scroll will be crooked or zigzag (σκολιά) in shape (914a27) (**Figure 7.7**).

This much is clear, but the reason given for the shape and appearance of the scroll is difficult to reckon out. The author focuses on the slanted cut, points of which are differently positioned on parallel circles on the outer surface of the scroll as the cut reaches from a point closer to, then more distant from, its origin (914a30, a37). Also considered, however, are the circles in the same plane, i.e., the continuous rolls inside the scroll (a32). These circles, when unrolled, "make a line from themselves."[314] If

the cut were parallel to the base, then the line made by these unrolled circles would be straight. When the cut is slanted, the interior circles cut are not in the same plane as the circle of the original cut. Thus, the line they make when unrolled is not straight. It is a repeating curve, but

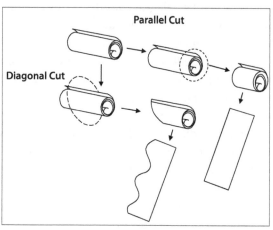

Figure 7.7

the period of the curve is progressively shortened due to internal rolls of the scroll having a shorter diameter. The edge is a smooth zigzag, because parts of a straight line cannot be in different planes (a39–40), the author says. Euclid makes a similar point in *Elements* XI.1: "A part of a straight line cannot be in the plane of reference and a part in a plane more elevated." Heath says that this is not really relevant since "the trace is anyhow in the plane on which the cylinder rolls" and the line can be considered a straight line in a plane cutting across right sections of the cylinder.[315] What would constitute a *dioti* account in this case seems considerably more involved and elegant that the author has envisioned. Indeed, it seems he does not consider the problem for the nature of its mathematical solution. What is his aim, then?

It is worth noting that the unrolling of the crosscut scroll complements the two cases already given in *Physical Problems* XVI, the rolling cone and the rolling cylinder. The shape of the edge of the crosscut scroll when unrolled corresponds to the path of a rolling elliptical section of a

---

314 τὴν ἐξ αὐτῶν ποιήσουσι γραμμήν.

315 *Mathematics*, 265. Flashar thinks that the mathematical account Heath goes on to give of the non-parallel cut is not reliable and presents an explanation by B. Artmann (Flashar, *Problemata*, 584).

cylinder. The rolling elliptical section provides an alternative case to the circular motion of either the cone or the rolling cylinder of chapter 5, both of which involve in their explanations right sections of their respective solids. It is interesting to consider if this case may have had an application, as the other two cases did.

In a fragment ascribed to Aristotle's *Constitution of Ithaca*, the Spartans reportedly used a pair of sticks as a simple encryption device (the so-called Spartan dispatch, σκυτάλη). A long piece of leather (ἱμάς) was wrapped around a stick of a particular diameter, and a message was written on it. The message could not be read without being wrapped around the corresponding stick. This was done, it is reported, to prevent those bearing the message from learning its contents. The word σκυτάλη, rod or roller, came to connote the message, not the stick.[316] That the *skutalê* was an encryption device appears more in the later Greek literature than the early.[317] Indeed, Aristotle's account of the device seems implausible as a method of encryption of the message itself, since it would be easy to decode without a corresponding stick. Perhaps it would impede furtive curiosity on the part of the messenger. Both Xenophon and Thucydides treat the σκυτάλη as insuring the official capacity of the messenger.[318] In this connection, we can note that crosscutting a scroll would certainly have produced *sumbola*, corresponding parts intricate enough to certify identity in the holder of the corresponding part.

The Aristotelian fragment gives another version of the *skutalê* as it was used in financial transactions in Sparta. Dioscourides cut the *skutalê* in the presence of witnesses and wrote *to sumbolaion*, the corresponding part, on each segment to signify a contract or bond. He would give one part to one of the witnesses and keep the other himself.[319] This suggests what might have been a more precise function for *sumbola* in wartime. Crosscutting a rolled text in advance of official dispatches would have

---

316 This fragment comes from Photius. See Aristotle, *Fragments* 509 (ed. Rose, 320.10–22).

317 Stephanie West questions that the σκυτάλη, as message stick, had a cryptographic role at all. See "Archilochus' Message Stick."

318 Xenophon, *Hellenica* 5.2.34 and 3.3.8–9; Thucydides, *Historiae* 1.131. Thucydides says of the Spartans dealing with Pausanias, who tarried abroad and engaged in intrigue with the barbarians, "the ephori forebore no longer but sent unto him a public officer with the scytale commanding him not to depart from the officer and, in case he refused, denounced war against him (trans. T. Hobbes, 1890).

319 Aristotle, *Fragments* 509 (320.22–26).

ensured identity of the message bearer sent to the general holding the other part. The jagged parts of a cut strip of papyrus would be complements nearly impossible to fake.[320] The content of the text that was cut could in this case be anything—an aphorism, a joke, a picture. This could account for why early textual references to the message stick do not convey the cryptographic connotations the word had later. As a means of conveying the official gravity of a message or its authenticity, the *skutalê* could have simply accompanied the message.[321] The real message might have been transported wrapped around a stick with the *sumbolon*. This would be consistent with West's suggestion that convenience of transport was a function of the stick. The association of the *skutalê* with riddles or fables might have been fostered by its involving *sumbola*, which are incomplete taken alone. Completing the sense of one half of anything written is a riddle. It seems likely, in any case, that it would be the shape of the edge produced by a rolling cross-wise section of a cylinder that would make cutting the scroll of practical interest to the ancients rather than the path described by a rolling body with an elliptical edge. The interest is the shape of the scroll when unrolled. In contrast, the path of a moving point or line is the concern in the author's treatment of the rolling cone and rolling cylinder.[322]

Among the chapters of *Physical Problems* XVI considered so far, chapters 3 and 12 have to do with the revolution of a body in forward motion. This phenomenon is explained by transferring the focus of attention from the movement of the body as a whole to the movement of parts within it. The author considers paths of points on opposite sides of the body. From this standpoint, the moving radius principle provides an explanation consistent with the experiential element of what happens in throwing an unbalanced body. Parts further from the "fulcrum" center

---

320 Βιβλίον means a strip of papyrus, βύβλος, thus a scroll.

321 *Sumbola* are a staple of authenticating trustworthiness in every age. Yuri Modin, the handler of the Russian spies Burgess, Philby, and Maclean in Britain, describes how he established his credentials with Melinda Maclean prior to her defection eighteen months after her husband's defection: "All we needed to do was drive ahead of her, pull up in a suitable spot—and show Melinda half of a postcard. The other half had been handed to Melinda by her husband a year and a half before with orders that she should trust nobody who did not produce its match. I had this second half in my possession" (*Cambridge Friends*, 225–226).

322 An elliptical slice off the end of a cylinder affects the trajectory of a material cylinder. The elliptically sectioned cone drifts in its trajectory toward the side of the elliptical cut, presumably because the cut results in unequal distribution of weight on that side.

move faster, i.e., describe a greater arc, than parts nearer the unmoved center. The chapters we have just considered, especially chapter 5, give one way of accounting for the moving radius principle as mechanical, i.e., involving motion. Indeed, in *Physical Problems* XVI.6, there is a gesture at mathematical completeness in contrasting the cone to the paths laid down by a rolling cylinder, and then contrasting both of these to the shape of an edge of a scroll (nested cylinders) cut crosswise. We recall from the treatment of animal motion in *Movement of Animals* 7 that Hero's term *isorrhopon*, used to describe the cone in his *Automatopoietica*, provides one key to the mechanical import conveyed by the image of the cone. The cone, being a stiff surface, distributes force evenly along its point of contact with the plane on which it rolls. The cone thus illustrates that the same force produces greater effect, a greater speed, in one part than in another. In contrast, the cut scroll seems not to involve issues of force at all. When the nested cylinders of the scroll are cut across right angles to the axis of the cylinders, thereby creating a new plane, a completely different shape of the edge of the scroll, neither a circle nor a straight line, is the result.

Everything we find in *Physical Problems* XVI.5 and 6 is consistent with the moving radius principle being known to the Aristotelian author of these chapters in its simpler formulation: concentric circles travel faster or slower in proportion to their longer or shorter radii. Chapters 3, 4, and 12 all bring into play a conception of circular motion as a resultant of two rectilinear movements. In all the chapters treated (excepting perhaps 6) the preoccupation is mechanical—the effect of force distributed evenly in rigid bodies. We now turn to chapter 9, in which the proclivity toward circular motion of bodies subject to natural force is placed in a new natural context, growth. This is very interesting, since the implication is that not just locomotion but an organic process is subject to the constraints tending to circular motion. The chapter is of considerable historical interest because the basic idea it presents is ascribed to Archytas. The language of the chapter is likely a combination of Aristotelian and Archytan terminology. One thing that will emerge from consideration of this chapter is that the Aristotelian author of *Physical Problems* XVI has some idea of a proportion governing balance in force and speed that was different from the proportion of arcs to radii.

Archytas on the Shape of Growth

Properties of the circle in natural motion appear again in *Physical Problems* XVI.9 but in a different way, because the moving subject is living and the type of motion considered is growth.[323] The question is why the parts of plants and animals that are not organs are all curved or circular (περιφερῆ), like stalks and shoots of plants, or limbs and the thorax in animals. The passage specifically excludes triangles and polygons as possible natural shapes for growth. It reads as follows:

> Why is it that the parts of plants and of animals that are not organs are all round—of plants the stalk and shoots, of animals the calves, thighs, arms, and chest? Neither a whole nor a part is triangular or a polygon. Is it, just as Archytas said, because there is in natural movement the proportion of equality (for he said all things move in proportion), but this [movement] is the only one that returns to itself, and so makes circles and curves, when it comes to be?[324] (915a28–33)

The Greek text of the last sentence is this:

> Πότερον, ὥσπερ Ἀρχύτας ἔλεγεν, διὰ τὸ ἐν τῇ κινήσει τῇ φυσικῇ ἐνεῖναι τὴν τοῦ ἴσου ἀναλογίαν (κινεῖσθαι γὰρ ἀνάλογον πάντα), ταύτην δὲ μόνην εἰς αὑτὴν ἀνακάμπτειν ὥστε κύκλους ποιεῖν καὶ στρογγύλα, ὅταν ἐγγένηται;

---

323 The authenticity of this passage has been accepted since Frank's treatment of it (*Plato und die sogenannten Pythagoreer*, 378). The passage is treated at length by Frank and by Huffmann (*Archytas*, 516–540). It is also mentioned by Cambiano, "La meccanica di Archita," 323, and treated briefly by Flashar, *Problemata*, 587. Huffman's explication of Archytas on motion is as comprehensive as possible, given the sparseness of the evidence. I concur in his view that Archytas believed motion to have the kind of order rendered by proportionality and that Aristotle followed his lead in this respect (*Archytas*, 537).

324 Both Huffman and Forster translate ὀργανικά as "instrumental." My translation is "organs." Compare *On the Soul* II.1, 412a27–b5, where the connotation of ὀργανική is organized into a whole. Huffman says that Archytas uses the term in a sense not fully compatible with Aristotelian usage (*Archytas*, 522). The contrast of specialized parts, like the liver or heart, to limbs and thorax, i.e., parts made up of homeomerous tissue like bone and flesh, seems clear enough, though, and not foreign to Aristotle. My judgment is that Archytas has in mind a fairly simple and obvious contrast of specialized and non-specialized parts.

This sentence gives all the answer to the problem that the author presents. The answer begins with "whether," possibly implying an unexpressed alternative. Most answers to *dia ti* questions in *Physical Problems* XVI begin with ἢ ὅτι or ἢ διὰ τί, "is it because?" The brevity and wording could mean that Archytas' explanation is included for its interest and its relevance to the topic of natural circular motion rather than because the author fully endorses the answer.[325] But what is the answer?

The general import of the passage is that, without over-riding specialization of function, parts of living things grow into rounded, indeed circular, shapes. According to the passage, Archytas explicitly excludes triangular or polygonal shapes. This is interesting, since triangulation is as common in nature as circular patterns. It is a natural strategy for adding structural strength and is ubiquitous in the building of shelters by humans throughout the ages.[326] Furthermore, one particular polygon, the hexagon, would have been well known because of the ancient craft of beekeeping.[327] The implication of the passage, however, is that circularity is universal in natural forms left to develop without overriding specialization and this is why body parts grow naturally curved in shape. In what follows, I will start with the most general interpretation of this passage and then add more content to the meaning, based on reasoning about evidence I bring forward.

In the first part of the passage, Archytas said that there is a proportion of equality (τὴν τοῦ ἴσου ἀναλογίαν) in circular motion and that all things move in accordance with a proportion. The διά and γάρ clauses

---

325 Huffman notes that the passage does not make it explicit that Archytas addressed circular growth himself (*Archytas*, 527). The author of the chapter may be taking Archytas' idea that regular movement always exhibits some proportion and applying it to growth. This caveat noted, I will treat the growth problem as if it were Archytas' own, as Huffman himself does. If in fact the problem of circular growth is that of the author of *Physical Problems* XVI, this strengthens my case for early Aristotelian interest in a mechanical account of circular motion.

326 See natural versions of triangulation, such as bone structure in birds, in Williams, *Origins of Form*, 46–47. Some of these should have been visible to the observant ancient naturalist. In *Parts of Animals*, Aristotle addresses bone density (πυκνόν) and flexibility but not this sort of internal structure. He was attentive to the presence or absence of marrow in the bones. Thompson notes that the mechanical function of the apparently spongy internal structure of bone was not understood until well into the nineteenth century (*Growth and Form*, 231).

327 Hexagonal cells in a honeycomb are like circles, of course, in that they maximize internal surface area, as a circle does. They are superior to a circle in this context, because they leave no interstices and so no unused storage area.

suggest that the proportion of equality is a term for any proportion and that perhaps all motion, but certainly all natural motion, has a proportion of equality.[328] A baseline interpretation is readily at hand for these sentences. Mathematical relations in general provide order in nature. This is Burkert's view. The analogy of equality is "the power of mathematics that governs the world."[329] This general interpretation can be made more specific, however.

In ancient mathematics, proportions brought heterogeneous quantities into a relation of similarity. The ratio of circumferences of circles are to one another as the ratio of their diameters, for instance. In this way, quantities that cannot be compared directly, curved lines and straight lines, are similar, by having the same ratio to another within their own type: $C{:}c \propto D{:}d$. Proportional reasoning is the basis for approximation techniques like squaring the circle, and comparison of speeds in astronomy. Plato and Aristotle use both means (proportions that share a term) and proportions without a mean term as a kind of equality. Plato drew on the geometric mean in the *Gorgias* (508a) and the harmonic mean in the *Republic* (431d) to describe the equality (ἰσότης) possible among men or within the soul. Proportion was readily drawn into discussions of justice, because it could involve in equality things that were themselves unequal. There was instead, as Morrison aptly puts it, "a fair system of what we should call differentials between powers that are in fact unequal."[330] In speaking of justice in *Nichomachean Ethics* V.3, Aristotle makes explicit the value of proportionality for political thought, saying that the equal (τὸ ἴσον) is a mean (1131a14) and that proportion is an equality of ratios (ἰσότης λόγων) (1131a31). Given what a proportion was understood

---

328   Huffman understands the explicative γάρ sentence to encompass all motion, not just natural motion and compares Archytas to Aristotle in this respect (*Archytas*, 537–538). Aristotle believes, however, that what distinguishes natural and forced motion is the orderliness (τάξις) of natural motion and that this order is ratio (λόγος) (*Physics* VIII.1, 252a11–14). In *Mechanics*, the rectilinear path of motion brought about by a push on the end of a balance is in accordance with nature (*kata phusin*) in contrast to the constraint toward the center, which is described as contrary to nature (*para phusin*) (*Mechanics* 1, 849b4–5). Yet, the two movements enter into a proportion. The author of *Physical Problems* XVI.4 says that all things naturally (φύσει) proceed in straight lines (913b9). In an Aristotelian context, then, there is wide latitude in what qualifies as natural motion, and the present testimonium may reflect this Aristotelian background.

329   *Lore and Science*, 78n156.

330   Morrison, "Plato's Philosopher-Statesman," 213–214. For more on the use of Archytan proportion in political philosophy of the fourth century BC, see Huffman, *Archytas*, 192.

to be, then, Archytas may be asserting that any orderly movement, but especially natural movement, has the kind of equality to be found in proportional relation of some of its discernible elements or parts. This makes Burkert's view more specific by explication of what proportionality is. At the same time, it does not require that we take the proportion of equality to be any specific pattern or relation—some particular mean, for example.

Knowing that proportion meant the sort of equality possible for things involving parts or aspects in relation sheds light on the very method for rationalization of motion. Eudemus said that Aristotle shared Archytas' criticism of definitions of motion as the unequal, uneven, or indefinite.[331] Archytas said these are rather causes of motion. Motion originates from the unequal or uneven (τὸ ἀνώμαλον), but the unequal is not identified with motion. Indeed, I would suggest that, for Archytas and Aristotle, proportion in motion indexes a natural tendency of movement to regain balance or attain order out of disequilibrium. So, just as there are achievement or success actions ("seeing" or "scoring"), there are achievement or success ratios for movements. Success for a ratio means the particular terms involved in a movement and brought into ratio do indeed form a proportion with another ratio of some other corresponding terms of the movement. The proportion can be shown to index or describe orderly motion of a particular type.[332] This understanding of motion is illustrated by the "settling into" circular movement that is described in *Physical Problems* XVI.3 and 12. The disequilibrium of rectilinear movements constraining one another is reconciled in a circular shape of motion. This shape of movement can be described by some proportion. It has equality of some sort as a property.

There is a question concerning the passage quoted as to whether Archytas means that all motion, all natural motion, or only circular motion has the proportion of equality. The most natural reading of the last

---

331 These definitions are ascribed to Plato and the Pythagoreans (*Physics* III.2, 201b16–202a2). Simplicius points out that, in the *Timaeus*, Plato says that inequality is the cause of the unevenness (ἀνωμαλότης) of motion (57e), not that these two are the same (Simplicius, *in physicorum, CAG* 9, 431.4–16). See Huffman's commentary on this passage, which is A23 of Diels–Kranz, *Fragmente* 1, Archytas (Huffman, *Archytas*, 508–515). Huffman turns to the connection Archytas makes between concord and equality in his political philosophy and to Aristotle's specific examples of Archytan definition of physical things to conclude cautiously that Archytas believes motion participates in equality though its causes are inequality, unevenness, and lack of concord (515).

332 Huffman believes that Archytas has different types of proportion defining different sorts of motion (*Archytas*, 519).

sentence would single out the proportion of equality as descriptive of the only kind of movement (ταύτην δὲ μόνην) that "turns back on itself so as to make circles and curves, whenever it comes to be" (915a31–33). Only circular motion has a proportion of equality, then. The first part of the sentence does seem to associate the proportion of equality with every natural motion, however. The two parts do not conflict if we understand that every natural motion has a proportion of equality but that its exact nature differs, depending on whether the motion is curved or rectilinear. This classification need not connote that there are two simple and mutually exclusive natural motions but could be wide enough

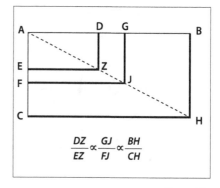

Figure 7.8a

to include a mathematical connection between circular and rectilinear motion, such as the one given in *Physical Problems* XVI.3 and 12. Can anything be said about what the proportion is that Archytas has in mind for circular motion?

The most direct and obvious meaning of "proportion of equality" in relation to motion would be the parallelogram of movements of *Mechanics* 1 (**Figure 7.8a**). A movement can be characterized by a sequence of ratios of sides of a parallelogram constructed around it. As *Mechanics* 1 shows, for rectilinear movement, this ratio is the same whatever point along the path of movement has yet been completed. The fact that the proportion is the same for every point along a straight line is a reason to single out this proportion, among all others that establish similarity of ratios (e.g., means), and give it the name proportion of equality. The problem is, of course, that this most obvious meaning of the proportion of equality describes motion in a straight line, not a circle. We have already seen, in Chapter 2 above, what is the proportion governing circular motion. Rectilinear elements taken from within the circle form a ratio that is the same ratio for *all* concentric arcs covered in the same time. One element taken for each circle is a perpendicular extended from the circumference to a point on a diameter (in **Figure 7.8b**, KG and FH). The other element is the segment of that diameter from the perpendicular to the circumference (in **Figure 7.8b**, BK and XF). For concentric circles, the ratio of these elements is always the same for arcs covered in the same time. So, this proportion correlating arcs of different circles, as it appears in *Mechanics* 1, has the dimension of equality too, like the parallelogram of movements though not in precisely the same way. Are there reasons to think Archytas knew of both proportions that could be called proportions of equality? An approach to answering this question need not be entirely conjectural. There are clues in *Physical Problems* XVI that bring Archytas closer to the context and concepts of both *Physical Problems* XVI and *Mechanics*.

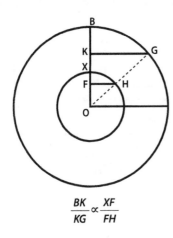

$$\frac{BK}{KG} \propto \frac{XF}{FH}$$

Figure 7.8b

Put succinctly, (*a*) Archytas must be relying upon some elements of the circle to form ratios that are the same respectively for different circles, and (*b*) it is most likely that these elements are straight lines—radii, perpendiculars to radii, tangents—drawn from the geometry of the circle. Both parts of this claim must be argued for, but the two parts are obviously connected. I will provide context for this bi-part claim by considering two scholarly interpretations of Archytas' proportion of equality, those of Fritz Krafft and Carl Huffman.

Krafft makes a case in general terms for there being a close relation between Archytas' methods and the proportion for correlating different concentric circles given in *Mechanics* 1. He believes that, in the 5th–4th centuries BC, there existed a writing on mechanics known to Plato that presented the ratio of curvilinear speeds as following the ratio of diameters. This is the rule found both in *Laws* X and *On the Heavens* II.10. He assumes that Archytas wrote this treatise.[333] He notes that Archytas makes use of movements composing a resultant motion in his way of finding the

---

333 Krafft cites the likelihood that Plato and Archytas met when Plato was in Syracuse, as well as the connection between the lower Italian school of mathematician/philosophers and the machines of war made for Dionysius. See *Betrachtungsweise*, 145.

two mean proportionals between given lines. The composition of rectilinear elements to make a curve in *Mechanics* 1 shows a strong kinship to Archytas' method and could also be his work, he believes. Krafft does not offer an interpretation of the proportion of equality as such, but he does suggest that the other parts of *Physical Problems* XVI we have examined may be the work of Archytas. Apart from the fact that there is no evidence of a treatise on this topic, the correlation of arc-speeds to diameters of circles to which Krafft appeals is a more general formulation of the principle of the lever than the correlation of arcs by means of the proportion of perpendiculars dropped to the diameter, the proportion which is given in *Mechanics* 1. The cases in other chapters surrounding Archytas' proportion in *Physical Problems* XVI concern curved motion coming about as a resultant of rectilinear movements. The question about Archytas' connection to the rest of *Physical Problems* XVI must be whether his proportion of equality involves some proportionality of lines taken out of the state of affairs itself, which represent contributors to the circular shape of growth.

It does seem that Archytas shares the concern with composition of motion found in the earlier chapters of Book XVI. A reason to think this is his referring, in *Physical Problems* XVI.9, to circular motion as the only motion in accordance with the proportion of equality that turns back on itself (εἰς αὐτὴν ἀνακάμπτειν). In *Physical Problems* XVI.3 and 12, the author says something similar about the revolving unbalanced body. In chapter 12, he uses the terminology of turning inward (εἰς τὸ ἐντός) to describe the movement of both the lighter and heavier parts (915b13). The motion turns back from a path that it would otherwise have taken, namely, the path extending further along a straight line. In the next sentence, he says the part further from the point of exertion of force by the thrower is the one that turns toward the thrower (πρὸς τῷ ἀφιέντι).[334] The language in the Archytas chapter is different but the idea is the same. The inclusion of εἰς αὐτήν (toward itself) presents the same picture of motion that would otherwise extend along a straight line bowing back instead. He says *this* (ταύτην) is the only movement that turns back on itself. Some proportion explains this. So, the association of a bending back sort of motion with an accommodation of linear motion is a possible

---

334 In the introductory question itself that is common to chapters 3 and 12, there is a similar idea. The author says that one throws the die, turning back (στρέψας) the lighter part toward oneself (913a38, 915b10). It is not clear if one simply begins the throw with the lighter part toward oneself or throws it in a slightly different way. There is the same implication, however, of motion curving back around.

link between Archytas and the connection of balance, straight lines, and circular motion in *Physical Problems* XVI.

Nevertheless, the term ἀνακάμπτει, turning back, in chapter 9 is unique among the chapters and is not typical Aristotelian usage. Ἀνακάμπτειν in general means "return," in particular, "bending back." Aristotle uses the word in *Physics* VIII.8 to describe return to a point of origin by reversal of the direction of motion. Rectilinear motion cannot be one and continuous indefinitely. This is because extent or distance in the universe is limited, and so motion in a straight line must turn back in the opposite direction to carry on (261b32). If it turns back, it also must stop first. There is a type of circular motion, which is not a continuous unrolling (συνείρειν) but reverses course to return to its origin. This circular motion also must stop when it reverses (262a12–18). So, genuine circular motion, ἡ κύκλῳ, revolving motion, does not turn back at all. It does not cover the same arc proceeding in an opposite direction.[335] Archytas' idea is not Aristotle's retracing a path but is rather an idea of turning back and inward to make a curve.

In *Mechanics* 1, a weight subject to a force would proceed at a tangent to a circle but is drawn toward the center instead and thus describes an arc (849a16). In *Mechanics* 1, the turning back is said to be "just as if it were drawn back" or drawn in a contrary direction[336] (849a12). The author of *Mechanics* reinforces the connotations the modern reader is quick to perceive of force being exerted on the object, by saying it is ruled more (κρατεῖται μᾶλλον) and so moves more slowly, the closer it is to the center of the circle described by the balance movement (a19). So, the language of the Archytas chapter of *Physical Problems* XVI is not really that of *Mechanics* 1 either. I would suggest that ἀνακάμπτειν is Archytas' own word, not the choice of the Aristotelian writer of this testimonium in *Physical Problems* XVI. The idea of movement turning back so as to make a circle may originally have belonged to Archytas, and the states

---

335 In *Physics* VIII.8, Aristotle uses a similar notion but in a figurative way. He analyzes whether what is causing motion in another must also itself be in motion of the same kind. He believes that the mover might be moved with a different species of motion but denies that it can be moved with the same type of motion it is causing. He also rules out a "bending back" of the series, whereby a mover causing locomotion has in its backward series of movers for itself another mover in locomotion (257a8). In *On Generation and Corruption* II.10, he uses the word to refer to the return of elementary water back to water through a cycle of the change of elements into one another (337a5).

336 ὥσπερ ἀντισπώμενον εἰς τοὐναντίον.

of affairs examined in *Physical Problems* XVI.3, 4, and 12 make use of this conception.

It should be noted, however, that a similar conception is used by Aristotle in *Progression of Animals* 9 with the word, κάμπτειν, without the prefix. He is making clear that forward progression of animals requires an unmoved point and says:

> Flexion (κάμψις) is a change from a straight line to a curve (περιφερές) or an angle, straightening (εὔθυνσις) a change from either of these to a straight line. Now in all such changes, the flexion or the straightening must be relative to one point. Moreover, without flexion there could not be walking or swimming or flying. (708b22–25)

So, animals bend or flex their limbs in locomotion, changing rectilinear motion into curved motion by bending. This passage does not use a notion of bending back, but it does concern the conversion of rectilinear to arc movement. An early meaning of καμπτήρ is "angle" in the sense of "turning point." Both καμπτήρ and κάμπτειν are used regularly in the context of turning at the post in a chariot race.[337] So, the recognition of a curve being akin to the "corner" made by straight lines is not new with *Physical Problems* XVI and *Mechanics*. It is an older conception than the idea of curved and straight as mutually exclusive kinds of magnitudes and motions.

Let us now consider a very precise claim about the meaning of the proportion of equality that addresses the meaning of "turning back." This is Carl Huffman's account, which does involve a connection between rectilinear and curved motion.[338] Huffman presents an interpretation of the proportion of equality as being the arithmetic mean. The most reliable and complete of the fragmentary evidence we have about Archytas makes him a transmitter of the theory of means and one who drew out some mathematical traits of mean ratios in music theory.[339] In the arithmetic

---

337 See *L-S* ad loc.

338 *Archytas*, 508–540. Huffman points out that modern commentators have not attempted a definitive interpretation of "analogy of equality" (518). He notes, however, how important it is for providing evidence of Archytas' theory of motion.

339 See the testimony of Ptolemy's *Harmonics* in Huffman, *Archytas*, A16, 402–428. The three means—arithmetic, geometric, and harmonic—are defined in a surviving fragment of Archytas' work on music (Huffman, *Archytas*, Fr. 2, 162–181). Archytas is reported to have renamed the subcontrary mean the harmonic mean. By later accounts, he

mean, the difference in subtraction between a first and second term is the same as the difference between the second and the third. In a geometric mean, the first term is the same part or parts of the second as the second is of the third. In the harmonic mean, the mean "exceeds and is exceeded by the same part of the extremes."[340] That is, by whatever part of itself the first exceeds the second, the second exceeds the third by that same part of the third.

In interpreting Archytas' proportion of equality, Huffman considers the means in terms of ratios of lines, an approach certainly not foreign to Archytas. He says the harmonic mean is least likely to qualify as a proportion of equality, because the slope defined by the ratio of lengths of successive lines conforming in the comparison of their magnitudes to the harmonic mean is a curve opening indefinitely.[341] Either the geometric mean or the arithmetic is a more likely candidate.[342] In the geometric mean, the *ratio* of terms remains the same, while in the arithmetic mean, the *difference* between terms remains the same. He says that either the arithmetic or geometric mean could be called a proportion of equality.[343]

In the geometric mean, what is the same is the multiple by which one term exceeds another in ratios that share a term. In the arithmetic mean, the difference between terms on either side of the equality is the same numerically. The geometric mean applied to distance covered in motion, however, yields rectilinear motion. The author of *Mechanics* understood that sameness of ratio over a motion was the mark of rectilinear motion, though he did not refer to this sameness of ratio as the geometric mean. The diagonals taken for successive distances that share an arithmetic difference, on the other hand, would when taken together be a curve—or rather a series of straight lines approximating a curve. At any rate, the

---

was one discoverer of some of the additional means. Nicomachus reports that Archytas was involved in the development of the means subcontrary to the harmonic and that he used means involving four terms (Huffman, *Archytas*, Fr. 2, 162–181). This indicates the range of experimentation around the idea of making terms equal through mediation. See Huffman, *Archytas*, 74, 168–177, and Heath, *History* 1, 84–89.

340　This is Heath's terminology. Heath lists all the means known to the Greeks, including ones developed later than the fourth century (*History* 1, 87).

341　The idea of "slope" is anachronistic, bringing into play plots on a graph. It would be better to treat the locus of successive ratios as a diagonal of a rectangle, an approach Huffman includes but without establishing its historical relevance or more exact ancient conception.

342　*Archytas*, 533.

343　*Archytas*, 530.

overall trajectory of the motion in accordance with an arithmetic mean would, in comparison to motion conforming to a geometric mean, "turn back" as the passage says the proportion does.[344]

This rendering of "proportion of equality" has the virtue of staying close to what we know from ancient authors is an achievement of Archytas, articulation of the mathematical means. Huffman gives no strong reason why means should be involved in the explanation of circular motion, however.[345] The strongest reason is just the large role they play in Archytas' harmonics. *Physical Problems* XVI gives another context, however, within which Archytas may have been thinking about mechanics. Huffman links the arithmetic mean to the circle by means of the curving figure plotted by the diagonals made by successive pairs of lines that enter into arithmetic proportion. He takes the pairs of lines from a parallelogram of movements. He refers to the model presented in *Mechanics* 1. The coincidence between the sameness of ratio for the geometric mean and the sameness of ratio for rectilinear movements along a diagonal of a rectangle makes him think some other mean must be involved in the circular motion of the proportion of equality. Other geometric proportions not mediated by a mean term share this characteristic with the geometric mean, however. Ratios of the respective successive distances along the diagonal of the parallelogram in no way need to *share* a term in order to be the same. So, the proportion of the parallelogram of movements is not actually a geometric mean. Huffman must think that Archytas had established the sameness of ratio for rectilinear motions but only in terms of a shared term.[346] A mere glance at the diagonal of the parallelogram would suffice for Archytas to know that the geometric mean is unnecessary to the conception of the parallelogram of movements. So, the basis for seeking the proportion of equality in the arithmetic mean is fragile. Indeed, it would make sense to seek Archytas' proportion in other proportional relations developed as variations on the geometric mean—a proportion involving multiples but not involving a common term.

---

344 *Archytas*, 532, 538–539. Huffman sometimes treats the arithmetic proportion as a mean and sometimes just as defining a series of terms in ratio by the arithmetic difference between them. Flashar takes ταύτην in the sentence to refer to the motion not the proportion. Huffman says it is the proportion itself that is characterized as turning back (*Archytas*, 538). For more on this, see below.

345 Huffman cites some limitations of his own account (*Archytas*, 533).

346 His figure is drawn and the example is given in terms of the conception of a geometric *mean* (*Archytas*, 539).

There are other reasons not to regard the proportion of equality as an arithmetic mean. As Huffman notes, the arithmetic mean does not yield a circle but a flattening curve. Given Archytas' mathematical sophistication, it seems unlikely that he would count this as "turning back" in the way a circle continuously curves. Stems and tree trunks come remarkably close to true circles in their growth patterns, the circular shapes being disturbed mainly by environmental factors like terrain and physical trauma. The comparable turning inward of *Physical Problems* XVI.3 and 12 explicitly refers to circular motion. Furthermore, to derive a curve from a series of arithmetic means of sides of rectangles depends on the curve being made up of short straight lines. If Archytas meant for the arithmetic mean to define a true curve, he would have needed to conceptualize it in the way the author of *Mechanics* conceives the ratio descriptive of the arc of a circle—at no time does the ratio of contributing elements remain the same.[347] There is always an arithmetic mean but the value of the ratios constituting the mean equality is always changing. Archytas may have so conceived the curve, but a related problem remains. Huffman understands ταύτην in the sentence to refer to ἀναλογίαν, not the motion under consideration. Huffman interprets this to mean that it is the proportion itself that turns back. Turning back is the property that distinguishes an arithmetic proportion from a geometric proportion. The motion is characterized in some general way by the arithmetic proportion, to which the property of turning back belongs. This seems unsatisfactory, since the proportion is then not clearly tied to things in the situation or elements of movement. The question is: what are the discrete quantities from the situation that are in the continuous proportion that is the arithmetic mean? What is being brought into ratio?

In his interpretation, ratios are formed by sides of a rectangle, on the model of the parallelogram of movements. If turning back applies to the ratio not the motion, then the straight lines relevant to the resultant circular motion do not come from the circle. We no longer have a rectangle of movements, unless the circle really is a series of straight lines. It seems implausible that Archytas would seek to explain circular motion in terms of rectangles without at least reference to elements of the geometry of the circle—tangents, chords, diameters, and perpendiculars to a diameter. The arithmetic proportion is not part of the geometry of the circle. Rectilinear elements are constructible within the circle, however—chords

---

347 φερόμενον ἐν μηθενὶ λόγῳ μηθένα χρόνον.

and perpendiculars dropped to diameters—in ways that would have been well known to Archytas.[348]

An Aristotelian Argument for the Proportion of Equality

Huffman's particular suggestion that the proportion of equality is the arithmetic mean seems unlikely for the reasons given, but the overall setting he gives to the problem seems right.[349] Means were the original mediated equalities, and the proportion of equality for circular motion may have developed out of the basic idea of mediate equality. Archytas, or his successors like the author of *Mechanics*, moved from consideration of different kinds of means to what I shall call a *characteristic proportion* that did not have a term shared in the ratios. A characteristic proportion makes use of magnitudes proper to the situation to be explained—radii, perpendiculars dropped to a diameter—that are different from the ones for which a relation is sought. A characteristic proportion is a selector, test, or sieve for magnitudes that are related in the way being sought—for instance, arc-distances covered in the same time. Let me offer concrete details of how a characteristic proportion could become the alternative for mediating different sized arcs.

Archytas is asking how a kind of motion more elusive of explanation than locomotion, namely growth, is ordered motion—i.e., how growth manifests some sort of equilibrium—and so why it assumes the shape it does. He seeks an account covering both (*a*) increase in size of unspecialized tissues, and (*b*) the circular shape of the increase. The two tasks are obviously related, and indeed there was already known to Plato and Aristotle a direct proportion believed to characterize circular shape. This was the proportion of ratios of circumferences of circles to the ratio of their diameters. Stating the tried and true proportion a different way—two shapes are circular if the ratio of perimeters is proportional to the ratio of diameters, assuming the diameters remain unchanged and that each diameter rotates around its midpoint.

---

348 Euclid makes regular use of perpendiculars to the diameter and radius of a circle, e.g., *Elements* III.3: "If in a circle a straight line through the centre bisect a straight line not through the centre, it also cuts it at right angles; and if it cut it at right angles, it also bisects it."

349 Huffman highlights the centrality of proportion for Archytas, coming to the conclusion that proportion, not arithmetic, became the foundation of definition for Archytas (*Archytas*, 494). This is an indication of how thoroughly relation was taken by Archytas as the source of explanation.

These parameters suffice to define the circular shape of stems and limbs, but the problem is why and how growth maintains the shape. We are dealing with movement in progress and achieved. The case of circular growth is illustrated by growth rings of a tree (**Figure 7.9**). Giving a proportion for circular growth will focus on the distance between X

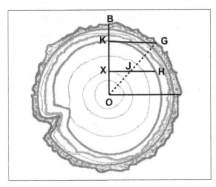

and K, and K and B, if ring BG is taken as successive to KH. In the form of statement closest to the relation of circumferences and diameters, consider the following supposition: the organic matter laid down between the rings takes a circular shape if the perimeters of the respective shapes have the same ratio as KX:BK for any radius OB that is taken.[350] So, the girth of the tree

Figure 7.9

at the time it was cut down is related to its circumference at an earlier date in the same ratio as the distances between successive growth rings for the present and the earlier date under consideration. The problem is that this supposition is too wide to pick out circular growth as opposed to growth in quadrilateral shapes or for that matter, growth as an unshaped mass. There would need to be some way to reference the center of the circle as part of the proportion in order to screen ratios of radius segments that cannot contribute to an explanation of circular growth. The example of *Physical Problems* XVI.3 and 12, however, suggests that there may have already been other rectilinear elements involved in the proportion, since growth would have disparate influences to bring into equilibrium somewhat like the uneven weight of an unbalanced body in motion.

Chords of the circle are another "part" of a circle (**Figure 7.10**). Chords might represent lines of influence or increase that interfere or compete with increase along a radius. The problem of circular growth itself defines the relevant chords. They are the ones that are also tangents to some preceding growth circle. The relevant chord is tangent to an interior

---

350   One reason for approaching the proportion of equality in this way is its obviousness and simplicity. It is also the case that a proportion of similar elements of different circles is presented as a consequence of the main proportion of interest in *Mechanics* 1 (849b4–6). What is there presented as a consequence, gotten by alternating proportionals, may have come first historically. See Chapter 8 below.

ring and extends out to a more recent growth ring, as do the half-
chords, KG and XH (**Figure 7.9**).
There was no special word for a
geometrical chord of a circle in
the fourth century BC. Of drawing a chord, Aristotle says, "let a
line join (ἐπιζεύχθω ἐφ᾽ἧς ΒΓ)
points" along a circumference
(*On the Heavens* II.2, 287b8).
Aristotle uses a verb for yoking
pairs (ἐπιζεύχθω from ζευγίζω
and ζυγόν), which suggests some
sort of balancing opposition for

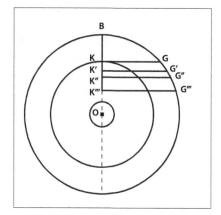

Figure 7.10

the pairs. *Zugon* is the crossbar of a yoke. The author of *Mechanics* 1
calls a chord a *diametron* (849a4). *Diametros* was used for lines joining
any points opposite one another in a figure. Aristotle also bears witness

to the Pythagoreans' attempt to
make the distance of a heavenly
body correspond to what would
be a length of gut strung on a lyre
or τρίγωνόν (**Figure 7.11**)—in
their belief that the heavens produce harmonious sound in their
movements.[351] These examples
suggest that the elements were in
place even before Aristotle's time
for turning to chords of a circle or
to perpendiculars to a radius (half
a chord) in measuring circles.

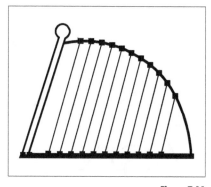

Figure 7.11

Chords alone, though, cannot establish any proportion of equality
that indexes circular shape as such. The singling out of the chord tangent
to a smaller ring and extending to the circumference of a larger ring yields
a ratio, $\frac{KG}{XH}$ (**Figure 7.9**), which is overly inclusive as an index of circular
growth, just like the comparison of segments of the radius.

We could try matching a ratio of portions of a radius with a ratio
of corresponding half-chords. It would seem that sometimes the ratio of

---

351 *On the Heavens* II.9, 290b12–13, 291a8.

radius segments to the ratio of chords would be the same ($\frac{BK}{KX} \propto \frac{KG}{XH}$), but whether this proportion, when it occurs, is relevant to the form of circular growth would still be a question. So, while one would wish the matter were so simple as circular shape being a function of the ratio of either a pair of the parts of a radius from one ring to the other or a pair of tangents from one completed ring to the later ring—this proportion would not hold most of the time.

It seems that some narrowing of the possibilities for proportion would occur by forming ratios of a segment of ratio to a segment of chord. The situation would be as in **Figure 7.10**. Do different perpendiculars from a single radius to the same circumference—KG, K′G′, K″G″, etc.—have the same ratio with the radius at the different points at which they contact the radius (**Figure 7.12a**)? In other words, is $\frac{BK}{KG} \propto \frac{BK'}{K'G'} \propto \frac{BK''}{K''G''}$ for a single circle? Are these ratios all the same ratio? It seems clear they are not, unless each K stood at O, so that every construction replicated the quadrant BOG (**Figure 7.12b**). This would be the tautologous case, since all radii are the same length, and the value of the ratio is 1.

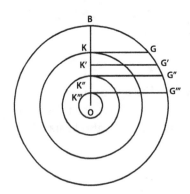

Figure 7.12a

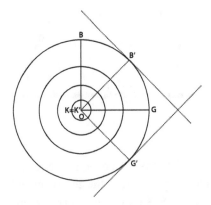

Figure 7.12b

These "unsuccessful" combinations of ratios are worth considering, because they are natural extensions of the successful direct proportion of ratios of circumferences with ratios of diameters or radii that Plato and Aristotle knew. The unsuccessful trial ratios use rectilinear elements involved in the circle. Moving to parts of radii and to chords shows what might have been the course of pre-demonstrative investigation of the reasons for circular motion in physical situations. Indeed, in *Mechanics* 1, the author forms a proportion of ratios of segments of a radius to ratios of perpendiculars to the radius segment where it is cut as a variation on the version of the proportion that "succeeds" in correlating arcs that are covered in the same time (849b4–6).

Once both tangents (chords of circles) and segments of a radius are involved in understanding the circular motion that is growth, however, a way opens for addressing both of the tasks (*a*) and (*b*)—how to explain both increase and the shape of increase in growth. We can imagine KG being *always at a tangent* to the same growth ring and extending outward as a chord to the circumference of the tree trunk but *at different positions* along the circle to which it is tangent. BK would be the distance, held constant, from the tangent at K to a point on the outer circumference. Geometrically, this would be like moving these rectilinear elements along the path of

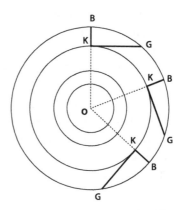

Figure 7.13

a moving radius (**Figure 7.13**). The series of ratios would say something about the curvilinear path that is bounded by B and G in each successive case. If the ratio of the distance along one radius and the distance at a perpendicular to that radius (BK:KG) is *unchanged*, then the path of increase in growth has been circular. This "moving ratio" may have been the first version of the proportion of equality for circular growth. One thing that would mark it as prior and primitive is that, while it provides a proportion for determining the shape of growth, it does not address increase or comparability of magnitudes, which would involve further comparison of properties of two concentric circles.[352]

For this reason, it is significant that Aristotle already knew one dis-

---

352   The length BK is held constant in the scenario I portray, because there could be ratios that are the same as BK:KG but involve multiples or fractions of BK. So, if the lengths changed, the curve would vary widely from the curve of one circle to another, each with a different radius length. This is one reason why, from its first consideration, a proportion descriptive of growth would have involved two concentric circles, capitalizing on the heritage of the lever and balance of unequal beams.

criminator that would sort ratios in the context of comparison of arcs. He says in *On the Heavens* II.8 that, for distances along outer and inner heavenly spheres to be covered in the same time, the arcs compared must be subtended by the same two radii (290a2–5). This statement, seemingly innocuous out of context, shows that there was a way of eliminating ratios of rectilinear elements of circles that were not relevant to explaining speeds or growth. Aristotle does not give, however, a reason or rationale for excluding other ratios of rectilinear elements of circles, something the characteristic proportion of *Mechanics* 1 does do. The demonstration in *Mechanics* 1 establishes exactly which ratios of rectilinear elements pick out arcs covered in the same time. Knowing the "subtended by the same radii" rule of *On the Heavens* II.8, however, the demonstration of *Mechanics* 1 is oddly redundant to the modern eye. From the standpoint of reconstructing the history of *Mechanics* 1, however, it is significant that Aristotle already had a means of narrowing down the chord-tangents and parts of a radius that would correlate arcs covered in the same time. His references to *automata* and carts shows that he knew the rule covered translations into other planes and spaces.

The two radii rule found in *On the Heavens* II.8 could have come from the "moving ratio" of **Figure 7.13**. The radius OG (**Figure 7.9**) can be constructed, once the limitation of holding BK constant is in place. At that point, we have two radii, OB and OG, selecting ratios of the same rectilinear elements, BK and KG, along the concentric circles. In fact, the two-radii rule of *On the Heavens* II.8 suffices to generalize the discussion of the proportion of equality for circular motion to any concentric circles at all that can be constructed. With this rule, the investigation of successive segments of a radius in relation to tangents to an interior concentric circle ceases to be the context for argument. To see how this is the case, I will revisit the overly broad attempts to account for circular shape and growth in terms of cohort ratios of chords to segments of radii (**Figure 7.9**).

Keeping in mind we are trying to explain increase as well as the shape of growth, it would make sense to ask if the "moving ratio" $\frac{BK}{KG}$ could be the same as any preceding interior growth ring ratio. Each taken alone could regulate the growth it mediates as circular. Yet will it then be the case also that $\frac{BK}{KG} \propto \frac{KX}{XH}$?

We may at this point use a simple *reductio* argument to show this proportion would not hold. Let us suppose that the ratios of additions to a radius of successive growth rings (XK and KB) to their respective tangents from the previous growth ring to the most recent, $\frac{BK}{KG}$ and $\frac{KX}{XH}$, are the same (**Figure 7.9**). By the "subtended by the same radii" rule given in Aristotle's *On the Heavens* II.8, those ratios would also be the same as some ratio KX:XJ, where X is a point of termination of a perpendicular that intersects the second subtending radius OG at point J (**Figure 7.9**). KX:XJ would be the same as BK:KG and so, on the supposition being tested, also the same as KX:XH. KX cannot have the same ratio to XJ as it has to XH, however. This is absurd. So, the requirement of sharing two radii for tangents to circles of growth just does exclude *most* ratios involving perpendiculars to the radius from being candidates for the proportion governing the shape of movement or growth that is circular.

Indeed, XJ bears no particular relation to the BK:KG pattern under consideration in **Figure 7.12a**, which would need to involve XH not XJ in its rationale. To try to continue the rationale of comparing portions of a radius to *tangents* from an inner to an outer circle, we would have to bring into play another concentric circle not evident in the visible growth ring pattern. At this point, the better strategy for getting at a proportion defining the shape and magnitude of cognate arcs is to drop the reference to tangents in the problem of cognate parts and to work simply with any perpendiculars dropped to a radius for a pair of concentric circles. This is the standpoint taken by the author of *Mechanics* 1. This standpoint, however, makes less evident the connection of the problem of *Mechanics* 1 to the Archytan proportion of equality.

We can see in these considerations concerning ratios of different rectilinear elements within the circle a way that Aristotle's winnowing style of argumentation could have been fruitful in finding a characteristic proportion for correlating arcs or circumferences. A proportion to govern movement is approached by whittling away at the range of alternatives and narrowing the field of possible accounts. The shared radii require-ment of *On the Heavens* II.8 and the involvement of rectilinear com-ponents of circular motion in *Physical Problems* XVI.3 and 12 join in dovetail fashion in the historical background to *Mechanics* 1. If there was a definite proportion of equality for circular motion, it is likely to have involved shared radii, halves of chords of a circle, and segments of a radi-us defined by the perpendicular chord tangent to a smaller interior circle. The proportion of equality need not have been exactly the proportion of *Mechanics* 1, however, and this has been one reason for exploring ratios of tangents and segments of radii relevant to growth.

The Rounding of Shells in the Surf

The idea of mechanical explanation as seeing into the structure of disparate motions of a body also plays a role in *Physical Problems* XVI.10. The picture of motion presented in chapter 10 appears at first to give an answer to its problem that is uncharacteristically ideal in comparison to the chapters already examined. The question is simply put: why do things always become rounded at their extremes? The answer is: because nature makes all things as excellent and fair as possible (ὡς δυνατόν) from the resources available (ἐκ τῶν ἐνδεχομένων), and this shape is the fairest, being the most uniform possible (915a32–36).[353]

The passage draws upon the idea of a circle as the noblest and fairest shape, being completely symmetrical with itself. Nature makes things in accordance with this shape insofar as materials permit. At first glance, this answer is teleological in a mundane way. Nature aims at the noblest shape and possibly falls short due to weakness in the materials or an impediment. A fuller treatment of the stated problem appears in *Mechanics* 15, however, in terms that draw upon the lever principle in the way we have seen in other passages of *Physical Problems* XVI. The author of *Mechanics* asks why pebbles on the beach[354] are all rounded, though they start out as elongated stones and shells. The answer is that parts of the rock or shell further from its center are moving faster. He continues:

> For the middle is a center, and the distance [to the extremities] is the [line] from the center [i.e., radius]. From an equal movement, the greater [radius] describes a greater circle. What travels a greater distance in an equal time moves faster, and things moving faster in an equal interval strike more forcefully (σφοδρότερον τύπει). And things striking [other objects] more are themselves struck more. So that the parts further from the middle must be broken in pieces (θραύεσθαι). As this happens to them, they become round. In the case of pebbles, because of the motion of the sea and the objects being moved with it, they are always in motion and strike against one another as they roll (κυλιομέναις προσκόπτειν). This effect must be greatest at the extremities. (852b32–954a4)

---

353   The last phrase is τὸ αὐτὸ αὑτῷ ὁμοιότατον. Translation is by Forster (*Works*, ed. Ross, 7).

354   αἱ καλούμεναι κρόκαι.

This is a remarkably detailed application to a natural process of the principle of faster movement further from a central point. The faster motion is explicitly described as circular motion in the last lines where the author adds that the objects roll as they strike one another. The explanation is, however, an account of why edges become round. We should recall that Aristotle himself says that a point moves faster the further it is from its origin, whether the movement is rectilinear or circular. Being off balance, the shells rotate, the longer end moving faster. Innumerable hits on the shell, especially at the longer and faster moving end, finally produce a round object rolling smoothly in the surf. The key to the shape of the shell here is reiterative circular movement. The series of impacts tends to produce motion in a straight line, but imbalance in the body makes for circular motion. The overall effect of all the impacts, whether from a rectilinear movement or a curved one, is a rounded shape.

The similar question in *Physical Problems* XVI is extremely brief, but with its dual reference to natural feasibility (ἐκ τῶν ἐνδεχομένων and ὡς δυνατόν) the answer highlights the underlying level of necessity associated with circular form in movement, which is treated more extensively in *Mechanics* 15. This theme also underlies the explanation of the tumbling of a body given in chapter 3. There, differences in weight seemingly pull against one another within a body, and opposite parts assume a circular motion as a natural accommodation to their different speeds. In *Physical Problems* 10 and *Mechanics* 15, it is external blows that produce a circular shape in the object itself, which has extremities at different distances from a middle. The brief answer to the question about rounded edges in *Physical Problems* XVI.10 is not platitudinous, as might appear at first glance, but instead offers a succinct summary of the priority of circular motion as the first resultant of rectilinear movements constrained by lack of balance in a body.

We might think that if circular motion is composed from other motions due to constraint, it could not also receive the mantle of being the noblest shape for motion, but chapter 10 would indicate that the beauty of circular motion is not compromised by its being reliant on a matrix of underlying materials and their tendencies to movement. Circular motion is the fairest by virtue of its shape being the most uniform (915a31). Flashar has taken this chapter of a piece with the account from Archytas preceding it and believes the thought belongs to Archytas. Whether this is a correct interpretation or not, we see here one of the reasons why

215

Aristotle would have been so interested in Archytas.[355] He himself mentions Archytas as one who included matter along with form in definition (*Metaphysics* H.2, 1043a22). This passage suggests that even circular form relies on conditions originating in body. It does appear that, for the author of this brief chapter of *Physical Problems* XVI, the beauty and symmetry of circular shape are enhanced by the circle's emerging from the very processes of nature.

Summary and Results

Surveying the chapters of *Physical Problems* XVI, it becomes clear that chapters 3, 9, 10, 11, and 12 all treat circularity, or curvature based on the circle, as a shape of movement into which changes are naturally channeled, changes that have been caused in a variety of ways—natural or forced locomotion, growth and increase, incremental attrition of bodily magnitude, increase or decrease of force of motion on a body. Circularity is a natural form for motion and is the shape of things generated by natural processes, but it is not thereby without contributing causes.

Chapter 4, concerned with rebound of objects from a surface, might be construed to have little to do with the lever, except for its reference to the experience of falling backward when hit in a forward direction. Kinesthetic awareness of leverage is clearly involved with this insight about the upper body falling in the opposite direction. Indeed, falling this way is an experience already structured as a state of affairs with internal necessities to the extent that the human being undertakes appropriate coping action without deliberating about it. The fall is a *phainomenon* in the sense explicated earlier in a different context, the observation of the occultation of Mars.

The fall provides a background for understanding the axis of balance treated in the earlier cases of *Physical Problems* XVI.4. This axis and its displacement in rebound have in common with chapter 3 the unbalanced body in movement. In chapter 3, there is a *meson*—a fulcrum point or point of balance within the body—between weights conceived as opposite one another in the revolving forward motion of the unbalanced body. In chapter 4, the line of balance is something like a middle of the body in the analysis given. In chapter 4, the author does not complete any analysis of why angles of rebound are equal, but he is sure the reason for their

---

355 Aristotle is reputed to have written three books on Archytas (Huffman, *Archytas*, 4).

being acute involves this axis of balance. The line of balance is brought to bear also in chapter 11 with its aerodynamic account of why a projectile begins to fall. Again, curvature of path is an outcome.

Chapter 5, which treats the rolling cone and the rolling cylinder, clearly explicates the underlying principle of the lever but has a different topic from chapters 3 and 4. It treats the differences in the locus of circular motion as a function of how circles are present in the surfaces of the cylinder and cone. The stiff surfaces of cone and cylinder exemplify the presence of the same amount of force at all points along the surface. Chapter 6, with its crosscut scroll, reinforces and completes the theme of variations in the locus of circularly shaped bodies in motion.

Although issues of mechanics appear most transparently in the chapters that suppose circular motion as a natural niche for interplay of movements (3, 9, 11, 12), the rolling cone was itself a trope for mechanical advantage, as we have already seen in Aristotle and Hero. The earlier chapters of *Physical Problems* XVI are more highly contextualized uses of the principle than the mathematical formulation of the rolling cylinder and cone.

One reason for dating these more contextualized variations on leverage phenomena (chapters 3, 4, 9, 10, and 12) to Aristotle's collaborators is, first of all, the simple historical principle that one could expect the contextualized reference to be present earlier than an abstracted mathematical account. Since the mathematical formulations of the cylinder and cone were known to Aristotle, the more contextualized accounts probably were also. Rougher and less complete, they may have been research topics for discussion in his school. Another stronger reason is the connection to Archytas, Plato's contemporary and an innovator in using the mechanical feint of shapes in motion to solve mathematical problems.[356] Chapter 3 and the Archytan chapter 9 share a supposition of the circle as a shape depending on a substratum of rectilinear elements in combination. In chapter 3, this shape is the result of the smoothing and rebalancing of forces bound to one another and otherwise tending toward disequilibrium. The disequilibrium is made explicit in chapter 3, but this is the import also of proportionality being a form of equality in the naturalness of circular growth for Archytas.

---

356 Aristotle's reference in *Movement of Animals* 1 to those who fictitiously make mathematical objects move (καὶ γὰρ τὸ κινεῖσθαι, ὥς φασί, πλάττουσιν ἐπ'αὐτῶν) may be a reference to Archytas and his procedures (698a25–26). The immediacy in the wording "as they say" (ὥς φασί), taken in the context of what precedes it, may mean he has taken the simple diagram he has just presented from these mechanicians.

I take this proportion to signify in the physical situation a "second" balance, because it is a balance by which a body retains equilibrium in motion despite the disparate natural tendencies of its contributing movements. I have argued that recourse to rectilinear elements within or around circles as making up the proportion is built into the very claim that a proportion governs circular motion. Chapter 3 is about forced locomotion, while chapter 9 treats growth. This shows some account of leverage was at the time of Archytas and the writer of chapter 3 already a crossover principle—a principle applied analogically. Its application in *Physical Problems* XVI to different kinds of motion, locomotion or growth, mirrors Aristotle's untroubled use of leverage as explanatory in the host of different kinds of change within the animal body. Given the background of the moving radius principle in kinesthetic awareness and simple machines, it is quite possible that this universal application of leverage experiences antedated the mathematical version of the principle clearly expressed in Plato's *Laws* and Aristotle's *On the Heavens* and *Movement of Animals*. The mathematical principle was not *applied* to new situations of motion. It began as a commonality noticed in experience of many natural phenomena and was refined by the mathematical formulation.

As providing a context for the natural philosophy of Aristotle himself, *Physical Problems* XVI offers both unsettling differences from what are taken to be standard doctrines of Aristotle and shafts of new light on the meaning of some doctrines. The biggest question about *Physical Problems* XVI in relation to Aristotle's more frequently treated works of natural philosophy concerns the composition of circular motion. In *Physics* and *On the Heavens*, there is hardly a doctrine stated more clearly nor marked as more fundamental than the doctrine of circular motion as simple, not mixed.[357] How is that Aristotelian starting point related to what seems a very different treatment of natural circular motion in *Physical Problems* XVI? One answer would be that this part of *Physical Problems* is late and that Aristotle's school has strayed quite far in its school discussions from the master's approach.[358]

---

357 *On the Heavens* 1.2, 268b17–24; *Physics* VIII.8, 261b28–29.

358 Studies by which a contrast of the philosophy of mathematics of Books XV and XVI might be made are Mayhew, "*Problemata* 15" and Acerbi, "*Problemata* XV–XVI." Mayhew analyzes manuscript evidence for titles of Book XV and compares the view of mathematics and astronomy expressed there to Aristotle's. Acerbi also treats primarily Book XV and evaluates terminology and the nature of the mathematical arguments. He briefly compares XV.5 and XVI.3 with respect to the issue of uniform velocity (137–138).

The materials of *Physical Problems* XVI suggest another answer. A key to the issue of circular motion as simple or composed is weight. In *On the Heavens*, Aristotle understood weight to be the tendency of any body made of earth to move toward the center of the universe.[359] Weight would be continually present as this downward drag in any state of affairs where natural materials figure. Weight seems to have had a different Aristotelian life history, however, in the literature stemming from understanding of the balance and lever. We have already seen that this understanding finds its way into some of the traditional natural philosophy texts of Aristotle. It is not something new with the author of *Mechanics*. In this context, weight is one factor in a system in which the force (*rhopê*) of weight is modified by other factors, like length of a rod, a balancing weight, a glancing blow to a body, or unequal tendencies to motion belonging to different parts of a magnitude. *Physical Problems* XVI is a model for this treatment of weight in system. The principle of proportionality, whether submerged or clearly expressed in these chapters, is a principle of conservation of force in a system. Weight acts like force in a relation of opposition with another weight all within a thrown object. As in *Physical Problems* XVI.11, even the air around the projectile may figure in the calculus of forces in balance. As in chapter 9, the constraints may not be weight but other tendencies productive of different kinds of change than locomotion. It is important to carry the results of this investigation of *Physical Problems* XVI into the more traditional corpus of Aristotle's natural philosophy, in particular his *Physics*. First, however, we should finish the story of the proportion that picks out arcs of different circles that are covered in the same time. This is the general problem of determining speeds of different-sized wheels that are turning together by virtue of contact or sharing a common axis.

---

359   *On the Heavens* IV.1, 308a14–17; IV.3, 310b3–5; IV.4, 311a18–24.

Chapter 8

The Maturity of Kinematics in the Aristotelian *Mechanics*

Physical Problems XVI and Mechanics 1

One of the most important things to come out of the analysis of *Physical Problems* XVI is a historically grounded interpretation of the meaning of "proportion of equality" for Archytas. In seeking sameness of ratio for circular growth, it would be reasonable to compare (*a*) successive additions of new growth (additions to a radius), or (*b*) segments of chords within a growth circle that are tangents to earlier growth rings. No sameness of ratio for growth was forthcoming, however, by comparing ratios of *any* additions to a radius or ratios of successive tangents to earlier growth rings. Both modes of comparison are too broad to determine whether there is any proportion, or following upon that, which ratios taken from larger and smaller circles constitute a proportion of equality for circular growth. The proportion would be expected to index the shape of growth or the magnitude of additions.

Nevertheless, one of the things sought—an explanation for the consistent shape of circular growth for a single curved body—is given by a specific ratio that takes an element from each of the two classes, additions to a radius and segments of a chord. The addition to the radius laid on by growth (distance *r*) enters into a ratio with the tangent to the smaller growth ring extended to some point on the larger ring (distance *s*) (**Figure 8.1**). For one pair of concentric circles, this ratio will be the same all around the two circumferences (**Figure 7.12** and **8.1**). Indeed, the ratio so taken would be consistent *for any pair* of concentric circles that are taken together. So, we have a precise proportion of equality from the size of one circle to the size of another larger one. One might contend that the different *r* to *s* ratios should not be distinguished by subscripts, since there is

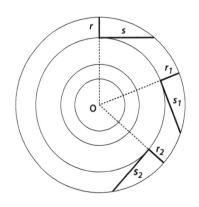

Figure 8.1

really no difference among them. They are the identical ratio and so not informative. In the context of explaining circular *growth or expansion*, however, that the ratio is identical for any point taken along the two rings is informative. This ratio will be the same between two points of growth whenever the shape of growth is circular.

This combination of *r* and *s* provides something like a 2-place function descriptive of circular growth. For any two circles the difference of whose radii constitutes an addition by growth, the function is a constant.[360] We must note, however, that the proportion of equality for circular growth of a single addition cannot accept multiples as proportions usually do, e.g.,

$$\frac{r_1}{s_1} \propto \frac{r_2}{s_2} \propto \frac{m}{n} \cdot \frac{r_2}{s_2},$$

and still remain a regular increase in circularity of the sort we see in tree rings. That is, there is no rule for the ratios of specific later pairs of rings being the particular ratio that held for an earlier pair of growth rings. This is a sign that the account of the proportion of equality gained from this reasoning is not generalizable to other applications of the moving radius, e.g., to the distances covered by opposite arcs of the beam of a lever.

Furthermore, there is not a reason for a *different set* of growth rings in a single tree trunk to have the ratio another set has. Accordingly, we *cannot* set the proportion $\frac{r_1}{s_1} \propto \frac{r_2}{s_2}$ equal to another ratio of distances between circles and chord lengths for the same circle. That is, the following proportions are not possible:

---

360 Its numerical value in a given system of measure remains the same for the two circles: $\frac{r_1}{s_1} \propto \frac{r_2}{s_2}$.

$$\frac{r_1}{s_1} \propto \frac{r_2}{s_2} \ \ldots \ \propto \frac{w_1}{x_1} \propto \frac{w_2}{x_2} \ \ldots \ ,$$

where the ratios come from any two sets of circles with the same center (**Figure 8.2**). To this extent, the proportion descriptive of the circular shape of growth is no better a guide to matching up ratios of arc-lengths than were the ratios composed solely of radius-segments or chords.

Nevertheless, it should be the case that *some other* ratios $\frac{radius\ segment}{segment\ of\ a\ tangent}$ from within the circle are in proportion with the original set (**Figure 8.3**). As we have seen, Aristotle knew that arcs covered in the same time were ones that shared two radii. From Figure 8.3, it is clear that the radius lengths (y and r) for a pair of circles do not automatically form a ratio with a tangent from the smaller circle to the larger ($\frac{r}{s} \propto \frac{y}{z+f}$), $z+f$ being the distance along the tangent to one circle to a point on the circumference of a larger circle with which it is paired. Rather, the ratios that are the same are $\frac{r}{s}$ and $\frac{y}{z}$. This is further indication that the present line of thinking about circular growth has reached a limit as a model for investigation of the le-

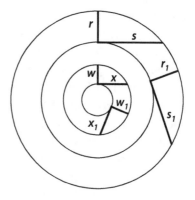

Figure 8.2

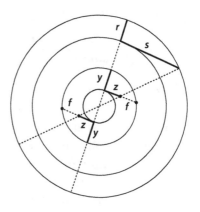

Figure 8.3

ver. The author of *Mechanics* makes no mention of the sharing of radii, perhaps because he is concerned with techniques in which effects of the lever are displaced through a succession of devices. He needs to compare arcs that may not be on the same center but are linked in some way. Accordingly, he seeks a proportion of lines as an index of arc distances covered. A generalizing account of why the proportion holds would make the correlation of arcs and rectilinear elements of the circle applicable beyond concentric circles—e.g., to transmission of effect by means of axles or gears, to calculations of the speed of a wheel given a particular magnitude of force exerted, or to the distance travelled in revolution by unbalanced projectiles. Put simply, giving a reason why would extend the kinematics of weight and force beyond the physical situation of either growth or the lever.

The argument of *Mechanics* 1 provides a way of finding ratios that are equal from *different* two-member sets of circles. To this extent, *Mechanics* 1 completes the winnowing argument traced in Chapter 7, the route of reasoning from Archytas to the Aristotelian author or compiler of *Physical Problems* XVI. There are passages of *Mechanics* 1 that point to a historical connection between it and the winnowing argument presented in Chapter 7. One comes at the end of the passage where the author of *Mechanics* 1 has established which arcs of different-sized concentric circles are covered in the same time (in **Figure 2.10** and **7.8b**). He takes the ratios of rectilinear elements, $\frac{r}{s} \propto \frac{y}{z}$, and alternates the proportion (849b4–9), so that the radius segment of one concentric circle is to the radius-segment of the other as are the perpendiculars from those circles dropped to the radius—i.e., $\frac{r}{y} \propto \frac{s}{z}$ in Figure 8.3. This is the proportion

$$\frac{radius\ segment}{radius\ segment} \propto \frac{segment\ of\ a\ tangent}{segment\ of\ a\ tangent}.$$

The alternation shows that, *once the algorithm is in place for picking out the correct rectilinear segments forming a proportion*—i.e., exactly which ratios of straight lines correspond to arcs covered in the same time—ratios of similar rectilinear elements *do* form a proportion. They simply must be drawn from the right concentric circles.

This concluding move could be simply a flourish added because the alternation is possible. Nevertheless, this is where we began—with ratios of *similar* elements—in considering what ratios would form a proportion so as to explain growth kinematically. The argument of *Mechanics* 1 is, to this extent, the final winnowing in a project that had begun much earlier. There is another clue in *Mechanics* 1 that supports the line of development I have sketched. It is the role played by the quadrant of a circle in the author's transition in *Mechanics* 1 from the parallelogram of movements to the geometry of the circle.

In the analysis of circular growth presented in my Chapter 7 as pre-dating the *Mechanics*, the quadrant was the single case in which ratios of radius segments and semi-chords to the radius would always be the same, regardless of which radii or tangents to the circle were taken. The quadrant could be considered the tautologous case, because the "chord" is simply another radius; the ratio of the two is always 1:1. In my own analysis, consideration of this case set up a *reductio* argument refuting that *any combination at all* of ratios of radius segments to chords for concentric circles would always be the same. Dealing solely with the materials of *Physical Problems* XVI, a route of reasoning that could finally eliminate unsuccessful combinations of ratios in favor of the single correct proportion of equality for compared circles remained obscure. The trail went cold. In *Mechanics* 1, consideration of the quadrant of a circle is a step in determining the correct proportion governing circular growth and also what arcs of different circles are covered in the same time in locomotion. We can now turn to examine the argument of *Mechanics* 1 in detail and see its relation to the line of thinking outlined so far.

The Demonstration of *Mechanics* 1

Briefly put, the argument of *Mechanics* 1 is this. Both rectilinear movement and movement in a circle, i.e., the distances covered in each case, can be characterized as a ratio of two other movements that are identified by straight lines. When these two movements are in the same ratio throughout a given time, the actual movement that takes place is rectilinear (848b11). When their ratio varies, the movement that takes place is not a straight line.[361] The author is especially interested in arcs of a circle, for which (he claims) the ratio of component movements is different, whatever segments of the arc one compares. Whether the movement is straight or circular, however, the author is able to specify rectilinear distances, constructible in a geometrical picture surrounding the movement, which provide the ratio for the two contributing movements.[362] Accordingly, the argument, though compressed, is systematic in

---

361 Contributor movements are not realized apart from their combination in a resultant movement. The author does not discuss how motions combine nor does he use the language of mixture. For the most part, he is careful to distinguish something moved or a line described by a moving object from the motion itself (φορά). Use of the cognate accusative, φέρεται δύο φοράς—moved with two movements—is typical.

362 In the case of circular motion, the continually changing ratio is meaningful because

that it establishes a common mathematical treatment for rectilinear and circular motion. In both cases, straight lines index or represent two movements, which are not realized separately in the case under consideration but which nevertheless contribute to an actual movement.[363]

There are three cases through which the author progresses in a short space:

1. movement in a straight line, whose ratio of surrounding equilateral sides remains the same (848b11–24),

2. curvilinear (περιφερές) motion, where the ratio does not remain the same (b24–34), and

3. circular movement, a more specific case of curvilinear motion (848b34–849a6).[364]

The transition from rectilinear to circular motion takes place in the passage cited in (3), where the author applies the parallelogram of movements model to the chord of a quadrant of a circle. Let us consider the three cases in order.

In his initial treatment of rectilinear motion, the author says that when the ratio of the two movements is the same, an object moves in a straight line (b12). He takes a distance traveled and makes it the diagonal of the quadrilateral (σχῆμα, τετράπλευρον) whose sides are straight lines (848b12–14, 20). Then, as in **Figure 8.4**, if A travels as far as Δ in its movement along AH, it has also gone as far as E, and the ratio $\frac{DZ}{EZ}$ is the same as $\frac{BH}{\Gamma H}$ (b16–19).[365] That the ratio of the sides meeting the diagonal remains the same all the way along the diagonal is a property of any

---

of its relation to the arc of a different but concentric circle. Because the context of explanation is the lever, the aim is to make a comparison of arc-distances on different circles. Arcs of circles covered in the same time will be those that have the same ratio of corresponding rectilinear elements for a given time taken. Accordingly, the fact that the ratio is continually changing in circular motion does not detract from the explanatory value of the account. On this point, see below.

363 On the argument of *Mechanics* 1, see articles by De Groot, "Modes of Explanation," and Schiefsky, "Structures of Argument."

364 Commentators are divided as to whether the term περιφερές must refer to circular motion or the more general case of curvilinear motion. For references, see the commentary of Bottecchia Dehò on 848b34 (*Problemi*, 148).

365 **Figure 8.5** is constructed by word with these Greek letters in *Mechanics*. It is the Aristotelian author's version of **Figure 7.8**.

parallelogram. The author expresses this by saying that the smaller parallelogram is similar to the larger (b19–20), and that the movement along the diagonal of the smaller is represented by a segment of the diagonal of the larger parallelogram (b21).
By making these points, the author shows that it is possible to contextualize *any* rectilinear motion as the diagonal of a parallelogram. The parallelogram of movements is a kinematic generalization. The author's approach thus opens an avenue for treating any movement in terms of a ratio

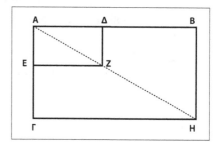

Figure 8.4

of element-motions contributing to it. He says it is impossible (*adunaton*) for motion to be in a straight line if there is no constant ratio for the sides of the constructed parallelogram (848b25–27). The first contrast the author makes, then, is between rectilinear and curved motion. Motion is curved when the two contributing motions do not form a consistent ratio for any time taken (b34).[366]

The generality of the argument he has given for sameness of ratio for any segment of a rectilinear movement makes the author sufficiently confident to offer a *reductio* argument against the proposition that any rectilinear movement could be composed from movements without the same ratio. He says that, if a line without a common ratio of the sort described were a straight line, when this line is taken as a diameter and the sides of a quadrilateral are expanded or filled out around it (παραπληρωθεισῶν τῶν πλευρῶν), the moving object would be moved in accordance with the ratio of those sides (848b29–30). Then, the rectilinear distance covered would both have and not have the same ratio for its different segments.

The terminology, παραπληρωθεισῶν, used by the author to describe construction of the sides of the parallelogram is interesting, because it is similar to terminology used by Euclid. In *Elements* I, prop. 43, Euclid speaks of parallelogram complements (παραπληρώματα) that fill out a larger parallelogram whose diameter has been cut at a point K, as in

---

366   The author's language, δύο φερόμενον φορὰς ἐν μηθενὶ λόγῳ μηθένα χρόνον (848b34), seems to rule out that a curve is composed of a series of very short straight lines. Any curvilinear line, whether irregular, elliptical, circular, etc., would be characterized in the same way in terms of its ratio of components *always* varying from one segment to another.

Figure 8.5.[367] By drawing lines to two sides of the parallelogram from this point, two smaller parallelograms, AEKH and KGCF, are constructed within the larger one. At the same time, there are created additional parallelograms, the complements EBGK and HKFD, which have areas equal to one another. The complements are, as Heath puts it, "figures put in to fill up (interstices)."

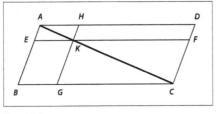

Figure 8.5

Heath comments that the terminology—παραπληρώματα, complements—"implies that the complements as well as the other parallelograms are 'about' the diagonal."[368] That is, the diagonal is the focal element around which figures internal to the parallelogram are created and other lines within the parallelogram are brought into relation. Something like this—filling out a geometrical context around a diagonal—is the procedure of the author of *Mechanics* 1 in constructing the parallelogram of movements. The movement taking place or accomplished is first placed as a diagonal, and then the sides of the parallelogram corresponding to that diagonal are instrumental to the presentation of the movement as a ratio.

The author of *Mechanics* uses the terminology of complementarity loosely in comparison to Euclid.[369] The sides of the parallelogram are filled out, not areas, and the only smaller parallelograms considered are similar parallelograms constructed along shorter segments of the diagonal. Nevertheless, the term yields insight into the geometric method of the author and his kinematic conception of motion. Movements are given by their distances completed. We place a movement, known in this way, within a geometric figure and then take cuts of that distance, now under-

---

367   *Elements* I, prop. 43: "In any parallelogram the complements of the parallelograms about the diameter are equal to one another." If ABCD is a parallelogram, as in **Figure 8.5**, with diameter AC, and AC is cut at K, then EH and FG are parallelograms, and complements BK and KD are equal to one another.

368   Heath, *Elements* 1, 340–341.

369   The relation between *Mechanics* and Euclid's *Elements* is a matter of conjecture. The similarities noted here are consistent with Heiberg's view (reported by Krafft in *Betrachtungsweise*, 91) that *Mechanics* was written before Euclid had made mathematical terminology technical and consistent. The author of *Mechanics* may have been familiar with theorems and methods that went into the *Elements*, however.

stood as a diameter. Additional geometrical properties are brought into relief by lines related to the cut.

Having shown in this way that a rectilinear movement always has a consistent ratio, the author turns to circular motion. He says it is clear that from these things,[370] i.e., from the contrast of a consistent ratio for distance covered versus a ratio that changes, *a line describing a circle is moved with two motions*. Why is this clear? It seems that, if every movement either has or lacks the sameness of ratio characteristic of the sides of the parallelogram constructed around the movement, then it must be possible to characterize a true circular arc or even an irregular curve in terms of this model of two motions and sameness or lack of sameness of ratio. So we must be able in some way to test the curve by the parallelogram of movements. This is the point at which the author turns to the quadrant of a circle, building rectilinear elements around it.

He offers further support (καὶ ὅτι) for the composition of curved motion from the fact that a point borne in a straight line "arrives at a perpendicular (*katheton*), so that it is again perpendicular to the center" (849a1). This sentence has presented considerable problems of interpretation throughout the history of *Mechanics*.[371] To understand it, the sentence must be taken together with what follows:

> That the line describing a circle moves with two motions simultaneously (φέρεται δύο φορὰς ἅμα) is obvious from these considerations, and because what moves along a straight line (κατ'εὐθεῖαν) arrives at a perpendicular, so that it is again (πάλιν) perpendicular to [a line drawn] from the center (ἀπὸ τοῦ κέντρου κάθετον). Let ΑΒΓ be a circle, and let the endpoint Β [of a radius] (τὸ δ'ἄκρον τὸ ἐφ'οὗ Β) be moved to Δ; it arrives sometime (ἀφικνεῖται δέ ποτε) at point Γ; if it moved in the ratio of ΒΔ to ΔΓ, it would move along the diagonal ΒΓ. But, as it is, seeing that

---

370 φανερον ἔκ τε τούτων καὶ . . . (848b36).

371 My reading follows the text of both Apelt and Bottecchia Dehò. The latter claims that the problem is not that the text is corrupt but that the meaning intended for *katheton* is not entirely clear. *Katheton* is ambiguous between "perpendicular to" and "tangent." See her commentary in *Problemi*, 148–149. My analysis gives at least one reason for the ambiguity in the term and also a reason why the ambiguity would be retained by the author of *Mechanics* and regarded by him as unproblematic. For more on the diversity of meanings taken for the passage, see below.

it moves in no ratio, it travels along the arc ΒΕΓ (τὴν ἐφ᾽ ἧ ΒΕΓ).[372] (848b35–849a6) (**Figure 8.6**)

Forster translates τὸ δ᾽ἄκρον τὸ ἐφ᾽οὗ Β as "a point above the center," so that the πάλιν signifies a return to that position on the circumference.[373] This translation provides a coherent picture of motion constrained throughout a cycle of radius movement. To achieve this meaning for the passage, however, Forster omits κατ᾽εὐθεῖαν, when there is not a good textual basis for excising it. Furthermore, there is not a clear-cut reference in the text to motion returning to a particular point. The πάλιν may mean something else in the passage. One question has been—to which straight line does the author refer when he says, "what moves along a straight line arrives at a perpendicular" (848b36)? Candidate straight lines are ΒΔ, ΔΓ, or the diagonal ΒΓ.[374]

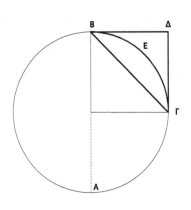

Figure 8.6

It is most likely that the straight-line movement is along ΒΔ, since the author refers directly to

---

372   As many have noted, the diagram accompanying this text in the Loeb edition (Hett, *Minor Works*, 341) is not to be relied upon. Bottecchia Dehò reproduces the variety of diagrams that have accompanied the text of the passage or its interpretation (*Problemi*, 150–151). Her text and translation includes Van Cappelle's diagram, as does Apelt's text and my own interpretation.

373   His translation reads, "and because the point from being vertically above the center comes back to the perpendicular, so as to be again perpendicularly above the center" (*CWA* 2, 1301). The movement of B is thus along the circumference of the circle, completing a full circuit. Hett keeps κατ᾽εὐθεῖαν and understands the passage as introducing two straight-line movements that represent "a balance of centripetal and centrifugal forces" (*Minor Works*, 341). Bottecchia Dehò translates the passage so as to refer to two tangents to the circle, at B and at Γ (*Problemi*, 65). Krafft takes the rectilinear movement to be from B to Δ (*Betrachtungsweise*, 25).

374   It seems unlikely to be the rotating radius itself, since the phrase κατ᾽εὐθεῖαν refers not to displacement of a line from one location to another but to a type of line or to the path generated by movement of an endpoint. Reading ἐπ᾽ εὐθεῖαν would not significantly change the meaning. Contrast 848b15, in the parallelogram of movements passage, where the author says, "Let the line ΑΓ move toward B."

this line ("let the endpoint B be moved to Δ"). He constructs this line as a tangent with his description of the line concerned as *katheton*. From Δ, a second tangent to the circle can be constructed that touches the circle at Γ. It is possible that the author refers to this tangent, when he says, "it [the point moving from B] arrives sometime at Γ (ἀφικνεῖται δέ ποτε ἐπὶ τὸ Γ) (849a4). On this interpretation, when he says something is once more (πάλιν) perpendicular to a line from the center, he has in mind the path of a point moving along ΔΓ to regain a position on the circumference.

It is important, however, that the author uses these perpendicular lines in the way he used segments of sides of the parallelogram earlier. Sides of the parallelogram provide the measure of the motion-elements of the actually occurring motion.[375] Similarly, in the case of circular motion, the author does not suppose that the point B is traveling the route of perpendicular lines. Rather, the lines BΔ and ΔΓ provide the ratio descriptive of the motion of B, if B moved along the straight line, BΓ, a chord of the quadrant. The author describes the path of B to Γ as a diameter (*diametron*), if its ratio is BΔ:ΔΓ (849a4). In this case, the path of the moving object is straight.

It is clear, then, that the reason for drawing a line to Δ outside the circle is to create, in the style of the parallelogram of movements, a complement to this diameter, the chord of the circle. The rectilinear trajectory of a moving point to which he refers at 848b36 may be BΔ—or it may be BΓ, the actual movement accomplished along a chord which can be described by the ratio of its constructed sides, BΔ and ΔΓ. The important point for interpreting the language of the passage is that an object moving from B—whether along the chord or the arc BEΓ—does indeed return to a tangent to the circle, i.e., a perpendicular to the radius at Γ (849a1).[376] This would be the meaning of πάλιν in the passage—returning to a tangent for the quadrant considered, not returning to the same point on the circle. This interpretation fits the contrast initially given by the author between movements characterized by a sameness of ratio for rectilinear movements versus movements having a ratio that is changing for non-lin-

---

375 Compare 849a3 to 848b15–17.

376 The author is concerned with an object that descends on a balance or a point on the circumference that commences moving. In the counterfactual case of that point moving in a straight line, we need not consider that the point remains the end of a radius, since a radius describes a curved path.

ear paths. In the spirit of his *reductio*, for whatever path the ratio keeps changing for the sides of a rectilinear figure constructed around the movement, that movement will not be a straight line.

This use of the quadrant might seem different from the quadrant as a special case of a ratio of radius segment and semi-chord presented in Chapter 7. The chord BΓ is not treated in *Mechanics* 1 as a tangent to any interior circle, though it could be so construed by constructing a new circle at the point where a radius bisects the chord.[377] The author is cast-

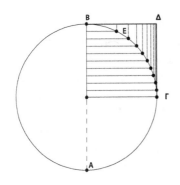

ing his eye backward to the parallelogram of movements he has just presented, not toward narrowing down the ratios of heterogeneous rectilinear elements of the circle that might qualify as the same. On the other hand, he does take advantage of the properties of a tangent to a circle in his contrast of the chord and an arc it subtends. The lines BΔ and ΔΓ give components of an actual motion. The question is whether the quadrilaterals constructible between B and Γ on the arc maintain the same ratio between the sides or vary. The author knows that they vary, because of his earlier *reductio* argument in favor of the parallelogram of movements. This could also be inferred from a construction like **Figure 8.7**.[378]

Figure 8.7

This passage, with its application of the parallelogram of movements to the chord of a quadrant, provides both continuity with the analysis of a straight line and also a sharp contrast to motion along the curve of the same quadrant. Importantly, ratios of component elements for the arc will

---

377 For bisection of a chord, see Euclid, *Elements* III, prop. 3.

378 Representing a component of motion was also the role the tangent played in the rationale, given in Chapter 7, for finding kinematic elements for circular growth (**Figure 7.13**). In that analysis, the quadrant was the limiting case (**Figure 7.12b**) in ruling out that any ratios at all taken from within the circle will correlate arcs covered in the same time. The quadrant is for the author of *Mechanics* also a limiting case. It has the demonstrative force of being the simplest case, the one where both components of motion can be taken as tangents. In that case, we are dealing with a single circle. For the purposes of rigorous argument, though, we would think it better not to use the square, which is a species of parallelogram. Because the square is a more specific case, it would jeopardize the demonstrative force of the argument as it is carried forward into the case of the circle.

be different for different points along the arc. This contrast by itself is broad and leaves circular motion in the same class kinematically as any sort of curved motion or even irregular paths of movement. As the author proceeds, he takes advantage of the mirroring inside the circle of rectilinear elements constructible outside it, which he has introduced with his analysis of the arc and chord of the quadrant. He makes his argument in terms of those elements inside the circle.

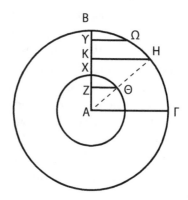

Figure 8.8

The argument that follows (849a36–b18) is the heart of the demonstration of the principle of the lever and it has two parts, both of which turn on discerning *which* ratios of rectilinear elements constructible within concentric circles form a proportion of contributing motions for circular motion. In the first part (849a29–b7), it is shown which rectilinear elements of circles being compared in fact cannot enter into a proportion. In the second part (849b7–18), it is shown which elements do have the same ratio.

Figure 8.8 is a drawing to which the author refers in the text.[379] In the drawing, X and B are endpoints of radii for smaller and larger concentric circles respectively. For arcs on concentric circles swept out by a single moving radius, the component of rectilinear forward motion is represented by a perpendicular (*kathetos*) dropped from the completion point of the arc movement to the radius taken at the starting position of the moving object—so, for the smaller circle, for instance, from Θ on the circumference to Z on the vertical radius. As representing a rectilinear component of arc-movement, this distance could also be a tangent to the smaller circle at X. As a tangent, it would more readily model the force or push exerted at a point on a wheel or at the end of a balance. That the author understands ΘZ as a force exerted at the perimeter is clear in this passage and in the applications of the principle, which follow in *Mechanics*. It is important to note, however, that as a tangent, ΘZ would not extend

---

379   This drawing is equivalent to **Figures 2.10** and **7.8b**. It is presented here with all the linear components and Greek lettering of the text of *Mechanics* in order to aid readers following the Greek text.

all the way to the correlate outside circle, a construction that was important in reasoning about circular growth. Instead, the perpendicular extends outward to the circumference of *its own* circle. The length of the tangent/perpendicular is regulated by this, and by the length of the radius segment taken. As mentioned before, this difference—the tangent does not reach to the outer circle—is an important departure from the Archytan context. It is certainly one that would obscure the pre-history of the achievement recorded by the author of *Mechanics* 1.

The perpendicular ΘZ drawn within the circle divides the radius of the smaller circle into two segments, AZ and ZX. The segment ZX will turn out to be the measure of constraint exerted by the rigid beam itself in keeping the movement of its ends tending inward. The author does not point this out immediately, however. Instead, he shows that there can be the same component of motion for the larger circle, ΩΥ, which corresponds to ΘZ.

Being equal, the lines ΘZ and ΩΥ contribute to some arc-movement on their respective circles. YB and its correspondent on the smaller circle, ZX, are taken to represent the amount of constraint toward the center undergone by B and X in moving to Ω and Θ respectively, when the bodies at these positions are moved with the same tangential motion. These two components have correlates outside the circle and so could be represented in terms of a parallelogram of movements (**Figure 8.4**). The author says B is drawn less toward the center. The reason he gives, however, is simply geometrical: "For (*gar*), equal lines extended from unequal circles perpendicularly to the diameter, cut a shorter segment of the diameter for the larger circles" (849a36–b1). The construction shows that the effect of constraint is less for the larger circle, because YB is shorter than ZX (849a36). The author takes this to be the reason that arcs BΩ and XΘ will not be distances covered in the same time. In seeking to understand the argument of *Mechanics* 1, emphasis has often been placed on interpreting the dynamic notions of force and constraint. The idea of constraint mainly contributes, however, to ruling out a length as suitable for the ratio sought.

The comparison of YB and ZX is itself only mediate to the author's aim, however, and here the second part of the argument begins. The problem is which rectilinear components of the circle provide a ratio descriptive of actual movement and of arc-movements covered in the same time. If BΩ and XΘ are not arcs covered in the same time, this is because the

234

movement at the perimeter is equal but the constraint toward the center is not the same. So there is no proportion between the ratios of these motion-elements for each circle. In fact, in the time a point moves along the arc XΘ on the smaller circle, a point moving along the circumference of the larger circle will have reached H (849b7). So, the appropriate motion-element entering into the ratio for the larger circle will be KH. And the motion-element of constraint is appropriately larger too. It is KB (b12). One thing of interest about this account is that constraint, as a cause of motion, has now effectively ceased to be an issue of interest, since even a faster movement has a larger component of constraint. The gist of the argument remains the taking of ratios of lengths. What matters is choosing motion-elements, representable as straight lines in some geometrical framing scheme, that will yield a sameness of ratios for arcs covered in the same time.

The author has pointed out in his treatment of the quadrant that the ratio of rectilinear elements for the arc will be always changing. Now, however, he has isolated which rectilinear elements will, at each moment of the arc movements, be the same for arcs covered in the same time. Even continual change has its regularity, when the change is circular motion. The claim for a proportion across arcs for ratios that vary continually is the heart of the author's argument and is not unconvincing taken in its own kinematic terms. The segment KB of the diameter AB, cut off by dropping a perpendicular to AB from the end of an arc, approximates the difference between a rectilinear movement originating at B and the curved motion BH that in fact is accomplished. It accounts for the element of curvature toward the center. The perpendicular KH represents another contributor to arc-movement, the product of a force exerted at point B on the circumference.

KH has been constructed by a method similar to that of *Elements* I, prop. 43, drawing lines from a point on the actual path of movement to the figure constructed around that path. The measures of constraint—ZX, YB, and KB—are like complements too, lines filled out around the actual path of a point along the circumference. This approach is a conceptual advance over the way of thinking about the composition of circular motion or growth that was outlined in Chapter 7. It is more comprehensive, bringing the puzzles of leverage into a coherent frame for problem solving. Nevertheless, this method of filling out complements around an arc-distance works upon all the same materials involved in analyzing circular growth and revolution in projectile motion: straight lines essential to the circle (radii and their segments) or those constructible with reference to the circle (tangents and chords perpendicular to a radius). The aim is to find a proportion descriptive of a continually changing set of ratios. Insofar as the value of the proportion continually changes, this is a true problem of mechanics, the science of motion.

As pre-figured in the original question about circular growth, the ratios have to involve two circles. The author of *Mechanics* has not produced a formula for constancy of ratios of travel along a single circumference taken alone. This was already accessible (**Figure 7.12**), and the author of *Mechanics* builds upon it. Explanation of the lever does need different sized arcs lying opposite one another. The dual circles of this account contrast markedly to the single path analyzed in the parallelogram of movements, and this feature has made modern understanding of the argument elusive. The dual circles are, nevertheless, the most prominent indication that Archytas' problem of circular growth was already understood as one with analysis of the lever and balance. The association, made by the writer or compiler of *Physical Problems* XVI, of the revolution of an unbalanced body with Archytas' proportion of equality for growth reinforces that these problems belonged together in the time after Archytas and up to the writing of *Mechanics*.

The Scholarly Context

I have treated the argument of *Mechanics* 1 as a kinematic account without yet giving much attention to the author's references to force (*ischus* or *dunamis*) and to constraint (*ekkrousis*) toward the fulcrum or center of the circle (849a6–14, 18–20). This is because the author's reasons for the proportion governing similar arcs derive from the geometry of the circle (e.g., 849a2–6, a23–b4). The kinematic aspect of *Mechanics* 1 is the coherent and systematic account in the text. The dynamic aspects of the text are weaker and under-conceptualized. Indeed, the chapter presents two different accounts overlaid as the continuous text from 849a36–b16 shows. The central account treats of movements as distances covered in a time, with these distances related geometrically. Overlaid on this kinematic account is an explanation in terms of impulse or force (*ischus*) and constraint (*ekkrousis*). The fundamental notions of the dynamic account, force and constraint, do not contribute to a coherent theory that incorporates the kinematic account.[380]

The author of *Mechanics* 1 introduces force and constraint immediately before his presentation of the correct governing proportion for
movement of the balance or lever. The author thus departs briefly from
his kinematic account and then returns to it (849a6–22). He considers the
case of two things moved by the same force but deflected in their movement by a constraint. When one is deflected (ἐκκρούοιτο) more and the
other less, it is reasonable that the one deflected more moves more slowly
(849a7–9). This is the case, he says, with larger and smaller concentric
circles:

> For, on account of the extremity of the lesser radius being
> nearer the stationary center than that of the greater, being as it
> were pulled (ἀντισπώμενον) in a contrary direction, toward
> the center (ἐπὶ τὸ μέσον), the extremity of the lesser moves
> more slowly. This happens in every [movement] describing a
> circle, and [the extremity] moves naturally along the tangent
> (εἰς τὸ πλάγιον) and unnaturally towards the centre. And the
> lesser radius is always moved more in respect of its unnatural
> motion; for being nearer to the retarding centre it is more con-
> strained.[381] (849a11–20)

The end of the radius is drawn more toward the center in the case of the
smaller circle, because it is nearer the center (a11–12, 18–20). The author
calls this "as it were being pulled in the contrary direction"[382] (though the
deflection in fact operates along the normal to the projected tangential
motion). To say the nearer point is drawn more toward the center introduces a physical reason why a smaller circle moves more slowly. Indeed,

---

380 For a definition of kinematics as contrasted with dynamics, see Clagett, *Science
of Mechanics*, 163. Kinematics "studies movements taken in themselves, i.e., the spatial
and temporal aspects or dimensions of movement without any regard for the forces which
engender changes of movement" (163). Kinematics relies on geometry but treats lines and
arcs as trajectories of movement. Meli believes that the distinction between kinematics
and dynamics does not serve us well for understanding mechanics before the nineteenth
century (*Thinking with Objects*, 8). Martínez, following Ampère, argues that kinematics
has been neglected as a distinct branch of physical science and that this neglect obscures
important aspects of the history of mechanics (*Kinematics*, ch. 1). I have been presenting evidence that a kinematic treatment of movement made an important contribution to
Aristotle's way of thinking about nature.

381 This is Forster's translation in *CWA* 2, 1301, slightly altered.

382 ὥσπερ ἀντισπώμενον εἰς τοὐαντίον (849a12).

the deflection toward the center is called contrary to nature (*para phusin*) (849a17), while the motion at a tangent to the circle is in accordance with nature (*kata phusin*). This contrast holds, even though movement in accordance with nature is the result of a push or external inducement. The author uses the language of force again, in saying that the end of the shorter radius is dominated or influenced to a greater extent (κρατεῖται μᾶλλον) by the constraint toward the center (849a19). We could say this is why it describes a tighter curve. Constraint outweighs tangential motion, keeping the path described nearer the center.[383]

This passage is often treated as a straightforward enunciation of forces as causes of two different kinds of movement. One force is a push (*ischus* or *dunamis*) at the periphery and the other is a pull toward the center. Yet how would a force of constraint located at the center of the circle aid a *physical* explanation of the lever? First, how does a point, the center of the circle, constrain movement, since points have no power?[384] Surely, it is something about the rigid beam of the lever that does the constraining. If we geometrize the beam as a radius with points, why not consider any point along the beam as an origin of constraint? The answer, of course, is that the author's account continues to be grounded in a geometrical treatment of a circle with one center. But in that case, again, the natural direction of explanation would proceed *from* a correlation—centripetal force as a function of distance from the center—to the fact and degree of constraint, rather than the other way around.[385] To place em-

---

383 The passage quoted above is open to interpretation in its first sentence. The hypothetical clause beginning "as it were" (ὥσπερ) could be read as translated so that the center is understood as a focal point of pull toward itself. Transferring the ἐπὶ τὸ μέσον, "toward the center," to the following sentence, it could be read to say that the smaller circle moves more slowly toward the center because of its motion contrary to nature. On the second reading, being under a greater influence of constraint, the end of the shorter radius moves more slowly. But why would a greater constraint make the extreme of the near radius move more slowly toward the center? It seems it could just as easily make it move faster, for otherwise it would fall into the center. Forster, Hett, and Bottecchia Dehò all translate the passage so that the phrase in question goes with the ὥσπερ clause: "as it were being pulled back in the opposite direction *toward the center*." The best interpretation is that constraint is an impediment to natural motion, the rectilinear movement along the tangent and away from the circle, and this is why a point or segment of the nearer circle moves more slowly. In either construal, however, there are problems with making the passage an analysis of the circle in dynamic terms, i.e. in terms of forces.

384 Aristotle says that the poles of the earth do not have power because they are points. See *Movement of Animals* 3, 699a20–21. Additionally, in *On the Heavens* III.1, 299a27, points are said to have no weight.

385 Aristotle takes this approach, speed a function of distance, in the passages from

phasis on force or constraint as the explanatory elements in the account strains the credibility of the text itself.

A resolution of the meaning of constraint and force in the text is perhaps found in the fact that the words are always embedded in a context where *movements* in accordance with or contrary to nature are treated as causal. This does not come through clearly in Forster's translation, since he uses the word "radius," which has no exact parallel in the text, to translate phrases where the feminine appears without a governing noun: e.g., πάσῃ μὲν οὖν κύκλον γραφούσῃ and ἡ ἐλάττων. Either line (*gramma*) or movement (*kinêsis*) could be intended. It seems most likely that the author intends *kinêsis*, in which case we read:

> This happens in every movement that describes a circle, and [the extreme] moves on the one hand naturally and on the other hand contrary to nature, to the side and to the center. But the movement of the smaller is always moved to a greater extent with the motion contrary to nature. (849a14–16)

The reiteration of movement words and use of the cognate accusative ("being moved with a motion") in the last sentence is common in Aristotelian texts. This reading shows to what extent the author is thinking in terms of combining movements not forces. The extremity of a radius drawn more toward the center is the one moving to the greater extent with a contrary-to-nature movement generated by and along the beam as a whole. Any radius is simply moving with two movements that have different directionality. It is reasonable that the effect of motion *para phusin* diminishes with distance from the immobile fulcrum around which revolution takes place, since the experience and observation is that concentric circles more distant move with a greater speed than interior ones. Casting movements in geometrical terms provides a kinematic rationale for this. It is possible, then, to understand constraint without supposing the geometric center of the balance to possess or to be the center for some sort of force.

Nevertheless, these dynamic notions have been a focus of interest for those wishing to place this first surviving treatise of mechanics as part of the history of mechanics that includes Galileo and Newton. In interpreting *Mechanics* 1, De Gandt places emphasis on the notion of constraint

---

On the Heavens II.8 and 10 already cited.

(*ekkrousis*) in the author's decomposition of circular motion into rectilinear components. This analysis of circular motion into component motions is the greatest achievement of *Mechanics*, he thinks, not surpassed until Huygens or Newton. Accordingly, he finds the central claim of the text—the assertion of a characteristic proportion for arcs of different-sized circles covered in the same time—to be less convincing than the claim that a combination of forces produces a resultant curved motion.[386] De Gandt says that, in *Mechanics*, the difference in velocities of larger versus smaller concentric circles is not taken as "un fait géométrique" since it is treated as requiring an explanation involving forces. The concept of force in the treatise is thus fundamental to the argument for De Gandt. Accordingly, the reference to the circle as the source of all mechanical marvels (847b16, 848a12) at the beginning of *Mechanics* is a rhetorical flourish and not the enunciation of a fundamental principle.[387] De Gandt's interpretation of *Mechanics* 1 is the centerpiece of his reevaluation of Duhem's brief but influential rendering, in his *Origins of Statics*, of the proportions presented by the Aristotelian author of *Mechanics*.[388] De Gandt's exclusion of the argument from proportionality is one way he defuses Duhem's reading of *Mechanics* 1. Let us consider in more detail the history of interpretation of *Mechanics* 1 to which De Gandt responds.

Duhem considered *Mechanics* as part of the pre-history of the science of statics, or equilibrium. He recognized that a proportion for movement was the aim of *Mechanics* 1.[389] Equilibrium resulted when no motion was produced. Importantly, he found in *Mechanics* a principle of motion that he believed to be present throughout Aristotle's natural philosophical works. This principle is that, for the same force acting on different bodies, the velocities imparted are inversely proportional to the weights of those bodies. Although this proportion of ratios, taken as a general law, is erroneous, he says, it allows for the following inference:

> Thus, two forces will be considered equivalent if, when
> moving unequal weights at unequal velocities, they cause

---

386 De Gandt, "Force," 123–124. The passage at issue is 849a31–849b15.

387 De Gandt, "Force," 119–120. I disagree with this thesis both in its devaluation of the argument by proportionality and in its making the concept of force fundamental to the import of *Mechanics* 1.

388 Duhem says more about aspects of Aristotle's dynamics in *Système du Monde* 1, ch. 4 and 6.

389 Duhem, *Origins*, 11–13.

the product of the weight times the velocity to have the same
value. (12)

This equivalence Duhem uses to interpret the geometrical proportions appropriate to the lever: "When the lever rotates about its point of support,
the two [unequal] weights move with different velocities. The weight fur-
thest from the point of support describes, during the same interval, a larger arc than the weight closest to the point of support (12)." The upshot is
that, to compare the effect of the two weights, one must compute for each
the product of the weight and the length of the arm of the lever. The one
with the greater product will descend. Duhem thus combines an account
of paths described by ends of the balance beam or lever with ideas of
weight and moment of force. Duhem's interpretation captures the co-variance that makes proportionality informative, but his rendering of it in
terms of a product of heterogeneous quantities (*force* ∝ *velocity* × *weight*)
is anachronistic.

Duhem is right, nevertheless, that the treatise introduces in a systematic way a principle applicable to nearly all mechanisms: "mechanicians
will be able to account for the various effects produced by these diverse
machines simply by considering the velocities with which certain arcs
of a circle are described" (12). Apart from its usefulness in relation to
machines, however, Duhem takes this formula, force is proportional to
velocity times weight, to be the historically first principle of rational mechanics, and so of great importance. He believes the principle is found
throughout Aristotle's physical treatises, including *Physics* and *On the
Heavens*, where it notably fails as a description of free fall, i.e., bodies fall
faster or slower in accordance with their greater or lesser weight.

Crucially, Duhem assumes that the forces or weights, the speeds and
times involved in movement are factors universally accessible in antiquity as in modern times. Aristotle really is talking about the elements of
mechanics. This is the chief point on which Carteron criticizes Duhem in
his comprehensive study of the notion of force in Aristotle.[390] Carteron
argues that notions of force (*ischus, dunamis, rhopê*) in Aristotle's treatment of motion—even of locomotion—are not independent of the type
of substance or body under consideration.[391] One indication of this is that
Aristotle says a greater body of fire will move more quickly upward. This

---

390 Carteron, *Notion de force*.

391 *Notion de force*, 21–22, 24.

is because fire possesses the quality of lightness not weight. A greater amount of a light body will have greater *dunamis* for movement, greater *rhopê* (actualized force of motion), and so greater speed.[392] Making use of a bit of explicative anachronism himself, Carteron says that force for Aristotle is a scalar quantity allied to some substance, a scalar "expliquant le movement réalisé, non la realization du movement" (22). This last comment pertains to Duhem's ascription of a rudimentary concept of work to the account of the movement of the balance in *Mechanics*. One need not produce change to know what would be accomplished by a particular combination of force with other elements. From this standpoint, one can also determine the conditions for equilibrium. The idea of virtual motion is especially important to an interpretation of *Mechanics* 1 as being about equilibrium, which was Duhem's great interest.[393] Carteron was emphatic that there is no Aristotelian statics. Aristotle did not make a distinction between statics and dynamics. For there to be an Aristotelian statics, Aristotle would have to discern in force some other function than producing speed.[394]

Duhem believed that the cogent principle he had found in *Mechanics*,

$$force \varpropto velocity \times weight,$$

was also enunciated in other works of Aristotle's natural philosophy. This claim gained credence from Drabkin's careful work on an array of passages in Aristotle's natural philosophy that have distinctive common features. In these passages, Aristotle uses letters to name different factors entering into motion—mover, moved thing, distance, time—and reasons by proportionality from changes in one of the factors to a corresponding change in another. For example, if the mover, or its force (*ischus*), is doubled, the mover will cover the same distance in half the time. If the resistance to movement is increased, the speed with which a body moves through the resisting medium will be proportionally decreased. Passages

---

392 *On the Heavens* I.8, 277b4, IV.4, 311a21; Carteron, *Notion de force*, 17.

393 There are two senses of virtual motion relevant to considering the influence of mechanics on Aristotle. The first is associated with the concept of work. The second is the idea of movement that is not realized in accordance with its own nature (e.g., a power of rectilinear motion) but that contributes to the actualization of another type of motion, e.g., curved motion. In this case, the rectilinear contributor is a virtual motion. This second sense of virtual motion is simpler than the first but is involved in explaining or defining work. For this reason to reject virtuality of motion in the first sense, work, often entails a commentator's rejecting the second as well.

394 Carteron, *Notion de force*, 13, 15.

sharing these features of analysis can be found in *Physics* IV.8, VII.5, and VIII.10, and in *On the Heavens* I.6 and 7, III.2, and IV.1.[395] From these passages, Drabkin culled what he called a "law of proportionality."[396] Cohen and Drabkin's *Sourcebook in Greek Science* is most closely associated with the claim that Aristotle developed a mathematical mechanics. Drabkin freely uses terms like "Aristotle's laws" of motion and the "equations of Aristotelian dynamics." He ascribes abstraction to the passages where Aristotle presents proportions of force, weight, distance, and time.[397]

In his landmark work, *Science of Mechanics in the Middle Ages*, Clagett cautiously endorses the line of thinking of Duhem and Drabkin. He treats *Mechanics* in terms of the later science of statics: "unlike the Archimedean treatises, it takes a dynamic approach to problems of statics."[398] By "dynamic" in this context, Clagett means that *Mechanics* treats *movement* of arms of the balance and lever as prior to an account of equilibrium. Most fundamentally, the velocity of a weight on a balance arm increases the longer the arm.[399] Clagett treats the geometrical argumentation of *Mechanics* 1 as "imprecise." There is nothing here approaching mathematical proof. Accordingly, Clagett explains motion along a circular arc as a function of the "continual interference with the tangential motion by the varying motion of constraint toward the center" (6). He highlights the notions of force and constraint but also focuses on the resulting paths of motion. Movement on the balance is a "constrained system" (5). This is a better formulation of the co-variance expressed in proportionality than Duhem's product of velocity and weight. As we have seen, the revolving unbalanced body presented in *Physical Problems* XVI is an ancient interpretation of the lever as a constrained system. Clagett, like Drabkin, culls proportionalities from the relevant passages to find an underlying "formula" of motion.[400]

---

395   See Drabkin's, "Laws of Motion," and Cohen and Drabkin, *Sourcebook*. For listings of relevant passages, see Drabkin's "Laws of Motion," and Carteron, *Notion de force*, 11–12.

396   Drabkin, "Law of Motion," 62.

397   Cohen and Drabkin, *Sourcebook*, 203–212. Drabkin responds to what he calls "Carteron's extreme view" in "Laws of Motion," 63–64.

398   Clagett, *Science of Mechanics*, 4.

399   Both Duhem and Clagett take the Archimedean principle of equilibrium as their reference point.

400   Clagett, *Science of Mechanics*, 432.

De Gandt grants a larger role to the concept of force in *Mechanics* 1 than does Clagett. He says that practically no treatise of astronomy before Kepler included notions of force, but force was always part of pre-modern mechanics.[401] De Gandt argues in particular against Duhem's claim that the principle enunciated in *Mechanics* 1 matches Aristotle's proportions of mover (force), moved thing (weight), distance and time in other treatises. He points out that the combination of velocity and weight together, which Duhem finds in *Mechanics*, appears first in the history of mechanics at the end of Hero's *Mechanics*. It is not even a first principle of that treatise. A conception approaching Duhem's is thus a late development of ancient mechanics.[402] As De Gandt sees it, the move from the parallelogram of movements in *Mechanics* 1 to an account of circular motion, which has no constant ratio, is accomplished by means of the introduction of notions of force. Differences in the velocity of circular motion "requiert une explication qui devra se placer sur un terrain dynamique: une même force obtient des effets différents" (120).[403] This mechanical *idea*—the same force produces different effects—is never approached in the passages treated as Aristotle's dynamics, he believes.

As can be seen from this brief survey of scholarship, the interpretation of *Mechanics* 1 became bound up with the fate of the "dynamics" believed to reside in Aristotle's narrative natural philosophy. Interpretation of different issues became entangled as the question assumed importance: did Aristotle have a dynamics worthy of comparison to early modern mechanics up to Newton? Aristotle's use of proportions in natural philosophy, the purpose of the passages that share a vaguely mathematicized form and content, the very meaning of the proportion special to *Mechanics* 1 became issues treated together.

Given this context, De Gandt undertook an important task as part of his interpretation, namely, the separation of the Aristotelian *Mechanics* from the group of dynamics texts in the traditional corpus. He analyzes two key passages, *Physics* IV.8 and VII.5, pointing out limitations of the

---

401   De Gandt, "Science des machines," 97.

402   This composed quantity, which Duhem dubbed power, *dunamis*, is not easily arrived at without the working through of mechanical ideas found only later in the Middle Ages and early modernity, De Gandt says ("Science des machines," 118). On this point, he agrees with Duhem, *Origins*, 13, and Drabkin, "Laws of Motion," 68–70.

403   In this passage, "dynamic" connotes forces acting as causes. "Dynamic" sometimes connotes simply an account in terms of movement, not stasis, and especially the combining of movements.

dynamical interpretation. In *Physics* VII.5, for instance, to reformulate the proportions in these passages in even the simplest modern notation tends to overstep the ancient proscription against direct comparison of heterogeneous quantities. Also, the proportions represented by letters are more like a template into which particular variations, e.g., of force and weight, can be fitted. The point of the proportions taken generally is simply the assurance that a proportion can be formed: "On se contente d'affirmer qu'il doit y avoir proportionnalité et donc rapport" (110). This commitment is fundamental in Aristotle and is allied with his commitment to order in nature. What De Gandt finds in *Mechanics*—a causal hypothesis of force and constraint opposing one another—he does not find in Aristotle's treatises on natural philosophy. The presence of these mechanical ideas in *Mechanics* 1 signals, De Gandt says, the inclusion of *Mechanics* in a different tradition, founded in practical problems and the construction of machines.

De Gandt's position on the dynamics passages could be placed in the line of commentary on Aristotle's dynamics initiated by Carteron. The trend of recent English language scholarship has been toward the interpretative stance of Carteron, not Drabkin.[404] This has to do partly with G. E. L. Owen's refutation of Drabkin on a number of points. Drabkin proved especially vulnerable with respect to his claim that Aristotle engages in an abstraction of mathematical physics that isolates weight, force and a homogeneous resistant medium. Owen points out that in *Physics* VIII.10 and *On the Heavens* I.7, the *dunamis* Drabkin translates as "force" Aristotle understands to be the power responsible for any kind of change (heating, sweetening, etc., as well as pushing) and specific to that change, whatever it is.[405] If these passages define *dunamis*, they define it not quantitatively, Owen says, "but so as to cover any alteration in any quality."

An exception to this trend away from a dynamical interpretation of the passages is Hussey, who speaks of "Drabkin's pioneering work" and who himself reassesses the passages.[406] He formulates Aristotle's proportions in *Physics* VII.5 to say that the power of an agent is (*a*) inversely proportional to the time of a change, (*b*) in direct proportion to the weight moved, and (*c*) in direct proportion to the amount of the change, e.g., distance covered. Hussey also provides a sketch of how the parallelogram

---

404 See, for instance, Wardy, *Chain*, and Berryman, *Mechanical Hypothesis*.

405 Owen, *Mechanics*, 321.

406 Hussey, "Mathematical Physics," 215–217.

of movements of *Mechanics* 1 could be integrated into an understanding of power consistent both with Aristotle's dynamical passages and with a common sense part of Newtonian physics to which Aristotle's insights run parallel. I will return to Hussey's interpretation in the next chapter.

Drabkin's search for laws of motion was undertaken in an atmosphere of early twentieth century philosophy of science that understood physics as the model for all sciences. Deduction from laws or law-like statements was the paradigm of adequate science. Certainly, Drabkin would be wrong to interpret *ischus* and *dunamis* too much along the lines of Newtonian force. Whether Aristotle pioneers a dynamic conception of power in his natural philosophy remains an interesting question, however. A dynamic conception would understand power in terms either of movement (not equilibrium) or causes of movement, or of the two together. If Aristotle has a dynamic conception of motion, the modern notion of work is the more likely avenue than force for an accurate interpretation of his natural philosophy in mechanical terms.[407]

To argue that there is an Aristotelian dynamics in *Physics* IV.8, VII.5 and similar passages is not at all my brief in the present context. I would wish, like De Gandt, to separate Aristotle's so-called laws of motion from the meaning and import of *Mechanics* 1. I have not found it possible, however, to effect a clear and complete separation of the dynamical passages in the traditional corpus and *Mechanics* 1. The questions to be addressed for the dynamical passages are these: Do these passages have a common aim? What makes them seem to share elements with modern dynamics? I would begin a reply to these questions by pointing out that there are at least four different things at work in these passages.

First, some passages do contain a genuine claim about the mathematical properties of motion. This claim is both supported by and consistent with the principle presented in *Mechanics* 1. The simplest formulation of this claim is that the same force, action, or impetus produces different effects on different bodies or in different circumstances. This feature was highlighted by both Duhem and De Gandt. Just as important as the

---

407 Scientists in the post-Newtonian tradition of mechanics regarded the concept of force as problematic. Physical ideas of d'Alembert and Lagrange were developments of the kinematic aspect of mechanics, which revealed that there was no sharp boundary between statics and dynamics. It should be noted that to associate Duhem with Drabkin in the interpretation of Aristotle's mechanics would be a mistake. This is because Duhem is thinking more in terms of the limitations of the force concept, while Drabkin seeks to clarify the notion of force in Aristotle.

statement of the variation, though, is what Aristotle makes of it, particularly with respect to similarity in excess, defect, or equality. As Chapter 9 will show, what lies behind the analysis of movement in Aristotle's physics is a dynamic analysis of the balance. Different effects stem from differences in weight or position of a body in a pattern of interacting bodies.[408] Indeed, Aristotle cannot account for differences in speeds without recourse to other bodies affecting or modifying the action of a mover.

In the collection of passages at issue, however, this principle usually appears in the context of a more fundamental analysis by Aristotle of the very possibility of change. Almost every passage includes a foundational analysis of continuity that is without mechanical content. These passages instead demonstrate by example that magnitude, motion, and time are all continuous and that the correspondence of continua precludes the infinite or nil from entering into proportion. This concern with how to rationalize change and exclude from it the infinite is the *second* and most important commonality in the collection of texts deemed Aristotle's dynamics.

Third, some of the passages directly address the quantities or non-quantitative analogates that can enter into change. In this context, the identity criteria for change and the parameters for distinguishing movements (*kinêseis*) from change taken generally (*metabolê*) are most prominent. This concern, like the second listed above, has the aim of clarifying conceptual foundations for change. For my purposes, it is the most important theme, since it introduces the question of the suitability of proportional reasoning for all types of change.

The *fourth* feature of these passages is Aristotle's use of letters to name the elements entering into the proportions that index variations in weight, applied force, distance covered, or time taken. His use of letters has reinforced the belief that these passages belong together and has encouraged their characterization in terms of abstraction or mathematical law. As much as I would like to explore this fourth feature of the passages under consideration, I will limit my efforts to clarifying the first three, as I argue that the influence of mechanics on Aristotle lies elsewhere than in laws of motion that involve force. The analysis of *Physics* VII.4–5 in particular is relevant in showing the

---

408 "System" might be a better word than "pattern," since Duhem is correct that a change in a feature of one body, weight or loss of acceleration means a proportional change somewhere else in the system. It would be misleading, however, to think system, for Aristotle, means being in possession of a wide-ranging set of related theorems of movement.

route to Aristotle's appropriation of mechanics in the ways I presented in Chapters 4–6.

In the next chapter, I will argue that, to account for Aristotle's conception of locomotion, we should not use the language of "laws" of motion but substitute instead the ideas of background knowledge or patterns brought to bear upon the explanation of particular phenomena.

Chapter 9

Did Aristotle have a Dynamics?

An Interpretive Frame

This chapter will examine the context of Aristotle's putative dynamics, or laws of motion, in several prominent passages. Three of the four aspects of Aristotle's concerns listed at the end of Chapter 8 are pursued in these passages:

1. the character of Aristotle's mechanical thinking,

2. his discussion of continuity, and

3. his criteria for comparing movements and establishing identity and similarity among movements.

It will be argued that Aristotle's mechanical thinking and his discussion of continuity are finally linked—but not by laws of motion. They are linked by a topological mode of thought that treats the lever principle as manifest differently in different situations of change.

"Topological" used in connection with Aristotle is usually a reference to his treatment of continuity in the different things involved in motion—magnitude, motion, and time.[409] Topology also concerns, however, properties preserved under continuous deformation of objects.[410] Aristotle

---

409 See, for instance, White, *Continuous and Discrete*, 7, 23.

410 E.g., a toros (a donut shape) by receiving just two cuts, one horizontal and one vertical, becomes a disk. It is important that continuous deformation can be effected in any number of dimensions. Though Aristotle is not treating surfaces or objects, he varies the

is very interested in issues of deformation but not deformation of objects or surfaces. He "deforms" the principle of the lever, producing transformations of a situation of change. Assuming the historical sequence is correct, we could say that once Aristotle found the moving radius principle fruitful for celestial mechanics and animal movement, he realized this was the way to understand forced and natural locomotion as well.

celestial

It has been seen already in Chapter 2 that the principle of leverage and its mathematical expression, the moving radius, are pleonastic in their appearances and that the ancients had no trouble recognizing the same principle in different contexts. We have also seen how the author of *Physical Problems* XVI.3 and 12 imagined in the revolution of an unbalanced thrown body something like a beam rotating about a "middle" within the projectile. In a similar way, Aristotle repackages leverage to apply to situations where forces or weights are changed or naturally vary. This strategy for understanding movement comes out of an acknowledgment of leverage as being a system in equilibrium. With respect to locomotion, we would say in modern terminology that Aristotle's deformation thinking involves four variables. Magnitude, force, weight, and time mutually diminish and increase in a system of movement where an overall equilibrium holds. This strategy for giving an account of movement is the subject of the first section of this chapter, "Multi-variant Analysis of Movement."

Aristotle thus introduces into the account of movement a mechanical principle involving several factors. Once acknowledged, it is clear that this implanting of a relatively plastic principle within different situations is one reason Aristotle would labor so assiduously to establish continuities that correspond among distance, force, weights, and time. Continuous increase and decrease of each of these factors is the condition for deformation that preserves equilibrium within a movement. Everything has to be on a sliding scale, so to speak. If the lever principle is present in different situations of change, then clearly one reason for Aristotle's correspondence of continua is to serve this physical conception of kinematic equilibrium. It is important, then, that there are two lines of discourse in Aristotle's thinking about mechanics, leverage talk and continuity talk. These lines of discourse are linked by the requirements of the deforma-

principle of leverage using usually two of three or four possible variables. It should be noted that deformation as a general mathematical term does not carry any negative connotation of distortion or denaturing.

tion strategy. The second section of this Chapter, "Continuum Reasoning Without Mechanics," lays out this link.

This section also considers the purpose and meaning of *Physics* VII.5, which is the centerpiece of Drabkin's interpretation of Aristotle's dynamics. It becomes clear that what Aristotle takes from Eudoxus' theory of ratio and proportion in *Physics* VII.5 and similar passages is general in import. Aristotle is most interested in the Eudoxan ratio's ability to define a continuum as such, so that there is no impediment to any correspondence at all of finite multiples or divisions of factors contributing to change.[411] Aristotle's interest in the shiphaulers in *Physics* VII.5 (many haulers move a ship though a single shiphauler does not move the ship at all) is his recognition of an unmitigated physical constraint upon the carrying through of mutual variation in these factors contributing to change. The considerations in this section, "Continuum Reasoning Without Mechanics," reinforce the deformation interpretation of Aristotle's kinematics presented in the immediately preceding section, Multi-variant Analysis of Movement.

Remarkably, Aristotle takes his strategy of deformation with equilibrium further than the analysis of locomotion. Recognizing in leverage a highly fruitful invariance leads Aristotle to treat change as a family of similar "subjects-with-structures." Change itself (*metabolê*) is one such subject.[412] So also, generation and alteration share the structure of "continuity plus a deformable invariance." This new direction for deformation thinking—working across *different* subject matters—makes the projected invariance more remote and even attenuated. The invariance is remote,

---

411   Since Aristotle usually gives specific multiples, even doubles or halves, of some factor contributing to change in order to track a covariance, we cannot suppose that he had in mind in his correspondences a continual ongoing deformation of some situation of change. His arguments from multiples and divisions presuppose there always being a finite cohort in distance or time taken for any change in force or weight. So, the continuity is important to guarantee equilibrium as a strategy. In some passages, however, Aristotle does consider continuous variation within a short span of time or movement. See the treatment of projectile motion in *Physics* IV.8 below.

412   This is a feature of a topology. The parent set includes itself as a subset. See Benke et al., *Fundamentals* 3, 2–3. The ill fit of set theory with the ancient *mathêmata*, geometry and mechanics, fosters caution about describing Aristotle's physical theory as topological. The comparison is nevertheless worth making, because continuity and leverage-equilibrium thinking in Aristotle turn out to have more in common than one might have thought. On the differences between Aristotelian and 19th–20th century formulations of continuity, see White, *Continuous and Discrete*, 179–187. White says, "Aristotle . . . does not accept the point-set ontology of continuous magnitudes" (33).

because in different subject matters, there are not factors common to different situations that, so to speak, wax and wane with deformation.

This extension of the strategy based on the lever thus presents new problems to solve. Aristotle needs a conception of pleonastic invariance that can be sustained without sameness of a subject matter and without a single recurring set of corresponding continua. In the terms of the *Categories*, sameness would be synonymy as to species or genus. In *Physics* VII.4, Aristotle seeks in the similar (*homoios*) a way to characterize a structural sameness, or a sameness of pattern, that is not synonymy.[413] In this project of conceptualization, Aristotle retains from the situation of leverage the equilibrium of diverse contributors to change, but the specific sort of balance characteristic of locomotion must drop out. The equilibrium of generation, for instance, is more like a tension between matter and form. The problem of extension of the deformation

---

413   Sameness is expressed by Aristotle with the word ταὐτό (pl., ταὐτά) a crasis from τὸ αὐτό (pl., τὰ αὐτά). Both singular and plural morphologies are frequent in Greek. The word means "the same thing(s)." Τὸ ἴσον, "the equal," has something of the import of ταὐτό in *Physics* VII, but Aristotle distinguishes it from equality, ἰσότης, which he limits to quantity. "Similar" is ὅμοιος, and "comparable" is συμβλητός. (For non-Greek readers, "the same" is *tauto* (*tauta*); "similar" is *homoios*; "the equal" is *to ison*, and "comparable" is *sumblêtos*.) Comparability connotes also mathematical commensurability, and ἀσυμβλητός is the word used for incommensurability of the diagonal and circumference of a circle.
It is important for *Physics* VII.4 that sameness need not mean things are identical as individuals or in species. One reference point for thinking about these issues in *Physics* VII.4, however, must be the *Categories*, since in *Physics* VII.4 Aristotle considers alternatives to change being just synonymous. There are clear differences among locomotion, alteration, generation, etc. (On this point, see *Physics* III.1. Change is in different categories but is not itself a category [200b31–201a9].) Aristotle treats sameness together with similarity in Book VII to the extent that we should sometimes read "similar" as "same." This is important, since sameness is considerably more consequential than similarity, which can be loose or strict depending on the criterion of similarity. Similarity is also subject to the "third man" problem. Proportions are not immune to the third man problem for similarity: the regress begins with the question by virtue of *what* the relation exemplified in one ratio is *like* the relation in another ratio. The regress is avoided by saying the relational structure is *the same*. One cannot say sameness of ratio is just similarity, because the Eudoxan proportion self-defines as a way of thinking same or equal. This places it as a mathematical conception, as qualitative mathematics. Aristotle's recourse to proportions for his physics is due to his awareness of this fundamental feature of approximative proportions. For more on sameness of ratio, see the last section of Chapter 10.
Aristotle treats criteria for the sameness of movement in *Physics* V.4, where he begins: "Movement is said to be one (μία) in many ways" (227b3). What is at stake in *Physics* VII.4–5 is the sort of adjectival one (the same) by which different kinds of change have one and the same principles. On one, same, and similar, see *Metaphysics* Δ.6 and 9. (I am grateful to an anonymous reviewer for suggesting the treatment of similar as same.)

strategy, particularly as it concerns similarity and sameness, is the subject of the section entitled Homonymy in *Physics* VII.

If the foregoing sketch of Aristotle's thinking is borne out in the textual argumentation that I draw together to support it, then to understand Aristotle on locomotion, we should not use the language of laws of motion but rather the idea of background knowledge, or an already known pattern, to interpret the passages involving lettered proportions that appear in Aristotle's physical treatises. Drawing on background knowledge, one discerns a well-known correlation appearing in new circumstances. For the moving radius principle and its repetition in lever phenomena and locomotion, I propose calling the pattern a "descriptive mode." From a philosophical standpoint, "description" and "mode" may not seem very content rich. A modular system, however, is one in which apparently different patterns are mapped upon one another, or seen to correspond, by means of a prime or lead pattern.[414] The word "descriptive" invokes the distinction between qualitative and quantitative mathematics. The qualitative in mathematics is the mathematical idea or concept. All mathematics involves the qualitative in this sense. Some areas of mathematics are entirely qualitative, because they do not deal with numbers or use numerical calculation.[415]

The principle of the lever can be viewed as a descriptive (qualitative) mode (invariance) found throughout locomotion and, for Aristotle, present in a more attenuated way as equilibrium in all types of change. The characteristic proportion given in *Mechanics* 1 is the best or most complete expression of the invariance. It is important, however, that this characteristic proportion need not be grasped in its entirety in earlier applications of the lever in order for some of the properties belonging to that best expression to be manifest in the earlier applications. The descriptive mode, not the characteristic proportion of *Mechanics* 1, is what we shall expect to find in *Physics* IV.8.[416]

---

414 A modular system is one in which polynomials are mapped onto another by means of a prime polynomial. See Kline, *Ancient to Modern* 3, 825. A similar notion of mode can be gained from point-set topology.

415 Brauer and Nohel claim that the recognition of qualitative mathematics is closely associated with the development of Newton's mechanics by means of differential equations (*Qualitative Theory of Ordinary Differential Equations*, ch. 1). The distinction also appears in analysis of the development of mathematical skills in children. Sousa says, about the mathematical skills belonging to very young children, that there is already a distinction between number sense and counting, on the one hand, and the development of conceptual structures for calculation, on the other (Sousa, *How the Brain Learns Mathematics*). The latter is more qualitative. Qualitative mathematics may still involve symbolization.

416 An example of *properties* of the more complete expression of the lever principle ap-

Multi–Variant Movement in *Physics* IV.8

Physics IV.8 is one of the most important sources for Aristotle's dynamics. It is relatively long and consistent in the subject it treats. The chapter treats both natural and forced locomotion and takes into consideration also the role of resistance in movement. It presents a number of proportions of elements involved in locomotion, each symbolized by letters. In an important passage in *Physics* IV.8, Aristotle compares movement through different media:

> A, then, will move through B in time C, and through D, which is thinner, in time E (if the length of B is equal to D), in proportion to the density of the hindering (ἐμποδίζοντος) body. For let B be water and D air; then by so much as air is thinner and more incorporeal than water, A will move through D faster than through B. Let the speed have the same ratio to the speed, then, that air has to water. Then if air is twice as thin the body will traverse B in twice the time that it does D, and the time C will be twice the time E. And always, by so much as the medium is <u>more incorporeal</u> and less resistant and more easily divided, the faster will be the movement. (215b1–12)

As the resistance is less, a body will move faster subject to the same force. Aristotle goes on in *Physics* IV.8 to apply this analysis to the relation of greater and lesser weight, or relative lightness:

> Insofar as the media differ through which the bodies move, these things occur. The following depend upon an excess of one moving body over another. We see that [bodies] having a greater <u>impulse</u> (*rhopên*) either of weight or of lightness, if they are alike in other respects, move faster over an equal space, and in the ratio which their magnitudes bear to each other.[417] (216a13–16)

A greater force of weight issues in a faster movement. Aristotle continues that it is impossible that these bodies would move the same way in the void, where there is no resistance, but "[i]n moving through *plena* it must

---

pearing in abbreviated form earlier is Aristotle's statement that the arcs of a moving radius that are covered in the same time will be those that share two radii (*On the Heavens* II.8). This topic was treated in Chapter 7.

417   Translation by Hardie and Gaye (*CWA* 1, 367) slightly modified. They translate the first line of the quotation as: "These are the consequences that result."

be so; for the greater divides them faster by its force (*ischui*)." A heavier body has a greater force of division of what lies in its path.

By common consensus, these passages of *Physics* IV.8 refer to the weight of a *falling body*. This interpretation follows easily from Aristotle's including lightness as subject to a similar analysis. He would be talking about rising and falling.[418] That Aristotle addresses the free fall of bodies in these passages seems to be reinforced by the fact that he begins *Physics* IV.8 by talking about the natural movement of simple bodies. Earth moves downward, fire upward. Nevertheless, considering these passages within the whole of *Physics* IV.8, it is clear that the direction of movement of the simple bodies figures only indirectly in the points Aristotle makes.[419] *Physics* IV.8 is a series of arguments against movement in the void. Aristotle aims to show that nothing would move in the void, or else bodies, once set in motion by force (βία), would never cease movement (214b12–215a24). Forced movement, the relatively heavy, and different effects of weight all figure in stages of the argument. In this context, Aristotle treats locomotion in general in terms of interacting opposed movements.

Early in the chapter, Aristotle seeks to disarm the intuition that a body, to move at all, must move into an empty place (214b29). His argument on this point is a piece of critical rationalism. The reason why

---

418   It is possible that, in *Physics* IV.8, 215b1–12, Aristotle means to compare water and air as light bodies and only the things going through them as the heavy bodies. I do not explore this interpretive option.

419   By contrast, in *On the Heavens* IV.1, Aristotle is clearly talking about movements upward or downward: "By lighter or relatively light we mean that one, of two bodies endowed with weight and equal in bulk (ὄγκον), which is exceeded by the other in the speed of its natural downward movement" (IV.1, 308a31–33). The lighter body is the one that, equal in volume to another, does not fall as fast. Other passages that refer directly to the speed of bodies falling include *On the Heavens* I.8, where Aristotle says that the greater the mass of fire or earth the quicker is its speed toward its own place (277b4). The context is argument against force or extrusion (ἔκθλιψις) as causing movement of the cosmic elements. Aristotle states the same relation of mass or volume and speed of the elements in *On the Heavens* IV.2, 309b12–15, in the context of arguing against those who distinguish weight and lightness by the presence of void in body. In this passage, he reiterates the difference between what is light by nature and the relatively light, which itself has weight. In *On the Heavens* II.8, however, Aristotle addresses a commonality of weight and lightness, saying that whenever bodies are moving with their proper motion the larger moves more quickly. It is easier to read all these passages as addressing free-fall than it is to read *Physics* IV.8 as concerned with free fall. The principle that a body moves faster with its own proper motion in proportion to its bulk (*On the Heavens* II.8) applies to both rectilinear and circular motion (290a1). This generalization is found also in *Physics* VIII.9, 265b11–16.

bodies would not move at all in the void is like the reason given by some pre-Socratics as to why the earth is at rest in the universe. It is because the earth is equally poised within the universe. The earth is located similarly in all directions (214b30–215a1). The parallel to weight is that, *if there is a void*, anything with weight is at rest in it. Every body would be similarly disposed in every direction, because there are no differences of place in the void. Aristotle says that if bodies were to move in the void, then they all would travel at the same speed, but this is impossible, he says (216a16–21). No body shall move faster or slower than another, because in the void there is no difference (214b34).

On this account, every movement in the void would be a forced motion. There is no natural motion in a void because there is nothing to define different inclinations to movement. That the void precludes natural motion and that nothing could go faster or slower than another body in the void are points that go together for Aristotle. Speeds are different due to differences in relative weight or relative lightness. Just as the infinite has no up or down just because it is unbounded, so also the void has nothing to distinguish up from down. Aristotle presents the alternatives starkly: either there is no natural motion, or if there is, then there is no void (215a12–14).

Continuing his line of thought, Aristotle could give a rationalist reason why there must be natural motion rather than the void. He himself believes the universe, as a sphere, has a center and a periphery. Downward is toward the center; upward is toward the periphery. He presents this reasoning in *On the Heavens* IV but not in *Physics* IV.8.[420] Instead, he shifts to a more empirical style of reasoning, in two arguments starting at 215a14 (introduced by ἔτι νῦν) and a24 (introduced by ἔτι . . . ὁρῶμεν). The first argument speaks to projectile motion:

> Further, in point of fact things that are thrown move though what pushes them is not touching them, either by reason of mutual replacement, as some maintain, or because the air that has been pushed pushes them with a movement quicker than the natural locomotion of the projectile wherewith it moves to its proper place. But in a void none of these things can take

---

420 He does give another rationalistic exclusion of the void at 215a19–22. No one would be able to give a reason why some body stops moving in the void and why it stops one place rather than another. Either a body shall remain at rest or keep moving indefinitely in the void.

place, nor can anything be moved save as that which is carried is moved.[421] (215a14–19)

Here, Aristotle says that a mutual interplay of bodies sustains projectile motion in some way, a possibility entirely foreclosed to explanation of movement in a void. The air, being lighter than the projectile, moves more quickly than the heavier thrown object, so much so that it impedes the natural tendency of the thrown object to fall.

This explanation of projectile motion has always seemed implausible and strange, because it is viewed from the standpoint of a metaphysically styled natural philosophy. Air as a substance is an unlikely recipient of a simple power to move a heavier weight. To interpret air's ability to move a heavier object, we are thrown upon the shoals of *Physics* VIII.10, where the air is endowed with both movement and the ability to be a relatively unmoved mover (266b27–267a20). In this passage, the movement of air may cease before its ability to move the projectile leaves off (267a5–7). So, being in motion and being a mover are separable in conception for the moving thing. Being in motion as such is "a kind of actuality but incomplete."[422] Nevertheless, there is enough achieved actuality for the moving thing to be a mover with respect to an adjacent body.[423] When the air has been moved in the measure of its own initial mover's impetus, its being a mover will dissipate, and then the object so far sustained by the air's moved thing/mover complex falls. This account in *Physics* VIII.10 I would call "high end" natural philosophy. It is closer to metaphysical reasoning and correspondingly more opaque with respect to its empirical dimension.

At this juncture, it helps to recall *Physical Problems* XVI.11, where the author includes the locus of a projectile's motion and explains sus-

---

421 Translation by Hardie and Gaye (*CWA* 1, 365) modified to reflect the subject of the genitive absolute, "the one pushing" (τοῦ ὤσαντος) (215a14), which they translate "that which gave them their impulse."

422 *Physics* III.2, 201b31–33. Aristotle says the reason for motion being an incomplete actuality is that *the potential* of which the actuality is, is incomplete. During movement, the potential is still not completely actual. That Aristotle defines movement as an actuality at all indicates that he regards motion as a state or at least as conceivable as a whole.

423 Possibly, the reason for a moving thing being a mover is that is has achieved in completion *some part* of what will be its overall achievement in moving (*Physics* VI.6, 236b32–237b13). In any case, Aristotle says in *Physics* III.2, that the mover has form—which connotes completion—and form is the principle and cause of its moving something, when it does. He also says that whatever moves another by contact itself undergoes some movement or change from that with which it is in contact (202a5–12).

tained movement and its cessation in terms of even or uneven force (*rhopê*) exerted by the air around the body. The author of *Physical Problems* XVI.11 considers a circular body that he says will travel straight forward as long as the force of air around it is the same on all sides. When the object inclines to one side because the force of air around it is uneven, then it describes a curved path. This passage resonates with *Physics* IV.8 in presenting projectile motion and fall of a projectile in terms of an interplay of movements or forces of movement. Both these passages manifest what I have called Aristotle's deformation strategy. Interpreted in terms of *Physical Problems* XVI.11, *Physics* IV.8 says that the air around the projectile pushes on the travelling body (as the thrower pushed it also) due to the faster speed of the air. By its pushing, the air counters the downward tendency of the weight. The body gradually comes to outweigh the air's energy of movement and so falls downward on a curved path. This would be a case of Aristotle's considering a continuous deformation over a short time of a correlation of force or speed to weight.

Along with *Physical Problems* XVI.11, Aristotle's account in *Physics* IV.8 indicates that air both above and below the body sustains its movement initially. *Physics* IV.8 differs in ascribing this sustaining of movement to faster movement of the air, not even and uneven *rhopê* due to the air. Aristotle's account in *Physics* IV.8 is nevertheless receptive to an interpretation of the movement of the air as adding motive power to the situation of projectile motion. A sign of this is the fact that, in *Physics* IV.8, Aristotle says a body having a greater force of weight (*ischus*) will divide a medium faster (216a12–13). He also mentions the *rhopê* belonging to the thrown object as a source of greater speed in cleaving the medium (a19). The fast moving projectile is a missile, setting up a commotion around it as it divides the air. A feather does not have the weight to do this. In the case of the feather, the air itself has more motive energy from the throw than the projectile feather. In the case of the missile, the commotion imparted to the air falls into an orderly pattern determined to some extent even by the shape of the body (a19). Aristotle recognizes the force of throw as adding *rhopê* to the situation. *Rhopê* is a word difficult to translate in *Physics* IV.8. We fall back on terms like force, pressure, or energy that have their proper connotations in modern physics. Certainly, one connotation of *rhopê* in *Physics* IV.8 is the *excess* of motive energy that a body possesses over against its moved thing, which might otherwise move it. The important point is that Aristotle is thinking in terms of something like the energy of movement, which is either in balance or is in what amounts to opposition. At the least, we can say that this part of *Physics* IV.8 shares with *Physical Problems* XVI.11 a treatment of projectile motion in terms of excess or deficit of competing movement states.[424] Speed and horizontal or vertical displacement co-vary along with the force of throw and agitation of the air. This amounts to a continuous gradual deformation of the entire situation of movement.

Aristotle's treatment of projectile movement in this passage of *Physics* IV.8 relies on implicit notions of balance, dominance in the context of balance, increase and decrease of force, or other notions built around leverage, advantage in force or weight, or equilibrium. For the moment, let us focus on the pervasiveness of equilibrium in Aristotle's account, which involves ratios that must be the same. Aristotle's equilibrium axiology for projectile motion can be compared to two modern accounts of flight. Here the relevant projectile is an airplane or its wings. The best known account of why airplanes stay aloft draws upon a principle of Bernoulli. Put simply, the principle is as follows:

> An increase in the speed of a fluid (or flowing gas) is accompanied by a *decrease* in the pressure or a decrease in the fluid's potential energy.[425]

This principle linking increase in speed to decrease in potential energy is taken in conjunction with the fact of the wing's shape. The wing is curved on top, thus offering more surface area to be covered by the air passing over the wing than under the wing. Since the air must go faster over the larger expanse of the top of the wing, pressure is lower above the wing than below it. The greater pressure below the wing means the wing rises and along with it the aircraft.

---

424   In his commentary on *Physics* VIII.10, Simplicius reports that Alexander of Aphrodisias ascribes the *antiperistasis* theory of projectile motion to Plato, while Alexander himself says the cause of motion is unevenness and inequality (τὴν ἀνωμαλίαν καὶ ἀνισότητα) (*in physicorum*, CAG 10, 1351.28–33). This would allow interpretation of the passage from *Physics* VIII.10 in terms harmonious with the understanding of *Physics* IV.8 given here.

425   For Bernoulli's achievement relating pressure and movement of gases, see Holton and Roller, *Modern Physical Science*, §21.6, 324–375. For its theoretical application to projectile motion, see Anderson and Eberhardt, *Understanding Flight*, "Introduction" and Appendix B.

259

Aristotle's account shares with Bernoulli's the idea that a body's *staying aloft* or *falling* is due to opposing force or pressure of air around it. (For simplicity of reference, I will call Bernoulli's the *B*-account and Aristotle's in *Physics* IV.8 the *A*-account.) The *B*-account relies upon conservation of energy within a system. This part of the *B*-account means that the *A*- and *B*-accounts share the aspect of a *balance* of contributing motive impulses, or the co-variance of contributing forces. Each yields in its own way a multi-variant *proportional* sameness. The co-variants are speed and some version of motive energy, whether due to weight or pressure. On the *A*-account, the speed of air has motive energy, gained from the thrower, that adds to the motive energy of the heavier body. This motive energy keeps the body aloft when without that extra push it would fall. The *B*-account relates lift and pressure inversely. Despite the differences in reasoning about what the air does and the apparent incommensurability of the notions of *rhopê* and pressure, the two accounts are similar in their treating some aspect of the air as a cause of flight by means of the notion of equilibrium within a system.

The other modern explanation of flight is by Newton's three laws. Scientists who offer this alternative criticize the *B*-account as inadequate to explain the tremendous transfer of air that would be required to keep a heavy aircraft aloft. Conservation of energy within a system is not enough. Energy must be added to the system of air-and-moving-heavy-body.[426] This point is key to an overlooked aspect of Aristotle's account.

In the Newtonian account (*N*-account), an airplane adds energy to a system created by the propulsion of the fuselage and wing through the air.[427] Energy is continually imparted to the air in front of the plane by the plane's speed and shape. The forcing upward of air by the wings and fuselage, and the speed imparted by the jet engine draws additional air from above, creating a downdraft along the wing. The downdraft continues steeply off the wing to the rear. This picture of lift draws on Newton's first and third laws. A change in velocity, or from rest to motion, is a sign of a force acting, and every action has an equal and opposite reac-

---

426 Interestingly, this criticism of the *B*-account, the most often cited explanation of flight, is similar to the criticism perennially leveled at the *A*-account: moving air is not enough to propel a body heavier than air. Directed at the *A*-account, this criticism has been taken as a reason for saying Aristotle's physics lacks empirical grounding or even the most obvious fact checking.

427 Anderson and Eberhardt, *Flight*, ch.1.

tion.[428] The *N*-account is causal and dynamic. It provides for an input of energy into the system sufficient to transfer large amounts of air, decreasing pressure above the wing and increasing pressure below and behind the plane. The *N*-account to this extent incorporates the *B*-account, but it relies on Newton's laws to explain the energy added to the system.

I have noted similarities between the *A*- and *B*-accounts. The difference between the *B*- and *N*-accounts highlights elements of the *A*-account that are similar to the *N*-account. In *Physics* IV.8, speed is an index of push against the weight of the thrown object. Either shape or volume may add to the power speed has to divide the air (216a19). What has this power of dividing the air to a greater extent (it cuts the air quicker) also moves faster, presumably creating more motive energy. The physical system of moving body and air in projectile motion that Aristotle puts forward in *Physics* IV.8 shows that he was thinking about projectile motion in terms of mechanical influences operating when movement is underway. So, empirical considerations of a perennial sort were robustly relevant to his own explanation of the phenomena. He was working out the mechanical tendencies of movements in or out of balance. The comparison to more thorough and readily understandable modern accounts helps to show that. Furthermore, we see that Aristotle's thinking about locomotion shares a *type of explanation* with many later accounts in mechanics. Galileo and Newton traced their own scientific heritage to the ancient craft of machine making. Why should it be surprising that Aristotle was similarly influenced by mechanics and machines, to the extent these were present in his own culture and in accordance with the state of mathematical knowledge at the time?[429]

---

428 "The key thing to remember about lift is that it is a reaction force caused by the diversion of air down" (Anderson and Eberhardt, *Flight*, 39). It is important that air below the wing is not being *pushed down* by the wing. Air is diverted downward (downwash) from around the front of the fuselage and from well above the plane's wings (*Flight*, 2).

429 It might be claimed that to compare an Aristotelian account to a modern one of the same phenomenon is always an instance of the terminal fallacy. It is "Whiggish," the current term of preference for backward looking intellectual history. Not every reference to a clearer and later scientific account is Whiggish. We should not be so intent on avoiding "precursorism" that we fail to take advantage of opportunities to understand a scientific period in its terms rather than our own. There is a much greater danger of historical inaccuracy in projecting an early modern conception of metaphysics onto Aristotle's science than from investigating his thinking as genuinely empirical. Aristotle's understanding of projectile motion may well have been misinterpreted for a long time by taking *Physics* VIII.10 as a starting point and by taking that passage in a particular way. I touch on this topic again in Chapter 11.

To return to the point at hand, Aristotle argues that the system of dynamic equilibrium he has presented is not even possible of realization in the void. The idea introduced by this first empirical argument against the void, then, is that there is possible in a void no impetus or motive energy (*rhopê, ischus*), no countervailing motive energies, nor overcoming (ὑπεροχή) of an opposite motive energy.[430] Movement does not take place without these factors in play. Aristotle has not said that these factors *cause* motion. Causes, however, are on his mind. He entertains the idea that the void is a cause (*aition*) of motion, if it is a condition of bodies changing place at all (214b16–22). In reality, he insists, the multiple factors he introduces are the conditions for there being potency for motion. These factors could not be brought into existence in a void. So, these factors, rather than the void, could be considered the material cause of motion.

The second empirical argument against the void that takes advantage of mechanical insights begins at 215a24 with "we see." The same word used in the perfect tense, "we have seen," introduces the *phainomenon* of the moon's occultation of Mars, a simple but striking observation freighted with import for the order of the moon and planets. This time the verb introduces an observation that is common and nearly unavoidable for reflective human beings:

> We see the same weight or body moving faster than another for two reasons, either because there is a difference in what it moves through, as between water or earth, or between water or air; or because the moving body differs, other things being equal, owing to excess (ὑπεροχήν) of weight or of lightness. (215a24–29)

The weight, texture, viscosity, or fineness of that through which a body moves affects the body's speed, as we know from the contrasting experiences of running and swimming. Aristotle elaborates on this by saying the medium impedes more when it moves in the opposite direction, but it also impedes when it is simply in place (a29–30). On the other hand, a body moves faster than another because of its excess of potency for motion. Excess is a relational term, implying comparison to another

---

430 For the formulations of these ideas in close proximity to one another, see *Physics* IV.8, 215a24–31.

body.[431]

Aristotle immediately offers proportions based on the first contention: a lighter medium impedes the moving body less in proportion to the difference of density of two media being compared, when other factors are held equal. Accordingly, the body will move faster through the thinner medium in the same time. The point of these proportions is that the void enters into no ratio with an impeding body, just as nothing has no ratio to a number (215b12–13).[432] Aristotle follows up this argument with another set of proportions showing that between any two movements there is a ratio, because each takes some time, but there is no ratio of void to full (216a8–11). Each argument against motion in a void makes use of the fundamental correlations among mover or force, moved thing, distance, and time. What *we see* about faster and slower movements has a narrow import in this context. The observations ensure by their empirical universality what is expected of movement in the void. Since the statements are things we see, Aristotle does not put them forward as laws underlying all phenomena but rather as *phainomena* in the sense we have already encountered in his astronomy. They are observations whose import is crucial in a context. Weight is exhibited in motion as outweighing or being outweighed by something else pushing it.

In what follows next, Aristotle takes the second thing we see, that a difference in the moving thing itself can make for different speeds. The passage, quoted more completely above, is as follows:

> We see that [bodies] having a greater impulse (*rhopên*) either of weight or of lightness, if they are alike in other respects, move faster over an equal space, and in the ratio which their magnitudes bear to each other. (216a13–16)

This passage has been taken to be Aristotle's assertion that bodies with weight fall faster or slower in proportion to their weight.[433] This reading

---

431 I follow Ross (*Aristotle's* Physics, 589–590) in interpreting the second case as a comparison to another moving body when the resistance of the medium is the same for each. As Ross notes, lines 216a12–21 develop this comparison.

432 In each case, Aristotle uses letters to stand for factors that affect speed. Factors include a body, heavier or lighter, that is moving, time, distance, and an impeding body, difficult or easy to divide. These are considered in relation to the void, which cannot figure in ratio because it has no quantity of resistance.

433 Drabkin, "Laws," 66, 76. Drabkin understands the passage treats a more general case

is, at the least, an over-interpretation of the passage. For one thing, like its sister observation concerning the effect of different densities of media on speeds, Aristotle brings the statement to bear immediately on the question of the void: "So that also [this will be true of motion] through the void" (216a16). The import of the statement is limited: bodies of greater and lesser weight should manifest the same differences of speed in the void, i.e., whatever underlies these persistent and universal observations, it would have to obtain also in the void. No proportions follow, however. Aristotle's point is made sufficiently by recalling his rationalist criticism that there would be no reason for movements to be faster or slower in the void (216a17). Again though, we are given a glimpse of the conditions of equilibrium, excess and defect that are found in movement: "for the greater divides more quickly by its force (*ischuï*)" (a18). A body, whether of the heaviness or lightness variety, has the power not only to fall or rise but also to divide bodies of different densities and viscosities. To this dividing, shape and volume would be relevant. Especially relevant, though, is the excess of motive energy (*rhopê*) that the moving thing has with respect to the body it cleaves (216a19–20). Here, *rhopê* means the advantage of force—in a particular arrangement of objects and at a particular point in their movements with respect to one another—that makes one weight exceed another in the determination of actual movement and the direction of the movement.

In this important passage, there is no direct reference to the fall of weights. Indeed, what "we see" concerns "things having greater force of weight or of lightness." The implication is that two (or more) things of weight or things that are all light are being compared. We notice some of these things travelling the same space (τὸ ἴσον χωρίον) more quickly (216a15). There is nothing to exclude the space being along a horizontal or an incline, or being the distance covered by something thrown. Reason to include these other cases is Aristotle's evident interest in a range of phenomena in which we see a common way of acting. As we have already seen, Aristotle treated projectile motion earlier in the chapter, setting the terms for weight conceived as *rhopê* that carry over into this passage, where he uses the word *rhopê*.

Aristotle signals by his language and argument that the *phainomena* of bodies moving faster and slower through different media carry import for what basic framework holds in analysis of motion. These two obser-

---

of locomotion but sees this more general application as an extension from the fundamental case of free fall.

vations lead to excluding an illicit physical concept, the void. Aristotle's way of thinking here can be illuminated by one line of twentieth century discussion of natural law. Ayer and Braithwaite both cite the importance of the subjunctive conditional to a minimalist strategy for distinguishing nomic generalizations from among all other contingent empirical generalizations.[434] A subjunctive conditional runs as follows: *A* does not exist (is not the case), but if *A* existed, then *B* would be the case. Braithwaite insists that in a Humean universe the inference $A \supset B$, based on the counterfactual *A*, is not contradictory or empty if it is derivable from higher-level premises in a deductive network of scientific assertions. Aristotle makes a similar move insofar as he says that, if there were movement in a void, it would have to accommodate the faster and slower movement we see obtain in movements through media or over against impediments. After setting up the observation at 216a13–16—heavier bodies move faster than bodies with weight but lighter—Aristotle then says, "Therefore, they will also move through the void with this ratio of speed. But that is impossible; for why should one move faster (216a16–18)?" Aristotle uses this counterfactual situation to point to a background pattern (in modern terms, regularities or higher level laws) to which the *phainomena* that he cites conform. Returning to his formulation at 215a28, there must be excess of weight in one body and falling short with respect to weight in the other body in order for there to be movement.

Following upon the role of counterfactuals for Braithwaite, Scriven's analysis of explanation by deduction fits Aristotle's procedure more closely, because Scriven allows for an event concerning which there is some doubt to be evaluated in terms of something familiar that already fits into a "pattern":

> When we are trying to locate events with respect to what we know and understand, we often look to see whether they represent departures from patterns we know and understand, and these patterns are the laws. Their importance lies not in the *precision* with which they trace the characteristics of events or substances but in the fact that they provide a readily identifiable pattern. The event in question either conforms to a known pattern or it does not. If it does not, it (probably) needs

---

434   Ayer, "Law of Nature," and Braithwaite, "Laws of Nature and Causality." The counterfactual conditional is endorsed by Popper (*Conjectures*, 374–375).   *ck*

> explaining; if it does then either it is not puzzling or the
> puzzle involves the origin or relation of the patterns.[435]

In this sort of account, background understanding is key. We can bring to *Physics* IV.8 Scriven's insight that more basic principles are presupposed by familiar observations that are themselves integral to what we already know and understand. The observations are placeholders for a more general pattern expressed in many occurrences.

Aristotle could not be so confident of his "we see" in *Physics* IV.8, if the events he describes were for him no more than repeated instances. They bring with them some background knowledge, which he expresses in terms of countervailing weight and *rhopê*. Given the pattern of different speeds, and exceeding or falling short in speed, it is clear that the background knowledge has to do with the dynamic conception of equilibrium that he learned from leverage phenomena and the moving radius. We have already seen that there was some level of scientific development of leverage and balance phenomena current in Aristotle's school. This historical claim based on material earlier and later than Aristotle is reinforced by seeing that the power of the lever appears in other of Aristotle's works. The counterfactual character of Aristotle's argument against the void shows him pursuing a strategy of allowing what we see to stand in for what we know.

On the basis of *Physics* IV.8, we cannot say that Aristotle must regard the salient observations as part of a full *system* of explanation. It is not necessary that the argument of *Mechanics* 1 be already known to him. *Physics* IV.8 does show, however, that weight figures in movement in ways reaching beyond simple downward tendency and that the concepts Aristotle uses to address these other functions of weight reflect the terms of *Physical Problems* XVI and *Mechanics* 1.

In general, not every reference to weight and movement made by Aristotle should be taken as referring to free-fall. Many relevant passages do not specifically mention weights falling to earth—sometimes do not even mention weight. The Greek reader is required to supply "body" or "thing" to complete the sense. The clearest examples of weight signifying a force of falling come from *On the Heavens* IV.1, where Aristotle defines weight in terms of the character of its natural motion. Weight and lightness are powers (*dunameis*) of movement. The actuality of the pow-

---

435   Scriven, "Explanations," 101.

er has no name, unless one believes that it is *rhopê* (307b28–33). Here, *rhopê* includes a connotation of actuality, as movement is actuality, and a connotation of power sufficient to effect the actuality of movement, whatever impediments have heretofore been in play.

Aristotle's competence as an observer is intimately involved with the question of how passages like *Physics* IV.8 should be interpreted. Aristotle's understanding of free fall is a particularly prominent issue. When Aristotle is thought to have a dynamics and a particular (mistaken) claim about the rate of free fall, it is also said that he has failed to be a good observer on this very point of free-fall. His science shares too much in the *a priori* of essence or the naïve naturalism of qualitative characteristics. In response to this familiar charge, Hussey asks if we are to suppose that the meticulous observer of phenomena in Aristotle's works on biology only made his appearance after *On the Heavens* and *Physics* were written.[436] Concerning free fall, Hussey says about experience and observation:

A's observation

> In the first place, Aristotle had no way of measuring short time-intervals accurately, and must have known quite well that he did not. In the second place, it is a matter of common observation that heavier bodies do not in general fall noticeably faster than lighter ones.[437]

Hussey comments that, as a practical matter, heavy versus light would be measured on the balance. Accordingly, he offers the hypothesis that "it is the starting speeds *on the balance* that Aristotle has in mind, when he says that the heavier weight is that which 'moves downwards faster'" (225). Wardy and Berryman are both wary of this hypothesis because of the seeming paucity of evidence in favor of it.[438] There is evidence for

---

436 Hussey, "Mathematical Physics," 225n30.

437 Hussey, "Mathematical Physics," 225. In contrast, Drabkin says that Aristotle's instruments for measurement of movement were the equal of Galileo's ("Laws," 69).

438 Wardy critiques Hussey's point of view in *Chain*, 305–308. Berryman gives a sage assessment of the difficulties confronting Hussey's interpretation in *Mechanical Hypothesis*, 98–103. Hussey, Wardy, and Berryman are all looking for a quantitative treatment of weight phenomena when they speak of mechanics. They take this to be necessary to a mathematical mechanics. One part of my argument is that mechanics for Aristotle was mathematical in its type of account or explanation, even though it was not characterized by direct quantizing of factors involved in movement. Quantity was a narrow category for Aristotle.

math but not exactly quantified

it, however, in *Physical Problems* XVI.3 and 12 where the author treats the revolution of a body of uneven weight as if it were two weights—one heavier, one lighter—with a motionless middle. In *Physical Problems* XVI, the body has been thrown. In this case, weight is not simply manifesting its natural downward movement but has the character both of an anchoring constraint on something else and of a body tending to reel off along a path of its own.

Analyzed in light of *Physical Problems* XVI, the account of projectile motion in *Physics* IV.8 also lends support to the idea that the descriptive mode Aristotle brings to both projectile motion and free fall is the correlation of speeds on the balance of unequal beams, or work (in a non-technical sense) done with a lever. From the standpoint of the deformation strategy introduced at the beginning of this chapter, we can say that Aristotle in *Physics* IV.8 presents what can be known about bodies influencing one another in locomotion by drawing from background knowledge about mechanical advantage and its theoretical expression in the moving radius. From this knowledge, he infers that, in a void, no body would cease moving or be subject to change of speed or direction (or, we might add based on *Physical Problems* XVI, alter from a rectilinear to a curved path). In this, Aristotle infers soundly from certain critical phenomena to what we would observe under conditions that do not hold. Because his approach to the content of rules governing motion is conducted in such close association with the Eudoxan conditions for continuity, he also concludes that the void, as nothing, introduces a surd into proportional thinking about motion. That we cannot think about physics if there is void renders the very notion of the void suspect. My references to Scriven and other philosophers of science reinforce one of the main reasons I introduced topological considerations in evaluating Aristotle's analysis of movement in *Physics* IV. From the standpoint of the notion of a descriptive mode, it is not surprising if consequences of some first principle of movement might be arrived at in advance of a full and clear enunciation of those very principles. This follows from there being an invariance that is manifest differently in different situations.

Background knowledge that is strongly substantiated both experientially and mathematically is the best resource for analysis of locomotion by thought experiments, which is basically what Aristotle undertakes in his lettered proportions of *Physics* IV.8 and his treatment of projectile motion in that chapter. My aim in this section has been to show that in

Physics IV.8 Aristotle draws upon the mode of thinking displayed in *Physical Problems* XVI.3, 11 and 12. Claimed for dynamics by Drabkin, *Physics* IV.8 does make use of mechanical ideas, though not of laws of motion. What has garnered more scholarly attention than the mechanical contribution in these passages, however, is the foundational analysis that is without mechanical content. I turn now to that analysis.

Continuum Reasoning Without Mechanics

In almost all of the passages where Aristotle presents proportions involving force, weight, speed, etc., the proportions are involved in a *reductio* argument against the infinitely small, the infinitely large, the void or the weightless. The bedrock of Aristotle's analysis of motion and the basis for these arguments is the Eudoxan ratio according to which, even when two definite quantities do not share a single *common* measure, they can still form a ratio. The Eudoxan ratio is formulated as a ratio of magnitudes, not numbers, in Book V of Euclid's *Elements*. Euclid gives the Eudoxan ratio as follows:

> Magnitudes have a ratio to one another, which are capable when multiplied of exceeding one another.[439] (*Elements* V, Def. 4)

Thus, a and b have a ratio if $ma > b$ and $nb > ma$.

The Eudoxan ratio allows that any multiple of a definite quantity is of the same species as the quantity itself. The ratio thus works as a license to infer the existence of a definite quantity that is a multiple (or fractional multiple) of an original given quantity. It yields a definition of the continuous as any non-gappy subject. The Eudoxan ratio is perhaps most clear to modern understanding when rendered in terms of division. Any two quantities of the same kind, a and b, may be divided by appropriate divisors so that the two definite quantities can be brought as close together as one would wish. In this Eudoxan conception, continuity is not conceived numerically but in terms of magnitude. The Eudoxan ratio leads quite naturally to a conception of sameness of ratio:

---

439   Heath, *Elements* 2, 120.

Two ratios, a/b and c/d, are equivalent, if a and c, when multiplied by the same multiples, alike exceed or alike fall short of multiples of b and d respectively. (*Elements* V, Def. 5)

Thus, $ma > nb \leftrightarrow mc > nd$, or

$ma = mb \leftrightarrow mc = nd$, or

$ma < nb \leftrightarrow mc < nd$.

It can be a stumbling block to conceive how ratios can be the same by cohort members both exceeding or falling short of the other member of their respective ratios. The key is Euclid's "alike exceed or alike fall short." When the multiples m and n bring the two members of a ratio together in a pattern that is the same in another subject matter, then the ratios are deemed the same ratio. The definition of proportion thus includes the possibility of correspondence of patterns of successive multiplication or division. This is the import of De Morgan's account of proportionality, quoted by Heath.[440] Accordingly, one compares a *ratio* of definite magnitudes within a type of magnitude to a ratio of definite magnitudes in another type of magnitude. One does not compare the cohort quantities, a and c, or b and d.

The footprint of a Eudoxan conception of ratio and the continuity established by it is readily discerned in Aristotle's physical treatises in statements of what is called the Axiom of Archimedes. One instance of the principle is its statement in *Physics* III.6:

> For if we take a determinate part of a finite magnitude and add another part determined by the same ratio (not taking in the same amount of the original whole), we shall not traverse the given magnitude. But if we increase the ratio of the part, so as always to take in the same amount, we shall traverse the magnitude; for every finite magnitude is exhausted by means of any determinate quantity however small. (206b6–12)

Another is *Physics* VIII.10:

> By continually adding to a finite [magnitude] I shall exceed any definite [magnitude] and similarly by continually subtracting from it I shall arrive at something less than it. (266b2)

---

440   Heath, *Elements* 2, 122–123.

A formulation of Archimedes himself makes plainer what is at stake:

> [O]f unequal lines, unequal surfaces and unequal solids, the
> greater exceeds the lesser by such a magnitude as, when add-
> ed to itself, can be made to exceed any assigned magnitude
> among those which are comparable with [it and with one an-
> other].[441]

A magnitude smaller than either of two magnitudes being compared,
when added to itself enough times will finally exceed the larger of the
two magnitudes. If repeatedly subtracted from the larger, it will finally
be smaller than the lesser of the two magnitudes. In Aristotle's simpler
formulations, additions of the same quantity, however small, will finally
exceed any magnitude, however large. The Axiom of Archimedes is certainly in the spirit of the Eudoxan ratio, though it is also possibly consistent with ratio techniques that antedate Eudoxus.[442]

For Aristotle, the key element of the Eudoxan ratio and the Axiom of
Archimedes is that there is always some definite magnitude to be found
that can be brought into ratio with any other definite magnitude of the
kind of magnitudes being compared, whether weight (movers or moved
things), forces other than weight, distances covered, or times. In *Physics*
IV.8, arguments reliant upon the Axiom of Archimedes are used to refute that there is a void and also to prepare for the correspondence of the
continua of magnitude, motion, and time that Aristotle puts forward in a
surprisingly routine way in *Physics* IV.10.[443]

Aristotle's arguments about movement that make use of the Eudoxan
ratio have two steps. *On the Heavens* I.7 illustrates the pattern. It is impossible for something infinite to be acted upon or to act upon something
limited (274b33). The infinite that is acted upon is *A*. The limited thing
that acts is *B*. In some other passages, Aristotle calls the one that acts a
force if mover, or a weight if moved, but here he leaves out these words.
In *On the Heavens* I.7, the time in which the infinite or finite thing is
moved is *C*. Let us take a single case from *On the Heavens* I.7, where
the moved thing *A* is infinite (275a1). If the limited mover *B* moves the

441 Archimedes, *Sphere and Cylinder*, Assumption 5 (*Works of Archimedes*, trans.
Heath, 4).

442 On *anthyphairesis* and other early means of approximation as they compare to Euclid
and Archimedes, see Knorr, "Pre-Euclidean Proportion Theory."

443 219a12–14.

infinite A some distance in the time C, let a lesser force D move a lesser weight E the same distance in the same time. This is the first step, the first comparison, which compels the infinite A into a ratio with the finite E:

$$(1) \quad \frac{finite\ B}{finite\ D} \propto \frac{infinite\ A}{finite\ E}$$

Given the ratio of B and D, however, we can infer on Eudoxan principles that

$$(2) \quad \frac{B}{D} \propto \frac{something\ finite}{E} \quad . (275a6)$$

This is the second step. There will be some *finite* thing greater than E that will be moved by B the distance that in the same time the infinite A was moved (275a8–10). So, E has the same ratio with A, something infinite, that it has with something finite. But this is absurd.

Aristotle generalizes the argument, in the course of giving it, by applying it to an alteration and as he says, any other sort of change (275a3). He says that a warmable object is not infinitely warmable by a finite heat source, for if it is, a lesser application of heat will warm the object to some definite lesser extent. This means that, in a time equal to the infinite heating of the object, it could be heated some larger but finite amount. Aristotle concludes, "Clearly the infinite shall be moved by no limited object in any time at all" (275a10–11). No proportion is even possible where one infinite is included in the proportion. Aristotle goes on in *On the Heavens* I.7 to argue that the infinite also cannot itself move any limited thing.[444]

The Eudoxan background of these sample passages is typical of Aristotle's presentation of the proportions at issue. Also typical is his use of them to refute that the actual infinite, or its opposites, the empty or nil, enter into natural science. In *Physics* IV.8, Aristotle uses the two-step argument in showing that, if a body travels some distance through a void in a given time, there is some medium through which the body would travel that distance in the same time. The medium may be thin, but it is still full (πλῆρες) (215b22–216a4). Movements through denser and lighter media can be compared. Movement through the void would have to exceed every ratio of this type. If that through which a body moves is

---

444 The entire argument of lettered proportions extends from 275a1–275b3.

as thin as could be, still it would have no ratio to the void, since there is no ratio of a number to nothing (215b10–13). With these proportions, Aristotle is putting in place a framework for valid comparisons by means of corresponding continua. This grounding of motion in continua is not mechanics but meta-science.

There is one passage, *Physics* VII.5, which does not fit this profile of elimination of the infinite or nil, when proportions of this sort are presented. In *Physics* VII.5, Aristotle plunges without apparent prologue into the following account:

> Since whenever anything produces movement, it moves something (τι) in something (ἔν τινι) to something (μέχρι του) (by 'in something' I mean 'in time', and by 'to something', 'to a certain distance': for it is always the case that the mover at once produces and has produced movement, so that there will be a certain amount of distance which has been traversed within a certain amount of time), if then A is the mover, B is what is moved, the distance which has been traversed is C, and the time is D, then it follows that a force (*dunamis*) equal to A's will move half of B twice distance C in an equal time, and will move it distance C in half the time D: for in this manner there will be an analogy. And if the same force (*dunamis*) moves the same thing such-and-such a distance in a given time and half the distance in half the time, half the impulse (*ischus*) will also move half the thing an equal distance in an equal time.[445] (249b27–250a7)

Here the correlation of mover, moved thing, distance, and time is not involved in any *reductio*, and Aristotle freely substitutes words connoting force or power (*dunamis, ischus*) for the mover (τὸ κινοῦν).[446] Aristotle continues in this vein in the lines that follow the quoted passage, halving both the power and the resistance or weight of the moved thing. In this case, the same distance would be covered by a half-weight moved by the

---

445   The translation is by Wardy (*Chain*, 66–67) but is slightly modified to exclude the interpretation of the neuter pronoun as "load." I translate it as "the same thing" and "half the thing."

446   On this substitution, see Wardy, *Chain*, 315–316. Wardy says that Aristotle does not dispense with substances as movers, and he still treats the movers as efficient causes. Nevertheless, proportionality requires treating *dunamis* as a quantum, he contends.

halved force.[447] This passage does not conclude with the exclusion of the infinite from comparisons of movements. To this extent, it does not have as its aim the clarification of the structure of the continuum as do the passages dependent on a Eudoxan analysis. For those seeking a mechanics in Aristotle, this passage states something like mechanical laws and serves as the model for reading mechanics into the other passages where proportions do serve a *reductio* argument.

In a famous part of this chapter 5, Aristotle acknowledges that forces cannot be continually reduced with the result that some correspondingly reduced movement always follows. As in the case of shiphaulers, where many men can move a ship, a single man acting alone can produce no movement at all (250a18). The shiphaulers could be taken to reinforce the supposition that Aristotle takes the preceding correlations as stating laws, or highest generalizations, of motion: with the shiphaulers, Aristotle establishes in principle a limit of the laws' applicability. In a given case, there will be some minimum exertion of force, below which there will be no effect of movement at all. Drabkin does not take the passage in so positive a light, however. He treats the passage as a problem, since Aristotle is "forced to make an exception and to limit his equation."[448]

To understand the shiphaulers, we should place the proportions of *Physics* VII.5 in their proper context of Aristotle's problems and solutions about movement, bearing in mind that the proportions in this passage are unfettered by involvement in a *reductio* argument about the infinite or nil. Toward this end, it is worth noting that, next after the shiphaulers, Aristotle addresses whether a single grain of millet inevitably makes a sound in falling, if a whole measure (μέδιμνος) does. The question comes from Zeno, whom Aristotle refutes by saying that any portion of

---

447   For an exposition of the proportions in the passage, see Wardy, *Chain*, 314.

448   Drabkin, *Sourcebook*, 203n3. Drabkin's explicit modernizing of Aristotle in the *Sourcebook* must have something to do with the book's intended audience. Owen gives little attention to the shiphaulers case, saying that in *Physics* VIII.10, Aristotle has forgotten all about it (Owen, "Mechanics," 330). Owen cites the passage at 266a13–23, where Aristotle treats a part D of a whole mover A, which is moving a part E of a moved thing B. The assumption is that the whole A moves the whole B in an infinite time C. By adding to D, Aristotle says "I shall use up A, and [by adding to] E, I shall use up B, but I shall not use up the time by dividing it equally, for it is infinite." The principle of the argument is the Axiom of Archimedes and emphasizes again that the infinite cannot function in proportion with a ratio of finites. In answer to Owen, I would place this passage among the foundational arguments without mechanical import. The shiphaulers case in contrast locates a logical mistake concerning parts and whole.

a measure is only potentially a portion of that whole (250a20–25). That is, the inexorable logic of dividing an effect in proportion to the divisions of its parts could be considered only insofar as the portion is actualized *as a part of this whole measure*. A grain of millet, though, is just a single grain. There is no logical necessity that a grain makes some slight noise just because dropping a large measure of grain makes a noise.[449]

In this place, Aristotle deploys a dual argument against Zeno. On the analogy of the shiphaulers, there is a minimum to the portions capable of producing any sound in falling, and that minimum is not a single grain. Neither can a single sailor haul a ship. Additionally, a single grain is not, as such, a portion (μόριον) of a whole measure anyway. The reference to Zeno is a reminder of the extent to which the motion books of the *Physics* (IV–VI) unfold against the background of Zeno's paradoxes about motion. In specifying the factors of mover, moved thing, distance, and time, Aristotle initiates a rationalization of motion. He provides the basis for seeing how the paradoxes are mistaken in their assumptions. Seen in this light, the proportions of *Physics* VII.5 recall *Physics* V.1, where Aristotle lays out the specifications of change and motion.

In *Physics* V.1, change may be accidental or *per se* to the subject of change, but every motion takes a mover, moved thing, a time of movement, and a "from which" and a "to which" (224a34–b1). The "from which" and "to which" are contraries, and there is a substratum of change that is not itself altered. These components of change allow for the comparisons by Eudoxan finite ratios that are needed to defeat Zeno—comparisons of movements in which one or more factors is varied, making for different but definite finite speeds. In *Physics* VI, this foundational sketch comes into its own in grounding every sort of comparison between movements based on the shared structure of continua. In *Physics* VI.2, Aristotle writes:

> By continuous I mean that which is divisible into divisibles
> that are always divisible: and if we take this as the definition
> of continuous, it follows necessarily that time is continuous.
> For since it has been shown that the quicker will pass over an
> equal magnitude in less time than the slower, suppose that A

---

449   There has been much discussion concerning the logical principle of the argument—whether it is a sorites, a *reductio* from proportionality, or a part/whole argument. Wardy canvasses contemporary commentary in *Chain*, 317–327, opting with some reservation for a part/whole interpretation (323–326).

is quicker and B slower, and that the slower has traversed the magnitude CD in the time FG. Now it is clear that the quicker will traverse the same magnitude in less time than this: let us say in the time FH. Again, since the quicker has passed over the whole CD in the time FH, the slower will in the same time pass over CJ, say, which is less than CD. And since B, the slower, has passed over CJ in the time FH, the quicker will pass over it in less time: so that the time FH will again be divided. And if this is divided the magnitude CJ will also be divided in the same ratio; and again, if the magnitude is divided, the time will also be divided. And we can carry on this process forever, taking the slower after the quicker and the quicker after the slower, and using what has been demonstrated; for the quicker will divide the time and the slower will divide the length. (232b24–233a8)

The continuity of all three—motion, magnitude, and time—Aristotle uses as an arsenal of argumentation against Zeno in the same chapter of Book VI. He asserts that there are two senses of the infinite for length and time, the quantitative infinite or the infinitely divisible (233a24–28). An infinitely divisible length *can be* gone through in a finite time, and indeed, a time is infinite in this way. On this basis, the infinite in time can be matched to any finite distance covered.

All of this is well known to students of Aristotle's natural philosophy. The consistency of the themes should be brought to bear, however, on the evaluation of whether *Physics* VII.5 is a standout among the passages collected by Aristotle's use of letters for the elements of movement entering into ratios and proportions. *Physics* VII.5 follows closely the relation between *Physics* V.1 and VI.2 in its presentation of the mover, a certain moved thing, the "in which," and the "to which" (249b27–28). Mover, moved thing, distance, and time are all continuous. In both *Physics* VI.2 and VII.5, the argumentation is made in order to deny some claim of Zeno about movement. The dismissal of Zeno in *Physics* VII.5 could be taken as special to the extent that it relies not strictly on a continuum argument but on an appeal to a principle of proper parts of a whole. Neither a single shiphauler nor a single grain of millet is actually a portion of a whole, except when each acts completely in concert with the whole. Neither individual is a part produced by division. Nevertheless, these pronounced similarities in argument between *Physics* V–VI and *Physics* VII.5 testify to the natural inclusion of *Physics* VII.5 among Aristotle's other arguments that rationalize movement in the defense against Zeno's excess of rationalism. *Physics* VII.5 is one of the passages concerned with foundations in senses (2) and (3) given at the beginning of this chapter. Aristotle offers a clarification of foundations that conveys no mechanical content (2), and he addresses criteria for comparability of movements (3). Thus, I would argue that *Physics* VII.5 is not, by virtue of its exclusion of a *reductio* of some sort, the paradigm case for an Aristotelian dynamics. Indeed, *Physics* VII.5 provides even less support for laws of motion than *Physics* IV.8. As we have seen, *Physics* IV.8 does refer its cases back to unarticulated but well-known characteristic behavior of bodies in motion.

Wardy has argued against *Physics* VII.5 as a part of an Aristotelian mechanics but in a way different from the way presented here. Examining one aspect of his interpretation of *Physics* VII.5 can bring into sharper relief the behavior of bodies to which Aristotle appeals in *Physics* IV.8. In refuting that the shiphaulers case is involved with any Aristotelian laws of motion, Wardy expands upon insights of Carteron and Wieland. Carteron regards the power of the single shiphauler to be a force too feeble to act. What happens to the force is a puzzle. Carteron says, "it returns to the subject from which it comes, whose energy it constitutes."[450] Wardy takes the force too weak to act—the force of one man pushing the ship—to be a completely frustrated force: "If nothing perceptible happens, nothing happens."[451] In this, he follows Carteron, who says it is as if the force did not exist.[452] Everything I have presented in this Chapter militates against this interpretation, which understands power solely as a kind of active attribute of a substance. Substance itself operates according to mysterious rules: e.g., powers return to it (presumably unscathed) when unable to act. I do not mean to ridicule this point of view but to point out, in Wittgensteinian style, that it presents a picture of *dunamis* that cannot be carried through consistently. The picture is far removed from

---

450   Quoted by Wardy, 318n28, in Sorabji's English translation, which uses the word "blocked" for checked power.

451   Wardy, *Chain*, 318n28.

452   It is worthwhile consulting Carteron's original text for the expressions I have placed in italics: "Pour que la force produise son effet sur tel mobile, il faut qu'elle dépasse un certain minimum, au dessous duquel *elle est comme si elle n'était point . . . Que devient cette force trop faible après son échec?* C'est ce qu'Aristote ne nous dit pas; il est clair qu'*elle retourne au sujet d'où elle est partie* et dont elle constitue l'énergie" (*Notion de force*, 22). Carteron says that, for a checked power, it is as if it did not exist. It is too feeble to act and returns to its subject of which it is a part.

Aristotle's actual motivation and intellectual practice in his analysis of movement.

Wardy's interpretation links expression of power to perception. Nothing happens, if a power is not converted to an action for which it is immediately recognized as the power. So, as with Carteron's interpretation, power is checked; it retreats or dissipates. This answer to the question of what happens to a frustrated power makes power uncomfortably entitative in connotation. It also leads us back, as interpreters, to Molière's "dormitive power" representation of potentiality—the idea of power as the ability to produce a single effect that has already been identified. It is true that powers are discovered by deeds, but the point of physical investigation is to learn how a power expressed in one way is effective in other ways.

It is remarkable how often Aristotle and his followers say a body simply moves with two motions. Aristotle and the respective authors of *Physical Problems* XVI and *Mechanics* do not describe composition of movements nor do they give causes as accounting for combined movements. Kinematic accounts were explanatory to them. This fact sheds light on a striking feature of Aristotle's analysis of locomotion in *Physics* IV–VII—its parsimony. Even though movements may issue in change not distinctively the identity of the original impulse to change, powers or forces are known by manifest action. This style of reasoning shows something about what it means to bring a mathematical style of reasoning into narrative. *Physics* IV–VII models a way of thinking that is not primarily concerned to lodge causes of motion in entitative beings. Certainly, there are initial forces or active powers (*ischus* or *dunamis*). A kinematic invariance reaches deeper for its cause, however, to a power consistent with the invariance and widely enough conceived to account for many phenomena. Because of its origin in kinematic considerations, an explanation by powers is not extravagant or florid but is on the contrary minimalistic.[453]

Wardy endorses the view that power returns to its source when checked in order to avoid placing Aristotle anywhere near Duhem's idea that the underlying principle of Aristotle's proportions is a forerunner of the physical concepts of work or virtual velocities. In the same place, Wardy says, "Aristotle does not even consider the possibility of postulating 'virtual' forces, impulses not productive of effects manifest to the

---

453 I address the meaning of minimalism in mechanical thinking in Chapter 11.

entitive

senses." The virtuality of motion was, however, a live and provocative idea among Aristotle's predecessors and contemporaries.

The author of *Physical Problems* XVI.3 and 12 relies upon one meaning of the virtuality of movement—that a movement can be expressed in action without following its own identity or its own directionality of movement—to explain how rectilinear movement becomes circular movement. There are similar instances in texts that more clearly belong to Aristotle. In *On the Heavens* II.8 and 10, circular movements—of the sphere of fixed stars and of the circles proper to each planet—act contrary to one another with the result that the planets describe a different path than would be expected based on either the moving radius principle or the speed of the planets' own circles. There is an instance presented in *Physics* VII itself, in chapter 2, where δίνησις—whirling—is taken back to pushing and pulling (243b17). So, Aristotle seems definitely to have considered the possibility of virtual motion in this sense.

With respect to the issue of combined movements or powers that appear not to have acted, one might counter that the different movements in the heavens are at least expressed in some way in action, even if not as rectilinear movement, or with the particular speed belonging to the planet's own circle. This is different from a force that does not issue in perceptible action at all, as occurs in the case of the shiphaulers. Admitting any cases of virtual motion, however, raises the question of what counts as expression of a power. We have seen that conversion from one type of change to another is a power of the animate; it is involved in animal response to a sense percept (*Movement of Animals* 7). For which kind of change, then, is the *dunamis* the power? The answer should be that *dunamis* may express itself across a range of actions the limits of which can be determined only by investigation. This was the view put forward in Chapter 5 above. We have seen that Aristotle uses *dunamis* in the plural, *dunameis,* as he capitalizes on an idea of pent-up power that may act either effusively or with persistence in an orderly succession, when an efficient cause acts on what possesses it. Accordingly, we should not eliminate prematurely notions like contributory powers, mixed movements, partially realized powers (movement itself) or circumvented powers.

Physics IV.8 lends itself to interpreting the force that does not issue in action in Book VII as a real force acting. Excess or defect of a motive force in relation to an inertial weight can both explain the inaction and also show how the same principle is operative in other cases. Opposing forces act but one overmasters the other. In this respect, *Physics* IV.8 could be related also to passages surrounding the definition of motion in *Physics* III.1–3. In *Physics* III.2, Aristotle says that what acts is also acted upon, since the two are in contact (202b5–7). In the calculus of equilibrium, motive energy may be cancelled by an opposing force of impediment. But in cancellation, something still takes place—the opposition of two motive actors. The power does not return to its subject, because it acts. So did the single shiphauler expend his energy to the point of exhaustion, and the ship exerted its weight in return both against the ground and against the single hauler.

We might say that, to the extent that *Physics* IV.8 can interpret it, the shiphaulers case is not without mechanical content. The issue in physical science treated directly in *Physics* VII.5 is the wholeness of combined effort. A key passage in the chapter comes after Aristotle has presented the proportions involving factors contributing to movement (249b27–250a16) and the puzzle from Zeno (240a16–23). Aristotle says first that a kernel is only potentially part of a whole measure and then returns to the strategy of proportion:

> If there are two movers each of which separately moves one of two weights a given distance in a given time, then the forces (*dunameis*) in combination will move the combined weights (τὸ σύνθετον ἐκ τῶν βαρῶν) an equal distance in an equal time; for in this case the rules of proportion apply (ἀνάλογον γάρ). (250a25–28)

Here he draws upon both issues he has already introduced to draw a conclusion about how increase of force in the mover works when the weights are combined as well as the forces exerted. The combined weight will move under the combined force "an equal length and in the same time" as the weights were moved separately.[454] The wholeness of combined movement is consistent with Aristotle's general interest in mixing movements.

The mixing of movements fits the strategy of deformation of situations of change that I have advanced as the model for passages in *Physics* IV.8. If both forces and weights are combined, the result is the same as it was for each force and weight taken separately. Below a certain division of force, exertion upon the same weight will not be effective at all. Also,

---

454   The proportion will also hold in the case of alteration (250a28–b7).

as we have seen in Chapter 7, mutually constrained rectilinear forces in certain circumstances will naturally fall into a circular pattern. All these cases exemplify the same concern with equilibrium among the factors contributing to change.

Homonymy in *Physics* VII

There is more to say about why the proportions in *Physics* VII.5 are placed where they are, with the other material of Book VII and in the simplest form of their presentation, without a *reductio* against the infinite in motion. The relevance of the passage to defeating Zeno's paradoxes about motion should not be underestimated. Wardy rightly insists, however, that the significance of *Physics* VII.5 must be found in its relation to the rest of Book VII.[455] Determining the significance of chapter 5 for the rest of Book VII is not the easiest task, since the chapters taken together are something of a puzzle in their own right.[456] In the analysis that follows, two interpretative themes will be reinforced. The first is the connection of chapters 4 and 5 of Book VII to *Physics* V. The other is Aristotle's reluctance, in this place consciously articulated, to separate the subject matter for comparisons of movements from the physical things themselves. Aristotle's aim is to articulate a sense for the sameness of change that is not bound by synonymy with respect to the subject matter of change itself. In this task, the topological features of Eudoxan proportion theory are especially useful to him.

We saw that the beginning of *Physics* VII.5 gives a précis of the elements entering into analysis of motion. These contributors to motion—mover, moved thing, distance, time, from which and to which—are presented with greater thoroughness in *Physics* V.1, where Aristotle is

---

455 Wardy, *Chain*, 88. The greatest interest in Book VII has been its version of an argument for a first unmoved mover. Book VII is almost universally regarded as inferior to Book VIII in this regard. There are two versions of Book VII. Version α is the longer one; version β does not include chapters 4 and 5, though Simplicius' reference to it indicates it was originally longer. Wardy believes chapters 4 and 5 of version α are meant to support the argument for the unmoved mover in chapter 1 of Book VII. The extant longer text, version α, is included in Ross's edition as Book VII. The existence of two versions occasions speculation that, perhaps, the shorter is an example of Aristotle, the philosopher, at work, or that version β was a response from someone in Aristotle's immediate circle to version α. My study of Book VII suggests to me that its materials are taken more directly than other books of the *Physics* from discussions of Aristotle with his collaborators. It could be an associate's draft of a work that became Book VIII.

456 Wardy, *Chain*, 90–91.

cf Glasner

concerned to show their applicability to all sorts of change. He says a change (*metabolê*) is named rather by that into which the change occurs than by that from which it proceeds (224b7). His example for this is a corruption, which is substantial change and the opposite of generation.

He organizes kinds of change in relation to the subject (*hupokeimenon*) (224b35–225a20). There is change from subject to subject, from subject into non-subject, or from non-subject into subject. Change from non-subject to non-subject does not exist, he says, for non-being has no contraries. Indeed, even generation is not a *kinêsis* but rather a *metabolê* since it is change between contradictories. *Kinêseis* are all changes from subject to subject. These are change as to quality, where and when, relation, quantity, acting and undergoing (225b5–9). As Book V proceeds, Aristotle treats the common features of the different *kinêseis*, with respect both to continuity and to criteria of identity and contrariety.

In *Physics* VII.4, Aristotle shows a similar concern for the universality of the criteria for analyzing movements of different kinds. He asks whether every movement is comparable (*sumblêtê*) to every other—not just different instances of locomotion, like straight versus curved movement, but also if locomotion is comparable to alteration, for instance. The comparison of straight and curved movements is problematic enough. But one cannot say that, because an alteration and covering a distance take the same time, an alteration is equal to a particular locomotion. This is impossible, for how is an affection (*pathos*) similar to length (248a10–18)?

Even for comparisons within a kind of movement, like alteration, can different alterations be of equal speed? To take an example, is the fading of a surface in the sun (paling or whitening) comparable to the regaining of health? The times in which the changes occur may be equal, but are they neither the same, equal, or similar? Ought we to compare that in which the *pathos*, the affection received, lies in each case, or even the affections themselves (249a29–249b16)? Aristotle says that whether generations or corruptions are comparable requires investigation (249b20). He ventures that alterations must have something more than just a same time in common to be comparable. If the subjects differ in species, for instance, so do the movements.

This flurry of questions is the style of chapter 4 in general. How to assess similarity and sameness is the chief topic of chapter 4, and most of it reads like a set of discussion topics put together by a collaborator of Aristotle. The topics very naturally lead, however, to Aristotle's crisp summary at the beginning of chapter 5: a "mover moves something in something to something" (249b27). The proportions, employing letters for analogates in ratio, immediately follow. There is in *Physics* VII.4–5 the connection already noted between analysis of sameness or similarity of movements (*Physics* V) and the proportions possible among different continua (*Physics* VI.2). Importantly, Aristotle's concern is not identity but sameness and difference, similarity and comparability.

There is an important difference, however, between *Physics* VII.4–5 and the more extended treatment of the earlier motion books of the *Physics*. Chapter 4 of Book VII turns attention to more problematic and particular issues than appear in *Physics* V. The writer, we shall say Aristotle, spells out what is counterintuitive about being unable to compare straight and curved trajectories of locomotion. He provides a brief of the difference between equality and similarity, and tackles the problems of degrees of similarity among qualitative changes.[457] He observes the distinction of the *Categories* that quantities, like substances, are not themselves more and less but rather that "more and less" belongs to the category of relation. That comparability (more and less, double and half, prior and later) is not dependent on abstracting quantity is the most important thing to understand about *Physics* VII.4, where Aristotle undertakes a series of queries concerning homonymy for terms of sameness or similarity. If the subject of comparison is not quantity, how are things comparable? As I understand the chapter, it considers a series of flawed options, which were topics of discussion at the time.

The first comparison of different kinds of motion that Aristotle considers is the comparability of different types of locomotion. There will be a circumference (περιφερής τις) equal to a straight line when they take the same time (248a12), an apparent absurdity. Similarly, alteration and locomotion cannot be comparable simply by taking the same time (248a13–15). Aristotle then offers a series of closely packed implications:

---

457 The extreme aporetic character of the chapter could reflect either its having been written before *Physics* IV–VI or Aristotle's assuming the more general treatment of comparability of movements in *Physics* V–VI as a basis for further exploration of a thicket of remaining issues. Morison and Seel write, "Book VII does not belong with books V, VI, and VIII, and Eudemus did not have a book corresponding to it in his *Physics*" ("Preliminary Remarks," *Reading* Physics VII.3, 37). Their statement reinforces my belief that Book VII represents a school discussion text or cooperative working through of a problem.

> Then is it the case that whenever things are changed an equal
> amount in an equal time then (τότε) they are changed at
> the same rate (ἰσοταχές), but an affection is not equal to
> a length, so that (ὥστε) an alteration is neither equal to nor
> less than a locomotion, so that not all changes are compara-
> ble? (248a16–18)

There is equality of speed when things change the same amount in the
same time. But alteration has no "length" that makes for sameness of
amount between a distance covered and a subject altered. So, alteration
cannot be either equal to or more or less than some instance of locomotion. So, this very case apparently disproves that all changes are comparable.

Aristotle believes both that alteration and locomotion do not exhibit
sameness in amount *and* that many motions that are apparently incompa-
rable really are comparable. (Later, Aristotle says we must think in terms
of similarity not equality.[458]) He goes on to treat equality and "more and
less" together. He explicates the possibility that not all changes can be
compared, by considering a more difficult case:

> For it is odd if it is not possible to be moved such-and-such
> a distance alike on both a circle and a straight line, but rather
> it be necessary straight off that one of the motions be either
> faster or slower, just as if one were downhill, the other, uphill.
> (248a19–22)

Aristotle here considers what must have been one alternative addressed
in school discussions concerning comparison of straight and curved—
namely, that if an arc and straight line cannot be made equal, then they are
always related by longer and shorter. On this view, it is strange to *deny*
that circular and straight motion cover the same distance in a given time,
since curved and rectilinear movements are both movements from place
to place exhibiting a distinct path. If they are comparable as to more and
less, then there should be a place for equality in their relation also.

The problem with this alternative, Aristotle says, is that the difference between curved and straight has not been understood as the rad-

---

458 Τὸ γὰρ ἴσον οὐκ ἔστιν ἐνταῦθα λεγόμενον, ἀλλ᾽ ὡς ἐν τῷ ποσῷ ἰσότης, ἐνταῦθα
ὁμοιότης (249b2).

ical difference it is. The reference to the road up and the road down[459] in this passage recalls *Physics* III.3, where the same participles are juxtaposed to distinguish the action of an agent from the undergoing of the patient upon which it acts.[460] In this case, the two are different aspects of a single movement, opposite ways of conceiving it—from the standpoint of the agent or of the patient. Only rectilinear motion, however, can be defined by opposite characterizations of the starting and ending point of the same substratum distance. There is no such opposition for circular motion.[461] Its difference from rectilinear motion is more profound than simply having opposite starting and ending points.[462]

That the movement in the same time along an arc and a straight line cannot be equal follows from the fact that no straight line can be made equal to a circle. This is the point with which Aristotle summarily concludes the examination (248b6), stating as a provisional conclusion that things not synonymous are all incommensurable.[463] In light of this, it should be the case that curved and straight trajectories would not be comparable as faster and slower either. So, the passage considers a possibility that Aristotle elsewhere takes to lie well outside elementary geometric plausibility.

Within this alternate universe of speeds that Aristotle momentarily considers, where straight and curved are compared, Aristotle presents the reasoning that goes along with the insistence upon "if faster and slower, then equal." It is that whatever can be more and less must also be capable of being equal:

459 ὥσπερ ἂν εἰ κάταντες, τὸ δ᾽ἄναντες (248a18–19).

460 *Physics* III.3, 202a19 and 202b13.

461 *On the Heavens* I.2, 268b20–24, *Physics* VIII.8, 261b31–36.

462 The road up and the road down may also call upon the sensible intuition that an uphill climb would be slower than covering the same distance going downhill. So also, a curvilinear path to a given point seems longer than a rectilinear path to the same point. Accordingly, movement along the arc of a large circle may seem to the eye faster than movement accomplished in the same time along a corresponding chord (compare ΒΓ and ΒΕΓ in **Figure 8.6**). The intuition is very familiar. In English, we sometimes say a line of argument does not get to the point but is "circuitous."

463 Wardy says that speeds of curved and rectilinear movements could be comparable while the distances along curved and straight lines are not (*Chain*, 267). While this may be a theoretical possibility outside an Aristotelian context, Aristotle's own claim that time and motion are continua following magnitude (*Physics* IV.10) grounds his resolution (248b5–6) of the apparent antinomy of "not able to be equal" versus "being more and less." His resolution is that neither equality nor more and less is possible for comparing curvilinear and rectilinear movement.

285

Nor does it make any difference to the argument if one asserts that it is necessary straight off that one of them be moved either faster or slower, since then the circular line will be either greater or smaller than the straight one, so that it can also be equal. For if in time A the one traverses B while the other traverses C, it might be that B is greater than C, because that was how 'faster' was described. Accordingly it is also faster if it traverses an equal distance in a lesser time, so that there will be a part of time A in which B goes through a portion of the circle equal to what C goes through in the entire time A. (248a22–248b4)

Here, Aristotle embarks upon proportional reasoning but within the flawed model of comparing circular and straight. The model is Brysonian. By the most reliable reports, Bryson reasoned that, while increasing the number of sides of rectilinear figures that both circumscribe a circle and are inscribed within the circle, we could still always say that the circle is smaller than every circumscribed regular polygon and greater than every inscribed regular polygon.[464] Aristotle is so critical of Bryson that he must take this to be saying that the circle will finally coincide with a polygon.[465] The idea that more and less embrace equality fits within Aristotle's dismissal of Bryson. Also Brysonian on Aristotle's reading is the idea that a curve and a straight line are not so very different as to preclude coincidence. Aristotle criticizes Bryson in *Posterior Analytics* I.9 because he does not proceed from premises at the level of commensurate universality, the geometrical, that could solve the problem he addresses.[466]

We can note that a proper formulation would reason, as Archimedes did, that the difference between the circumference of the circle and the perimeter of the polygon can be made as small as one wishes. Circumference

---

464 This is Themistius' report. See Heath, *Mathematics in Aristotle*, 49.

465 *Sophistical Refutations* 11, 171b12–18, 171b34–172a7.

466 *Posterior Analytics* I.9, 75b36–76a2. Wardy takes most of the passage under consideration to be a straightforward articulation of views Aristotle accepts, and so he finds many errors (*Chain*, 266–271). He says Aristotle accepts that a "greater than/less than" comparison entails also "equal to." But Aristotle explicitly separates "equals" from "greater than/ less than" in chapters 6 and 7 of *Categories*, an early work of Aristotle. Definite quantities can be placed equal to one another, but quantity as such does not admit of more and less (5b15–17). More and less puts us in the category of relation. Furthermore, he drops the whole problem in *Physics* VII.4 when he insists upon the incommensurability of the *magnitudes or distances* of curved and straight. Without comparability of distances, there is no comparability of changes (248b5–6).

and perimeter never coincide. It is generally held that Archimedes' account is superior to any articulated in Aristotle's time. Nevertheless, the inexhaustibility of the difference between circle and polygon would have been understood through means of approximation that antedate Archimedes. So, formulating the basic insight of the inexhaustibility of the difference between circle and polygon does not need Archimedes' superior rendering. Given Aristotle's references to Bryson elsewhere, it is reasonable to think that Aristotle is rejecting Brysonian reasoning here because it does not partake of the geometrical insight that would preclude absolute equality for what can be shown to be greater than and less than.

The affirmation of the incommensurability of straight and circular lines in *Physics* VII.4 is interesting juxtaposed to chapter 2 of *Physics* VII, where Aristotle treats straight and curved motion in somewhat different terms. In fact, he treats circular motion as coming out of a combination of rectilinear movements.

Aristotle says in *Physics* VII.2 that there are three kinds of motion: in place, quality, and quantity, and so three kinds of movers. Locomotion is the first of motions (243a40). Everything moved in place is moved by itself or another. Being moved by another is of four kinds: dragging, pushing, carrying, and rotating (whirling).[467] All movements in place go back to these (243a15–19). Aristotle's immediate concern in chapter 2 is that, for all these movements, the mover is in contact with the moved thing. This is a condition of Book VII's argument for the first mover in chapter 1. Nevertheless, Aristotle goes into some detail concerning the analysis of all movements into these four. Shoving along is a kind of pushing where the mover follows along what it has pushed. Pushing away, a single shove, so to speak, occurs when the mover does not follow along with the moved thing. Throwing occurs when the mover produces motion more violent than the motion in accordance with nature and the propelled object continues as long as that motion rules.[468] Aristotle continues on to more cases, e.g., pushing apart or together (243a20–243b16).

This passage has been of considerable interest to students of Aristotelian mechanics, because it is the rare passage where a writer we take to be Aristotle himself composes a circular movement from rectilinear movements. He says that rotation (*dinêsis*) is composed from drag-

---

467 The Greek words are as follows: ἕλξις (dragging), ὦσις (pushing), ὄχησις (carrying), and δίνησις (rotating or causing a whorl).

468 Shoving along translates ἔπωσις; pushing away, ἄπωσις. Throwing is ῥῖψις.

ging and pushing (244a2). The mover making the whorl both pushes a part of the body away from itself or him/herself while at the same time drawing a part toward itself (a4). We should imagine the experience, involved in many tedious tasks, of stirring a thick mixture—tar, mortar, a stiff batter. The thicker the mass the more one's movements become a series of rectilinear movements at right angles to one another or along an imaginary hypotenuse of a right angled triangle.

A ubiquitous vortex phenomenon for sailors and those living by the sea in ancient times would have been the gradual formation of whirlpools in straits of the Mediterranean Sea and near rocks. These whirlpools originate from sea waves that strike rocks in straight waves but at an angle to the rocks. The breaking up of the wave creates a partial void near the obstacle, into which other water rushes. The agitation stabilizes when parts of the water maintain through time their respective positions within a circular movement.[469] Floating bodies moving at a slower pace than the circulating water will tend toward the center of the whirlpool—hence Odysseus' problem at Charybdis.[470] From an empirical standpoint, it hardly seems unusual that Aristotle would describe whirling motion as a combination.

---

469   That different parts of a body are pulled and pushed in whirling motion does not mean that Aristotle had in mind the application of force producing motion in different directions on opposite sides of a whorl, or wheel, as Wardy portrays (*Chain*, 136). Formation of a whorl depends on closely situated parts of a fluid being moved in different and somehow opposed rectilinear paths. (In *Mechanics* 1, movements at right angles are regarded as opposed.) This would be the case on any Aristotelian construction of the passage, even one that antedates *Mechanics*. In Aristotle's uses of the cognate term, *dinê*, a whorl is a motion that results in objects carried by the whorl tending toward the center (*On the Heavens* II.13, 295a13, *Physics* II.4, 196a26). This points to an understanding of forces operating within the whorl, not at its rim. Both these passages of Aristotle criticize pre-Socratic conceptions of the heavens. This reply to Wardy is not meant to endorse Ross's inflated dynamic interpretation of the passage (quoted in Wardy, *Chain*, 135), which Wardy criticizes.

470   For an analysis of Odysseus' path between Skylla and Charybdis in terms of the dynamics of the whirlpool, see Vatistas, "Floating Body Dynamics" and "Vortices." The advice given to Odysseus for avoiding Charybdis reflects craft-based nautical understanding of what Odysseus must do to avoid the whirlpool. His ship must be travelling in a straight line and faster than the revolution of the outer edge of the vortex. He has to glance off the vortex. It should be noted that, even away from shore, differences in temperature and salinity can create eddies, by initiating pressure gradients in adjacent masses of sea. This is a relatively high probability occurrence in the Mediterranean, which is highly saline, and in the Atlantic Ocean just outside the Mediterranean, where waters mix.

Physics VII.2 is not alone, in Aristotle's works, in showing curved motion as coming out of rectilinear.[471] The passages where Aristotle reasons in this way, however, do not serve as fundamentals of Aristotle's cosmic picture, it is generally agreed, in the way that the opposition of curved and rectilinear as simple movements does serve. Aristotle's pronouncements in *On the Heavens* on the simplicity of the circular motion of the heavens take precedent in the history and present evaluation of his natural philosophy. The situation as Aristotle presents it in *On the Heavens* is nuanced, however. First, Aristotle does not take simple bodies as the *starting points* of analysis of motion. The assumption has been that Aristotle hypothesizes a special substance, the aether, in which he lodges simple circular movement. Admitting the kinematic aspect of Aristotle's thinking on natural motion, however, raises the possibility that he had recourse to the aether as a kind of explanatory placeholder.[472] His ever-reliable mechanical principle accounted neatly for many of the features of phenomena in the heavens. There was needed a medium that could sustain the features of movement of which this kinematic principle gave an account. What was needed in particular were parts being in contact that can communicate movement without resistance or dissipation of motive energy.[473] Also, the medium should be rigid, since the expression of the

---

471 See the references in my Chapter 7.

472 There is an important issue here concerning whether Aristotle multiplies substances where he needs some physical connection and then makes the substance immune to scientific investigation. In a related point, Berryman holds that the *automaton* model for organisms, which was analyzed in foregoing chapters, is not mechanistic in any real sense: "Aristotle himself does not understand these mechanistically—inasmuch as he attributes the workings, in the case of the organism, to a theoretical substance with stipulated powers that are not susceptible to the kind of investigation and manipulation characteristic of mechanics" (Berryman, *Mechanical Hypothesis*, 206). The procedure Berryman describes as Aristotle's does not fit the character of Aristotle's science as I have been developing it, and it is contrary to Aristotle's criticism of multiplication of substances in other contexts (see *Metaphysics* B.2 and Chapter 10 below). Berryman develops the theoretical substance view further in reference to the connate pneuma (see her "Aristotle on *pneuma*"). Berryman contrasts her view to that of Hankinson who also uses the term "placeholder" for Galen's powers language (Berryman, *Mechanical Hypothesis*, 206n95). Rist makes a somewhat more modulated point along the lines of Berryman's but concerning the aether: "We can see Aristotle striving for a unity in the cosmos, for general explanations of all 'phenomena,' and for basic physical substances which are to 'underlie' (as 'matter') or 'overlie' (as God—the final or efficient cause)" (*Mind of Aristotle*, 17). The question is whether Aristotle supplies mysterious substances with stipulated powers or hypothesizes placeholder entities in a structure of explanation already going forward. In the latter case, the placeholders are subject to further investigation.

473 In the late nineteenth century, it was thought that there must be a universal impercep-

moving radius principle in the trope of the rolling cone presupposes rigid lines and surfaces that distribute mechanical effects evenly. Consistent with this interpretation is the fact that, in *On the Heavens*, Aristotle does not use the word aether to refer to anything in his own cosmology.[474] He refers to a heavenly immutable medium without naming it, in *On the Heavens* II.7, in terms of there being something whose natural movement is circular[475] (289a15). In this context, he says that it seems more important to argue for a simple body for circular motion than to argue for simple bodies for the rectilinear movements, since the latter are more readily observable in things around us (269a30). For both heavenly and sublunary movements, then, the kinematic aspect comes first.

When considering Aristotle's accounts of circular motion, a second question should give us pause. This is what Aristotle means by "simple" for movement, body, and magnitude. In *On the Heavens* I.2, Aristotle says that there are only two simple motions because there are only two simple magnitudes, the straight line and the curve (268b17–20). So, magnitude possesses the original simplicity—that of shape. If simple movements follow shape, then there must be a simple body that is naturally inclined to move in a circle (269a5–8). With the cognate repetitiveness possible in Greek, Aristotle drives home that the naturalness of a simple motion implies that it belongs to some body as that body's *principle* of motion: ἀναγκαῖον εἶναί τι σῶμα ἁπλοῦν ὃ πέφυκε φέρεσθαι τὴν κύκλῳ κίνησιν κατὰ τὴν ἑαυτοῦ φύσιν ("It is necessary that there be some simple body that is naturally inclined to move with a circular movement in accordance with its own nature") (269a5–8).[476] The question is whether

---

tible medium in the universe to sustain a very plausible and well-accepted wave theory of light. The Michelson-Morley experiment was designed to detect this medium, called the aether. This connection of a notion of the aether to theory and experiment is what I mean by the aether serving as a placeholder rather than an inaccessible substance with stipulated powers. The Michelson-Morley experiment failed in the sense that the flow of the aether could not be detected. If there were no aether, this raised the question in relation to *what* the speed of light could truly be measured.

474 The four occurrences of the word, αἰθήρ in *On the Heavens* appear at I.3, 270b22 and 25, II.13, 294a25–26, and III.3, 302b4. Each time the word is used in reference to pre-Socratic cosmologies.

475 τι εἶναι ὃ κύκλῳ φέρεσθαι πέφυκεν.

476 In his "Natural, Unnatural, and Preternatural Motions," Hankinson argues against the view that Aristotle thinks every simple motion has a simple body. According to Hankinson, Aristotle's position is that, since the heavens cannot contain corruptible elements, it must be composed of an element whose movement is by nature circular and does not have contraries.

this means such movement is elemental, with no aspect of composition from either other movements or other elemental materials. Issues treated in the next chapter will provide more context for evaluating this question.

One thing that is clear from examination of *On the Heavens* I.2 is that there is no bar to circular motion in the sublunary realm being composed from rectilinear movements. Movements here below are usually mixed (μικτή, μικτάς), and circular movement, as a resultant movement, could exist among things whose natural movements are rectilinear. In that case, the circular movement is not properly called unnatural (παρὰ φύσιν). If it is fire that is moved circularly, circular movement is not the opposite of fire's upward motion, since downward motion is its proper opposite (269a7–15). This position on circular movement dovetails with remarks made in *Physical Problems* XVI.3, 11, and 12 about circular movement of a projectile. In both chapters 3 and 11, circular movement has a kind of simplicity by its being a natural niche into which the reconciliation of competing movements fall. It is possible that the simplicity of circular motion in the heavens is the simplicity of the natural default setting for the behavior of all bodies in movement but particularly the heavenly bodies, which manifest circular motion in a spectacular way. In any case, it is possible to say that the occurrence of curved movement, in the terms formulated by the author of *Mechanics*, presents no particular problem for Aristotle's treatment of types of movement in *On the Heavens*. Accordingly, the composition of δίνησις from pushing and pulling in *Physics* VII.2 need not be an aberration from Aristotle's other teachings on motion.

Leaving these questions about *On the Heavens* aside, we have gained an important point from Aristotle's inclusion of δίνησις in *Physics* VII.2. At the time of writing this chapter, Aristotle already had in hand a conceptual tool that figures importantly in the demonstration of *Mechanics* 1— the resolution of circular motion into rectilinear components. In *Physics* VII.2, the context is strongly physicalistic. In *Movement of Animals* and *On the Heavens*, his references to the principle are more cleanly kinematic. The physicalistic context of *Physics* VII.2 is appropriate, because it lends itself to a causal account, which is itself suited to the announced topic of Book VII, the necessity for a first mover.

Returning to *Physics* VII.4, we note that, after his consideration of comparing circular and rectilinear movement, Aristotle goes on to more difficult issues of synonymy and difference. We return to Aristotle's flat assertion that things that are not synonymous are not comparable (248b7). We do not say a wine, a pencil, and a high note are comparable because they are all called sharp. So also, swift or quick (τὸ ταχύ) does not mean the same thing in relation to rectilinear and circular motion, and even [less so] for alteration and locomotion compared (b10–12). On the other hand, "much" means the same thing (τὸ αὐτὸ σημαίνει) in reference to water and air, which are not comparable. Even if "much" did not mean the same in these cases, at least "double" (two in relation to one) does, even if the doubled things are not comparable. Then, Aristotle asserts more definitively, "In fact (καὶ γάρ), 'much' is homonymous" (b16). It would seem that he has in mind connected homonyms, since he goes on to a more disjunctive homonymy, "But of some things (ἀλλ'ἐνίων), even the definitions are homonymous." This could be true for usages of "much." The "equal" and "one" then, might each happen to be unconnected homonyms (248b12–20).

This passage recalls *Categories* 1, where Aristotle defines homonymy as the same word having different definitions. This is equivocation (for words), or disjunctive homonymy (for things). Nevertheless, the example he gives in *Categories* 1, "man" and "picture" (τὸ γεγραμμένον) as both ζῷον, living thing, bears interpretation as an example of connected homonyms, "man" and "picture of man."[477] The passage in *Physics* VII.4 raises the possibility that Aristotle is mindful of the ambiguity surrounding homonymy in *Categories* 1 and regards it as interestingly benign. He presents the two kinds of homonymy close together in both passages. Wardy translates the text under consideration in *Physics* VII.4 as depicting something increasingly unacceptable:

---

477 Ζωγράφημα (from ζωγραφέω, paint from life) also means picture, so Aristotle may consider τὸ γεγραμμένον as connected to this word for picture that incorporates the root ζω- for "animal." Commenting on this passage, Ackrill writes, "The example Aristotle uses for both homonymy and synonymy, 'ζῷον' can signify either an animal or a picture (whether of an animal or not)" (13). There is considerable discussion as to whether Aristotle means to invoke connected homonyms in *Categories* 1. Ackrill thinks so; Wedin does not. See, for instance, Ackrill's translation of 1a2–3: "both a man and a picture are animals (ζῷον)" and his commentary on *Categories* 1 (*Aristotle's* Categories, 71–72), as well as Wedin, *Theory of Substance*, 12–27. On Wedin's reading in accordance with what he calls strong homonymy, the man and the picture have nothing in common. I am calling this disjunctive homonymy. This companion passage in *Physics* VII.4 provides evidence that Aristotle was well aware of how disjunctive homonymy yields readily to the nuance of connected homonyms.

"[W]ere one to say that 'much' is such-and-such an amount
and more, the amount would be different in different cases.
And 'equal' is homonymous, and perhaps 'one' as well immediately becomes homonymous." (248b17–19)

So, if amounts are not comparable for "much," nothing prevents "equal"
and "one" from having multiple meanings. In comparing things so disparate, there would be no reason (διὰ τί) some things are comparable and
others not, since the nature would be all one (248b21). In this case, there
would be one supergeneric substratum for all comparison, and it would,
Aristotle says, disclose no contours leading us to compare things. He says
"even double" would be homonymous. Double is important, because it is
a prototype relation (πρός τι) that transcends many differences already,
without our being tempted to think it has a different definition in each
case.

Aristotle rejects the one nature for comparability and offers an alternative of incorporating synonymy in apparently different things.
Sameness of recipient (δεκτικός) can make things comparable, in the
way that the paleness of a horse and a dog are comparable, because it is
always and only surface that receives paleness (248b21–24). But does
this mean that comparable things are never homonyms? Must comparables share a differentia, so that only things the same in species are comparable (249a3–5)? Aristotle finally concludes that one cannot give a single
differentia for the genus of movement (249a22). He makes the interesting
remark that many candidates for comparability escape notice by falling
outside or alongside the genus (παρὰ τοῦτο λανθάνει πολλά), which is
not one thing[478] (249a22–23). That is, the subject matters in which their
movements take place do not fit obvious genera, although they may resemble another genus. He introduces a wider range of comparability:

Of homonymous movements, some differ widely, others have
a certain resemblance, while others again are closely related
either in genus or by analogy, which is why they do not seem
to be homonyms although they really are. So is the species different when the same characteristic is in different recipients,

---

478 Wardy translates, "And this argument indicates that the genus is not one single
thing: but apart from the genus of change there are many other cases which go undetected"
(*Chain*, 64). The Oxford translation of Hardie and Gaye reads, "and this discussion serves
to show that the genus is not a unity but contains a plurality latent in it and distinct from it"
(*CWA* 1, 416).

> or when different characteristics are in different recipients? And what is the mark of differentiation? By means of what shall we judge that white and sweet are the same or differ- ent—is it because they appear different in different recipients, or because they are altogether not the same?[479] (249a23–29)

This ending to a passage full of argumentative switchbacks has seemed to some to be not a resolution but rather the specter of Aristotle abandoning well-defined subject matters for the natural sciences. It is unlikely that this is the thread of meaning in the briefly presented alter- natives. The point is that, if the phenomenon of connected homonyms is multi-faceted, the subject matter for being the same may often be anony- mous, without a name (249b24). Comparability does not require synon- ymy by species.

By showing the elasticity of similarity for movement, Aristotle effec- tively transfers the structure of magnitude to any subject matter in which change takes place. Having sketched this result at the end of chapter 4, he proceeds immediately to the proportions at the beginning of *Physics* VII.5. These proportions we can understand as applying broadly under the criteria of sameness and difference given in *Physics* V and at the be- ginning of *Physics* VII.5. Aristotle concludes chapter 5 by returning to the issue of alteration. Thus, as it is a prelude to *Physics* VII.5, chapter 4 also shows that the lettered proportions of *Physics* VII.5 concern equality and similitude and what lies between them, not mechanics. Put in terms of Aristotle's deformation strategy, *Physics* VII.4–5 provides the *rationale by which* some invariance may be transformed in different circumstances. One might say that the rationale substitutes for outright foundations.

In *Physics* VII.4, Aristotle is showing why establishing criteria of sameness by which to compare movements is not needed to support iso- morphism across subject matters. Settling the question of the definition of subject matters is a lesser prize for Aristotle than disclosing the contours of nature across subject matters. We can infer this from his telling remark that pursuing single nature homogeneity for comparables submerges the *reasons* things are comparable (248b20). A single nature makes every- thing one. Being the same in some way, on the other hand, shows up against the background of difference, and difference comes in more guis-

---

479   Wardy's translation altered to reflect the plural feminine case of ὁμωνυμίαι, homon- ymous things, which I understand to be movements, κινήσεις.

es than can be catalogued. So, the treatment given to similarity in *Physics* VII.4 shows the character of VII.5 as providing a framework for understanding change. Within this framework, we seek a physical invariance, the investigation of which is more in evidence in *Physics* IV.8.

It may not be immediately obvious but is nevertheless true that the sequence of topics in *Physics* VII.4 reflects Aristotle's commitment as an empiricist. I have argued that the ancients became progressively more aware of the lever principle as a mathematical whole embedded in nature, the moving radius in its many manifestations. Aristotle extends the mechanical reasoning behind leverage phenomena to his accounts of animal movement, perception, and embryological development. In *Physics* VII.4, Aristotle reflects upon the grounding for this sort of explanatory proliferation. The homonymy Aristotle depicts in *Physics* VII.4 suits the embedded character of mathematical relations in nature but also suits the explanatory proliferation of the relation to other natural circumstances. Aristotle neither separates what is invariant across cases from its immediate context nor treats the invariant as univocal, a "same thing." This is possible because what is invariant is relational, what I have called a descriptive mode. Homonymy provides a broad but productive middle ground between synonymy and disjunctive homonymy. The stretching of the basis for comparison that is present in *Physics* VII.4 is just what one would expect to find in Aristotle if he pursues the explanatory strategy I ascribed to him in earlier chapters. To Aristotle's mind, there is no loss of explanatory power or inner detail in exercising the option of analogy.

By upgrading similarity in change to anonymous sameness, Aristotle provides a rationale for comparability keyed to the reason things are comparable:

> [W]e must consider the same question in the case of becoming and perishing: how is one becoming of equal velocity with another? They are of equal velocity if in an equal time there are produced two things that are the same and specifically inseparable (ἄτομον), e.g. two men (not two animals). (249b19–21)

Here, Aristotle says that equal velocity can be judged sometimes by time and an outcome of the same indivisible species. He immediately goes on to say, however, that "if in an equal time something different comes about (for we do not have some 'two' in which the otherness is expressed, like a dissimilarity [in species])," then one becoming is faster than the other

(249b21–23). In this case, the difference is not in species but is anonymous. He continues:

> If substances were numbers, there would be a greater number and a lesser number within the same species; but what is common is anonymous, nor are there terms to express either of them separately in the same way as we indicate greater affection or excess by 'more', or a quantity by 'greater.' (249b24–26)

Between subjects that are not the same individually or in species, there still is something that is the same but anonymous. If similarities are not in a species or genus, they are still valid analogically by virtue of some commonality (249b25).[480] Aristotle distinguishes the equal (τὸ ἴσον) for similarity (ὁμοιότης) from equality (ἰσότης), which is proper to quantity (ἐν τῷ ποσῷ) (249b2–3). He says, "What is equality in the category of quantity is similarity here." The context of the quotation is alteration. He thus makes it explicit that one may reason in the mathematical mode of relation without quantizing.

true?

Summary

The upshot of this long chapter is the following. In the passages of Aristotle's natural philosophy where he forms proportions using letters standing for forces, weights, speeds, distances, and times, he is drawing upon mechanical knowledge of a relational kind that had been known for a very long time to Greek thinkers in terms of proportions governing leverage and mechanical advantage. The moving radius or concentric circles principle was an early intellectualized expression of leverage. The form the principle takes in the analysis involving rectilinear elements of the circle in *Mechanics* 1 is the latest version explored here. There is an invariance that unifies these and other different expressions of the principle of the lever. The invariance I have dubbed a descriptive mode. One thing about a descriptive mode is that some features of later more mathematicized expressions of the mode may well show up as properties of earlier expressions but not systematically. This is one reason for drawing

---

480   Aristotle refers to a common feature that is without a name at 249b25. On the common (*koinon*) in relation to mathematical physics, see also *Posterior Analytics* I.7, 75b20 and I.9, 75b41, also I.13, 78b32–79a15. These passages are treated in the next chapter.

attention to the descriptive mode. We are not dealing with simple incrementalism in the growth of knowledge but with properties belonging to a principle, which are drawn out by the circumstances themselves in which the principle is manifest.

The descriptive mode for leverage involves ratios of the factors mentioned above participating in deformations in concert in such a way that an equilibrium in movement is maintained. I showed how, in *Physics* IV.8, the descriptive mode functions as background knowledge in extending the kinematic implications of leverage. Background knowledge is not the same as laws of motion.

The extension of kinematics into Aristotle's analysis of locomotion has been considered in relation to his discourse about the continuum, which is so prominent in the same passages that give lettered proportions. Sometimes the continuum analysis serves the clarification of the conditions under which movement is possible at all, thus being directed at Zeno. In other cases, the continuum analysis serves the extension of Aristotle's deformation strategy, which depends on continuity in a way cited by Aristotle himself.

The possibility for wide deployment of the principle of the lever as a descriptive mode for locomotion makes Aristotle ambitious to extend at least some aspects of the mode to all sorts of change. Hence, he investigates in *Physics* VII.4 what could constitute comparability of deformations across very heterogeneous types of change, like growth, alteration, and generation. Here again, continuity is the starting point for comparability among subject matters. It has been my contention that Aristotle recognizes an anonymous sort of sameness in congruent relation, the very basis of proportion. He has understood the import of Eudoxan proportion as defining sameness of ratio. This sameness is neither identity nor similarity in some respect. Sameness of ratio is *sui generis*, because what is the same is a *relation* between members of ratios homogenous within their respective domains.

Coda on the Sequence of Aristotle's Interests

Throughout this chapter, I have referred to the author of *Physics* VII as Aristotle. My readings of chapters 2 and 4–5 suggest to me, nevertheless, that Book VII is rougher than a first draft of Book VIII, which is Aristotle's more polished version of the argument for the first mover.

Both chapters 2 and 4 collect definite original ideas, which are not presented with so much brevity by Aristotle elsewhere. Chapter 4 in particular seems like a listing of key problems involved in transferring reasoning from one subject matter into another, and a probing of directions for their solution. The chapter sketches how one can reason by similarity without falling into the kind of mistakes (e.g., Bryson's) that would otherwise afflict proceeding without a basis for judging things synonymous. Book VII has the character of a collection of study materials. I would offer the speculative suggestion that these chapters were compiled on Aristotle's instruction by a collaborator.

These study materials reflect a new or at least different direction of research from Aristotle's earlier work in *Physics* I–II. It is likely that his teleology of nature, *Physics* II, was written during or at the end of his first stay in Athens.[481] *Physics* II is a product of Aristotle's reflection on Plato's philosophy. *Physics* VII lays out different commitments about motion, which are replicated with more detail and crispness in *Physics* IV–VI.[482] The biggest difference is Aristotle's focus, during his second stay in Athens, on locomotion as a prime exemplar of change.

At the beginning of *Physics* VII.2, Aristotle says explicitly he is not treating the cause for-the-sake-of-which but rather the efficient cause when he says that the first mover and the moved thing must be together (ἅμα) (243a32–35). Efficient cause produces an effect by contact. In terms reminiscent of *Physics* V.3 (227a1), he says that for an efficient cause to act, there must be nothing in between it and the moved thing. In *Physics* VII.2, he says furthermore that locomotion (φορά) is the first

---

481 Aristotle left Athens sometime around Plato's death in 347 BC. See Rist, *Mind of Aristotle*, 12. Macedonian destruction of Greek cities and Macedon's threat to Athens would have made Aristotle unwelcome there. He returned to Athens in 334. In the period between Aristotle's return to Athens and the death of Alexander in 323, when he had to leave again, Aristotle finished a great number of works in biology begun elsewhere, as well as the motion books of the *Physics* and the books of the *Metaphysics*.

482 Given the prominence at this time of principles from mechanics among Aristotle's working principles in natural philosophy, it is possible that a new collaborator joined him in Athens, someone familiar with the fifth century kinematics of southern Italy. A candidate whose name we know is Aristoxenus, a student of Aristotle's who was from Tarentum and who said that his father knew Archytas. Aristoxenus is best known for his specialty of harmonics (and an apparently hubristic character). See Burkert, *Lore and Science*, 106–107. It is always possible that others from southern Italy were in Aristotle's circle at this time. This suggestion is speculative, but the presence of a new collaborator would help to explain why these ideas, left unexplored in earlier years, assumed a more central role in Aristotle's thinking.

among movements (243a39–40). It is prior to qualitative or quantitative change. He then gives the catalog of pushes and pulls that are fundamental to other types of change, including circular locomotion. He completes the chapter by showing how what alters and what is altered are also in contact, as well as what causes quantitative change and what undergoes it. It is thus clear that the investigation of movement here is different from the one undertaken in *Physics* II. There are many reasons to think the motion books of the *Physics* were written during Aristotle's second stay in Athens, and so also possibly *Physics* VII dates to that period. What is important is to notice just how much the direction of his research during his second stay in Athens comes from a different source or inspiration than either *Physics* II or the biological works that were his preoccupation in the time he spent with research associates in Assos and Lesbos.

Certainly, Aristotle could have learned of the work in kinematics done by Archytas and others of the southern Italian school from the exchanges that accompanied Plato's travels to Sicily and southern Italy. Such exchanges within Magna Graecia would have been routine at any time but are even more to be expected when the leader of the Academy was traveling there.[483] This was when Aristotle was first in Athens as a young man. Yet, neither Plato nor Aristotle exploited the key kinematic principle until much later—at the end of Plato's life when he wrote *Laws* X, and when Aristotle returned to Athens well after Plato's death. The connections among the *Physics*, *Physical Problems*, and *Movement of Animals* that have been reconstructed here make the background for Aristotle's thinking at this time more like a fabric of connected crisscrossing interests. He is not a logicist analyzing in a dialectical way problems presented to him by Parmenides and Zeno. As important as these metaphysical problems are, he integrates them with his interest in simple mathematically based principles explanatory of weights in motion. One

---

483 Concerning the authenticity of Plato's *Seventh Letter*, where the author purporting to be Plato describes meeting Archytas, see Irwin, who says "many of the more straightforward and (for contemporaries) easily verifiable historical claims may be accurate" ("Intellectual Background," 78–79n4). See also Lewis, "Seventh Letter," 231–233 and n4 and n11. I take it to be true that (1) Plato went to southern Italy and Sicily for the purposes of educating a ruler, Dion, (2) that he met Archytas, ruler of Tarentum, at least once, and (3) that this or these meeting(s) could have issued in intellectual exchanges in person or by letter between Archytas or his companions, on the one hand, and members of the Academy, on the other. I am grateful to John Rist for confirmation of the likelihood of this sort of intellectual communication between the Greek cities and their colonies (private communication).

reason for this turn to practical mechanics is that he sees in this topic the promise of a unified treatment of the cosmos.

A key tenet of Aristotle's analysis of movement at this time is the proposition that a greater weight moves faster in the same time than a lesser weight subject to the same force. This proposition accompanies the analysis of revolution of an unbalanced projectile in *Physical Problems* XVI. The tenet is expressed clearly in both *Physics* IV.8 and *Physical Problems* XVI.3, though in neither is it an axiom or law. It is a highly contextualized comparative observation. The composition of circular motion discussed in kinematic terms in *Physical Problems* XVI is invoked in *Physics* VII.2 in the cataloging of *dinêsis* as derived from the pushing and pulling sort of efficient causes. A similar combination of movements figures in *Progression of Animals*. This background makes *Movement of Animals*, with its mix of topics on animal motion and first movers more understandable as part of an ongoing project of Aristotle's later period of concentrated scientific work. Aristotle is serious about kinematic principles in animal movement. This background also helps to explain why he would add references to mechanical puppets to works considered strictly biological. He is rethinking the inner dimension of generation. The references to *automata* are not oddities. They combine two new interests of Aristotle's later period of investigation in natural philosophy: (1) the succession of efficient causes in change, and (2) the inner dimension of dynamic equilibrium within a flux that could afford explanatory accounts of movement itself.

Chapter 10
Weight and Mathematical Science

This chapter treats Aristotle's explicit statements about the mathematical natural sciences of his time and the effort he made at a systematic integration of these with the mathematical disciplines that he called sep-arable in thought. I noted in the first chapter that a philosophy of mathematics—a systematic treatment of the different *mathêmata* and their ontological status—is one thing, while Aristotle's use of mathematics in his natural philosophy is something else. What he says and what he does might not be entirely consistent. In this chapter, I examine Aristotle's more systematic pronouncements about mathematics in light of his uses of ratio theory and mechanics in his natural philosophy. Given the range of topics relevant to my project in this chapter, my interpretation of Aristotle's systematic thinking in relation to his practice must remain a sketch. There is much interesting recent scholarship, however, on mathematics from the pre-Socratics through Aristotle that supports the key point I argue, namely, that <u>Aristotle did not regard separated mathematics as prior to the mathematical natural sciences.</u>[484] I believe Archytas is an influence on Aristotle's taking this view. I also offer the hypothesis that Aristotle worked from an initial Platonic handicap on the issue of weight.

Though I continue to argue strongly for the influence of mechanics on Aristotle's natural philosophy, for his use of a mathematical type of thinking, and for the highly contextualized nature of the mathematics

---

484   That Aristotle did not regard mathematical objects as prior to substances or other kinds of being that manifest mathematical traits is clear from *Metaphysics* M, 1077b1–11. This passage is treated by Cleary, "Terminology of 'Abstraction,'" 27. This position stated by Aristotle is not identical to my claim that Aristotle did not regard separated mathematics as prior to mathematical natural science, but it provides additional support for that claim.

available to him in the fourth century, I do not mean to deny a distinction between mathematics and natural philosophy for Aristotle. Although the influence of mathematical mechanics upon Aristotle's natural philosophy is quite direct—it is a conscious appropriation—at some point the very success of the structures transferred from the mathematical discipline to philosophy makes those structures the context for development of issues specific to philosophy. What I do claim is that Aristotle's philosophy of nature gains from mechanics a precision that came with its mathematical aspect, a particular range of topics to address, and a notion of function in one mathematical sense (the idea that when one thing varies, another thing changes also). Another very important aspect of mechanics retained by Aristotle's natural philosophy will be treated in the next chapter.

Let us note, to begin with, a certain stumbling block in addressing weight in its role among the mathematical sciences in Aristotle. In the *Categories*, Aristotle lays out what are the fundamental entities of the world, namely substances and their properties or attributes. It is noteworthy that the word "weight" (βάρος), or its adjectival "heavy" (βαρύς, βαρύ), appears nowhere in the treatise. If the *Categories* is an ontology, then weight is not a main division of the ontology nor apparently is it significant enough to be mentioned as falling within one of the main types in the ontology.[485] Aristotle gives number and magnitude as types of quantity, even language and time. He mentions both body (σῶμα) and solid (τὸ στερεόν) as quantity. States, conditions, and affections are types of quality. The omission of weight in either list is striking, seeing that all earthy bodies have weight and all bodies have either weight or lightness.[486] Neither does weight appear in the *postpredicamenta* (chapters 10–15) where contraries, prior and posterior, and change, are discussed. Presumably, weight's pairing with lightness and its involvement with change would make it an appropriate subject for the *postpredicamenta*.

Aristotle believes, I will argue, that weight belongs to particular bodies as a property or something attributed. When we measure it with con-

---

485 The interpretation of *Categories* 1–5 that is adopted here is that the treatise is about words as meaning or referring to things.

486 ,Ackrill suggests that Aristotle classifies types of quantities by ownership of the trait. For this reason, his list is not exhaustive. There is no single owner for weight as line is the owner of length, he says. If he is right, then *sôma*, body, is also a term whose categorical status needs clarification. It is not clear why body, or a type of body, earth, cannot be the owner of weight. See Ackrill, *Aristotle's* Categories *and* De Interpretatione, 91–92.

ventional units, we make it simulate quantity.[487] As it is defined in *On the Heavens* IV.1, though, weight is a power of movement and exists as greater or lesser than the weight of another body. As *dunamis*, it would be a quality but one that exists relationally. Heavy is "heavier than" another body with weight; light is "lighter in weight." Besides weight, however, there is also lightness (τὸ κοῦφον), a power of moving upward or to the extremity of the cosmos. "Lighter than," as the comparison of bodies intrinsically light, namely fire and air, is different from one *weight* being lighter than another. This chapter will show that weight has the being *relation* appropriate to relation. Weight is a relational quality inhering in some bodily substances.

Quantity in Aristotle's conception is fairly narrow in import, but its narrowness goes along with Aristotle's opening of the other categories to what receives measure and relation. It is a common assumption that Aristotle's failure to quantify weight adequately is a sign of his inability /14 R to treat motion mathematically. This is why his science is "qualitative." Looking for mathematical thinking in the category of quantity, though, is looking for it in the wrong place.

Quantity and Proportion

The range of *mathêmata*—arithmetic, geometry, harmonics, astronomy, optics, mechanics, surveying—were not conceived by Aristotle strictly as sciences of quantity. Quantity derived as a notion from the interrogative pronoun, πόσον, "how much?"[488] Although both Plato and Aristotle distinguished discrete and continuous quantity as the subject matters of arithmetic and geometry respectively, *more and less*—the core idea in both the various means and in proportionality—was not primarily quantitative for either philosopher. In a passage of *Republic* VIII, Socrates shows his interlocutor that he does not know what more and less really mean. The discussion concerns the idea of more or less filled. Plato dissociates the notion of filling up or being full (πλήρωσις) from quantity (585b9–c6) and associates it with sharing more in being (οὐσίας

---

487 Examples of units of weight are μνᾶ, σταθμός, τάλαντον. Even as conventionally measured, weight retained a relational meaning, because of being measured on the balance. The words τάλαντον and σταθμός mean a balance and by extension connote also what is weighed, and finally a unit or standard of weight.

488 In the *Categories*, Aristotle does not use an abstract noun for quantity, as he does for quality, ποιότητα.

303

τι μᾶλλον μετέχει): "And isn't that which is more, and is filled with things that are more, really more filled than that which is less, and is filled with things that are less (585d7–9)?" Socrates here leads Glaucon to a conception of "more" as ontological priority. Plato's discussion of more and less comes after a consideration of how what we call pleasure involves deliverance from pain (584b5–c7). He says this dependence is most like differences in place. Up, middle, and down are relative to the observer. He says:

> Do you suppose that a man brought from the downward re-
> gion to the middle would suppose anything else than that he
> was being brought up? And standing in the middle and look-
> ing away to the place from which he was brought, would he
> believe he was elsewhere than in the upper region since he
> hasn't seen the true up?[489] (584d6–8)

Plato's root insight is that judgments of more and less depend on percep-tion. Plato relates both difference in place and the limitation of quantita-tive notions to the preferences of one who lacks knowledge of the virtues (586a). He thus applies the insight very widely. He also counter-intuitive-ly makes the prior sense of more and less non-quantitative.

On a more mundane level, Aristotle says that quantity does not admit of more and less (i.e., there cannot be more or less of any given quantity, like three). Being three does not include being more than two. More and less is instead a relation. This does not present as much of a problem for doing mathematics as it might seem. Aristotle constructed proportions from sensible subject matters without a systematic base in a pure mathe-matics taken as prior. Furthermore, though quantity lacks more and less, it does receive measure; there is a quantitative aspect to anything that can be a multitude determined in accordance with a standard or unit. These two features of mathematical *praxis* in antiquity—quantity does not in-clude relation but it does receive measure—mean that much of what we might identify as calculation or function in the mathematical sense fell to subject matters not numerical or quantitative. Correspondingly, even though these two *mathêmata* were conceived by Plato and Aristotle as noetic subject matters—i.e., the subject matter of arithmetic or geometry is separable in thought from sensible things—the kinds of relation at work

---

489 Translations are by Bloom.

in the *mathêmata* were not the province of the noetic alone. This state of affairs was something that required an explanation only in retrospect.[490]

Klein draws attention to the retrospective view in his observation that the late Neoplatonic taxonomers of mathematics, Nicomachus and Theon, could not fit proportionality into either theory of numbers or calculation, the two divisions of arithmetic.[491] Klein ascribes this difficulty to the loss of Platonic logistic (λογιστική) as a mathematical discipline parallel to theoretical arithmetic. Both Archytas and Plato regarded logistic as the science of the relation of numbers.[492] Huffman has pointed out, however, that Archytas' understanding of logistic was more concrete than Plato's. Logistic was superior to geometry because logistic reasoning applied most widely and contributed to wisdom, including wise moral judgment.[493] Although Plato would seek a philosopher's logistic to contrast to ordinary logistic,[494] his was not the only voice on the matter. Both means and proportions would have been in the sphere of logistic, but the boundaries of the subject matter to which these applied were not agreed upon. Aristotle does not use the word λογιστική to flag arithmetic calculation as universal, in the way Archytas does. Aristotle follows Archytas' lead, however, in applying proportional reasoning to definition throughout physics.[495] Aristotle's practice in this regard is a sign of the plasticity of mathematical concepts as they were being drawn into the development of philosophy.

I have pointed to three aspects of the fluidity of thinking about mathematics from Archytas to Plato—first, Plato's making of more and less non-quantitative; second, the existence of another mathematical tradition, logistic, for ratio and proportion; and third, the lack of clear definition of the boundaries between different *mathêmata* at this time.

---

490   The retrospective view is dawning already in Aristotle's remark on his own procedure in *Movement of Animals* 1, of treating the movement of limbs as radial motion of a radius around a stationary point: "For the moving as they say is fictional (καὶ γὰρ τὸ κινεῖσθαι, ὥς φασί, πλάττουσιν ἐπ' αὐτῶν) for nothing mathematical moves" (698a25–26). Cleary suggests that the question of the ontological status of mathematical objects was only just emerging for Aristotle at the time of his writing *Posterior Analytics* ("Terminology of 'Abstraction,'" 18).

491   Klein, *Greek Mathematical Thought*, 31–32.

492   Huffman, *Archytas*, 243.

493   See Archytas Fr. 1 and 4 (Huffman, *Archytas*, 103–112, 225).

494   See below on the *Philebus* 55d–56d.

495   Huffman, *Archytas*, 75, 180.

In general, recent scholarship, beginning with Burkert's *Lore and Science in Ancient Pythagoreanism* and continuing with the work of Huffman, Mansfeld, and Zhmud, has shown that the divisions among the sciences recognized in present-day scholarship on Plato and Aristotle only became settled doctrines in the hands of the Platonists and Aristotle's successors, like Eudemus.[496] These divisions were carried through medieval philosophy up to the Renaissance. My aim is to evaluate Plato's pure mathematics (geometry and arithmetic), as well as Aristotle's mixed sciences (astronomy, harmonics, and optics) in their own contemporary contexts as attempts, more or less successful, to account for the logical structure of mathematical analysis and for the fact that mathematical principles are at work in nature. Accordingly, in what follows I will try to stay close to Aristotle's own language and avoid treating the various *mathêmata* as a contrast of pure and applied mathematics.

In the context I have sketched, weight presents an interesting case study. Weight was a very practical concern and was linked to the use of simple machines. Weight was linked with motion undertaken with an end in view. Nevertheless, the geometry of the circle was seen to be relevant to the motion of balance and lever. Weight thus falls between the Platonizing segregation of mathematical principles, which seemed irresistible given the constancy of the features of numbers and geometrical objects, and the contingency and practicality of overcoming natural obstacles. In the range of issues in fourth century philosophical reflection on mathematics, the notion of weight occupies unclaimed territory.

Weight in Plato

Weight's equivocal status can be seen in Plato's ambivalence about weight. In the *Euthyphro*, Plato gives a reason for weight to be included among the fortunate subjects susceptible to a precise account. Like counting (λογισμός) number, and measuring (τὸ μετρεῖν) larger and smaller, we can weigh (διακριθεῖμεν) heavier and lighter (7b6–c5). Plato thus places heavier and lighter with number and "larger and smaller" as fit subjects for measurement.[497]

---

496 Huffman, *Archytas*; Mansfeld, *Studies in Historiography*; Zhmud, *Origin*.

497 Depending on its translation, a passage in the *Timaeus* may repeat this triad. Any of the three—number, magnitude or bulk (ὄγκος) and power (δύναμις)—may enter into mean proportion (31c4–32a1), in this case a geometric proportion. The weight of scholarly opinion interprets these terms as direct references to different means. Number and magni-

In contrast, the *Phaedo* strikes a familiar Platonic theme in the association of weight with the less real visible realm (ορατόν). Weight is the heaviness that drags a soul back into the visible realm (89c9). Like Aristotle, Plato usually presents heavy and light together. The *Theaetetus* combines this duality with the *Phaedo*'s insistence on the unreality of ordinary things. In the *Theaetetus*, Socrates says that, just as there is nothing large that cannot appear small sometime, also anything heavy may seem light (152d5). Visible things can be measured, however. The measurability of body was a key assumption of the *Timaeus*. The receptacle, before it receives qualitative differentiation, has no equality of powers or forces but shakes, unevenly balanced in every direction, and is in general lacking in proportion and measure (52e1–53a9). Words having to do with weight and balance predominate in this description of the opposite of a measured condition in the original principle of body.[498] The contrast implies that, as we know body and normally encounter it, it is measurable. Heaviness, being bodily, merges in Plato's treatment with the tendencies of desire working against the person's true nature, against rationality. Yet, the idea of measuring out by comparison continues to figure in Plato's treatment of weight.

In the charioteer myth of the *Phaedrus*, Plato repeatedly uses the language of weighing, rising, and sinking to describe the fate of souls (246a6–248e1). In this treatise, the soul itself, and not body, is the source of the soul's heaviness.[499] A key element of the myth is that gods and men as charioteers are making circuits, the souls of men rising and falling as they strive upward toward the dwelling place of the gods. Both divine and human charioteers steer two horses. The gods have steeds that are obedient and equally balanced (ἰσορρόπως) (247b2), so that nothing impedes

---

tude are paired with δύναμις and ὄγκος respectively, plane and solid numbers. Cornford's translation of the relevant subordinate clause reads: "For whenever, of three numbers, the middle one between any two that are either solids (cubes?) or squares . . ." (*Cosmology*, 44). See Cornford's commentary in *Cosmology*, 46–47. Burkert interprets the passage similarly to Cornford (*Lore and Science*, 372n13). Krafft offers a different reading of the text, supporting it with a citation from Simplicius, who attributes the threesome, ῥοπή, μέγεθος, and πλῆθος to Archytas (Krafft, *Betrachtungsweise*, 147–149). This is worth noting since the triad—number, magnitude or bulk, and weight—became familiar in late antiquity. Huffman says Simplicius' quotation (*CAG* 8, 128.18–20) is based on a treatise on the categories that is spurious. Archytas did not write it (Huffman, *Archytas*, 78n13).

498 δύναμις, ἰσορροπεῖν, ταλαντουμένη, βαρέα, κοῦφα, ἀνωμάλως, ἀλόγως καὶ ἀμέτρως.

499 On this point, see Guthrie, *Greek Philosophy* V, 425.

their ascent. The teams of the men each have one noble horse and one disobedient and difficult to control. The latter, the horse sharing in the bad, is heavy (βρίθει γὰρ ὁ τῆς κάκης ἵππος μετέχων) (247b3). The language of weight and balance in Plato's rendering of the myth suggests that the circuit of souls is not an accidental feature of the myth, since both a balance and heavenly bodies move circularly. In the circuits of the myth, chariot teams rise or fall according to their component horses and the management of the charioteer. Human souls are being measured and show their mettle by their exceeding or falling short of others. A soul rises at one time and falls at another. The bad horse, in the case of the human charioteer, is heavy, sinks to the earth, and is weighed down by its upbringing (b4).[500] The climactic sinking is to be so weighed down as to lose the soul's wings,[501] the one bodily means of overcoming heaviness, and so to fall to earth (248c8). The wings have the power (*dunamis*) to lift what is heavy (246d5).[502] In the charioteer myth, weight is only partly a metaphor, because it is in fact the main attribute of the bodily nature that the desiring part of the soul seeks. Weight may be measurable, but it is inextricable from the perceptible and corruptible.

Partial insight on the charioteers' rise and fall is gained from the understanding of weight Plato presents in *Timaeus* 62c–63e. Plato understands the cosmos to be spherical and recognizes a difference between the center and periphery of the cosmos. He imagines someone able to stand at the circumference, where he takes away (ἀφαιρῶν) parts of the fire there and places them on opposite arms of a balance (πλάστιγγας). He will have to use force (ἕλκων, βιαζόμενος) to pull the fire into the air inside the circumference. If the parts of fire are unequal, the smaller portion of fire will yield to the force more easily (63a4–c1). In this situation, the larger quantity of fire is heavy and must be said to travel downward, as

---

500 Greek words are ἦρεν (rose), ἔδυ (fell), βρίθει (is heavy), ἐπὶ τὴν γῆν ῥέπων (sinking to the earth), βαρύνων (weighing down), βιαζομένων (being forced) (248a4–6).

501 βαρυνθεῖσα δὲ πτερορρυήσῃ.

502 The circuits take on the character of an assay (δοκιμασία) of souls as Plato describes a crashing scene in the apparently doomed effort of some to keep on an upward track (248a–b). Plato uses this term most frequently in the *Laws* to denote the scrutiny to which officers of the state must be put before approval (763e3–7 for example). He does not use this term in the *Phaedrus* myth, probably because the rising and falling of souls is a self-winnowing and so a natural sorting process. The verb also carries a connotation of judging horsemanship or assaying metals, either of which could be a metaphor for the separation of souls described here. Plato uses the language of weighing instead.

the movement of its end of the balance beam (ζυγόν) tends back toward the circumference. The smaller quantity of fire, at its end of the beam, moves into the interior air. It is called light in weight (ἐλαφρόν) and is said to move upward (ἄνω) (c5). So, even travelling toward the outer rim of the cosmos we might say in some circumstances is due to weight.

With this brilliantly conceived picture, Plato shows that up and down are not natural to the cosmos. They are natural to us. Weight and lightness follow up and down in our perception. So, weight, like up and down in the *Republic*, is a matter of perception.[503] The movement of the balance beam plays an important part in the credibility of this image. Taking this passage back to the *Phaedrus* myth, we understand that Plato, for the edification of his hearers, uses the language of perception for what is heavy and sinks. But also, the *Phaedrus* myth conveys that, depending on the more and less of its true being, the soul will tend toward the circles of the divine near the circumference of the cosmos or will tend toward earth. The weighing is by like to like, as the *Timaeus* too would have it.

In the *Philebus* 55d–56d, Plato addresses directly the question of rational knowledge of perceptible subject matters, saying that knowledge in the manual arts is less pure (ἀκαθαρτότερα) than knowledge aimed at education alone (55d7). He gives a triadic division of craft knowledge that follows roughly the division of the kinds of exact inquiry given in the *Euthyphro*. There are arithmetic, metrical, and statical crafts (ἀριθμητική, μετρητική, στατική) (55e1), which correspond to the *Euthyphro*'s counting, measuring, and weighing. The craft of weighing is here concerned with equilibrium, staying in place. All of these involve measurement in their own sphere, but he lauds the μετρητική of shipbuilding and housebuilding over measure in harmonics (ἀριθμητική), because the latter still relies on investigation of actual sounds to reach its standard harmonies. Finally, though, there must be two arithmetics, one for crafts practiced by the many and one for philosophers (56d5). There are also separate modes of calculating (λογιστική and λογισμός)[504] and a philosopher's version of μετρητική, namely γεωμετρία. He does not give a philosopher's version of statics, the science of equilibrium.[505]

---

503 I am indebted to O'Brien's treatment of this passage in detail in *Plato: Weight and Sensation*, ch. 2. See also O'Brien's "Heavy and Light," §V–VII.

504 On λογιστική in Plato, see (besides Klein) Annas, *Metaphysics M and N*, 5–7. On Archytas' understanding of logistic, see Huffman, 68–76.

505 In *Posterior Analytics* I.9, Aristotle understands geometrical accounts as applying also

In *Metaphysics* B.2, Aristotle took Plato to hold there are also separate objects for the philosopher's version of mathematical sciences—e.g., for astronomy, a non-sensible heavens—which are intermediate entities (τὰ μεταξύ) different from the Forms generative of mathematical objects.[506] Plato's pronouncements in this passage of the *Philebus* support Aristotle's ascription of this doctrine to Plato, as do Plato's remarks on the systematic relation of mathematical science in the divided line of *Republic* VI (509d5–511e5) and the discussion of astronomy in *Republic* VII (525d5–531d4). The scholarly literature on these passages from the *Republic* is large and need not be recapitulated here. A contemporary scholarly preoccupation has been the status of hypotheses in the mathematics unassisted by images in the highest division of the divided line. It is clear, however, that Plato regards the subject matter of mathematics primarily as objects of a particular sort, not hypotheses.[507] Furthermore, where there is a sensible subject matter as well as mathematical principles for a science, Plato follows his programmatic pronouncements of the *Philebus* and delineates a non-sensible object as the true object to which the mathematical principle pertains, even when the mathematical principle is a principle of motion. In this respect, *Republic* VII is consistent with the account Aristotle gives of Plato's belief in *Metaphysics* B.2.

In the case of movement in the heavens, whether the non-sensible objects make up an astronomy of ideal objects or simply a more perfect astronomy of the actual heavens, the resulting science has as objects not only spheres and circular tracks but also states of affairs corresponding to the proper accidents of the geometrical figures concerned. The moving radius principle as it appears in *Laws* X in relation to differences in speeds of the heavenly bodies provides such states of affairs.[508] Mourelatos

---

to mechanics (76a24). Mueller points to the testimony of Philodemus that Plato's school was interested in all sorts of mathematical disciplines, even mechanics ("Mathematical Method and Philosophical Truth," 172–173). Zhmud regards the notion that the Academy was a research institution and Plato a director greatly interested in mathematics as having been discredited by both philologists and historians of mathematics (*Origin*, 83n5–6).

506   For Aristotle's many references to Plato as believing mathematical objects are intermediate between Forms and sensible things, see Annas, *Metaphysics M and N*, 19n26. See in particular *Metaphysics* A.6 and B.1–2 besides Books M and N. Burkert ascribes to Plato belief in the existence of the intermediates. Plato's derivation of line, plane, and solid from numbers is not a reference to Speusippus or Xenocrates (*Lore and Science*, 23n41).

507   Mueller, "Mathematical Method," 190–193.

508   The risings and settings of the heavenly bodies as these differ throughout the solar year are also states of affairs treated by the geometry of circles inclined differently with

points to this principle of *Laws* X in considering the case for Plato's true mathematical astronomy as being a general geometrical kinematics.[509] Kinematics without force would be a worthy mathematical science, even though it involves motion. Nevertheless, *Republic* VII shows that there is a preference in Plato's systematic treatment of mathematics for the objects of mathematics to be without motion. A mathematical science of objects in motion ought to be built upon a science of solids without motion, and so he criticizes astronomy as practiced for being insufficiently grounded (528b1, e3). It is still better than harmonics, however, whose continued reliance on sensible things for its object ends up involving its empirical method of determining harmonic intervals (531a), something that Plato ridicules.

Plato's system, presented in *Republic* VII, for building a mathematical science of movement on stereometry seems a promising plan for mechanics, and his treatment of weight in the *Timaeus* does not oppose it. Nevertheless, his wedding of weight as perceived and experienced to what opposes and corrupts the noetic (the *Phaedrus* account) is a roadblock to further conceptualization of weight mathematically. Because weight is part of the visible realm, something reinforced in *Republic* IX, a science of weight as a mathematical discipline is problematic for Plato from the outset. In the *Philebus* where Plato mentions the art of the balance, he calls it statics, the science of maintaining position. Mechanics is better conceived as statics. Astronomy is about movement, but the heavenly bodies have reason to share the status of mathematical objects that weight cannot claim—their incorruptibility and the constancy of their movements in repetition and return. Plato's familiarity with the moving radius principle evident in *Laws* X makes it very unlikely that, at the end of his career, he did not know of the significance of the principle of the lever—he clearly knows that it underlies man-made wonders (*thaumata*). The principle is a bridge between the rising and falling of weights on a balance and the weightless motion of heavenly bodies. The charioteer souls of the *Phaedrus* similarly bridge heaven and earth. They strive to attain the circuits of the gods but rise or fall in accordance with the weight of their souls. To the extent that weight is subject to measure and

---

respect to the constant circle of the horizon in a place. See Autolycus, *Le sphere en mouvement.*

509   Mourelatos, "Astronomy and Kinematics," 3.

comparison for Plato, it renders the sensible life of the soul intelligible. Nevertheless, only flight to a heavenly circuit, escape from the materiality of weight, can break the cycle of rising and sinking.

Plato's association of weight with bodily bulk and with the human weakness attendant upon bodily desires leaves Aristotle, the scientist, with few leads on how to make weight as ordinarily experienced a part of mathematical science. The doctrines championed by Speusippus and Xenocrates after Plato's death separated Aristotle even more from the Platonists. Throughout his works but especially in the *Metaphysics*, Aristotle wrestles with the cosmological and mathematical issues surrounding weight that were left to him by the Pythagoreans and Plato.

Two points will emerge as important in the following section. One is a central insight for Aristotle, namely, that mathematical objects could never compose a physical body, because there is no way to derive weight from lines and planes. This is a point Aristotle directs against the Pythagoreans but also against the Platonists. A second fateful conclusion of Aristotle is that mathematical objects must be immaterial and separable. This conclusion is not only true to the nature of mathematical thinking but also necessary to avoid what he takes to be the Pythagoreans' confusion of the bodily and the mathematical.

This second point, however, which places Aristotle alongside Plato in his interpretation of the subject matter of mathematics, leaves Aristotle without a rationale for making the movement characteristic of sensible things part of mathematics. Immateriality goes with what is immovable, i.e. incorruptible. Weight demands a mathematical subject matter of its own, but what is mathematical as such does not move. Accordingly, the two points to emerge in what follows are to some extent at cross purposes with one another and in need of a strategy for reconciliation.

Aristotle's Criticism of Earlier Cosmology

In *Metaphysics* B.2, Aristotle asks, concerning what is posited as intermediate between forms and perceptible heavenly bodies, how these extra (τὰ μεταξύ) solids in motion could be at all. He brings in optics and harmonics, alongside astronomy, in making his point. It is unreasonable, he says, that there should be lines-in-themselves, lines, and sensible lines. Does this mean there are a sun and moon in a non-sensible heaven? It is hard enough to credit this, but to credit their moving is completely impossible (997b20).

312

He applies the same reasoning to optics and harmonics, saying "it is impossible these [intermediate objects of what optics and harmonics treat] should exist alongside the sensible objects of those sciences (τὰ αἰσθητά)" (997b22). Along similar lines, he says it cannot be the case that the only difference between geometry and surveying, for instance, is that the latter deals with perceptible things (997b27), while the objects of geometry are imperceptible. If this were the case, there would indeed need to be intermediate objects, not just for surveying but for living things and for an art like medicine (997b23–24), and so for everything sensible. There is a profound point underlying this criticism. The fantastic hypothesis of intermediate beings is not true, but the reason does not hinge primarily on whether the objects of mathematics are sensible or not. Whatever are the important differences between the types of *mathêmata*—e.g., arithmetic and harmonics—these sciences bring with them commonalities that amount to genuine interpenetration between separated mathematics, on the one hand, and astronomy, optics, harmonics, and surveying, on the other. This fact is just *why* the subject matter of mathematics and allied sciences is puzzling. Aristotle here takes the commonality between pure mathematics and a mathematical natural science without prior prejudice against the natural science.

He points out that surveying, a *mathêma* at the perceptible end of the spectrum of techniques, itself involves imperceptibles: "At the same time not even this is true, that surveying is of magnitudes that are sensible and corruptible; for then it would have perished when they [its objects] passed away" (997b32–34). By this, Aristotle means that a unit of measurement for surveying cannot be simply a perceptible thing belonging among the other perceptibles it measures. The measure that makes measuring possible is not something perceptible. So also, in medicine, some item of knowledge cannot be a perceptible that perishes (997b28–29). Aristotle thus acknowledges a measure that is incorruptible and not limited to being a sensible thing, but there is a problem. Coherence demands that there are standards or unit measures to explain even the activity of practical sciences rooted in sensible things. Yet to find the measure in intermediate objects will not work (997b12–34).

Aristotle goes on to say that neither is astronomy concerned with perceptible magnitudes. In this, both measurement and astronomy are like geometry, he says. No perceptible thing is either straight or curved (997b32–998a6). Perceptible magnitudes are subject to just the sort of limitations cited by Protagoras, that no sensible circle (κύκλος) touches a straight edge (κανών) at a single point (998a7–11). So, the accounts given by astronomy are not accounts of the very movements that the perceptible heavens in fact display, nor do points have the same nature as stars. Again, one cannot say, as some do, that there are intermediate mathematicals but they are *in* perceptible things (998a9). This, he says, would put Forms in perceptible things. It would make two solids be in the same place at the same time, and put what does not move in what does (998a12–15). In general, why would you posit intermediate substances and then put them in sensible things (a16)?

His criticism in *Metaphysics* B.2 treads near arguments he makes against the Pythagoreans from the point of view of weight. In *Metaphysics* A.8, he says that the principles of the Pythagoreans are even stranger than those of Anaxagoras and Empedocles. The Pythagoreans[510] draw their

---

510   Writing about the effect on scholarship of Burkert's *Lore and Science*, Burnyeat asks who is left to be the Pythagoreans that Aristotle writes about. His answer is Philolaus and Archytas ("Other Lives"), and particularly Philolaus because of his cosmology. An earlier figure, Hippasus of Metapontum is a contender by reputation. Burnyeat is talking about Pythagoreans of verifiable mathematical achievement. Burkert had shown how much of the tradition about Pythagoras' accomplishments was a creation of Platonists who sought to ground their founder's philosophy in an authoritative past that was both mystical and mathematical (*Lore and Science*, ch. 2). Burkert's point of view is reinforced by Zhmud, *Origin*, ch. 3. For a valuable summary of the evidence, see Hermann, *Like God*, ch. 2.

Iamblichus (AD 3rd–4th century) is taken to be more reliable than most doxographers in his more detailed testimony about who were Pythagoreans. He names Hippasus, Theodorus, Kurenaios, and Hippocrates of Chios (*Mathematical Sciences*, 77.25–78.1). Iamblichus says there were "two kinds of the Italian philosophy called Pythagorean" (*Mathematical Sciences*, 76.16). Followers were ἀκουσματικοί (eager hearers) or μαθηματικοί (mathematicians). The two groups were somewhat at odds as to which were the true Pythagoreans. The hearers, or *acusmatici*, traced the practice of the mathematicians to Hippasus (76.22) not Pythagoras. The *acusmatici* did not practice mathematics themselves for reasons Iamblichus explains. Iamblichus gives a longer list of Pythagoreans in his *Pythagorean Life* (Diels-Kranz 1, §58 [45] A [446–448]). Huffman sheds light on the sequence of teachers among the mathematical Pythagoreans of southern Italy in his *Philolaus*, 3–12. On the division of *acusmatici* and *mathematici,* see Burkert, ch. 2, §5.

In a passage significant for comparison to Aristotle, Iamblichus says the Pythagoreans loved the precision of mathematical arguments and believed the *mathêmata* alone to be the way for humans to achieve demonstrations. Seeing agreement equally in the *mathêmata* of harmonics through numbers and of optics by lines, they believed these were the causes of all things and the principles of these, so that anyone wishing to know how things are would pursue these disciplines. Iamblichus mentions in particular numbers, geometrical forms (τὰ γεωμετρούμενα εἴδη) of beings, and the arguments (λόγους) of mathematics (*Mathematical Sciences*, 78.8–18). On Iamblichus' sources concerning the Pythagoreans and Aristotle's lost work on them, see Burkert, *Lore and Science*, 29–30 and 29n5. For

principles from mathematics (whose objects are without motion) but they seek to explain all manner of change in the sensible world (989b29–990a1). Interestingly, he says they use up (καταναλίσκουσιν) their principles (a2–3), moving from sensible things to higher things without ever having adequately explained the natural movements of sensible things. The criticism is not that mathematical principles can in no way fit the project of explanation of the sensible world. Rather, the Pythagoreans erred in how they utilized mathematical principles. They move too quickly to what is higher, and the way they use mathematics produces explanations that are inadequate. Both these criticisms are linked to weight.

One thing Pythagoreans cannot explain is how weight and lightness belong to bodies, when mathematical objects have neither of these (990a12–14). Aristotle makes the point very explicitly in *Metaphysics* N.3: The Pythagoreans "construct natural bodies out of numbers, things that have lightness and weight out of things that have not weight or lightness" (1090a32–34). In *On the Heavens* III.1, he repeats the criticism, leveled again against the Pythagoreans—bodies cannot be composed from what does not have weight (300a19). Weight is a sort of minimum requirement for something to be a body, and it is not a property that appears from composition. The nub of the problem is that the Pythagoreans do not explain sensible things by anything proper (*idion*) to that realm (300a18). So, to move to mathematical explanation from the shape of bodies and not to consider weight is to move too quickly to higher principles. Mathematical principles are relevant in some other way to weight, because weight is something proper to sensible things.

In *Metaphysics* N.3, the point about weight comes in the context of a general assault on the Ideas. Aristotle says that the Pythagoreans seem to be forced to speak of another heaven and other bodies besides the sensible (a failing of the Platonists), but they claim to speak of this world. The Pythagoreans are right at least to say that mathematical objects do not exist apart. For if these were separated (κεχωρισμένων), their traits would not be in bodies (1090a30).[511] The solution, Aristotle says, is to adopt

a rare survey of the Pythagorizing Platonists of late antiquity, including Iamblichus, see O'Meara, *Pythagoras Revived*.

511 The import of Aristotle's criticisms of the Pythagoreans and those who hold to Ideas is an area of on-going research and conflicting interpretation. For the issues at stake, see Burkert, *Lore and Science*, ch. 1, §2. Burkert argues convincingly that Aristotle's account of the Pythagoreans is actually more reliable than the testimony of the Platonized Pythagorean tradition beginning with Speusippus and continuing through the Neoplatonic

his own point of view given explicitly in *Metaphysics* N.1 and 2. There are two key elements to his solution. The first approach is by way of the categories of being; the other is the fact that beings may exist potentially.

In his approach by way of the categories, Aristotle goes straight to the central issue, measure, saying that "one" (*hen*) is a measure (*metron*), and is something different depending on the substratum. *Metaphysics* N.1 presents a dense collection of notions related by quantity, quality, and relation. He includes weight along with harmony, magnitude, and rhythm, as what has a definite measure (σταθμός) chosen in whatever way (1087b33–37). So, weight can be measured, even though numbers, points, lines, and solids do not have weight. Measure is a notion that spans quantity and quality. A quantity is the measure of a quantity; a quality measures qualities. Measure is a "one," and what is important is that the measure be indivisible and be the same thing in every instance (1088a10). For example, of a man, a horse, and a god, the measure is perhaps living thing. Measure distinguishes individuals as countable but sometimes as part of a definition (thus individuals as included in a universal). Measure, then, is not limited to quantitative aspect. The measure is always indivisible, but in one case, it is indivisible as to form, in the other case, in relation to perception.[512] These comments may seem rather too general for a solution to the monumental problem of how mathematics applies to the world. It is important, though, that Aristotle thinks that so much of attributional being is subject to measure. This is one way that precision (ἀκριβεία) is introduced into philosophical analysis. Aristotle adds to the account by bringing into play the category of relation (*to pros ti*).

Aristotle addresses next in *Metaphysics* N.1 a series of relational terms—great and small, few and many, odd and even, smooth and rough, straight and concave. These come up because some thinkers have present-

---

Greek commentators (*Lore and Science*, ch. 1, §3). On this point, see also Huffman, *Philolaus*, 19–26, and Hermann, *Like God*, 23–24 and 90–92.

Aristotle seems to endorse the Pythagorean understanding of attributes of numbers as agreeing with attributes of things (*Metaphysics* A.5, 985b32–986a6). (See also Burkert, *Lore and Science*, 48.) For the empiricist, this is a starting point of great importance. Aristotle's following Plato in making mathematical objects immovable may result from his agreement with Plato on the subject matter of mathematics being incorporeal, not agreement that mathematicals are never subject to change of place. So, mathematical objects are for Aristotle not separate but separable (χωριστόν). The point of cleavage between Platonism and the earlier tradition of mathematical philosophy may be precisely the *mathêmata* inclusive of motion.

512 Τὸ μὲν κατὰ τὸ εἶδος τὸ δὲ πρὸς τὴν αἴσθησιν.

ed the indefinite dyad as a principle coming out of the great and small. Great and small, however, are not substrata but attributes (1088a15–19), and so are not candidates for principles. Aristotle's inclusion of smooth and rough in this list of relational attributes makes us think he might also include heavy and light in the list. He does allude to other pairs to which his discussion applies (1088a22). These pairs are all instances of relation, he says, and are posterior to quantity or quality.[513] Relation is an attribute (πάθος τι) of quantity (a24).[514] He may have in mind great and small here, since he reiterates the point that a relation is not a substratum. His main point is that nothing is a relation without also being something else (a27–29). Relational attributes are not substance. He does not here make a connection between relation and his immediately preceding topic of measure.

Continuing in *Metaphysic* N.1, Aristotle gives more reasons why relation cannot be substance. All the categories but relation are subject to change. Of relation alone there is no generation or corruption or movement (a30). In particular, there is increase and decrease of quantity, alteration of quality, locomotion for place, and absolute generation and corruption of substance. There is no change with respect to relation (a34). He explains this difference for the category of relation by saying:

> For without changing, a thing will be at one time larger, at another time smaller or equal, when another changes quantitatively. And the matter of each thing and so also of the substance must be potentially [greater or smaller in relation to the other], but relation is substance neither potentially or actually. (1088a34–b2)

Some thing, A, may assume a different relation to another, B, without A itself changing. If this is the case, then A must possess that different relation potentially. It is not the relation that has the potentiality or actuality, however. It is the substance A. A relation ceasing to hold is not a passing

---

513 Aristotle speaks of a relative, *to pros ti*, which is either of the two of what we would call a relation. So, as Annas says, "great" and "small" are relatives, and "great and small" only a conjunction of the two. See Annas, *Books M and N*, 198.

514 This is not true in every instance of relation. There is, for example, "father" and "son," "master" and "slave" and many other cases. Annas notes this (*Books M and N*, 198). The present context is mathematical where the expectation is that the category of quantity will be primary.

away of the relation, because there is no substratum for greater and lesser apart from the substratum of what is changing. This is usually substance but can be quantity or quality.

The immutability of what falls in the category of relation is interesting from the standpoint of Aristotle's refutation in *Metaphysics* B of intermediate mathematical objects. Relation actually meets Plato's requirement that the mathematical be immutable but meets it in a way undoubtedly too paltry to be relevant to mathematics from a Platonist perspective. Nevertheless, relation has non-Platonic strengths that enabled Aristotle to combine refutation of intermediates with an expansion of the possibilities of mathematical science.

Aristotle on Quantity and Relation

Read from the standpoint of weight, Aristotle's treatment of quantity in *Categories* 6 does actually clarify the status of bodily attributes like weight that are not purely quantitative but which nevertheless are the subject of a *mathêma*, a technique or mathematical method. He limits the connotation of quantity itself but in doing so considerably widens the range of terms like more and less in their application to other categories. These terms he admits seem at first to be quantitative (5b11–20).

Aristotle gives two genera of quantity and a number of species, or examples, of these. Quantity is of two types, discrete and continuous. He distinguishes continuous quantity from discrete quantity on two bases: (1) whether the parts making up the whole have position with respect to one another, and (2) whether the extremities of the parts touch. Discrete quantities have parts possessing neither position nor common boundaries. Continuous quantities, like the parts of a solid or things in place, have parts with both position and common boundaries (5a15–28). He gives only two examples of discrete quantity—number and speech. Speech is discrete quantity because it is measured by long and short syllables, which are definite and separate from one another (4b33). Continuous quantity has as species all the familiar geometrical kinds from line to body. The word for three-dimensional continuous quantity is *sôma*, body, not *to stereon*, solid. The latter term he reserves for a specific notion—a solid having parts with position. Time is continuous quantity.

It is important how many things Aristotle excludes from quantity. Quantity does not have opposites. This is because there is no way that one

318

definite quantity is the opposite of another (5b14). Furthermore, opposition requires a pair, and a quantity is taken by itself and not in relation to another (5b31). This is why the relational terms that seem quantitative—great and small, many and few—are not quantities (5b17). We see that these notions are non-quantitative by the fact that the same thing can be great or small depending on that to which it is compared, but quantity would not vary in this way. So, quantity always means "a quantity" understood to be definite and possessing a single connotation. Accordingly, to say an action is long means that the time in which it takes place is long, just as there is a great deal of white, because the surface area affected by the color is large (5b37–6a6).

To say a surface area is large, however, is to designate its quantity vaguely. The quantitative designation belongs to the thing possessing the quantity. The mountain is large by virtue of the place it takes up. Speaking more precisely, though, large is always larger *than*. It seems quite important that Aristotle chose to put all these terms (including much and little) in a category together and that the category is not quantity.[515] The move to relation allows comparisons to be expressed with conceptual precision without the subject matters of comparison being taken as quantitative first. This is important for weight, which resists reduction to sheer quantity.

Though not mentioned, weight is not far from Aristotle's mind when he apportions terms of number and comparison to different categories. In *On the Heavens*, weight is always paired with lightness and linked to distinctions of place in the universe. Aristotle says in *Categories* 6 that the oppositions we purport to find in quantity, but which really are relations, all go back to the original relativity belonging to place, i.e., up and down (6a13). These are judged in terms of the greater or lesser distance from the center or limits of the cosmos:

> But it is most of all with regard to place that there seems to be contrariety of a quantity. For people regard up as contrary to down—meaning by 'down' the region towards the centre—because the centre is at the greatest distance from the limits of the world. And they probably derive from these their definition of the other contraries also; for they define as contraries

---

515 Ackrill explores the implications of Aristotle treating "large" as always meaning "larger than," in *Aristotle's* Categories, 95–96.

those things in the same genus which are most distant from
one another.[516] (6a11–18)

Aristotle recognizes the analogical sense of distance implicit in the notion
of contraries, pointing out that contraries are always what are most distant
from one another in any genus. Nevertheless, the priority he gives to up
and down is more than a concession to the human dependence on con-
cretizing logical relations. Aristotle is not simply generalizing common
notions of up and down. The underlying issue is whether or not there
are distinctions of place in a sphere. Where the cosmos is concerned,
Aristotle believes, in contrast to Plato, that differences of place are not
just relative to us.

In *Timaeus* 62d, Plato sought to combat the notion that there are
distinctions of up and down in the universe, despite the presence of a
center and extremities in the spherical cosmos. His rationale is geometrical. Anyone moving from one part of a sphere distant from the center
to a position opposite within the sphere would have to regard what had
been down as now above. There simply are no up and down in a sphere
(63a). Aristotle directly discounts this criticism in *On the Heavens* IV.1,
saying that the extremity in general of the universe is above in position
(κατὰ τὴν θέσιν) relative to the center of its sphere. Just that the universe has extremity and center differentiates its space. The extremity is
also by nature prior, he says (308a17–24). In justifying the latter claim,
he refers specifically to common opinion (ὅπερ καὶ οἱ πολλοὶ λέγουσι),
saying it is correct but not sufficient, since it supposes only the hemisphere above us as the universe (a26). One must suppose in addition
(προσυπολαβόντες) the hemisphere extending in a circle with a center
equidistant from the whole extremity. That the universe is spherical is
key to the whole debate. Aristotle thus regards up and down as relatives
primary in the orders both of experience and of cosmic place.

The definitions of heavy and light ἁπλῶς, or *simpliciter*, bear the
mark of the debate concerning whether there is up and down in a sphere.
The relational character of weight and lightness follows up and down, the
point of departure in *Categories* 6. Comparability as to speed—literally,
being faster (θᾶττον)—follows heavy and light being relational terms.
In *On the Heavens* I.3, where Aristotle gives a definition of weight
"sufficient for present needs," he defines the heavy as a tendency toward

---

516 Translation is by Ackrill.

the center and the light as a tendency away from the center (269b20–28). Thus, the reason why weight cannot be a quantity in a straightforward way is that things are heavy or light in relation to one another (b28). Even "heaviest" is defined as what never rises in relation to any other body, and lightest as what never sinks (296b24–26). These are later called weight and lightness *simpliciter*,[517] terms usually translated as "absolute" weight and lightness. "Absolute" is not a good adjective to translate *haplôs* (ἁπλῶς), however, since the connotation of "absolute" removes the intrinsically relational character of the terms. We should think of ἁπλῶς as giving the superlative for weight and lightness in the following sense. There are "having weight," "being heavier," "being lighter" and "being heaviest." As Aristotle says:

> By light *simpliciter*, then, we mean that which moves upward or to the extremity, and by heavy *simpliciter* that which moves downward or to the center. By relatively light (πρὸς ἄλλο δὲ κοῦφον) or lighter, we mean that one, of two bodies having weight and equal in bulk (ὄγκον), which is exceeded by the other in the speed of its natural downward motion. (308a29–34)

Aristotle distinguishes homonymous senses of heavy and light here. A body with weight can be lighter than another body with weight. But we can also say that fire is lighter than air, another intrinsically light thing. Does it also make sense to *compare* fire and earth as lighter and heavier? A reason for saying "no" is that each is light or heavy *simpliciter* in its own domain. *Haplôs baru* is that heavy thing of which nothing is heavier.[518] To this extent, the relational character of weight defines weight, and this fact has sometimes been obscured by the connotations imparted to absolute weight and lightness. Clearly, though, the relational character of weight invites further investigation of it in terms of ratio. The possibility exists that much of interest to mechanics could be developed within the category of relation without compromise of the mathematical features of mechanics.

---

517 Τὸ ἁπλῶς βαρὺ καὶ κοῦφον (*On the Heavens* IV.1, 308a7).

518 Ἁπλῶς may have additional connotations. On the difficulties of deciphering relative and absolute weight and lightness as Aristotle meant them, see O'Brien, *Democritus: Weight and Size*, 49–56. One question is whether different earthy materials have different weight in themselves or whether every equal quantity of earth has the same weight.

Relation has, from a philosophical standpoint, a weakness that masks the considerable strengths it offers to mathematical practice. It is important, as Aristotle says in *Metaphysics* N.2, that things in relation are the least of all candidates to be a certain nature or substance and that they come after both quality and quantity (1088a23–24). This is what I mean by relation being weak. Ontologically, relation is dependent even on other attributes. On the other hand, relation is flexible enough to include multiple features of a situation of change. Furthermore, it can belong to substance, quantity, or quality. These features are strengths, since relation provides for structure and conceptual precision in an account without having to involve quantity. Furthermore, some ubiquitous qualifications, like large, are just inherently relational even when we think they are not.

Let us briefly consider Aristotle's definitions of relation in *Categories* 7. There are three definitions of "relative" that Aristotle gives in *Categories* 7:

> **Def-1**. Relatives are those things called what they are *of* or *in relation to* something else (6a36). For instance, a father is father "of a son."
> **Def-2**. All relatives are spoken of in relation to correlatives that reciprocate (7a22). The translation "correlative" follows from the single word for "things reciprocating" (ἀντιστρέφοντα). So, father and son reciprocate. Father is "of a son" and son is "of his father."
> **Def-3**. Relatives are that for which being (τὸ εἶναι) is the same as being somehow in relation to another (τῷ πρός τί πως ἔχειν) (8a32). By this definition, one is a father because he has offspring. The being of father is having a son or daughter. The being of fatherhood is in relation to another.

In giving **Def-3**, Aristotle says that the **Def-1** is not what makes relatives what they are (8a35). It is simply true of all of them. So, **Def-3** is more fundamental. By **Def-1**, parts of the body, like head, can be taken as relatives. **Def-3** helps to explain why particular substances are never relatives. Particulars, primary substances, do not *exist* because of and as being in relation to anything else. This much is true also for relatives in other categories. They are first what they are and secondarily are relatives.[519] **Def-2**

---

519   The third definition excludes from the category of relation not just primary substances but also secondary substances like parts of an animal body (8a28–35). The fact that Aristotle excludes parts of secondary substances as relatives shows that he wishes to de-

separates out a large class of traits that are not true relatives. A rudder, for instance, belongs to a ship, but not every ship has a rudder, so rudder and ship do not reciprocate (7a8–10).

A strength of relatives is something Aristotle takes to follow from **Def-3**: "From these things, it is evident that if one knows definitely (ὡρισμένως) some one of the things in relation, one will also know definitely that to which it is related" (8a35–37). If the being of relatives necessarily involves their being related to another, then one cannot know the relative without knowing also its correlate. This implication of relation generalizes a feature of the Axiom of Archimedes as Aristotle used it in his physics. He could be sure to find a definite quantity to enter into ratio with another ratio of finites in one of his lettered proportions. With this procedure, he ruled out the infinite and nil in movement. This license to infer to a definite quantity is part of the Eudoxan ratio concept, and Aristotle defines relation in its strongest sense by this similar feature.

The chief problem that has been noted with Aristotle's account in *Categories* 7 is that it seems he should understand relations themselves as the relatives, but he speaks mostly of things as relatives. For example, "slave" and "master" are relatives. The relative is not the master-slave relationship.[520] The problem is evident in **Def-1.** Things in relation are those said to be just what they are (ὅσα αὐτὰ ἅπερ ἐστίν) *of others* or in some other way *in relation to another* (6a36–38).[521] It is not that Aristotle cannot conceive of the relation as having whatness. He can speak of a relation as what it is in itself—what makes relational attributes be in relation.[522] This definition as it is repeated later (6b34) seems to make substances themselves relational taken under a particular aspect. He says

---

lineate among things spoken of relatively a sub-class of things that are permanent relatives because their being is the same as being somehow related to something (τὸ εἶναι ταὐτόν ἐστι τῷ πρός τί πως ἔχειν) (8a31–33).

520   Relation remains anchored in subjects. When everything but being a master is subtracted (περιαιρουμένων) from the subject, then slave will still be said in relation to that (7a30–39).

521   This paraphrase follows the translation of Ackrill. On relations, see Mignucci, "Definitions of Relatives." A book-length treatment of relation in English is Hood, *Aristotle on the Category of Relation*. See also Morales, "Relational Attributes in Aristotle." Relation is not a topic in Wedin's *Aristotle's Theory of Substance*, though he refers to Mignucci's article (22n30), nor in Mann's *The Discovery of Things*. Relation is discussed by Modrak in *Language and Meaning*, 34–43.

522   In both *Topics* I.9 (103b31–35) and *Metaphysics* Z.4 (1030a22), Aristotle's allows use of the term *ti esti* in connection with categories other than substance.

that a mountain is large in relation to something else (6b8–10). Is it then *objects* under the aspect of being related to another that fall into the category of relation, or does Aristotle have in mind relational attributes as populating the category of relation?[523]

Despite the apparent intransigence of this puzzle about relation in Aristotle, it is in fact one context in which the significance of relation for Aristotle's method in natural philosophy can be seen. To indicate this briefly, I will use Modrak's treatment of the issue of relatives versus relation. My aim is to place relation as a sortal notion inclusive of the contextualized mathematical being Aristotle recognized in mechanics.

Following Aristotle's language and examples, Modrak focuses attention on the correlates that are in a relation.[524] Modrak is interested in how relations are non-substances:

> 'Socrates is a man' is true just in case 'Socrates' denotes a human being. The referent of the relative term 'father' is a complex state of affairs consisting of a primary substance standing in a particular relation to another primary substance and, for this reason, the relative cannot simply be identified with either the primary substance or the relation. Not only substances but also items falling under the other categories stand in various relations.[525]

A relative depends on substances and is an attribute of a substance, but it is not without reference to another substance. A relative is a complex state of affairs, because its being involves more than one substance. From the standpoint of the state of affairs, the relation itself between subjects plays a subordinate role to the subject's own being in relation, which is not the same relative as the attribute of the other substance to which it is related. That is, being the father of someone is not the same relative as

---

523 Mignucci thinks Aristotle aims in *Categories* 7 at a definition of "relational properties," and he offers a series of intentional definitions to explicate Aristotle's conception. *Pros ti* concerns properties fully and univocally determined by a formulable relation and not determined by that to which the relation belongs: "What is essential is that there must be a reference to a specific relation that alone or together with other properties characterizes the relative at issue" (Mignucci, "Definitions of Relatives," 104–105). Hood argues that Aristotle has in mind what we would call "two-place predicates" in his category of relation and that he aims to treat relations themselves rather than things in relation (*Relation*, ch. 2).

524 Modrak, *Language and Meaning*, 38.

525 Modrak, *Language and Meaning*, 39.

being a son of the father. Modrak cautions against thinking of a relational attribute as belonging to a single substance, since this makes the relation hold between two relational attributes (being a master and being a slave, for instance). Rather, the relative attribute itself involves another sub-stance. Modrak avoids relatives being too closely identified with singular substances but at the expense of *pros ti* being itself something simple or philosophically primitive as one would expect the first four categories to be (substance, quantity, quality, relation). A relative involves a state of affairs. She makes this point herself, saying that in the case of relatives, what is present in a subject "is not primary," because being a relative always depends on other more basic objects.[526]

Modrak's interpretation of relatives as necessarily based in states of affairs while yet being attributed to substances points to a positive aspect of what is usually taken to be a confusion or lack of clarity in Aristotle's account of relatives. The account is in fact a good description of the sig-nificance of items in ratio. Ratios and proportions remain in context. A term in a ratio may be contemplated alone (having covered a certain arc-distance), but the terms of a proportion (e.g., a ratio of distances cov-ered to times taken) cannot be contemplated alone and tell us something about the relation (sometimes multi-variant) from which it was taken. This is obvious, but it means that elements of a ratio have to reciprocate. There is reciprocation either if the ratio is taken by itself or if it is taken in proportion.

This connection between the notion of ratio and the idea of relation does provide a reason for the bi-focal vision Aristotle directs toward re-lation in *Categories* 7. On the one hand, a relational attribute belongs to something else, the substance, quality, or magnitude that would appear as something in ratio or as an analogate in a proportion. On the other hand, the relation itself is what is being defined in the proportion that holds between ratios.

---

526 Modrak, *Language and Meaning*, 40. Modrak enlists relatives to support the general ontology according to which primary substances have primary qualities (Socrates is pale); they do not have properties (Socrates has the [universal property] pallor). Neither does attribution language commit us to the existence of "kooky objects" like "the pale one" for a pale Socrates (37). Primary qualities are what have been called in other scholarly literature "non-substantial individuals."

Mechanics and *Phainomena* in *Posterior Analytics* I.13

In *Physics* II.2 and *Metaphysics* E.1, Aristotle presents the relation of the *mathêmata*, geometry and arithmetic, to "the more physical of the *mathêmata*" in the following way:

Chart 10.1

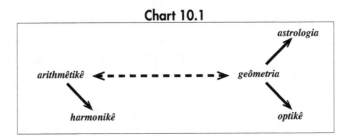

The chart conveys a minimum of information, as Aristotle himself does. He classes harmonics with arithmetic, because harmonics uses numerical ratios. Both astronomy and optics rely on geometrical shapes and their properties and on proofs drawn from geometry. From these, astronomers and experts in optics make their arguments about movement of the spheres of the heavenly bodies, on the one hand, and the effects characteristic in vision, on the other. So, the mathematical natural sciences take principles from the corresponding mathematical science that does not itself involve physical objects. In addition, it is clear that the natural science has mathematical principles distinctive to that discipline, as optics has the visual ray and astronomy has the movement of the sphere of fixed stars carrying around all movements within it.

In *Physics* II.2 and *Metaphysics* E.1, Aristotle in effect classifies arithmetic with geometry because of the nature of their subject matters. We can easily see, for example, the difference in subject matters of geometry and astronomy when we name their objects: planes, solids, points as opposed to the sun, moon, and these bodies' *per se* attributes (193b23–30). In *Physics* II.2, Aristotle is even-handed about the priority of one or the other level. Geometry investigates (σκοπεῖ) physical line, *qua* mathematical, and optics investigates mathematical line but *qua* physical (194a9–12). The mathematician (at this point narrowed down to the practitioner of geometry or arithmetic) considers physical objects, but without the movement properly belonging to physical things. He separates (χωρίζει) shapes or numbers and their traits. Most importantly, there is no falsity in his separating these features of natural bodies (193b35). This is something we just recognize about mathematical features, because some *per se* attributes follow along with shapes or numbers and not with the bodily, changeable nature of the thing. Nevertheless, the existence of *mathêmata* of natural subject matters shows that the separation of mathematical objects is not absolute. The equality of angles of a line reflected at a surface applies as much to optics as to geometry.

Another emphasis of *Physics* II.2 is the mathematician's separating mathematical features from the *matter* of physical things. At the other end of the spectrum from geometry, physics treats objects that are like snub, which is concavity belonging to only one type of object, nose. It is not entirely clear that Aristotle means to be treating shapes with this description of physical qualities, since we can separate the nose's shape as concavity. His point is ontological: physical attributes cannot be distinguished from matter without falsifying what the physical things are. Only noses are snub. This part of Aristotle's discourse in *Physics* II.2 is directed at the Platonists' separation of the forms of physical things (193b36).

In *Physics* II.2, arithmetic is not explicitly named alongside geometry, though some of the objects of arithmetic are named. In *Metaphysics* E.1, geometry again stands in for other branches of mathematics whose subject matter is immovable and separated. Separability and immovability pertain to some branches of mathematics, he says (1026a9). Astronomy and optics, as we met them in *Physics* II.2, are *mathêmata* whose objects are not separate and immovable. In *Metaphysics* E.1, Aristotle classes geometry and astronomy together insofar as each treats a particular nature, but the science universal to them, he says, is common to all (1026a27). Aristotle refers to such a science without naming it, at *Metaphysics* Γ.2, in the context of the search for the proper place to discuss being and one. He says, "For 'philosopher' is like 'mathematician'; for mathematics also has parts, and there is a first and a second science and other successive ones within the sphere of mathematics" (1004a6–8). In both passages, Aristotle is drawing an analogy between mathematics and the science of being, so he does not mean that what is prior in the order of mathematics is the science of being. Rather, geometry and astronomy are together comprehended by something common for mathematics, and different kinds of being are related to something more comprehensive in a similar way. Aristotle reinforces this relation among *mathêmata* in *Posterior Analytics* I.13 in more explicit terms of what is "above."

The points I have highlighted from *Physics* II.2 and *Metaphysics* E.1 do not amount to a summary of their content or a full analysis. My aim is to lay out in terms closest to Aristotle's own in these passages his cautious alignment of related *mathêmata* that have striking differences. In *Metaphysics* E.1, Aristotle is interested in how mathematics and physics are each theoretical pursuits in order to delineate what would be the subject matter of a prior theoretical pursuit, the science of being *qua* being. This context and the systematizing tendency in each passage have been taken to indicate that Aristotle here lays out his philosophy of mathematics. This view is by no means unreasonable. In general, Aristotle endorses Plato's commitment to the eternality and immobility of the subject matter of arithmetic, geometry, and stereometry. In *Metaphysics* E.1, he says, "Whether [mathematics] is about things immobile and separate is at present not clear; nevertheless, that some mathematics does treat of objects *qua* immobile and *qua* separate is clear" (1026a8–10).[527] We do not know if the *per se* objects of mathematics are all immobile and separate, but we know that some mathematics treats objects as if they were. This statement is consistent with Aristotle's position in *Physics* II.2 and is less an endorsement of mathematics as a separate subject matter than a recognition that mathematics is the method of a variety of subject matters that in some way overlap or interpenetrate with respect to their principles and demonstration.

In *Posterior Analytics* I.7 and 9, Aristotle addresses the structure of a science that uses premises from another science. The context is his insistence that each subject matter has principles proper to it and that the middle terms also must belong to the same genus as the first principles (75b2–11). The relation between some mathematical disciplines is the exception to this rule. These *mathêmata* hold "in relation to one another so that one is under the other (θάτερον ὑπὸ θάτερον)" (b14–15). Only here does Aristotle introduce the notion of one *mathêma* being over or under, higher or lower, than another. He mentions optics in relation to geometry and harmonics in relation to arithmetic. The idea is that the more physical *mathêma* employs connections of a mathematical kind that are developed

---

527 This statement is an interesting combination of what Aristotle affirms on the Platonist side—immobility and separability of mathematics—and what he would affirm in the Pythagorean view of mathematics, which is the commonality of principles and methods between mathematical natural sciences and noetic mathematics. See *Metaphysics* A.5, 985b32–986a6 and the characterization by Iamblichus of the Pythagoreans' commitment to mathematics (note 510 above).

in a more detailed way in geometry or arithmetic. He says that the conclusions in this case hold not by virtue of a genus proper to them (ᾗ τὸ ἴδιον γένος) but by virtue of a common element (ᾗ κοινόν τι) (75b20).

Posterior Analytics I.9 explicates the common element, adding to this basic description the distinction between *hoti* and *dioti* demonstration. Aristotle says that the demonstration "that it is" (*hoti*) for the natural science comes from "another science, because the underlying genus is different." For example, "Visual rays extend from the eye to the object seen," is a hypothesis of an underlying genus different from geometry, so one might demonstrate that visual rays are reflected from a polished surface from observations involving mirrors. On the other hand, the reason why (*dioti*) reflection is at equal angles comes from the science "above" (76a10–13). Aristotle introduces optics as an exception to hypotheses having to be proper to a science, but it does not remain an exception. After offering this difference in subject matters, he says this shows that demonstrations are only from principles proper to a subject matter. In the case of optics, the principles of the lower and higher subject matter have "the common element" (τὸ κοίνον) (a15). So, optics must have its own version of the relations so clearly and competently handled in the geometry relevant to optics. The exception is a special case of the rule. In these chapters of *Posterior Analytics* I, Aristotle makes explicit that arithmetic and geometry are "higher" than the natural sciences they direct in explanation.

It is odd, however, that even though what is *proper to* the subject matter is something physical, the physical is not the genus where demonstration through the *reason why* is made. The mathematical higher science is the source of the reason why. We could almost say the lower science borrows its principles except that Aristotle holds there is nothing accidental about the relation of these sciences (76a13, 8–10). Despite the oddity—principles proper to the subject matter do not provide the best kind of demonstration, the reason why—Aristotle does not resolve the divergence by saying there is a higher genus uniting arithmetic with harmonics or geometry with optics. Higher and lower *mathêmata* just have something common. This was also Aristotle's conclusion in *Metaphysics* E.1, where he makes a comparison to the science of being. Even mathematics is not something universal over all *mathêmata* (1026a23–27), but geometry and astronomy are each concerned with a particular nature (περί τινα φύσιν).

In these three passages, *Metaphysics* E.1, and *Posterior Analytics* I.7 and 9, Aristotle rotates usage of three terms—*idion, tis phusis,* and *to koinon*—in discussing the divergent subject matters of mathematics. *Idion* is an adjective denoting what is proper to a science, what belongs to its subject matter, whether object or attribute. *Tis phusis* means a certain nature. Roughly put, having a certain nature is the basis for ascriptions of what is *idion* to a subject. Having a particular nature means belonging to a genus. This may have ontological implications (1026a21). Certainly, belonging to the same genus suffices for attributes to be subject to demonstration from the same principles. Aristotle uses the third term, *to koinon,* what is common, to denote a less determinate basis for sharing principles of demonstration. He uses *koinon* in all three passages,[528] its connotation being mainly contrastive to the case of belonging to the same genus. The positive connotation of *koinon* in this context is that each *mathêma* has mathematical features that receive the same treatment. So, these features actually are in each different underlying subject matter. The mathematical traits belong to visual rays, and they belong to geometric lines.

Aristotle does not specify the mode in which geometry and arithmetic are "above" their cohort more physical *mathêmata*. We may infer from the treatment in *Metaphysics* E.1 that what is immovable and eternal is prior to what is changeable (1026a13), and so arithmetic and geometry would be prior to harmonics and astronomy to this extent. In the passage cited, Aristotle is defining the priority of a science concerned with what is both immovable and separable to either physics, whose subject matter is movable, or to mathematics, whose objects are sometimes immovable but "are probably not separable but exist as enmattered" (1026a10–16). So, the thrust of the discussion of priority in *Metaphysics* E.1 is not priority among the mathematical sciences themselves. We are left with the words "under" (ὑπό) and "above" (ἄνω) in *Posterior Analytics* I as our only real clues to the type of priority Aristotle has in mind for arithmetic and geometry.[529] Aristotle treats the topic again in *Posterior Analytics* I.13.

Posterior Analytics I.13 is extraordinarily rich with insights into Aristotle's demonstrative theory. Structurally, the chapter has two parts

---

528 *Metaphysics* E.1, 1026a27, *Posterior Analytics* I.7, 75b20, and I.9, 76a15. The word *koinon* is not used in this way in *Physics* II.2.

529 Above is compromised as a locator of "pure mathematics" insofar as arithmetic and geometry are sources of demonstration by virtue of something common they share with the natural science. The disparity is less acute if the references to above and below sciences pertain to the disciplines themselves but not the subject matters.

built around the two kinds of *hoti* demonstration: (1) demonstration through an observation (The planets do not twinkle) to the minor premise of the corresponding *dioti*, or *propter quid*, demonstration (The planets are near),[530] or (2) demonstration that has a *dioti* form but does not demonstrate through a middle term that is closest as a cause to what is to be explained. Aristotle refers to this case as the middle term being "outside" (78b13), so that the demonstration fails to give the cause.

The first kind of *hoti* demonstration, though generally rejected by modern scholars as having probative force, has nevertheless proven resilient in discussion of Aristotle's science, because it offers insight on how the empirical content of a conclusion is related to the middle term in a demonstration and also how it is related to definition. Certainly, the inference in this kind of *hoti* demonstration is sound, even if the significance of the whole demonstration is disputed.

The second kind of *hoti* demonstration Aristotle regards as a sound inference but potentially misleading. Aristotle's example of the second case is explaining why a wall does not breathe by saying it is not alive. The middle term is outside the range of relevant causation, because many living things do not breathe either, e.g., fishes and plants.[531] The cause is not entirely irrelevant but it is remote.[532] The example is unfortunate, be-

---

530   This kind of *hoti* demonstration is related to a *dioti* demonstration using the same terms (78a22–b3). Taking Aristotle's example, the *hoti* and *dioti* demonstrations respectively are:

What does not twinkle is near.	What is near does not twinkle.
The planets do not twinkle.	The planets are near.
The planets are near.	The planets do not twinkle.

The demonstration *hoti* (that it is) takes an observation as a minor premise, "The planets do not twinkle," and an immediate insight, "What does not twinkle is near," as the major premise and concludes through the observation as middle term to a conclusion otherwise uncertain, "The planets are near." This inference is the basis for constructing a demonstration through the actual cause of the non-twinkling, namely the nearness of the planets, which is the middle term of the demonstration *dioti* (the reason why). In the *dioti* demonstration, the major premise is converted as to subject and predicate, so that the cause precedes its effect—"What is near does not twinkle"—and the conclusion of the demonstration *hoti* becomes the minor premise of the demonstration *dioti*, "The planets are near." Appropriately, it is the observation, "The planets do not twinkle," that is the conclusion. The original observation is now understood in terms of its cause.

531   Breathing (ἀναπνεῖν) here means inhaling and exhaling not respiration in general.

532   Aristotle provides the logical argumentation against the reason given being the cause (78b16–29).

cause knowing that walls are not living things and thus not candidates for respiration would keep the question from being asked in the first place.[533]

Aristotle then treats a type of demonstration that might be interpreted to be by remote cause but in fact is not. This is the case of the *dioti* account coming from another science (78b35). This is the case we have been considering, in which sciences "hold in relation to one another as one under the other" (78b36), as Aristotle repeats the formulation of chapter 7. Aristotle goes further and gives a different catalog of related *mathêmata* in chapter 13, however. The set of lower and higher sciences he names in this inverted order:

Chart 10.2

$$\frac{optics}{geometry} \propto \frac{mechanics}{stereometry} \propto \frac{harmonics}{arithmetic} \propto \frac{ta\,phainomena}{astronomy}. \quad (78b37\text{--}39)$$

This account includes the usual relation of optics and harmonics to geometry and arithmetic respectively. Astronomy, though, which was also linked to geometry in *Physics* II.2 and *Metaphysics* E.1, is here made the cohort of geometry and arithmetic, the over-sciences. It has a science under it, which is "the phenomena." Putting *ta phainomena* in this position as a science in relation to another implies at the least that *phainomena* include some noetic registration of evidence in astronomy—the ordering of heavenly bodies or recognition of faster and slower speeds. These are already component *phainomena*.[534] Aristotle includes stereometry, the incompletely developed *mathêma* for solids, which Plato had made a predecessor science for astronomy in *Republic* VII. Aristotle does not place stereometry in relation to astronomy, however, but makes it the higher mathematics for mechanics. So, in this treatment of the mathematical natural sciences in *Posterior Analytics* I, mechanics is a *mathêma* in its own right.

---

533 Aristotle's second example is the observation of Anacharsis that the Scythians do not have flute-players because they do not have vines. An enigmatic statement, it is taken to mean that, not having vines, the Scythians do not have grapes for wine. Flute-playing in particular was associated with revelry and its attendant drunkenness, so without wine, there was no reason to have flutes or flute-players. Aquinas comments, "The middle term here is very remote; a closer one would be that they have no wine, and closer yet, that they do not drink wine. For drinking wine brings a joviality that leads to singing" (*Commentary*, I.24, commentary b [trans. Berquist, 110]).

534 This passage supports my argument in Chapter 3 that the *phainomena* of astronomy can be regarded as "the way things are" with the heavens, something that involves a framework of intelligibility organizing a set of most important empirical observations.

This placement of mechanics and *phainomena* as cohort terms in relation to a branch of separated mathematics is not simply an odd deviation from Aristotle's usual plan or from Plato's authoritative reflections on stereometry and astronomy in *Republic* VII. This part of *Posterior Analytics* I.13 is Aristotle's most explicit acknowledgment that the ancient inheritance of practical mechanics constitutes experiential knowledge comparable to the framework of *phainomena* in astronomy. This passage shows that Aristotle sees mechanics as being a source of intelligible experience, as being one of the *mathêmata,* and also as being related to higher *mathêmata.*

After presenting this proportional organization of mathematical sciences, Aristotle adds, "Many of these sciences are nearly synonymous, like astronomy that is mathematical and nautical science, or mathematical harmonics and "that which depends on listening to notes" (ἡ κατὰ τὴν ἀκοήν).[535] This too is something different from Aristotle's statements elsewhere. He associates the mathematical natural science closely with a phenomenal mathematical account like navigation or an empirical determination of ratios of musical strings by tuning. Harmonics and empirical determination of ratios in tuning are nearly synonymous, he says.

What does he mean by the word synonymous (συνώνυμοι) then? In *Categories* 1, Aristotle's distinction of synonymy and homonymy plays a role in his subsequent classification of words as denoting things. The categories group terms used synonymously. Does Aristotle mean, then, that a mathematical natural science and the more empirical, rule-based use of the mathematical are the same for a given subject matter? To some extent, yes, but we need a less inflated interpretation of synonymy for this passage than one with the ontological implications of the *Categories.* In fact, Aristotle is giving us valuable information on the lack of a clear boundary between mathematical natural sciences and their more practical or empirical partners at the time of his writing. They are not clearly distinguished. Perhaps they would not need to be further distinguished if we simply understand the role of the mathematical.

There is some overlap of basic principles in the mathematical and empirical treatments of a subject matter.[536] He says:

---

535 78b39–79a2. The quotation is Ross's rendering in his paraphrase, *Analytics*, 551.

536 Aristotle says at the end of chapter 13 that there is another science under optics, namely, theory of the rainbow. In general in this passage, he is juggling different descriptions of closely related pursuits in an attempt to introduce ordering in terms of which

> For here it is for the empirical scientists (τῶν αἰσθητικῶν)
> to know the fact and for the mathematical to know the reason
> why; for the latter have the demonstrations of the explanations
> (τῶν αἰτιῶν τὰς ἀποδείξεις), and often they do not know
> the fact, just as those who consider the universal often do not
> know some of the particulars through lack of observation (δι'
> ἀνεπισκεψίαν). (79a2–6)

An astronomer might have a demonstration relevant to the movement of
heavenly bodies but not know how it applies to real movements of the
heavenly bodies, because he does not have the familiarity with detail that
the observational astronomer has.[537] Yet, this would still be mathematical
astronomy. As Aristotle said in *Metaphysics* A.1, the knowledge of the
trained doctor can sometimes be inferior to the know-how of the man
of experience. We might think this an unusual occurrence. Aristotle's
remarks in *Posterior Analytics* I.13 indicate otherwise. The empirical scientist deals with experiential notions that he knows have mathematical
import and that he regards as mathematical. His practice involves actual experience, though, and this makes for a different perspective on the
mathematical than the theoretical astronomer has. Aristotle himself falls
into the class of the more empirical scientist when, in *On the Heavens*
II, he brings the occultation of Mars to bear on the order of the heavenly
bodies, an order important to him because of its confirmation of the concentric circles principle as a foundation of both mathematical and physical astronomy. So, the practicing scientist is working at the boundary of
mathematical and empirical. What is more, he knows it and may by this
awareness be able to add details that enhance the mathematical picture of
the natural phenomena.

Returning to the position of mechanics in Aristotle's placing of the
respective sciences, mechanics is like astronomical *phainomena*, mathematically formed intelligible observations, but it is also like harmonics.
Harmonics is more clearly a mathematical science and is usually paired
with astronomy. So, in the same chapter 13 where Aristotle speaks of

EDS ✳

---

sciences have universal principles and how they hold those principles.

537   Aristotle could have in mind his contemporary, Autolycus, who wrote a treatise *On
the Moving Sphere*, which includes demonstrations on this topic without regard to their
immediate application to risings and settings of heavenly bodies. The latter is the subject
of Autolycus' other surviving treatise. Aristotle might also have in mind Aristoxenus of
Tarentum, a student in Aristotle's own school who excelled in mathematical harmonics.

higher and lower relations among the mathematical sciences, he also blurs the boundaries between the mathematical natural sciences and rule-based empirico-mathematical pursuits. Taking another turn, Aristotle says at the end of chapter 13 that mathematics deals entirely with forms, which even if they are in a subject, are not treated as if they are in that subject (79a6–10). The mathematics of forms we surmise is what would be understood as separate. Certainly, it may be pursued without regard to a subject matter. The natural sciences, however, involve mathematics doing work in explanation, so that the gradations between them are more nuanced and varied. Aristotle then gives an example of a *mathêma*, the study of the rainbow, which is under optics as optics is under geometry (79a10–12).

Some things to notice about Aristotle's treatment of mathematics in the five passages examined are the following. The hierarchical relation of different mathematical sciences is less pronounced than the terms common in English language interpretation of the passages—subordinate, subaltern–would make it appear. The issue of priority in *Metaphysics* E.1 concerns the priority of a science of being to both mathematics and physics. It does not concern priority within mathematics. *Physics* II.2 actually avoids treating separated mathematics as prior. The chapters of *Posterior Analytics* I use the minimal terminology of "under" and "above" for a weak kind of priority among sciences.

With his expressions centered on *to koinon*, Aristotle stresses that mathematical traits belong to their natural subjects just as much as they belong to separated mathematical forms. In this, Aristotle seems to keep in play the Pythagorean insight that the mathematical traits and objects later separable in thought appear "live" in natural things and precede in experience the separable mathematical objects that provide demonstrations. There is a clearer distinction between a separated mathematics and a mathematical natural science that corresponds to it than there is between any given mathematical natural science and other natural sciences, like the optical science of the rainbow, to whose demonstrations optics provides aid.

Furthermore, at the level of natural science, the mathematical is also explored empirically. Mathematical traits emerging from investigation may provide clues to demonstration in the higher *mathêma* or may take demonstrations from it. Even the minimally hierarchical terms, "under" and "above," are applicable to related mathematical sciences insofar as principles (*archai*) can be propositions proper to demonstration. So, we need propositional principles from a science above for propositional knowledge in the logically ordered version of the lower mathematical natural science.

Finally, the noetic objects of mathematics are not prior (πρότερον, πρῶτον) to the objects (including properties) of a mathematical natural science. The cognitive process of acquisition of mathematical knowledge provides no support for an ontological priority of mathematics to physics. This is the point on which Aristotle finds the Pythagoreans particularly insightful. It is also a point where we can see the interplay of sensible seeing and rational insight that forms Aristotle's empiricism. Aristotle's placing a science of being that is genuinely first above physics and mathematics equally in *Metaphysics* E.1 supports this ontological deflation of the subject matter of separated mathematics.

Something else worth noting comes from juxtaposing these points with the preceding presentation of mathematics as it might belong to the category of relation. Mathematics has to do not just with a certain type of object but (perhaps even more so) with relational characteristics of things and with mathematical arguments.

Proportionality and Commonality

One conclusion I draw from the materials presented in this chapter is that Aristotle's common element (*to koinon*) between a mathematical natural science and a branch of separated mathematics is common to the *respective disciplines* he considers. That is, arithmetic and harmonics as organized mathematical pursuits have the common element. It is not the subject matters as such that have the common element. There may not seem to be much of a difference between the discipline and its subject matter, but making this distinction allows a clearer view of the fact that the geometrical traits belonging to the subject, e.g., visual rays, are traits of and in the natural state of affairs. Aristotle was not thinking in terms of mathematics being applied to physical problems. The entire problematic of his time for mathematical natural science was a movement in the opposite direction, from the natural science to separated mathematics. So, the common element that he addresses in *Posterior Analytics* I is not something identical in each subject matter but rather something the same by proportional ratios holding in the same way in each case.

336

Mechanics in this context is the science of weight whose cohort in noetic mathematics, Aristotle tells us, is the *mathêma* of ratio and proportion among solids (stereometry). As we have seen in Chapter 9, however, Aristotle extends the method of proportional reasoning even further than solids to include distances, times, and weights. In Chapter 8, I spoke of a proportion of ratios of different rectilinear elements of circles as being "successful" or "unsuccessful." A successful comparison of ratios is one where the relation of individuals entering into separate ratios is the same. That is, the *relation* of terms on each side of the proportion is similar and nearly the same relation. The relation is not unequivocally the same (identical), because the terms themselves in the two ratios—e.g., distances covered versus weights—are not the same. Given relations the same to the extent that this heterogeneity allows, we say that a proportion holds. The point of teasing apart these elements of proportionality is to show that there just is not direct equality or identity in proportional reasoning.

Proportionality is powerful reasoning nonetheless. A proportion asserted is a *proposal* that the heterogeneous things being compared have the same relation.[538] Sameness of ratios can of course be accidental or short term. What Aristotle seeks are ratios that endure as reciprocating throughout continued investigation and proportions that always hold. So, the achievement of proportionality first narrows the subject matter to a particular set of components to investigate and then reinforces the "always holds" as being, at the least, a property (*per se* accident) of the beings or terms entering into proportion.

For Aristotle's purposes in the *Physics*, sameness of ratio comes into its own when an element in a proportion is varied to demonstrate a covariance. The altered element remains inseparable from its ratio, but some change in the other ratio takes place to maintain proportion. Covariance in particular makes proportion an instrument of physical investigation. Covariance in physical factors that enter into change contributes toward winnowing the candidates for a characteristic proportion such as the one in *Mechanics* 1.

---

538   There are four elements of proportional thinking: (1) individuals entering into ratio, (2) ratios themselves which give a (3) relation holding between the individuals in ratio, and finally different ratios being (4) the "same ratio," which is what is meant by a proportion holding. A proportion "holds" can be glossed as "holds true," or one could say, "the ratios hold equally." Aristotle prefers to say that there is a proportion (*analogia*). In *Physics* IV.8, Aristotle uses the locutions κατὰ τὴν ἀναλογίαν (215b3), ἐχέτω τὸν αὐτὸν λόγον (215b6), ἔσται τι ἀνάλογον (216a7).

Since Aristotle grounds his foundational work in mechanics on co-variance, trying to define relations apart from what is in relation may go against the spirit of his natural philosophical enterprise, however much it may seem central to the clarification of relation more generally. Still, there is a being of the relation, and it resides in the reciprocating of the respective ratios. So, there is something it is proper to say is a relation, but one can never really separate the relation from its subjects. This incompleteness of abstraction has always been regarded as one of the chief assets of argument by analogy.

I have shown that Aristotle sought to apply proportional reasoning across very different kinds of movements. He sought a unitary account of movement in nature. To whatever extent his science has been superseded by more sophisticated scientific thinking, it has been shown that his strategy was not "qualitative science" in the sense usually ascribed to Aristotelian science. Aristotle hammered out a *methodos*, a research program, that would guide what elements to look for in every analysis of a change, and he sought this *methodos* in the mathematical innovation of his own time. He was looking for precision and a high level of universality in his resort to proportional reasoning across subject matters of natural science. I would suggest that what is clearly not superseded in this approach are all the advantages accruing to homonymous or analogical understanding in science over against the restriction of expressions of natural truths to literal and narrowly defined language.

Chapter 11

Aristotle's Empiricism in Cognitive History

The Fundamental Insight of Mechanics

The last chapter has shown that weight resisted assimilation into the emerging fourth century BC consensus concerning the subject matter of mathematics and of the mathematical natural sciences. Put most simply, movement was intrinsic to the mathematical treatment of weight, but the systematic formulation of the subject matter of mathematics excluded movement from mathematics. Even before the late fourth century BC, the phenomena constituted by weights in motion were understood by the Greeks to be highly receptive to mathematical formulation in terms of the rule we have examined. Substantiating this point has been part of the argument of this book. It has also been shown that leaving weight phenomena out of the discipline of mathematics did not prevent Aristotle from incorporating kinematic insights into his emerging science of motion. As Chapter 9 argues, the moving radius principle, which was the simplest gathering point in thought for all leverage phenomena, figures in the rationale of key passages in *Physics* IV–VII. Aristotle had the principle in mind. Because Aristotle shared Plato's dictum about the immutability of mathematical objects, a mathematical idea about weight and movement, rather than fostering the growth of mechanics as mathematical, instead became part of Aristotle's narrative natural philosophy.

This so to speak *enforced* route for the expression of a founding mechanical idea brought a habit of thought typical of mechanics into Aristotle's natural philosophy, namely the simple inference from action underway, accomplished, or altered (change in direction or speed) to some *principle* of that action, accomplishment, or change in the action. This very spare inference to a principle of change is also a feature of early modern mechanics in its most economical expressions and was very intentionally made an element of classical mechanics by a succession of its practitioners in the 17th–18th centuries: a change in a movement has some origin.

This formulation—a change in a movement has some origin—is open either to an ontological or a minimalist interpretation, depending on whether one takes the origin as a force (or cause) or simply as a function (placing the change within a system or structure).[539] I believe that the minimalist version of this inference is the core empirical insight that Aristotle gained from ancient mechanics. It guided his natural philosophy.

I assign to the inference characteristic of mechanics the shorthand moniker, *M*-inference. An indication of how widely the *M*-inference is recognized is its importance for C. S. Peirce, who refers directly to mechanics and its characteristic reasoning in these emphatic terms:

> [I]f the actual changes of motion which the different particles of bodies experience are each resolved in its appropriate way, each component acceleration is precisely such as is prescribed by a certain law of Nature, according to which bodies in the

---

539 For contrasting formulations of the principle of force in classical mechanics, see Lützen, *Mechanistic Images*, 24–26. Hertz sought to formulate mechanics without force (Lützen, 40–49). Also relevant is Boudri's reading of the problems surrounding interpretation of force in the eighteenth century. He contends that mechanics only just came into existence with Newton and did not achieve completion until the working out of a consistent metaphysics for mechanics. In this, Boudri opposes instrumentalist or positivist interpretations of the maturation of classical mechanics (*What Was Mechanical*, 15–17, 109–110). Boudri specifies that the new metaphysics of mechanics dropped the "scholastic residue" of substance notions. He connects d'Alembert, a central figure in the instrumentalist interpretation, to his own interpretation, seeing d'Alembert as seeking a purification of metaphysical foundations for mechanics (*What Was Mechanical*, ch. 4). On the shifting delineation of principles within classical mechanics addressed from the standpoint of a physicist, see also Lindsay and Margenau, *Foundations*, ch. 3. On d'Alembert in particular, see their §3.8 (102–109). Martínez addresses this topic from the standpoint of kinematics, which is a central theme also of this book. He points out that Newton's conception of force was distinct from the idea of physical cause. Newton "relied on the concept of force to account systematically for physical phenomena, that is, to deduce observed motions from mathematical principles, facilitating subsequent investigations of the possible causes of such phenomena" (*Kinematics*, 59). Thus, Newton resisted an ontological conception of force. In the terms used here, he insisted upon the minimalist interpretation of the origin of change. Martínez outlines the importance of kinematic considerations to the genesis of Einstein's special theory of relativity in his ch. 6.

relative positions which the bodies in question actually have at the moment, always receive certain accelerations, which, being compounded by geometrical addition, give the acceleration which the body actually experiences.

This is the only fact which the idea of force represents, and whoever will take the trouble clearly to apprehend what this fact is, perfectly comprehends what force is. Whether we ought to say that a force *is* an acceleration, or that it *causes* an acceleration, is a mere question of propriety of language, which has no more to do with our real meaning than the difference between the French idiom "*Il fait froid*" and its English equivalent "*It is cold*." Yet it is surprising to see how this simple affair has muddled men's minds. In how many profound treatises is not force spoken of as a "mysterious entity," which seems to be only a way of confessing that the author despairs of ever getting a clear notion of what the word means! In a recent admired work on "Analytic Mechanics" it is stated that we understand precisely the effect of force, but what force itself is we do not understand! This is simply a self-contradiction. The idea which the word force excites in our minds has no other function than to affect our actions, and these actions can have no reference to force otherwise than through its effects. Consequently, if we know what the effects of force are, we are acquainted with every fact which is implied in saying that a force exists, and there is nothing more to know.[540]

I quote this passage at length, because it describes the basic inference pattern fostered by acquaintance with mechanics. We know forces through the effects of forces. Furthermore, forces are known *precisely as* the effects they bring about. Peirce regards the inferential pattern to be so significant as to draw from it philosophical implications that found his own pragmaticism. The *M*-inference in Peirce's case takes on positivist overtones.[541] Peirce clearly takes a stand against forces as causes. He be-

---

540 C. S. Peirce, "Make Our Ideas Clear," 174. Peirce's insight may have to do with Kirchoff's newly published interpretation of mechanics as purely descriptive (*Mechanik*, 1876). On Kirchoff, see Lützen, *Mechanistic Images,* 24, 52–54. On the dating of this essay of Peirce, see Brent, *Peirce: A Life*, 69. Peirce was in Germany in 1877 presenting his work on the pendulum to the International Geodetic Association (*Peirce: A Life*, 119–120).

541 Peirce discusses his pragmaticism in relation to positivism in "What Pragmatism Is," 171. Pragmaticism he calls a prope-positivism. This is an expansive version of positivism that does not eschew some typically metaphysical problems, which Peirce regards as open to clarification and solution.

lieves the meaning of a term is nothing but its effects, and from this belief he develops his own theory of signs. The *M*-inference is, however, too basic to implicate inevitably a single philosophical position. It is simply minimal. The lesson is that inference to force from action taking place precedes ascription of causes or characterizations of force.

Some might think that the feature of mechanics Peirce seizes upon belongs to mechanical analysis only within post-Newtonian classical mechanics. Indeed, addressing Aristotle himself, someone might say that, surely, there are many sources for a notion so basic as "change requires a principle of change." One could, for instance, find a predecessor of the notion in Anaximenes' introduction of condensation and rarefaction as the source of differences in a natural world composed from aetherial air. Anaximenes is responding to the rational problem "Why does the one existing substance change? Why does it show different appearances?" Anaximenes' answer could be viewed as substance-based—the one thing compacts and disperses—and thus not reliant on something inherently dynamical, like proportional rules. It should be noted, however, that "change requires a principle of change" is not the same claim as "a change in change is an indication of some principle at work." The latter insight treats rest and motion together as related phenomena of movement and also treats rates of change as subject to change and thus as comparable.[542]

It is possible to establish ancient recourse to the style of inference I have highlighted by consulting Aristotle's own works and works of his school. As one would expect, the *M*-inference shows itself in the Aristotelian *Mechanics*. In that treatise, of the three terms—*ischus, dunamis,* and *rhopê*—*ischus* and *dunamis* are used more or less synonymously to mean force, a push, or an immediate external source of movement.[543] The act that is *ischus* or *dunamis* is intelligible in terms of the movement it brings about, which is represented in the mechanical conception of the Aristotelian *Mechanics* by lines of different lengths. *Rhopê*, on the other hand, is a more nuanced term in *Mechanics*. It connotes the influence

---

542   One may also point out, of course, that not everything in Aristotle's physical theory goes back to this principle as it developed in mechanics. I claim only that the principle of the lever in its larger context of mechanical thinking is a major, and relatively unexamined, line of influence on his thought.

543   For an example of *dunameis* in this sense, see *Mechanics* 3, 850a30 (μικραὶ δυνάμεις). For *dunamis* used in the singular for a push, see for instance 851b3: "ῥᾷον κινεῖ καὶ θᾶττον ἡ αὐτὴ δύναμις τὸ αὐτὸ βάρος." For a possibly dual use in the same sentence of *dunamis* as first signifying power and then a simple push, see 850b28–30.

due to position, weight, and added force, which will initiate movement or suffice to alter a movement underway. So, whereas *ischus* and *dunamis* are thought of as uncombined and individuated acts of agency, *rhopê* is an accumulated or combined power of movement at the point of its beginning to show itself. To this extent, the phrase "moment of force" is a useful and apt placeholder for *rhopê*, which has the connotation of a tipping point of influence. An example of this meaning of *rhopê* is the discussion in *Mechanics* 8 of how a balance beam situated vertically will move when disturbed. The author is discussing why larger circles are moveable with little effort. He says:

> Further, he who moves circular objects moves them in a direction to which they have an inclination as regards weight (ᾗ ῥέπει ἐπὶ τὸ βάρος). For when the diameter of the circle is perpendicular to the ground, the circle being in contact with the ground only at one point, the diameter divides the weight equally on either side of it; but as soon as it is set in motion, there is more weight on the side to which it is moved, as though it had an inclination in that direction (ὥσπερ ῥέπον). Hence, it is easier for one who pushes it forward to move it; for it is easier to move any body in a direction to which it inclines, just as it is difficult to move it contrary to its inclination (τὸ ἐπὶ τὸ ἐνάντιον τῆς ῥοπῆς). (851b26–33)

In this passage, the author treats inclining (*rhepein*) or inclination (*rhopê*) as an additive influence productive of movement. Points on a circumference are understood as being inclined downward due to weight on either side of a vertical diameter. In this condition, the inclination due to weight is equally balanced on either side of the diameter (851b29). A point at the top of the vertical diameter is thereby unmoved. If a mover adds inclination by pushing (ὠθεῖν) along the circumference (a push operating along the tangent to the circle), the effect is equivalent to adding weight to an already existing but equally balanced inclination (b30–31). By means of *rhopê,* the author gives an account of why circular movement turns out to be so useful in the crafts. As soon as the wheel is set in motion, it is after that easier to move forward by additional pushing. The force exerted (*ischus*) need not be so great. This is because its inclination is already in the direction of the manifest movement. *Rhopê* is a conception of a confluence of inducements to movement, which are made intelligible by means of perceptible *effect.*

343

Looking to Aristotle's own works, we can see that he makes use of a similar inference. Movements or activities, changes in movement, or transitions from rest to movement are prompts for inference to a principle. In *Physics* IV.8, Aristotle says repeatedly that differences in the movement of the same body signal some difference in at least one of the factors sustaining the movement. This is the unifying thread in his *reductio* against the void and the infinite, which uses proportions. As one part of this *reductio*, he says that movement without an impediment operating against it will continue indefinitely (215a20–22). The coincidence of this insight with Newtonian inertia is momentarily startling but should not be surprising. The coincidence is due to the fact that Aristotle too is thinking in the terms of mechanical notions available to him that concern changes within a system of movement. He is also thinking of force being correlative to perceived effects. In any case, the insight means that, if a medium affects movement by slowing it down, the absence of force will entail a movement continuing always at the same rate of change.[544]

A cognate of the *M*-inference is the inference to an origin or a principle, *archê*, which is so much a part of Aristotle's method. In *On the Soul* II.2, Aristotle distinguishes cause and soul, saying:

> Just as the nutritive power can be separated from touch and all sensation, so is touch separable from the other senses. The nutritive is the part (μόριον) of soul in which all plants share. It is obvious that all animals have the sensation of touch. By what reason (δι' ἣν δ'αἰτίαν) either of these facts is true we shall say later. For now, let this much be said: that soul is the principle (*archê*) of these

---

544   In the passage that follows in *Physics* IV.8, Aristotle goes on to emphasize the common observation that if the same weight, or body, moves faster in one instance than in another, this can be explained in two ways (διὰ δύο αἰτίας). It is due to a difference in what opposes it—the medium through which it travels; or it is due to the body's excess of weight or lightness with respect to some other body with which it is compared (215a25–29). From the standpoint of the inference under examination, the two cases are different in essentials. In the first case, faster movement indicates less of an opposing force. The slower speed of the body is proportional to the greater influence of resistance. In the second case, Aristotle adds a *ceteris paribus* clause, saying that all other things being equal, a difference in a body's speed is due to a direct ratio of the bodies as to weight or lightness. The heavier will move faster or the lighter will move faster. This seems a reference to heavy and light in their primary inclinations of moving downward or upward respectively.

mentioned [powers] and is defined by them: the nutritive,
the sensitive, the capacity for thinking, and movement.[545]

In this passage, activities or singular biological functions *occasion* the inference to a principle of that function, but the principle is itself closely identified with the activities. Aristotle says clearly in this passage that the inference to *archê* precedes giving reasons or assigning causes. So, he separates and highlights the minimalism of the original insight and then flags it as the inference to *archê*.

Aristotle does not simply transfer the *M*-inference into other natural situations. He adds that whatever is the principle of the change or characteristic activity, it is not a thing, event, or state of affairs, as is what it describes or names. It is important when engaging in *archê* talk, Aristotle tells us, not to lapse into treating the principle of natural things as if it is another natural thing (τὸ φυσικόν). In *Physics* I.2, Aristotle says that *archai* are not things, beings (τὰ ὄντα), but that beings have *archai*.[546] Not everything about nature can be treated with the philosophical grammar appropriate to beings. In this account from the *Physics,* then, *archê* is not a count-noun like "bicycle" nor is it the name of any natural substance, like water; it is not on the same plane as natural substances and artifacts. This raises the question on what plane of thinking the philosopher is when thinking on principles. Nevertheless, we should note a certain advantage accruing to the separation of principles and beings in the context of an immediate inference from action to principle. The advantage is that *archê*, being the inference primitive and prior to ascriptions of cause or delineation of modes of being, possesses the duality of belonging both in the *explanandum* and in the knower's knowing. A circle already moving has *rhopê* and we can tell this by it being easier to increase the circle's speed, even when we apply a lesser force than initially exerted. As Aristotle conceives *archê*, there is no rupture between thinker and his subject when the inference to a principle is made. Peirce is so adamant in his preference for how thinking is done in mechanics precisely because he wants to avoid the separation of knower and known thing. Peirce's semeiotic would recover this feature of Aristotelian principles. The duality of *archê* is aided

---

545 *On the Soul* II.2, 413b5–13. The translation follows Smith in *CWA* 1, 658.

546 *Physics* I.2, 185a4. Distinguishing principles and beings is made urgent by the mistakes of the monists with respect to being (185a20–30). See also *Physics* III.4, 203a1–10. Aristotle does not maintain a dogmatic separation of beings from principles. See *Metaphysics* Λ.7, 1072b4–14, where the first mover of necessity is a being and a principle.

by giving no actual definition to the notion beyond its being the origin of its activities or functions.

Archê can be compared to another ancient scientific term, γνώμων, the meaning of which is knower or what discerns.[547] In its meaning of what discerns, the *gnômôn* was the style, or perpendicular, on a sundial that makes known the time of day (**Figure 11.1**).[548] A *gnômôn* could, however, be a simple stick placed perpendicularly in the ground, casting a shadow that moves during the day. Some prominent and naturally occurring permanent features of a landscape, a vertical boulder or escarpment, could play the same role. For anyone who works outdoors all day, the shadow reaching a particular length as judged in reference to some other feature of the landscape, could signal the time to begin the trek home.

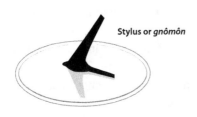

Stylus or *gnômôn*

Figure 11.1

Let us consider momentarily the boulder or escarpment, a natural promontory. In this case, since the discerner (*gnômôn*) occurs naturally, the shadow cast is not only a sign of the time of day (like the style's shadow on the sundial) but something more like a token of the sun's different positions. The difference is due to the fact that the promontory was never contrived to serve timekeeping. The natural promontory, the moving sun, and the moving shadow simply constitute a state of affairs. Other things are part of that state of affairs also—the height of the escarpment, its vegetation, the changes in location of the shadow through the seasons. Because of this, taking the shadow in its different locations or lengths as a sign is to treat one part of the state of affairs instrumentally, something the faculties of experience, craft or intellect can do. But the original naturalness of what is now a sign remains making the shadow in its newest configuration a *sumbolon*, one of a pair, and this is how a shadow is a token of the portion of the day already passed. To be as precise as

---

547 Heath says the literal meaning of *gnômôn* is "a thing enabling something to be *known, observed* or *verified*, a *teller* or *marker*, as we might say" (*Elements* 1, 370). Heath comments on Book II, Def. 2.

548 Herodotus says that the Greeks learned the *gnômôn* and the twelve divisions of the day from the Babylonians (*Histories* II, 109.11).

possible, let us say that the pair is "position of shadow/portion of sun's day." What discerns the pair, the *promontory*, now recedes within the newly constituted state of affairs that for the timekeeper includes solely the shadow and the portion of the accomplished day. Paradoxically, the *gnômôn* which provides the shadow nevertheless fades out of the time-keeper's frame of reference, insofar as it services as a *device*. This is a particularly trenchant example of our coming to ignore or look through what is the source of discernment and our focusing instead on an outcome of discernment as a token of what we seek to know. This makes the sign closely identified with what it signifies. The tool makes the two—which we could also characterize as "movement of shadow/movement of sun" —a natural pair. It is interesting that the *gnômôn* is not the sign; the shadow is. This interweaving of signifier and what is signified extends to the made object, the sundial. *Gnômôn*, the word, thus functions in much the same way that Aristotle uses the word *archê*. *Gnômôn* does not separate thought and thing. It brings them closer together.

One reason for bringing *gnômôn* into the present discussion is that the word had the connotation in early Greek science of being a marker *around which* the intelligibility of other things is constituted. The sundial's style functions this way, because without the style, there is no discernment of time of day at all. The *gnômôn* is also a focal point of intelligibility in the technique of figured numbers in Pythagorean science.[549] Figured numbers were laid out by arrangement of pebbles. In the simplest case, the addition of two pebbles around one, with the empty spot filled by another pebble, produces a surrounding array of three pebbles. The array makes a quadrilateral shape (see **Figure 11.2**). Continued addition of one pebble

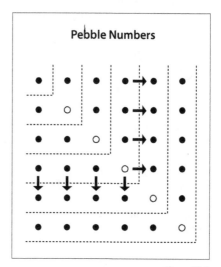

Figure 11.2

549   On this topic, see Heath, *History* 1, 76–86. Burkert affirms the tradition of pebble numbers as appearing "exclusively in the Pythagorean tradition" but associates it with no particular mathematicians of the tradition (*Lore and Science*, 427–428).

to replicated bars of the immediately preceding quadrilateral maintains the square shape of the original arrangement of three. This process yields the series of odd numbers). The sum of the numbers in the series up to any given odd number is always a square number, n^2. So, 1+3+5+7=16, a square number. Furthermore, the laying out of another series of pebbles by the method given (**Figure 11.2**) yields the next square number. These connections, and others like it for differently shaped series, were known before Aristotle's time. Calling the Pythagoreans by name, Aristotle said of their method, "When the gnomons are placed round the one and apart, sometimes the shape is different, sometimes it is one."[550] There is, however, considerable difference of opinion as to what kind of figural addition Aristotle refers to, and also what are the *gnômones*. They are certainly something other than individual counters—individual dots or pebbles. Iamblichus gives the clearest description, that the gnomon is "any number which, when added to a figurate number gives the next number of the same figure."[551] Consistent with Iamblichus, Heath describes the *gnômona* (pl.) as "the odd numbers successively added."[552] Presumably, this means each odd number as it forms another complementary layer in the quadrilateral array. From this standpoint, though, we could say (still consistent with Iamblichus) that the gnomon is 2(--) + 1, with 2(--) standing for the replication of sides from the last number generated. Whatever details are relevant to adjusting this picture of *gnômôn*, it is clear that, in the case of figured numbers, the *gnômôn* was associated with a pattern in which addition of an element produced a succession of pairs {(1,3) (3,5) (5,7) (7,9), . . .} that maintain the same type of complementary relation.

Intelligibility for the *gnômôn* then is at least the agreement highlighted in natural pairing. Uses of the word by pre-Socratic authors and by Euclid show that the agreement involves complementarity. Philolaus is

---

550 See *Physics* III.4, 203a13–15. The Greek reads, περιτεθεμένων γὰρ τῶν γνωμόνων περὶ τὸ ἓν καὶ χωρὶς ὁτὲ μὲν ἄλλο ἀεὶ γίγνεσθαι τὸ εἶδος, ὁτὲ δὲ ἕν. There is debate about the meaning of the passage and, hence, the interpretation of certain phrases, like καὶ χωρίς. For an extended discussion, see Ross, *Aristotle's Physics*, 542–545. See also *Categories* 14, 15a30.

551 This formulation is Ross's in *Aristotle's Physics*, 544. Iamblichus says, "In the representation (σχηματογραφία) of polygonal numbers two sides in all cases remain the same, and are produced (μηκυνόμεναι); but the additional sides are included by the application of the gnomon (τῇ τῶν γνωμόνων περιθέσει) and always change" (Iamblichus, *Commentary on Nichomachus' Arithmetic*, 62.10–14, trans. D'Ooge in Cohen and Drabkin, *Sourcebook*, 9).

552 Heath, *History 1*, 77.

reported to have said, "Number makes all things knowable and mutually agreeing (γνωστὰ καὶ ποτάγορα ἀλλάλοις) in the way characteristic of the gnomon."[553] Here, the *gnômôn* is the medium or conduit of knowability, and it induces knowing by showing agreement. The word ποτάγορα is Doric for προσήγορος, which connotes the agreement of address or appellation—what we might call naming by face-to-face opposition.

Euclid includes a connotation of agreement in his extension of the meaning of *gnômôn* in his second definition of *Elements*, Book II: "And in any parallelogrammic area let any one whatever of the parallelograms about its diameter with the two complements (παραπληρώμασι) be called a gnomon."[554] Euclid here carries the gnomon idea beyond the complementary figured numbers of the Pythagoreans to a geometrical context.[555] As we saw in Chapter 8, it is a notable feature of the parallelogram that it can be divided into other parallelograms drawn around the diameter of the original figure containing the complements (**Figure 8.5**). Euclid calls these internal parallelograms by the name *gnômôn*. He says, "[L]et any of the parallelograms . . . with its complements be called a gnomon." This formulation would seem to take each complement as a gnomon, or else it means that any complement can be the gnomon insofar as all the complements imply one another. This meaning seems to be a good example of the shift in meaning of gnomon from the generator of complementary tokens to the complements themselves.

---

553   See Diels–Kranz, *Fragmente* 1, 46 B11 (411.14–412.3). The passage is quoted in Heath, ed., *Elements* 1, 371. It is from Stobaeus' *Extracts* (*Eclogae*) (AD 5th? century). For information on *gnômôn*, see also Heath's discussion in *Elements* 1, 370–372, and Cohen and Drabkin's quotation of Iamblichus' report on *gnômôn* in the context of figured numbers (*Sourcebook*, 9, and 9n1). By analyzing its vocabulary, Huffman makes a convincing case that Fragment 11 is inauthentic. He believes the connection of knowability and agreement cited in the passage belongs to the early Academy, citing the similarity of language to *Republic* 546b7. Huffman acknowledges a doctrine of "being fitting together" (ἀρμοσθέν) in Philolaus (Fragment 7) but connects it to cosmology. He does not discuss the word *gnômôn* in Fragment 11. Huffman cites the reference to things limited and unlimited in the passage as conveying genuine doctrine of Philolaus (Huffman, *Philolaus*, 61–62, 347–350). Since Philolaus is associated by Speusippus with figured numbers, there is a case to be made that *gnômôn*, being a pre-Platonic word in natural philosophy, was used by Philolaus and that it had for him the connotation of organizing intelligibility by creating complements. In the case of figured numbers, these complements are successive. See Heath, *History* 1, 78 and 78n4–5 for earlier scholarly interpretation along these lines.

554   Heath, ed., *Elements* 1, 370.

555   See Cohen and Drabkin, *Sourcebook* 9n2, for a display of figurate numbers as spatially complementary.

Aristotle uses the word *gnômôn* only a few times in his entire corpus, whereas *archê* appears hundreds of times. He thus seems to have little use for the more ancient connotations of *gnômôn*. For the purposes of comparison to *archê*, though, the important point about *gnômôn*, the discerner, is the immediacy of its giving intelligibility to a thing or situation. As we experience *phainomena*, they cluster around a mark, because the phenomena cannot but take their meaning and expression from the *gnômôn*. This gnomonic complementarity—the immediate rendering of perceptibles as knowable complements to the *gnômôn*—is the central feature of Aristotle's inferences to *archê*. The parallelogram complements, though a late instance of *gnômôn*, still give some idea of how a *gnômôn* or an *archê* renders perceptible things as intelligible. Complementarity is naming by direct opposition, the establishment of *sumbola,* things mutually intending one another, each of which can be taken as a sign of the other.

The way Aristotle makes the empirical intelligible follows closely upon gnomonic complementarity. Yet there is a difference between *gnômôn* and *archê* that may account for Aristotle's preference for the latter term. The *gnômôn*, though a discriminator, is on the same plane of existence as what it explains. In figured numbers, the *gnômôn* is itself a number. The style of the sundial is a thing like the horizontal surface on which it casts a shadow. In the case of the stick that tells time, the perceptibles are the different positions of the stick's shadow and the *gnômôn* is the stick itself. An *archê*, on the other hand, is not something like the stick. *Archê* must be accessed *logikôs*—intellectually or by reason, even though the warrant for the inference to a principle is something empirical.

When I claimed in Chapters 5 and 6 that Aristotle's concept of *dunamis* is (*a*) a notion content-rich in physical terms, (*b*) a potency that is at the same time passive and active, and (*c*) a potency evident equally in natural changes and machine arrangements, I had in mind that the inference to *dunamis* belongs to the "principles club" of *gnômôn* and *archê*. In *Metaphysics* Θ.1, Aristotle refers to *dunamis* as *archê*. In this connection, it is significant that *gnômôn* as it was initially introduced to the Greeks (supposedly by Anaximander) was a device, some version of a sundial. The word then acquired the additional meaning of a tool for drawing right angles. This tool was a portion of a geometrical square or rectangle. That a notion has a connection to device in fact boosts the immediacy of its agreeing with the world, since device just does produce an effect or an action. It has meshed with physical reality. For Aristotle, *dunamis* has this same sort of agreement with the world, and the notion of *dunamis*, by being linked to the mechanical, enjoys the integral relation to reality that *gnômôn* and *archê* each have. Of the three related immediate inferences, gnomonic complementarity, inference to a principle (*archê*), and the *M*-inference, the last most lucidly portrays the minimalism of Aristotle's method of thought. This minimalism, as an aspect of later classical mechanics, came to characterize the method of mechanics above all else.

It is worthwhile to make one more point about the *M*-inference. Whenever it appears, the inference is involved with another feature of reasoning in mechanics. This feature runs throughout the mechanical references in *Physics* IV.8 and could be called the equilibrium-sum rule (**ES**):

> **ES**: Factors contributing to movement, whatever they are, participate in a system in which energy and movement taken together maintain some version of equilibrium.

One feature of **ES** replicated in Aristotle's inferences to *archê* is that any natural subject or phenomenon under consideration participates in a system of activity or movement. This is important to note, because the intelligibility brought into a situation by the *archê* or *gnômôn* is more than the opposition and separation of naming. In Aristotle's equilibrium-sum reasoning, it is not force or energy in heterogeneous kinds of things— movers, moved things, speeds—that is mutually interchangeable. That is, force is not passed along and transformed in its different subject matters. Rather, the equilibrium itself assumes many different forms. If one thinks within this picture of systematic relation, while avoiding the mistake of making force the interchangeable element, then one needs a strong rationale for tracking equilibrium as present similarly across different subject matters. Equilibrium (*isorrhopia*), like *archê*, is a notion that serves explanation in physics while remaining at a remove from physical things themselves or the concepts of physical things.

In summary and to draw this theme to a close, ancient mechanical thought, as I understand it influencing Aristotle, carried with it precision and a minimalism of content in thought. A mechanical style of thinking introduced equilibrium as an intellectual value. Translated into thought, equilibrium is system or structure. Yet, by means of its founding inference, thinking in mechanics maintained a close connection to what is explained. For Aristotle and probably some of his predecessors in natural philosophy, mechanics and attendant mathematical ways of organizing experience defined what would constitute intelligibility in nature. To this extent, the mechanical brought with it an epistemology in which sense experience and intelligibility were not alien to one another.

We have seen in the foregoing the immediacy of knowledge to the known in Aristotelian empiricism. An important ancillary theme of this book has been Aristotle's use of analogy to assimilate the fruitfulness of the mechanical style of thinking. It is possible to clarify and comment upon the conviction (πίστις) that accompanied his intellectual translation of mechanics-type intelligibility to thinking about change in other natural phenomena. Accordingly, I return to the examples from *Movement of Animals* 1–7 to show how they functioned in knowledge as similes or illustrations in Aristotle's time and place.

Proportional Reasoning and Versions of Action

What follows in this section is a brief account of how devices may well have functioned *cognitively* in Aristotle's science because of the precedent of emotive and rational acceptance of action as real in Greek theater. Let us begin with the device examples or similes for animate action that Aristotle offers.

In *Movement of Animals* 7, there are two kinds of what we as moderns would call analogy: (1) the proportional method of reasoning (*analogia* or *logos*) already explained in connection with *Physics* VII.4, and (2) concrete examples that run all through the treatise. Aristotle's references to boats and rudders, sticks and toy wagons, pegs and wires connecting the parts of *automata* have been taken as fairly *ad hoc* comparisons proper only to their immediate contexts. Treating them more systematically, Bénatouïl notes the number and variety of comparisons in *Movement of Animals* as remarkable and offers a classification of them by type. He rightly cautions against the tendency of repeated and casual usage to make comparisons and analogies into metaphors or identities.[556] Bénatouïl treats in particular the inter-specific analogies between parts of animals. He considers more broadly, however, the status of potentiality and actuality as concepts known by analogy and regards the reasoning of *Movement of Animals* as fitting within the analogical method explicitly

---

556 Bénatouïl, "L'usage des analogies," 81, 94–95, 112.

articulated by Aristotle in *Posterior Analytics* I.10 and *Metaphysics* Θ.6. There are principles (and theorems) called common in different sciences that do not appear as identical in each science but in a form adapted to the objects of each science.[557] It is always important to bear in mind, too, that what is similar in proportional analogy is the *relation* between terms of ratios brought into analogy. The ratios are the same, not the terms entering into ratio. These points, grounded in Aristotle's own method, inform my account of Aristotle's extension of the power of the lever to other kinds of change.

While *pros hen* analogy has occupied pride of place in scholarly philosophical treatments of Aristotle, proportional analogy has been regarded as an incomplete and weaker kind of analogical thinking.[558] *Pros hen* analogy connects the meaning of predicate terms to their single ground or primary sense. A diet or exercise regimen may be healthy. A gadget or scalpel may be healthy in the sense of promoting health, but the primary meaning of health is the health in a living body. So also is the primary meaning of "being" the being of substance. In many instances of his proportional reasoning, on the other hand, Aristotle does not identify a primary analogate in an anchoring first ratio to which other similar ratios are equal. The contexts where he seems to (e.g., *Physics* I.7, where Aristotle reasons to a substratum for substantial change[559]) are passages whose interpretation is disputed partly because of questions about the meaning of the analogical reasoning. Aristotle does not regard proportional reasoning as weaker than *pros hen* analogy, however. It has a very different epistemic function from *pros hen* analogy. It is heuristic reasoning, which means it works in an epistemic context where much remains unknown. It is significant in this regard that Plato and Aristotle both treat proportion as a kind of equality.[560] When terms cannot be compared directly, it may

---

557 Bénatouïl, "L'usage des analogies," 90–91.

558 Aristotle presents *pros hen* analogy, also called focal meaning, in *Metaphysics* Γ.2, 1003a33, Z.1, 1028a10–20, and Z.4, 1030a20–b3. Classic scholarly accounts of focal meaning include J. Owens (*Doctrine of Being*, ch. 3), G. E. L. Owen, "Logic and Metaphysics," and Irwin, "Homonymy." Berti gives a critical assessment of the history of interpretation of *pros hen* analogy in Anglo-American scholarship on Aristotle ("Multiplicity and Unity"). He sees Frede and Patzig as reviving the interpretation of J. Owens, which Berti identifies as a Platonizing interpretation influenced (in Owens's case) by medieval philosophy.

559 *Physics* I.7, 191a7–12.

560 For proportion as equality (ἰσότης), see Plato, *Gorgias* 508a, and Aristotle, *Nicomachean Ethics* V.3, 1131a31. Morrison ("Plato's Philosopher-Statesman") offers an

still be possible to establish a kind of equality among them by proportionality.

It is clear at least that, when Aristotle applies *dunamis* to different kinds of change in *Movement of Animals* 7, he relies on structural similarities. The structural features are dynamic regularities. The dynamic regularity we can think of as a rule of magnification of action along a line of effect, whether the effect is velocity, growth, or fear and desire. His analogies, the toy wagon and *automata*, serve to render *actions* analogous.

Aristotle's examples ally apparently different venues, childhood play and theatrical display, that are in fact not very different. Considering toys as technological achievements, de Solla Price notes the general observation of historians of technology that principles used in toys only much later figure in useful machines, before they finally issue in scientific generalizations.[561] The implication is that principles known in toys are inherently limited and even regarded by thinkers of the time as trivial. Peter Dear makes a contrasting observation that some references to children's games in early modern science rooted scientific observations in "commonplace experience." If a phenomenon was familiar to children, it had a universal character.[562] This seems the role of Aristotle's allusion to the toy wagon. The toy illustrates a principle whose multi-valence is already understood to extend to activities of commerce, shipbuilding and architecture.[563] The very universality of the toy's *logos* in experience is a reason to take its *archê* as extending analogically to other subject matters. This implicit rationale for extension of a principle is a cognitive feature of empiricism.

Theater in its turn was one of the original homes for device recognized as contrivance. Not unlike the automatic theater whose illusion depended on wheels, pegs, and cords, the outdoor theater used simple machines, like the pulley or crane (αἰώρημα, μηχανή) to raise or lower an actor, and all manner of contrivance that could inspire awe, but most especially the simple device of the mask (πρόσωπον). These are all part

---

interpretation of the ancient means—arithmetic, geometric, and harmonic—as kinds of equality, in the sense of "a fair system of . . . differentials between powers" (213–214). He makes a case for the influence of this kind of equality in Plato's philosophy.

561   De Solla Price, "Automata," 15.

562   Peter Dear, *Discipline and Experience*, 149.

563   Compare, for instance, *Mechanics* 11, where the author asks why heavy loads (τὰ φορτία) are easier to move on rollers (ἐπὶ τῶν σκυτάλων) than in carts (ἀμαξῶν).

of theatrical display, the non-linguistic features of theatrical re-creation and storytelling. These features are covered by Aristotle's term, ὄψις, in his classification of parts of tragedy in *Poetics* 6.[564]

Play is like theatrical display in simulating, or recreating, natural phenomena or life processes by the means nature makes available. One can make a thunder-like noise by rattling sheet metal or change one's face by paint and masks. The natural processes of play or theater may be different from actual life—a human being flies raised by a pulley or crane. Alternatively, the natural process may be miniaturized processes of the same kind. Playing at having a tea party is a simple miniaturization. Onstage simulation of steam coming from a fissure in the earth is most easily contrived with real steam and so is an elaborate miniaturization. Importantly, play and theatrical display are alike in being activities, not conceptual metaphors or conceptual simulations.[565] Activity is the sort of thing it must be feasible to carry out. When a marionette swings its arms like a human with a club, it has actually moved, and this movement has to have been "possible" within the frame of natural possibility. Though calling upon imagination in those playing or observing, neither play nor theatrical display is complete in thought alone. To this extent, both are dependent on nature for the resources to produce action.

Aristotle's toy wagon at first seems different from either imitative play or theatrical display, which present again the phenomena they portray. The wagon is a minor useless oddity, fun because it is quirky and aberrant. It simulates nothing, unless one could say it parodies a useful wagon. That it does not straightforwardly simulate something else makes it a bridge between natural things that Aristotle takes to be governed by the principle, on the one hand, and complicated devices crafted in accordance with the principle, on the other. The toy wagon displays the

---

564 *Poetics* 6, 1450a10. Display includes scenery as conventionally conceived, as well as machinery for special effects (this could include automatic theaters with simulacra of animals and people), as well as any kind of marvelous festival display of sound, light, and movement.

565 Metaphor is applying traits to a subject in thought with the understanding that the subject is not the sort of thing to actually possess the traits ("The road was a ribbon of moonlight"). Conceptual simulation is mapping one thing onto another by correspondence in thought. Conceptual simulation need not involve direct application in action. Descartes' understanding of the animal body as a machine is conceptual simulation. As the Cartesian example shows, conceptual simulation often constitutes a research program for filling out details of the correspondence between the concept and real things. On this issue in Descartes, see Des Chene, *Spirits and Clocks*.

natural principle even though it is something made. Indeed, the toy is a venue for improvisation upon the natural principle—think of skateboards. Aristotle's examples drive home that the boundary between nature and craft is lower when considered in relation to action than in simply regarding natural and artificial things as objects.

In this context, the words "likeness" or "image" (εἴκων, εἰκόνα) prejudge the degree of reality belonging to the re-presented action.[566] To simulate nature or to create an apparently unnatural display (a wonder, *thauma*) requires familiarity with natural principles and also an understanding of those principles as natural.[567] The utilization of natural phenomena in an *automaton* redeploys, or presents again, the original action. It is re-presenting precisely because it is action. No devised action can be purely artificial.[568]

Considering play or display from the point of view of nature, re-presented action is not a *likeness* of what had been produced by the unimpeded natural process but a *version* of it. Both a likeness and a version are "seconds." Indeed, theater would seem to involve both likeness and re-creation, since the spectators see the action; they do not take the action themselves.[569] A likeness, however, is not a guide to principles belonging

---

566 In Platonic conception, a likeness is like a reflection and always depends on some medium in which it is realized. This means a likeness exists, to the extent it does exist, in a way inferior to the Form, which is self-subsistent. In the case of the physical things Aristotle considers, however, the form is already enmattered and so is a different kind of original to start with. We cannot follow completely the Platonic model of original and inferior likeness in order to understand Aristotle's search for principles in this context.

567 Lloyd makes this point in *Magic, Reason*, 51.

568 That an end or intelligible action has to garner natural resources in order to become enacted in its re-presentation is a point usually noticed by Aristotle in terms of the utilization of materials, not principles of action, in natural processes. See, for instance, *Parts of Animals* I.1. For a straightforward statement of craft as following the same process or route as nature in producing ends, see *Physics* II.8, where Aristotle says that if crafted things were made by nature, they would be made in the way they are now made by craft, and vice versa. In this passage (199a8–20), he says that stages in a change are each for the sake of the next and that, in general, things done or undertaken in natural and craft processes respectively are done for the sake of something. "Craft perfects what nature is unable to achieve (ἀπεργασάσθαι), but craft imitates nature" (199a15–17). Although he contrasts nature and craft in other important passages, especially his definition of nature in *Physics* II.1, this passage is Aristotle's testimony to the ability of craft to uncover nature and its principles. It can do so because it trades on the same process and outcomes as nature.

569 The spectators are οἱ θεαταί, those who come to see. The theater, θέατρον—the place for seeing—is, as Nagy points out, "an instrument for seeing." The -ρον ending denotes instrumentality ("Subjectivity of Fear," 36–37). This point reinforces that theater is both a place for spectacle and a place of devising or contrivance.

to the original as an alternate version might be. Again, the difference is action. In Aristotle's thinking, the *hamaxion* and *automata* are both versions of living things that separate out the salient principle involved in structural similarities among kinds of changes. If an analogy is a version of portrayed action, then there is reason for it to carry conviction as a genuine portrayal. One way of putting this is to say that the moving figures in the automatic theater are like living things, not the reverse. My suggestion is that Aristotle's device analogies carry the resonance of being true to life in a way already understood by the Greeks in their theater.

It might seem to be an impediment to this view of re-presentation of the real that the representations are so incomplete. Being raised on a pulley is not flying after all, and neither does a flexing *automaton* arm have the suppleness of the real thing. We probably underestimate the degree of sophistication of the machinery underlying the moving animals of automatic theaters.[570] Still, animal-shaped figures in an automatic theater render only the smallest range of animate activity. Knowing the cause, no one would mistake the version for the real thing. Here the difference between a contrived actual version and an image (*eikôn*) is worth noting. Since the contrived action is to represent the real action, it is safe to say that no one expects in action the completeness possible in conceptual (imagined) simulation. Achieving in simulated action even a few of the purposive actions (ἕνεκα τινῶν) of animate behavior is significant, if one seeks guidance to principles of natural activity. The distinction between action and imagination is important. For us as moderns, what it is possible to imagine in the realm of action sets the standard for verisimilitude in action. But this was the case neither for theatrical imitation nor for the conception of physical processes in antiquity.

There is, however, something of a paradox belonging to the real powers of a theatrical contrivance. On the one hand, theatrical device aids the rendering of action, and action is what can span the boundary between imitation and reality. On the other hand, this occurs despite what we suppose is a marked inferiority of contrived action to imagination of the same. Let us investigate this issue in relation to the simplest device of theater, the mask.

---

570 Fostering this caution is the discovery and scholarly study of the Antikythera mechanism, dated to the first century BC. The device manifests a level of precision engineering of gears by the Greeks that was previously unknown. See de Solla Price, "Greek Computer," and Zeeman, "Gears." The device was an ancient calendar for tracking movements of the heavenly bodies, an astronomical clock. It receives its name from the island near which it was found.

Notably, in the 5th–4th centuries BC, there was no word for mask separate from *prosôpon*, face or countenance.[571] The mask was the countenance of the character as an agent and the countenance of his action and its consequences. Certainly, masks expressed a persona. Also, a mask was very assertive. The masked chorus gave a terse commentary or amplified emotional effects. In our own time, the Greek mask is rarely used successfully in theater, because it seems incompatible with the psychological naturalism of contemporary performance. Studies on Greek masks of the fifth century BC point to the distinctively Greek naturalism of the mask. Wiles reports the experiences of modern actors in performing Greek drama outdoors with masks. The outdoor theater changes how the actors project their voices and the mask leads them to move their bodies more slowly. With the mask, the voices of the actors resonate differently to themselves, both because walls do not affect the acoustics and because they hear their own voices differently in the mask. Wiles's view is that the mask "creates a link between human beings and the natural world. The boundary between an inanimate environment and the flesh of the human subject comes to be experienced as permeable."[572] In addition, Meineck points out that the spectator merges the mask, character, and action in his reception of the spectacle.[573] The porosity of the interface between nature and the human actor during performance is the important element in understanding the Greek mask. Far from being artificial or stilted, the mask makes the character alive through the "matter" of the actor's performance and the story (*muthos*).

In this context, *completeness* or near completeness in verisimilitude is far from being the most important factor in the believability of a performance device. A contemporary reference that carries back into ancient cultures reinforces this point. Early in his career, the twentieth-century

---

571 *L-S*, πρόσωπον; Wiles, *Mask and Performance*, 1. Aristotle uses *prosôpon*, not the later *prosôpeion*, in *Poetics* 5, 1449a36, to refer to a comic mask. Homer uses *prosôpon* only in the plural.

572 Wiles, *Mask and Performance*, 163. For a different expression of Greek naturalism, see Meineck, "Neuroscience of the Tragic Mask."

573 Thinking about the manner of effectiveness of the Greek mask in theatrical production is an exercise in exploring hylomorphism in a context other than philosophy. Citing Carr et al., Meineck writes that "our cognitive abilities to imitate, learn, speak, understand, and empathize are linked to embodiment—our minds and our bodies are connected in experiential cognition and we process the emotion of others through a system of 'action representation'" (§7.2). Meineck refers to the spectator processing the speech of the actor in mask.

sculptor Henry Moore was attracted to Cycladic and Mexican masks as art objects. These masks are not representational in the sense of reproducing a strict likeness. Moore nevertheless noticed delicate natural details captured by masks, like the fact that no face is entirely symmetrical. Moore made masks, using this detail to render the essence of a face through concentration on emotionally expressive features.[574] Conveying the essence of a face in this way will leave some details of the face indeterminate. It is not that the details left out are insignificant, but all one needs of other details is what contributes to the proportionality of the mask. The proportional relation is recognizably typical of what is being portrayed. So, it is possible for *blankness* to make a positive contribution to portrayal. The mask closes the deal on the reality of the face for the spectator by allowing the viewer to supply details of the face or character.[575] In this case, proportion is the natural scaffolding for the viewer's more complete imaginative or emotive presentation. It is clear then that device did not have to have all the details of its original in order to recreate the real.

The cognitive function of selective detail is operating within the framework of action in Greek theater. The threshold of difference between nature and craft is lower for action than for simply comparing objects as to likeness. The action portrayed, for a short space, made a credible claim on the spectator to be the action itself. It is reasonable to think that as Aristotle used mechanical analogies in his philosophy he drew upon the epistemic possibility, still active in his culture, of production (*poiêsis*) being a version of naturally occurring action (*kinêsis, energeia*).

The human capacity for making this epistemic identification is not easily dispelled by successive ages of reason. In modern science, a model with fewer actual correspondences between parts of the model and the natural reality it models may be better for conveying the important characteristics of what is being modeled. Schrödinger's cloud model of the atom is superior to the Bohr model in this way. Indeed, a model with a relational countenance is more hospitable to the mathematical aspect of what is to be understood, because it portrays only essentials or the chief implication of the mathematical account.[576]

---

574 Moore and Hedgecoe, *Moore,* 56–63.

575 For a treatment of how the mind supplies details not present in a mask, see Meineck, "Neuroscience of the Tragic Mask," §5–7.

576 The suitability of the image of a cloud for the electrons surrounding an atom is not in the objects that make up a meteorological cloud, particles hanging in the air, but in an

Any model works by the knower performing a mental feat of displacement of the knowing self over against the object to be explained. The viewer or knower faces the object. If knower and known thing are in opposition, there is some distance between them.[577] Paradoxically, this separation allows the knower to take the model as the thing without losing the original phenomenon. Through the model, the knower is aware of a thing as still being itself in a different mode of being presented.[578] The model is one appearance of the thing.

The theatrical mask is relevant to understanding this displacement of significance. *Prosôpon*, the word for face and for mask, is what presents itself in the view from opposition or *en face*. As Nagy says, *prosôpon* comes from the syntax of "looking straight at another person who is looking straight back at you."[579] So, just as the mask is the face, an epistemic model *is* the countenance of its reality. This moment of taking one thing for another is crucial to the emotional credibility of Greek theatrical performance. The moment of taking one thing for another is also an aspect of the empirical grounding of knowledge. Some sensible being is what is opposite the knower. It has a countenance familiar or re-lived, so that there is no breach between thought and thing. For Aristotle, the *autom-*

---

imagined appearance of the flurry of locations of the atom's electrons in a supposed change of place. The scientist cannot locate a particle at any single location. Taken this way, the cloud model also makes intelligible the fact that the electron is not the sort of thing to occupy positions, in the sense of being in a place over time. This seems to be more of a displacement of significance of meaning in the model than we find even in proportional reasoning.

Citing Thucydides on how reports of speeches given should resemble the actual speeches, the philosopher of science, Cartwright, likens physics to theater. She says, "It is important that the models we construct allow us to draw the right conclusions about the behaviour of the phenomena and their causes. But it is not essential that the models accurately describe everything that actually happens" (*Laws of Physics*, 140).

577   Interestingly, Heidegger's account of *Dasein* as truthful (being in accord) involves the elements of opposition of knower and the being to be known, together with an idea of separation between the poles of opposition, where the being to be known presents itself. *Dasein* must let things appear ("Essence of Truth," §2). It was important to both Husserl and Heidegger that no instance of presence shows everything about a being. The one perceiving supplies aspects hidden to present perception. Also, vague knowledge is not necessarily deficient knowledge.

578   For insight on how models are signs of their objects and not of thoughts or concepts about objects, see Sokolowski's *Presence and Absence*. He gives an extended treatment of re-presentation in the context of words and propositions. Also relevant is his "Picturing."

579   Nagy, "Subjectivity of Fear," 37. Nagy regards fear as the primal emotion engaged in the viewing of the theatrical spectacle (39).

aton in its own realm works according to the same relation of *dunamis* and action as a living thing. His examples are the faces of that relational reality in a living thing, not because they are mechanical in the sense of the mechanical philosophy but because they follow a mathematical rule that works throughout nature.

A Summation of Coming to Know

The two topics of this chapter—(1) empirically based reasoning around a principle of intelligibility, and (2) the cognitive power of a re-presentation of action—can be taken together to elucidate the character of Aristotle's thinking about movement and natural things. Aristotle combines the minimal conceptual content of the *M*-inference with the ability of device to renew natural actions in another medium. From an epistemological standpoint, this is the best of both worlds. The limitation of a literal account of an occurrence, a description or explanation in words or symbols, is the inevitable failure to achieve denotative specificity.[580] This failure is bypassed by the two features of ancient understanding given here. The *M*-inference specifies a minimal empirical content while keeping explanation economical. Device in its ability to renew action assures that there is no break between the knower and what is to be explained. Crucially, the *M*-inference begins explanation extremely close to nature. Because it anchors empirical intelligibility in a principle, it may then accept as explanation the elaboration of meaning possible in homonymous not synonymous language.

The mind is so constituted as to assimilate the intelligibility of device to the intelligibility of nature. Device utilizes natural principles even in accomplishing human purposes. There is, however, an odd perversity in the cognitive process, because device itself becomes occluded from view by the display it makes possible. Our reproducing natural action by device is first wonderful and then reassuring. To reproduce action shows it can yield to human understanding. To this extent, nature falls within comprehension and control. Having achieved this stage of instrumental understanding and utility, however, the mind loses touch with the original principle of intelligibility, the *gnômôn* or *archê*, which had made the mind able in the first place to make the correlation of

---

580   Quine has called this the under-determination of theory by facts. The relevant facts are not rich enough to conclusively verify or falsify any theory, whether scientific or of ordinary language (*Word and Object*, ch. 1, §6).

action and an organizing principle. At this point, there is not a fruitful opposition of mask and spectator, or of analogy and the knower, but a rupture between knower and the known. This is the human phenomenon of objectification.

Conclusion

Empiricism and Experience

In this book, I have attempted to give an explication of how experience is an origin of knowledge for Aristotle. That all knowledge comes from pre-existing knowledge, familiarity, or acquaintance is both a philosophical commitment for him and a way of proceeding in his own science and natural philosophy.[581] Aristotle says that the very first knowledge base, which he describes as an inborn critical power, is sensation.[582] He gives considerable importance, however, to experience (*empeiria*). I have argued that sensation and experience include the interactive knowledge distilled from kinesthetic awareness and practical pursuits. By consulting the early history of Greek science (Chapter 11), we have reason to think that a power allied to sensation is the ability to couple features of experience by means of an organizing significant marker, which is also an object of sense. The person experiencing and thinking uses a gnomon while barely recognizing it as such. Paradoxically, this feat of forgetfulness occurs in memory, where one *logos* comes from many percepts. Complementarity, the efficacious epistemic product of the gnomon, when once established has great staying power, so much so that it comes to substitute for the origin of discernment, the gnomon. So memory pairs the length of a shadow and time of day, a symptom and the underlying condition that makes it appear.

---

581 *Posterior Analytics* I.1, 71a1–2: Πᾶσα διδασκαλία καὶ πᾶσα μάθησις διανοητικὴ ἐκ προϋπαρχούσης γίνεται γνώσεως.

582 *Posterior Analytics* II.19, 99b25.

Complementarity builds upon previous instances of complementarity, supporting empirical intelligibility of increasing sophistication. In the example of Chapter 4, the occultation of Mars by the moon leaves no doubt of the relative distances of the two heavenly bodies, but this observation is interesting because of an empirically derived mathematical rule that is the prime candidate for governing the overall movement of the cosmos. It is the prime candidate, because it is a core common experience possessed of mathematical intelligibility. Aristotle understood mathematical intelligibility to be (*a*) something naturally occurring that was (*b*) highly prized (considered the best explanation) because of (*b1*) the simplicity, precision and clarity of the relations it established and (*b2*) their potential for universality. As we have seen in the specific case of parallelograms, Euclid built a purely noetic version of complementarity on this cognitive pattern that originated empirically.

The contemporary philosopher of science, Van Fraassen, has written with admirable breadth and acuity about empiricism.[583] He believes that empiricism must be a stance, not a philosophical position. Whether coming from *sensibilia* or ordinary experience, sensation and experience constitute the point of view from which to criticize rationalist claims in philosophy. Van Fraassen says that, in the modern period, this was the original role of empiricism, which should never have assumed the status of a foundation or *starting point* for philosophy. Van Fraassen draws upon and endorses the point of view of the logical empiricist, Reichenbach.[584]

As much as I admire Van Fraassen's fresh approach to the problems attendant upon modern philosophy and his analysis of historicism in connection with science, I am also impressed by the paucity of the results philosophically when sensation and experience are taken this way. Van Fraassen's point of view testifies to the continuing importance of Humean empiricism in Anglo-American philosophy since the time of Ayer and Reichenbach. Even discounting logical positivism, whether we see in Hume a skeptic or an early phenomenologist, his influence at best is to validate our ways of *speaking* about things.[585] Ordinary language philosophy, in its turn, depended historically on an agreement about the significance of symbolic logic as propounded by Frege and Wittgenstein.

---

583 Van Fraassen, *Empirical Stance.*

584 *Empirical Stance*, 39–40. See Reichenbach's essay, "Rationalism and Empiricism."

585 This is a possible criticism of Strawson's *Skepticism and Naturalism*, which analyzes Hume and Wittgenstein in connection with a validation of naturalism.

Already with Quine, it was clear that there was not agreement among logicians about the philosophical significance of the 19th–20th century developments in logic.[586] Yet, Van Fraassen mounts a strong attack against analytic metaphysics, something that might be considered an alternative to philosophy of language, as being simply more of the failed rationalism of the modern period.[587] In general, it would help the progress of philosophy at the present time to have a stronger version of empiricism.[588]

My aim has been to show how a philosophy of physical and biological nature has in the past received a crucial and credible contribution from actual experience. I have argued that the contribution of experience to Aristotle's philosophy is minimalist in import and also common to perspicuous seekers of knowledge about motion, regardless of the millennium. It has not been recognized before that *kinematics* plays a large role in Aristotle's thinking about nature. The cognitively primitive kinematic thinking of a "first mechanics" is the beginning of scientific empiricism. Aristotle's mechanical thinking is, at the least, one historical vector extending out from a core universal knowledge process. That knowledge process issued, in a different age, in classical mechanics. The process I have described culminated in a philosophy of nature that featured *dunamis* and *archê*.

A point that should be made is that Aristotle's natural philosophy of motion, as I described it in Chapter 9, turns out to be non-foundational in character. The invariance that Aristotle would carry through other forms of change depends for its explanatory power on the method of homology. At the beginning of Chapter 9, I defined a "descriptive mode" as an invariance, a simple function or a rule of how things change in tandem or as a group, which is expressed qualitatively not numerically. The lever principle, as expressed in the moving radius, the rolling cone, or the characteristic proportion of *Mechanics* 1, is a descriptive mode. We understand the descriptive mode well enough (even without a definitive demonstrative version of it) for us to have *anchinoetic* insight about its likely appearances.[589] That is, the well-prepared mind recognizes the properties

---

586 Quine, *Word and Object*, 3.

587 *Empirical Stance*, ch. 1.

588 Rationalist reconstructions of the relation of perception and knowledge are underway. See, for instance, McDowell, *Perception as a Capacity for Knowledge,* and Gupta, *Empiricism and Experience.*

589 Ἀγχίνοια is Aristotle's word for quickness of wit, the ability to grasp a cause or

of the mode without having to refer to the most complete version of it. We wait for and look for further showings of the descriptive mode. Non-foundational knowledge does not necessarily mean continually shifting knowledge. In Aristotle's case, doing mechanics-based philosophy of motion has the great strength that belongs to analogical reasoning. It employs a sophisticated method of reasoning while not abstracting from physical things. Furthermore, the pleonasm Aristotle recognizes in his basic principle allows for a cognitive refraction of that principle so as to follow the lines of a new subject matter where the invariance is seen to be relevant, e.g., in alteration or generation.

Within this context, Aristotle does not hesitate to use incompatibility with reason as a way of refuting certain claims of his predecessors. As Bolton has argued, Aristotle uses a combination of evidentiary argument (*phainomena*) and reasoned argument (*logikôs*) in his refutation of predecessors in *On the Heavens*.[590] At the nub of the conviction attending his reasoning, however, is the *M*-inference, which as I pointed out in Chapter 11 is the minimalist component of mechanics and the central empirical insight that opens the way to equilibrium-sum reasoning. One thing that must be acknowledged as an implication of this study is the dynamism that is part of Aristotle's conception of the structure of movements and their causes (Chapter 6). Movements make things happen, and there are structural relations between linked movements.

The Other Aristotle

For some, the materials presented in this book may seem jarring as part of an interpretation of Aristotle. Mechanism is the very thing to which Aristotle's whole philosophy lies opposite. I do not ascribe to Aristotle mechanism as a conceptual approach known to modernity. Instead, I show that Aristotle appropriated for his narrative natural philosophy a key mathematical formulation that belonged to a genuine though fragmentary mechanics that he knew. My perspective might also be mistaken to be antagonistic to traditional interpretations of Aristotle's natural philosophy based on substance, essence, form, and teleology. Surely, these are the topics central to Aristotle's natural philosophy, not an incipient mechanics that later nearly vanished from Aristotle's legacy.

---

unmediated scientific connection without prolonged investigation (*Posterior Analytics* I.34, 89b10).

590   Bolton, "Two Standards for Inquiry."

Nothing I have written is meant to sow doubt about the centrality of either substance or natural teleology for Aristotle. Much has been written on these topics, however, and less about Aristotle's interpretation of mathematical natural science, and very little on the presence of actual mechanics (something surely to be expected) in his philosophy of motion. I have placed Aristotle's regard for mathematical science in the context of his ontology of the *Categories*, showing just how broadly mathematical thinking can be deployed outside the category of quantity (Chapter 10). My development of the physical aspect of Aristotle's *dunamis* concept could be taken to fall within investigation of the puzzling divergences among Aristotle's logically based ontology, his matter-form ontology, and his reasoning by potentiality and actuality.[591] I have introduced a line of Aristotle's thought the probable date of which places it in the period when his later philosophy was maturing.

As for teleology, movement toward a *telos* is the very context for my consideration of the micro-structure of movement in Chapter 6. Concerning form, Chapter 5 treats the analogy between craft and fulfillment of natural *telos* in a comprehensive way. This chapter also leaves open a path along which mathematical intelligibility—the unity of a geometrical trope or formula—could be pursued as a means of understanding the unity of form.

Regarded systematically from the standpoint of teleology, the mechanics present in Aristotle's work could be seen as sharing the holism of teleology without the primacy of causal interpretation. Aristotelian treatment of the balance and lever is a rationing of movement, not a calculus for sustaining equilibrium. Accordingly, the starting point of the mathematical account is a distance covered or projected to be covered. The idea of distance covered includes a destination, something similar to the end-point of a teleological change. Furthermore, locomotion remains highly contextualized in Aristotle's writings that play upon the mechanical principle. In all locomotion, speeds are relative. Distances covered are conceived in terms of what is prior for the accomplishment of the movement and what comes later in the course of the movement. That is, movements have a directional component.[592] Even in mechanics, then,

---

591   On these topics, see Graham, *Aristotle's Two Systems*.

592   An example of this is Aristotle's treatment, in *Physics* VI.6, of continuity in terms of completions of successive parts of a distance to be covered. This topic was treated in Chapter 5.

Aristotle's approach is holistic, and this is an attribute commonly regarded as part of teleology, explanation by final cause.

I do not believe, however, that Aristotle proceeded in his thought from teleology to a de-natured version of it for locomotion. The importance of distance covered came with the very territory of giving mechanical accounts. This is true in *Mechanics* 1, and it is explained by the epistemic centrality of the *M*-inference. We must experience or have perceived a change. Relative distance covered is also an original given of astronomy. From this standpoint, it is very interesting that Aristotle would argue from a model of locomotion to other types of change, even biological change, in *Physics* V–VII. The interaction of teleology and the mechanical thinking that I have highlighted is a topic of considerable interest, but the lines of development of these two types of natural explanation seem at the present reading independent of one another in important ways.

Someone might ask, if Aristotle had recourse to the mechanic's art in so fundamental a way, why does he not just say so explicitly? One answer of course is that Aristotle did not say all sort of simple things that would clarify for us his meaning in important passages. More constructively, this question has at least two answers. One follows from the argument of Chapter 10: weight resisted assimilation into the evolving canon of sciences as conceived by Plato and Aristotle. The definition of the subject matter of mathematics as immovable made it harder to see the intrinsic mathematical character of nature itself, depriving intellect of a fluid vocabulary for *historia,* investigation of nature.[593] A separated mathematics as prior imposed on intellect a new and awkward self-consciousness when mathematical inferences were obviously conjunct with natural movement. It was mechanical *ideas*, including to some extent their mathematical component, which then entered into the fabric of natural philosophy by reasoning analogically. The vocabulary of mathematics in motion developed mainly in word and logical argument.

Along with this occluding of the dynamically mathematical in nature, there is another reason why Aristotle might not say more about his mechanical knowledge. This reason has to do with the ubiquity and anonymity of practical mechanics. The revolving wheel, levers, and pulleys were everywhere in Greek life, from transportation to throwing pottery,

---

593 Iamblichus reports that *geômetria* was called by Pythagoras *historia* (*Mathematical Sciences* 78.5). On *historia* in relation to Aristotle, see Lennox, "Data and Demonstration."

pumping water, moving building materials for monumental architecture, designing and using weaponry, and seamanship. The Greeks were a nautical people; they both fished and fought at sea. Almost every aspect of their life at sea involved mechanical tools—e.g., rudder, windlass, yardarm, and oar—yet we gain information about these tools, in the main, only indirectly from stories or visual representations.[594] The paucity of accounts of how the rudder works, for instance, cannot be ascribed entirely to the vagaries of preservation of texts or to the craftsman class being unlettered. Mechanical insight was taken for granted.

Polanyi tacit knowledge

There is also the issue of *how* notice would be given to mechanical *innovation*. Improvements in device were continuous with the function the device already served. A clever engineer is someone a ship's captain wanted at his side, but the cleverness of his subordinate did not mean the superior attended to any particular innovation or new assembly. Presumably, the helmsman would be interested, if he had to use the improved or repaired tool. He might himself be the innovator. As Usher says, though, in his *History of Mechanical Inventions*, "The changes are accepted without much conscious realization of the novelties involved."[595]

The anonymity of innovation is not as remote a phenomenon as one might think. Design in the mechanical arts is easily lost when a technique falls into disuse. In his 1868 catalog of mechanical movements, compiled for an American audience, Brown notes that one-quarter of the movements he describes are of American origin and never before published. Most of the movements are unattributed. He writes, "The want of a comprehensive collection of illustrations and descriptions of Mechanical Movements has long been seriously felt by artisans, inventors, and students of the mechanical arts."[596] In other words, it is a great value to the mechanic or engineer not to have to "reinvent the wheel," when the reinvention is a labor saving or elegant refinement. The anonymity of mechanical innovation is a serious impediment to the study of its history in antiquity. The anonymity, along with the perceived continuity of innovation with what already exists, does provide a reason, though, why Aristotle would not say more about his recourse to mechanical experience in natural philosophy. No one ever said much about mechanical experience.

---

594 On this topic, see Casson, *Ships*, 224–228.

595 Usher, *Mechanical Inventions*, 100–101.

596 Brown, *507 Mechanical Movements*, 3.

Fodor said, "The more global . . . a cognitive process is, the less anybody understands it." [597] I take this aphorism as relevant to the universality of the empiricism born of experience with mechanics. The "not understanding"—the transparency of device and contrivance—is there, but Aristotle captures the salient features of self-acquired mechanical understanding anyway—a sign that it must not be impossible to capture the global.

It can be difficult, though. The *gnômôn*, an original "instrument" and generator of intelligibility, loses even its name to the complements it enabled. Plato comments in his Allegory of the Cave on the unseen puppeteers who carry the made objects of ordinary understanding. More positively and methodically, Aristotle makes action indicative of a principle (*archê*). For what is a principle if not what gathers around it the intelligibility of the manifest? Aristotle delineates certain features of the action that discloses a principle. It is defined by differences (like the distinguishable functions of living things), and it possesses the telling clue of being the well ordered and regular in natural occurrences. Later, we say a principle is a complement—an item of knowledge matching something—and then we understand it less.

In general, I have presented the view that we cannot understand the philosophical ideas in Aristotle's natural philosophy by having only the range of his thought that runs from natural philosophy toward metaphysics. We need also the steel thread of emergent mechanical thinking that is present throughout the fabric of his natural philosophy. We need to look at the spectrum of Aristotle's thought from mathematical science to natural philosophy.

The separation I have labored to maintain between natural philosophy and metaphysics in Aristotle's thought will finally, I believe, serve a better understanding of how these two philosophies are related for Aristotle. I would venture to say that the thread of empiricism gained from mechanical experience is what anchors Aristotle's philosophy as an alternative to Plato. Aristotle's empiricism is neither skeptical nor seeking to avoid philosophical import. It is one instance of empiricism serving as a point of entry for gaining a philosophical position.

---

597 Fodor quoted by Netz, in *Shaping of Deduction*, 5. Fodor called this his law of the non-existence of cognitive science. For a brief description of "cognitive history" in contrast to cognitive science, see Netz, 5–7.

Bibliography

Primary Sources

Texts

Apollonius of Rhodes. *Argonautica*. Edited by Hermann Fränkel. Oxford: Clarendon Press, 1961.

Archimedes. *Opera Omnia*, 2nd ed., 4 vols. Edited by J. L. Heiberg. Stuttgart: B. G. Teubner, 1972 [1910–1915].

Aristotle. *Analytica Priora et Posteriora*. Edited by W. D. Ross, with preface and appendix by L. Minio–Paluello. Oxford: Clarendon Press, 1982.

———. *De Anima*. Edited by W. D. Ross. Oxford: Clarendon Press, 1974.

———. *De Caelo*. Edited by D. J. Allan. Oxford: Clarendon Press, 1973.

———. *Categoriae et liber de Interpretatione*. Edited by L Minio-Paluello. Oxford: Clarendon Press, 1974.

———. *Fragmenta*. Edited by Valentinius Rose. Leipzig: B. G. Teubner, 1886.

———. *De Generatione Animalium*. Edited by H. J. Drossaart Lulofs. Oxford: Clarendon Press, 1965.

———. *Historia Animalium*. Bekker text with revisions by A. L. Peck, 3 vols. Loeb Classical Library. Cambridge: Harvard University Press, 1965.

———. *Mechanica*. Tradizione manoscritta, testo critico, scolii a cura di M. E. Bottecchia. Padova: Editrice Antenore, 1982.

———. *Metaphysica*. Edited by W. Jaeger. Oxford: Clarendon Press, 1973.

———. *Aristotle's De Motu Animalium*. Text with Translation, Commentary, and Interpretive Essays by Martha Craven Nussbaum. Princeton: Princeton University Press, 1978.

———. *Parts of Animals*. Bekker text with revisions by A. L. Peck. In *Parts of Animals, Movement of Animals, Progression of Animals*. Loeb Classical Library. Cambridge: Harvard University Press, 1968.

———. *Physica*. Edited by W. D. Ross. Oxford: Clarendon Press, 1973.

. *De Plantis, de Mirabilibus Auscultationibus, Mechanica, de Lineis Insecabilibus, Ventorum Situs et Nomina, de Melisso, Xenophane, Gorgia,* edited by Otto Apelt. Leipzig: B. G. Teubner, 1888.

———. *Problems Books I–XXI.* Teubner text by Ruelle-Knoellinger-Klek, with notes by W. S. Hett. Loeb Classical Library. Cambridge: Harvard University Press, 1936.

———. *Problems Books 1–19.* Edited and translated by Robert Mayhew. Loeb Classical Library. Cambridge: Harvard University Press, 2011.

———. *Problèmes, tome II, sections xi à xxvii.* Texte établi et traduit par Pierre Louis. Paris: Belles Lettres, 1993.

———. *Progression of Animals.* Bekker text with revisions by E. S. Forster. In *Parts of Animals, Movement of Animals, Progression of Animals.* Loeb Classical Library. Cambridge: Harvard University Press, 1968.

Autolycus. *La sphere en mouvement; Levers et couchers héliatiques.* Testimonia; texte établi et traduit par Germaine Aujac avec la collaboration de Jean–Pierre Brunet et Robert Nadal. Paris: Belles Lettres, 1979.

Commentaria in Aristotelem Graeca. 23 vols. Berlin: G. Reimer, 1882–1909.

Diels, Hermann, and Walther Kranz, eds. *Die Fragmente der Vorsokratiker: griechisch und deutsch.* 3 vols. Berlin: Weidmann, 1956.

Euclid. *Elementa.* In *Euclidis Opera Omnia.* 4 vols. Edited by I. L. Heiberg and H. Menge. Leipzig: B. G. Teubner, 1883–1885.

Galen, *Klaudiou Galenou Hapanta / Claudii Galeni Opera Omnia.* Vol. 18. Edited by Karl Gottlob Kühn. Hildesheim: Olms, 1964–1965 [1821–1833].

Hero of Alexandria. *Automatopoietica.* In *Opera Omnia,* vol. 1, 334–453, edited by Wilhelm Schmidt. Leipzig: B. G. Teubner, 1899.

Herodotus. *Historiae. Thesaurus Linguae Graecae* [Ph.-E. Legrand, *Hérodote. Histoires.* 9 vols. Paris: Belles Lettres].

Homer. *Opera.* 2 vols. Edited by David B. Monro and Thomas W. Allen. Oxford: Clarendon Press, 1978.

Iamblichus. *De communi mathematica scientia liber.* Edited by Nicolas Festa. Leipzig: B. G. Teubner, 1891. Reprinted 1975.

———. *In Nicomachi arithmeticam introductionem. Thesaurus Linguae Graecae* [U. Klein (post H. Pistelli), *Iamblichi in Nicomachi arithmeticam introductionem liber.* Leipzig: B. G. Teubner, 1894. Reprinted 1975: 3–125].

———. *Vita Pythagorica liber. Thesaurus Linguae Graecae* [Edited by U. Klein (post L. Deubner), B. G. Teubner, 1937: 1–147].

Oppian. *Cynegetica, or The Chase,* and *Halieutica, or Fishing.* In *Oppian, Colluthus, Tryphiodorus.* Edited by P. Boudreux and F. S. Lehrs with notes by A. W. Mair, 2–534. Loeb Classical Library. Cambridge: Harvard University Press, 1928.

Plato. *Platonis Opera.* 5 vols. Edited by John Burnet. Oxford: Clarendon Press, 1900–1907 [reprinted 1989].

Stoicorum Veterum Fragmenta. Vol. 2. Edited by H. Van Arnim. Leipzig: B. G. Teubner, 1923.

Translations and Modern Commentaries

Apollonius of Rhodes. *Argonautica*. Translated by R. Cooper Seaton. New York: G. P. Putnam, 1930.

Aquinas, St. Thomas. *Commentary on Aristotle's* Posterior Analytics. Translation, introduction, and commentary by Richard Berquist. Notre Dame, IN: Dumb Ox Books, 2007.

Archimedes. *The Works of Archimedes*. Edited by T. L. Heath. New York: Dover Publications, 2002 [1897].

Aristotle. *Aristotle's* Categories *and* De Interpretatione. Translation with commentary by J. L. Ackrill. Oxford: Clarendon Press, 1963.

———. *Complete Works of Aristotle / Revised Oxford Translation*. 2 vols. Edited by Jonathan Barnes. Princeton: Princeton University Press, 1984.

———. *Aristotle's* Metaphysics *Books M and N*. Translated with Introduction and Notes by Julia Annas. Oxford: Clarendon Press, 1976.

———. *Metaphysica. A Revised Text with Introduction and Commentary*, by W. D. Ross. 2 vols. Oxford: Clarendon Press, 1958.

———. Metaphysics *Book Θ*. Translated with an introduction and commentary by Stephen Makin. Oxford: Clarendon Press, 2006.

———. *Minor Works*. Translated by W. S. Hett. Loeb Classical Library. Cambridge: Harvard University Press, 1980.

———. *Aristotle's De Motu Animalium*. Text with translation, commentary, and interpretive essays by Martha Craven Nussbaum. Princeton: Princeton University Press, 1978.

———. *De Motu Animalium* and *De Incessu Animalium*. Translated by A. S. L. Farquharson. In *The Works of Aristotle*, edited by W. D. Ross. Vol. 5. Oxford: Oxford University Press, 1912.

———. *Aristotle and Michael of Ephesus / On the Movement and Progression of Animals*. Translated with introduction and notes by Anthony Preus. New York: G. Olms, 1981.

———. *Marché des animaux: Mouvement des animaux*. Texte établi et traduit et suivi d'un index des traits biologiques par Pierre Louis. Paris: Belles Lettres, 1973.

———. *Aristotle's Physics: A Revised Text with Introduction and Commentary*, by W. D. Ross. Oxford: Clarendon Press, 1979.

———. *Aristotle's Prior and Posterior Analytics. A Revised Text with Introduction and Commentary*, by W. D. Ross. Oxford: Clarendon Press, 1949. Reprinted New York: Garland, 1980.

———. *Problemata*. Translated by E. S. Forster. In *The Works of Aristotle*, edited by W. D. Ross. Vol. 7. Oxford: Clarendon Press, 1927.

———. *Problemata Physica*. Übersetzt und erläutert von Hellmut Flashar. In *Aristoteles: Werke in Deutscher Übersetzung*. Band 19. Berlin: Akademie Verlag, 1991.

———. *Problemi meccanici*. Introduzione, testo greco, traduzione italiana, note a cura di Maria Elisabetta Bottecchia Dehò. Soveria Mannelli (Catanzaro): Rubbettino Editore, 2000.

Euclid. *The Thirteen Books of Euclid's* Elements. With introduction and commentary by Sir Thomas L. Heath, 2nd ed. rev. with additions. 3 vols. New York: Dover, 1956.

Galilei, Galileo. *Galileo's Logical Treatises*. Translation with Notes and Commentary of His Appropriated Latin Questions on Aristotle's *Posterior Analytics* by William A. Wallace. Boston: Kluwer, 1992.

Plato. *Complete Works*. Edited with introduction and notes by John M. Cooper. Indianapolis: Hackett, 1997.

———. *The Republic of Plato*. Translated with notes, an interpretative essay, and new introduction by Alan Bloom. New York: Basic Books, 1991.

Simplicius. *Simplicius on Aristotle's* "On the Heavens 2.10–14." Translated by Ian Mueller. Ithaca: Cornell University Press, 2005.

Secondary Sources

Acerbi, Fabio. "*Problemata Physica* XV–XVI." In *Studi sui Problemata physica aristotelici*, edited by B. Centrone: 115–142. Naples: Bibliopolis, 2011.

Aleksandrov, A. D., A. N. Kolmogorov, and M. A. Lavrent'en. *Mathematics: Its Content, Methods, and Meaning*, 2nd ed. 3 vols. Translated by K. Hirsch. Cambridge: MIT Press, 1969.

Anderson, David F., and Scott Eberhardt. *Understanding Flight*. 2nd ed. New York: McGraw-Hill, 2010.

Ayer, A. J. "What Is a Law of Nature?" In *Philosophy of Science: the Central Issues*, edited by Martin Curd and J. A. Cover, 808–825. New York: Norton, 1998.

Baldry, H. C. *The Greek Tragic Theatre*. New York: Norton, 1971.

Balme, D. M. "Aristotle's Biology Was Not Essentialist." *Archiv für Geschichte der Philosophie* 62, no. 1 (1980): 1–12. Reprinted in *Philosophical Issues in Aristotle's Biology*, edited by Allan Gotthelf and James G. Lennox, 291–312. Cambridge: Cambridge University Press, 1987.

———. *Aristotle's* De Partibus Animalium I *and* De Generatione Animalium I, *with passages from II.1–3*, 2nd ed. Oxford: Clarendon Press, 1990.

———. "Teleology and Necessity." In *Philosophical Issues in Aristotle's Biology*, edited by Allan Gotthelf and James G. Lennox, 275–285. Cambridge: Cambridge University Press, 1987.

Barnes, Jonathan. "Aristotle and the Method of Ethics." *Revue internationale de philosophie* 34: 490–511. Reprinted in Jonathan Barnes, *Method and Metaphysics: Essays in Ancient Philosophy* I, 174–194. Edited by Maddalena Bonelli. Oxford: Clarendon Press, 2011.

Beekes, Robert, with the assistance of Lucien van Beek. *Etymological Dictionary of Greek*. 2 vols. Boston: Brill, 2010.

Beere, Jonathan. *Doing and Being: An Interpretation of* Metaphysics Θ. Oxford: Clarendon Press, 2009.

Behnke, H. F., Bachmann, K. Fladt, and W. Süss, *Fundamentals of Mathematics*. 3 vols. Translated by S. H. Gould. Cambridge: MIT Press, 1983.

Bénatouïl, Thomas. "L'usage des analogies dans le *De motu animalium*." In *Aristote et le mouvement des animaux: Dix études sur le* De motu animalium. Edited by André Laks and Marwan Rashed, 81–114. Villeneuve d'Ascq: Presses Universitaires du Septentrion, 2004.

Berryman, Sylvia. "Ancient Automata and Mechanical Explanation." *Phronesis* 48 (2003): 344–369.

———. "Aristotle on *pneuma* and Animal Self-Motion." *Oxford Studies in Ancient Philosophy* 23, 85–97. Oxford: Oxford University Press, 2002.

———. *The Mechanical Hypothesis in Ancient Greek Natural Philosophy.* New York: Cambridge University Press, 2009.

Berthier, Janine. "Les apocryphes mathématiques du corpus aristotélicien." In *Mathématiques dans l'Antiquité*. Textes réunis et presentés par Jean Yves Guillaumin, 27–42. Saint-Étienne: Publications de l'Université de Saint-Étienne (Centre Jean-Palerne), 1992.

Berti, Enrico. "Multiplicity and Unity of Being in Aristotle." *Proceedings of the Aristotelian Society* 101, no. 2 (2001): 185–207.

Blair, Ann. "The *Problemata* as a Natural Philosophical Genre." In *Natural Particulars: Nature and the Disciplines in Renaissance Europe*. Edited by Anthony Grafton and Nancy Siraisi, 171–204. Cambridge: MIT Press, 2000.

Bodnár, István M. "The mechanical principles of animal motion." In *Aristote et le mouvement des animaux: Dix études sur le* De motu animalium. Edited by André Laks and Marwan Rashed, 137–147. Villeneuve d'Ascq: Presses Universitaires du Septentrion, 2004.

———. "The pseudo-Aristotelian *Mechanics*: the Attribution to Strato." In *Strato of Lampsacus: Text, Translation, and Discussion*. Edited by Marie-Laurence Desclos and William W. Fortenbaugh, 443–455. New Brunswick, NJ: Transaction Publishers, 2011.

Bolton, Robert. "Aristotle's Method in Natural Science." In *Aristotle's Physics: A Collection of Essays*, edited by Lindsay Judson, 1–29. Oxford: Clarendon Press, 1991.

———. "Essentialism and Semantic Theory in Aristotle: *Posterior Analytics* II.7–10." *Philosophical Review* 85 (1976): 514–544.

———. "Two Standards for Inquiry in Aristotle's *De caelo*." In *New Perspectives on Aristotle's* De caelo, edited by Alan C. Bowen and Christian Wildberg, 51–82. Leiden: Brill, 2009.

✓ Boudri, J. Christiaan. *What Was Mechanical About Mechanics: The Concept of Force Between Metaphysics and Mechanics from Newton to Lagrange*. Translated by Sen McGlinn. Dordrecht: Kluwer, 2002.

✓ Bowen, A. C., and B. R. Goldstein. "A New View of Early Greek Astronomy." *Isis* 74 (1983): 330–340.

✓ Bowen, Alan C. and Christian Wildberg, eds. *New Perspectives on Aristotle's* De caelo. Leiden: Brill, 2009.

Braithwaite, R. B. "Laws of Nature and Causality." In *Readings in the Philosophy of Science*, ed. by Baruch A. Brody, 55–63. Englewood Cliffs, NJ: Prentice Hall, 1970.

Brauer, Fred and John A. Nohel. *The Qualitative Theory of Ordinary Differential Equations: An Introduction*. New York: Dover, 1989.

Brent, Joseph. *C. S. Peirce: A Life*. Bloomington: Indiana University Press, 1993.

Brody, Baruch A., ed. *Readings in the Philosophy of Science*. Englewood Cliffs, NJ: Prentice Hall, 1970.

Brooks, Frederick P., Jr. *The Design of Design: Essays from a Computer Scientist*. Upper Saddle River, NJ: Addison-Wesley, 2010.

Brown, Henry T. *507 Mechanical Movements: Mechanisms and Devices,* 19th ed. New York: Dover, 2005 [1st ed., 1901].

Burkert, Walter. *Lore and Science in Ancient Pythagoreanism*. Translated by Edwin L. Minar, Jr. Cambridge: Harvard University Press, 1972.

Burnyeat, Miles. "Good Repute." *London Review of Books* 8, no. 19 (November 6, 1986): 11–12.

———. "Other Lives." *London Review of Books* 29, no. 4 (February 22, 2007): 3–6.

Cambiano, Giuseppe. "Archimede meccanico e la meccanica di Archita." *Elenchos* 19, no. 2 (1998): 291–324.

———. "The Desire to Know." In *Aristotle's* Metaphysics A: *Symposium Aristotelicum*. Edited by Carlos Steel, with a new critical edition of the Greek Text by Oliver Primavesi, 1–42. Oxford: Oxford University Press, 2012.

Carr, L., M. Iacoboni, M. Dubeau, J. C. Mazziotta, and G. L. Lenzi. "Neural mechanisms of empathy in humans: A relay from neural systems for imitation to limbic areas." *Proceedings of the National Academy of Science* (USA) 100 (2003): 5497–5502.

Carteron, Henri. *La Notion de force dans le système d'Aristote*. Paris: J. Vrin, 1923.

Cartwright, Nancy. *How the Laws of Physics Lie*. Oxford: Clarendon Press, 1983.

Casson, Lionel. *Ships and Seamanship in the Ancient World*. Baltimore: Johns Hopkins University Press, 1995.

Charles, David. *Aristotle on Meaning and Essence*. Oxford: Clarendon Press, 2000.

Clagett, Marshall. *Science of Mechanics in the Middle Ages*. Madison: University of Wisconsin Press, 1961.

Cleary, John J. "The Terminology of 'Abstraction' in Aristotle." *Phronesis* 30, no. 1 (1985): 13–45.

Cohen, M. R. and I. E. Drabkin. *A Source Book in Greek Science*. Cambridge: Harvard University Press, 1966.

Cooper, John M. "Aristotle on the Authority of 'Appearances.'" In *Reason and Emotion: Essays on Ancient Moral Psychology and Ethical Theory*, 281–291. Princeton: Princeton University Press, 1999.

———. "Metaphysics in Aristotle's Embryology." In *Knowledge, Nature, and the Good: Essays on Ancient Philosophy*, 174–203. Princeton: Princeton University Press, 2004.

Cornford, F. M. *Plato's Cosmology: The* Timaeus *of Plato*. Indianapolis: Bobbs-Merrill, 1975.

Daston, Lorraine. "Marvelous Facts and Miraculous Evidence in Early Modern Europe." *Critical Inquiry* 18, no. 1 (Autumn, 1991): 93–124.

Davidson, Donald. "On the Very Idea of a Conceptual Scheme." *Proceedings and Addresses of the American Philosophical Association* 47 (1973–1974): 5–20.

De Gandt, François. "Force et science des machines." In *Science and Speculation: Studies in Hellenistic Theory and Practice*, edited by J. Barnes, J. Brunschwig, M. Burnyeat, and M. Schofield, 96–127. Cambridge: Cambridge University Press, 1982.

De Groot, Jean. *Aristotle and Philoponus on Light*. New York: Garland Publishing, 1991.

———. "*Dunamis* and the Science of Mechanics: Aristotle on Animal Motion." *Journal of the History of Philosophy* 46, no. 1 (2008): 43–68.

———. "Eudoxan Astronomy and Aristotelian Holism in the *Physics*." In *Texts and Contexts in Ancient and Medieval Science*, edited by Edith Sylla and Michael McVaugh, 1–22. Leiden: Brill, 1997.

———. "A Husserlian Approach to Empirical Mathematics in Aristotle." *Proceedings of the American Catholic Philosophical Association* 80 (2006): 91–100.

———. "Modes of Explanation in the Aristotelian *Mechanical Problems*." *Early Science and Medicine* 14 (2009): 22–42. Reprinted in *Evidence and Interpretation in Studies on Early Science and Medicine: Essays in Honor of John E. Murdoch*, edited by William R. Newman and Edith Dudley Sylla. Leiden: Brill, 2009.

Dear, Peter. *Discipline and Experience: the Mathematical Way in the Scientific Revolution*. Chicago: University of Chicago Press, 1995.

———. *The Intelligibility of Nature: How Science Makes Sense of the World*. Chicago: University of Chicago Press, 2006.

Des Chene, Dennis. *Spirits and Clocks: Machine and Organism in Descartes*. Ithaca: Cornell University Press, 2001.

Dijksterhuis, E. J. *Archimedes*. Translated by C. Dikshoorn, with a new bibliographic essay by Wilbur R. Knorr. Princeton: Princeton University Press, 1987.

Drabkin, Israel E. "Notes on the Laws of Motion in Aristotle." *American Journal of Philology* 59, no. 1 (1938): 60–84.

Drummond, John J. "The Perceptual Roots of Geometric Idealizations." *Review of Metaphysics* 37, no. 4 (June 1984): 785–810.

Duhem, Pierre. *The Aim and Structure of Physical Theory*. Translated by Philip P. Wiener. New York: Atheneum, 1962.

———. *The Origins of Statics: The Sources of Physical Theory*. Translated by Grant F. Leneaux, Victor N. Vagliente, and Guy H. Wagener, with a foreword by Stanley L. Jaki. Boston: Kluwer, 1991.

———. *Système du Monde: Histoire des Doctrines Cosmologique de Platon à Copernic*. 10 vols. Paris: Librairie scientifiques Hermann, 1954.

———. *To Save the Phenomena*. Translated by Edmund Doland and Chaninah Maschler. Chicago: University of Chicago Press, 1969. Originally published as "ΣΩΖΕΙΝ ΤΑ ΦΑΙΝΟΜΕΝΑ." *Annales de philosophie chrétienne* 6 (1908): 113–139, 277–302, 352–377, 482–514, 561–592.

Düring, Ingemar. *Aristotle in the Ancient Biographical Tradition*. Göteborg: distributed by Almqvist & Wiksell (Stockholm), 1957.

Einstein, Albert, and Leopold Infeld. *The Evolution of Physics*. New York: Touchstone, 1966.

Fagles, Robert, trans. *Homer: the Iliad*. Introduction and notes by Bernard Knox. New York: Viking, 1990.

Feyerabend, Paul. *Against Method*. 4th ed. New York: Verso, 2010.

Forster, E. S. "The Pseudo-Aristotelian Problems: Their Nature and Composition." *The Classical Quarterly* 22, no. 3–4 (Jul.–Oct., 1928): 163–165.

Frank, Erich. *Plato und die sogenannten Pythagoreer: Ein Kapitel aus der Geschichte des griechischen Geistes*. Halle: Max Niemeyer, 1923.

Frede, Dorothea. "Stoic Determinism." In *Cambridge Companion to the Stoics*, edited by Brad Inwood, 179–205. Cambridge: Cambridge University Press, 2003.

Frede, Michael. "Aristotle's Notion of Potentiality in *Metaphysics* Θ." In *Unity, Identity, and Explanation in Aristotle's Metaphysics*, edited by T. Scaltsas, D. Charles, and M. L. Gill, 173–193. Oxford: Clarendon Press, 1994.

———. "Aristotle's Rationalism." In *Rationality in Greek Thought*, edited by M. Frede and G. Striker, 157–174.

Freeland, Cynthia. "Aristotle on Bodies, Matter, and Potentiality." In *Philosophical Issues in Aristotle's Biology*, edited by Allan Gotthelf and James G. Lennox, 392–407.

———. "Aristotle on Possibilities and Capacities." *Ancient Philosophy* 6 (1987): 69–89.

Furley, David. *Two Studies in the Greek Atomists*. Princeton: Princeton University Press, 1967.

Gerson, Lloyd. *Aristotle and Other Platonists*. Ithaca: Cornell University Press, 2005.

Gillispie, Charles Coulston. *The Edge of Objectivity*. Princeton: Princeton University Press, 1960.

Goldstein, Bernard R. "Saving the Appearances." *Journal for the History of* ~~date?~~ *Astronomy* 28: 1–12.

Gomez-Lobo, Alfonso. "The So-called Question of Existence in Aristotle, An. Post. 2.1–2." *Review of Metaphysics* 34, no. 1 (1980): 71–89.

Gotthelf, Allan. *Teleology, First Principles, and Scientific Method in Aristotle's Biology*. Oxford: Oxford University Press, 2012.

Gotthelf, Allan and James G. Lennox, eds. *Philosophical Issues in Aristotle's Biology*. Cambridge: Cambridge University Press, 1987.

Graham, Daniel. *Aristotle's Two Systems*. Oxford: Clarendon Press, 1987.

———. *Explaining the Cosmos: The Ionian Tradition of Scientific Philosophy*. Princeton: Princeton University Press, 2006.

———. "The Paradox of Prime Matter." *Journal of the History of Philosophy* 25 (1987): 475–490.

Grant, Edward. *A History of Natural Philosophy*. Cambridge: Cambridge University Press, 2007.

Grafton, Anthony, and Nancy Siraisi, eds. *Natural Particulars: Nature and the Disciplines in Renaissance Europe*. Cambridge: MIT Press, 1999.

Grayeff, Felix. *Aristotle and His School*. New York: Barnes and Noble, 1974.

Gupta, Anil. *Empiricism and Experience*. New York: Oxford University Press, 2008.

Guthrie, W. K. C. *A History of Greek Philosophy*. 6 vols. Cambridge: Cambridge University Press, 1975.

Hankinson, R. J. "Contrariety and the Argument for the Elements." In *New* ~~ck~~ *Perspectives on Aristotle's* De caelo, edited by Alan C. Bowen and Christian Wildberg, 83–118. Leiden: Brill, 2009.

Haskins, Ekaterina V. "Endoxa, Epistemological Optimism, and Aristotle's Rhetorical Project." *Philosophy and Rhetoric* 37, no. 1 (2004): 1–20.

Heath, Sir Thomas. *A History of Greek Mathematics*. 2 vols. New York: Dover, 1981.

———. *Aristarchus of Samos: the Ancient Copernicus*. New York: Dover, 1981.

———. *Mathematics in Aristotle*. Bristol: Thoemmes Press, 1998.

Heidegger, Martin. *Basic Writings*, rev. ed. Edited by David Farrell Krell. New York: Harper Perennial, 2008.

Hermann, Arnold. *To Think Like God. Pythagoras and Parmenides: The Origins of Philosophy*. Las Vegas: Parmenides, 2004.

Holton, Gerald and Duane H. D. Roller. *Foundations of Modern Physical Science*. Reading, MA: Addison-Wesley, 1958.

Hood, Pamela M. *Aristotle on the Category of Relation*. Lanham, MD: University Press of America, 2004.

Huffman, Carl. *Archytas of Tarentum: Pythagorean, Philosopher and Mathematician King*. Cambridge: Cambridge University Press, 2005.

———. *Philolaus of Croton: Pythagorean and Presocratic*. Cambridge: Cambridge University Press, 1993.

Hume, David. *An Enquiry Concerning Human Understanding*. Edited by Eric Steinberg. Indianapolis: Hackett, 1977.

Husserl, Edmund. *Crisis of European Sciences and Transcendental Phenomenology*. Translated by David Carr. Evanston, IL: Northwestern University Press, 1970.

Hussey, Edward. "Aristotle and Mathematics." In *Science and Mathematics in Ancient Greek Culture*, edited by C. J. Tuplin and T. E. Rihill, 217–229. Oxford: Oxford University Press, 2002.

———. "Aristotle's Mathematical Physics: A Reconstruction." In *Aristotle's Physics: A Collection of Essay*, edited by Lindsay Judson, 213–242. Oxford: Clarendon Press, 1991.

Irwin, Terence. *Aristotle's First Principles*. Oxford: Clarendon Press, 1990.

———. "Homonymy in Aristotle." *Review of Metaphysics* 34, no. 3 (1981): 523–544.

———. "Plato: the Intellectual Background." In *Cambridge Companion to Plato*, edited by Richard Kraut, 51–89. Cambridge: Cambridge University Press, 1992.

Jaeger, Werner. *Aristotle: Fundamentals of the History of his Development*. Translated by R. Robinson. Oxford: Clarendon Press, 1948.

Jaki, Stanley. *The Relevance of Physics*. Edinburgh: Scottish Academic Press, 1992.

Kitcher, Philip. *The Nature of Mathematical Knowledge*. Oxford: Oxford University Press, 1984.

Klein, Jacob. *Greek Mathematical Thought and the Origin of Algebra*. Translated by Eva Brann. Cambridge: MIT Press, 1968.

Kline, Morris. *Mathematical Thought from Ancient to Modern Times*. 3 vols. Oxford: Oxford University Press, 1990.

Knorr, Wilbur. "Archimedes and the Pre-Euclidean Proportion Theory." *Archives internationales d'histoire des sciences* 28 (1978): 183–244.

———. *The Ancient Tradition of Geometric Problems*. New York: Dover, 1986.

———. *The Evolution of the Euclidean* Elements: *A Study of the Theory of Incommensurable Magnitudes and its Significance for Early Greek Geometry*. Boston: D. Reidel, 1975.

Kosman, L. A. "Substance, Being, and *Energeia*." *Oxford Studies in Ancient Philosophy* 2 (1984): 121–149. Oxford: Clarendon Press, 1984.

Krafft, Fritz. *Dynamische und Statische Betrachtungsweise in der Antiken Mechanik*. Wiesbaden: Steiner, 1970.

Kuhn, Thomas S. "Objectivity, Value Judgment, and Theory Choice." In *The Essential Tension: Selected Studies in Scientific Tradition and Change*, 320–339. Chicago: University of Chicago Press, 1977.

———. *The Structure of Scientific Revolutions*. 3rd ed. Chicago: University of Chicago Press, 1996.

LaBarge, Scott. "Aristotle on Empeiria." *Ancient Philosophy* 26, no. 2 (Spring, 2006): 23–43.

Laird, Walter Roy, and Sophie Roux, eds. *Mechanics and Natural Philosophy Before the Scientific Revolution*. London: Springer, 2008.

Laks, André, and Marwan Rashed, eds. *Aristote et le mouvement des animaux: Dix études sur le De motu animalium*. Villeneuve d'Ascq: Presses Universitaires du Septentrion, 2004.

Landor, Blake. "Aristotle on Demonstrating Essence." *Apeiron* 19 (1985): 116–132.

Lang, Helen. *The Order of Nature in Aristotle's Physics: Place and the Elements*. Cambridge: Cambridge University Press, 1998.

Lear, Jonathan. "Aristotle's Philosophy of Mathematics." *Philosophical Review* 92 (1982): 161–192.

———. *Aristotle: the Desire to Understand*. Cambridge: Cambridge University Press, 1988.

Lefebrve, David. "La critique du mythe d'Atlas." In *Aristote et le mouvement des animaux: Dix études sur le De motu animalium*, edited by André Laks and Marwan Rashed, 115–136. Villeneuve d'Ascq: Presses Universitaires du Septentrion, 2004.

Lennox, James. *Aristotle's Philosophy of Biology*. Cambridge: Cambridge University Press, 2001.

———. "Between Data and Demonstration." In *Aristotle's Philosophy of Biology*, 39–71.

Lewis, V. Bradley. "The Seventh Letter and the Unity of Plato's Political Philosophy." *Southern Journal of Philosophy* 38, no. 2 (Summer, 2000): 231–249.

Liddell, Henry George and Robert Scott. *A Greek-English Lexicon*. 9th ed. Revised and augmented by Sir Henry Stuart Jones, with a supplement, 1968. Oxford: Clarendon Press, 1973.

Lindsay, Robert Bruce, and Henry Margenau. *Foundations of Physics*. New York: John Wiley & Sons, 1936.

Lloyd, G. E. R. *Aristotelian Explorations*. Cambridge: Cambridge University Press, 1996.

———. *Magic, Reason, and Experience*. Cambridge: Cambridge University Press, 1979.

———. "Saving the Appearances." *Classical Quarterly* 28 [continuous series vol. 71] (1978): 202–222.

Lützen, Jesper. *Mechanistic Images in Geometric Form: Heinrich Hertz's Principles of Mechanics*. Oxford: Oxford University Press, 2005.

Machamer, Peter. "Activities and Causation: The Metaphysics and Epistemology of Mechanisms." *International Studies in the Philosophy of
Science* 18, no. 1 (March, 2004): 27–39.

Machamer, Peter, Lindley Darden, and Carl F. Craver. "Thinking About
Mechanisms." *Philosophy of Science* 67 (March, 2000): 1–25.

Maddy, Penelope. *Realism in Mathematics.* Oxford: Clarendon Press, 1990.

Manin, Yuri Ivanovich. "Mathematical Knowledge: Internal, Social, and
Cultural Aspects." In *Mathematics as Metaphor: Selected Essays of
Yuri I. Manin,* 3–26.

———. "Mathematics as Metaphor." In *Mathematics as Metaphor: Selected
Essays of Yuri I. Manin,* 27–32. Providence, RI: American Mathematical Society, 2007. First published in *Proceedings of the International Congress of Mathematicians* 11 (1990). Kyoto, Japan:
Mathematical Society of Japan and Springer Verlag: 1665–1671.

Mann, Wolfgang-Rainer. *The Discovery of Things: Aristotle's* Categories
and Their Context. Princeton: Princeton University Press, 2000.

Mansfeld, Jaap. "*Physikai doxai* and *Problêmata physika* from Aristotle to
Aëtius and Beyond." In *Theophrastus: His Psychological, Doxo-
graphical, and Scientific Writings,* edited by William Fortenbaugh
and Dimitri Gutas, 63–111. New Brunswick, NJ: Transaction
Publishers, 1992.

———. *Studies in Historiography of Greek Philosophy.* Assen: Van
Gorcum, 1990.

Martínez, Alberto A. *Kinematics: The Lost Origins of Einstein's Relativity.*
Baltimore: Johns Hopkins University Press, 2009.

Maso, Stefano, Carlo Natali, and Gerhard Seel, eds. *Reading Aristotle's*
Physics VII.3: *What Is Alteration?* Las Vegas: Parmenides, 2012.

Matthen, Mohan. "The Four Causes in Aristotle's Embryology." *Apeiron* 22
(1989): 159–179.

Mayhew, Robert. *The Female in Aristotle's Biology.* Chicago: University of
Chicago Press, 2004.

———. "The Titles of [Aristotle], *Problemata* 15." *Classical Quarterly* 62
(2012), no. 1: 179–183.

Mazur, Barry. "Mathematical Platonism and Its Opposites." *European
Mathematical Newsletter* (June 2008): 19–21. Also available at
http://www.math.harvard.edu/~mazur/expos.html (accessed De
cember 13, 2013).

———. "When Is One Thing Equal to Some Other Thing?" In *Proof and
Other Dilemmas: Mathematics and Philosophy,* edited by Bonnie
Gold and Roger Simons, 221–242. Spectrum Series. Mathematical
Association of America, 2008. Also available at http://www.math.
harvard.edu/~mazur/expos.html (accessed December 13, 2013).

McDowell, John. *Perception as a Capacity for Knowledge.* Milwaukee:
Marquette University Press, 2011.

McMullin, Ernan. *The Inference That Makes Science*. Milwaukee: Marquette University Press, 1992.

Meineck, Peter. "The Neuroscience of the Tragic Mask." *Athens Dialogues: An International Conference on Culture and Civilization*. Stories and Histories. 2010. Also available at http://athensdialogues.chs. harvard.edu/cgi-bin/WebObjects/athensdialogues.woa/wa/dist?dis=82 (accessed December 13, 2013).

Meli, Domenico Bertoloni. *Thinking With Objects*. Baltimore: The Johns Hopkins University Press, 2006.

Mendell, Henry. "The Trouble with Eudoxus." In *Ancient and Medieval Traditions in the Exact Sciences*, 59–138. Stanford: CSLI Publications, 2000.

Menn, Stephen. "The Origins of Aristotle's Concept of 'Ενέργεια and Δύναμις." *Ancient Philosophy* 14 (1994): 73–114.

Mignucci, M. "Aristotle's Definition of Relatives in *Cat 7*." *Phronesis* 31, no. 2 (1986): 101–127.

Modin, Yuri. *My Five Cambridge Friends*. Translated by Anthony Roberts. New York: Farrar, Straus, Giroux, 1994.

Modrak, Deborah. "Aristotle on the Difference between Mathematics and Physics and First Philosophy." *Apeiron* 22 (1989): 121–139.

———. *Aristotle: the Power of Perception*. Chicago: University of Chicago Press, 1987.

———. *Aristotle's Theory of Language and Meaning*. Cambridge: Cambridge University Press, 2001.

Monfasani, J. "George of Trebizond's Critique of Theodore Gaza's Translation of the Aristotelian *Problemata*." In *Aristotle's* Problemata *in Different Times and Tongues*, edited by Pieter De Leemens and Michèle Goyens, 275–294. Leuven: Leuven University Press, 2006.

———. "The Pseudo-Aristotelian *Problemata* and Aristotle's *De Animalibus* in the Renaissance." In *Natural Particulars: Nature and the Disciplines in Renaissance Europe*, edited by Anthony Grafton and Nancy Siraisi, 205–247.

Moore, Henry, and John Hedgecoe. *Henry Moore: My Ideas, Inspiration and Life as an Artist*. London: Collins and Brown, 1999.

Morales, Fabio. "Relational Attributes in Aristotle." *Phronesis* 39, no. 3 (1994): 255–274.

Morrison, J. S. "The Origins of Plato's Philosopher-Statesman." *Classical Quarterly* N. S. 8 (1958): 198–218.

Mourelatos, Alexander P. D. *The Route of Parmenides*, rev. and exp. ed. Las Vegas: Parmenides, 2008.

Mueller, Ian. "Aristotle on Geometric Objects." *Archiv für Geschichte der Philosophie* 52, no. 2 (1970): 156–171.

———. "Mathematical Method and Philosophical Truth." In *The Cambridge Companion to Plato*, edited by Richard Kraut, 170–199. Cambridge: Cambridge University Press, 1992.

————. "Mathematics and Education: Some Notes on the Platonic Program." *Apeiron* 24, no. 4 (December 1991) (*Special Issue* ΠΕΡΙ ΤΩΝ ΜΑΘΗΜΑΤΩΝ): 85–104.

————, trans. *Simplicius on Aristotle's "On the Heavens 2.10–14."* Ithaca: Cornell University Press, 2005.

Murdoch, John E. "Pierre Duhem and the History of Late Medieval Science and Philosophy in the Latin West." In *Gli studi di filosofia medievale fra otto e novecento*, edited by R. Imbach and A. Maierù, 253–302. Rome: Edizioni di Storia e Letteratura, 1991.

Murdoch, John E. and Edith Dudley Sylla. *The Cultural Context of Medieval Learning*. Boston: D. Reidel, 1975.

Nagy, Gregory. "The Subjectivity of Fear as Reflected in Ancient Greek Wording." *Dialogues* 5 (2010): 29–45. Also available at http://chs.harvard.edu/wa/pageR?tn=ArticleWrapper&bdc=12&mn=3722 (accessed December 13, 2013).

Netz, Reviel. *The Shaping of Deduction in Greek Mathematics: A Study in Cognitive History*. Cambridge: Cambridge University Press, 2003.

Newman, William R. and Edith Dudley Sylla, eds. *Evidence and Interpretation in Studies on Early Science and Medicine: Essays in Honor of John E. Murdoch*. Leiden: Brill, 2009. Reprint of *Early Science and Medicine* 14 (2009).

Nightingale, Andrea Wilson. *Spectacles of Truth in Classical Greek Philosophy: Theoria in its Cultural Context*. Cambridge: Cambridge University Press, 2004.

Nussbaum, Martha Craven. "Saving Aristotle's Appearances." In *Language and Logos: Studies in Ancient Greek Philosophy Presented to G. E. L. Owen*, edited by Malcolm Schofield and Martha Craven Nussbaum. Cambridge: Cambridge University Press, 1982.

————. *The Fragility of Goodness*. Cambridge: Cambridge University Press, 1986.

————. "The Text of Aristotle's *De Motu Animalium*." *Harvard Studies in Classical Philology* 80 (1976): 111–159.

O'Brien, D. *Democritus: Weight and Size: An Exercise in the Reconstruction of Early Greek Philosophy*. Paris: Belles Lettres, 1981.

————. "Heavy and Light in Democritus and Aristotle." *Journal of Hellenic Studies* 97 (1977): 64–74.

————. *Plato: Weight and Sensation, the Two Theories of the* Timaeus. Paris: Belles Lettres, 1984.

O'Meara, Dominic J. *Pythagoras Revived: Mathematics and Philosophy in Late Antiquity*. Oxford: Clarendon Press, 1989.

Owen, G. E. L. "Aristotelian Mechanics." In *Logic, Science and Dialectic: Collected Papers in Greek Philosophy*, 315–333. Ithaca: Cornell University Press, 1986.

————. "Logic and Metaphysics in Some Earlier Works of Aristotle." In *Logic, Science, and Dialectic*, 180–199. Ithaca: Cornell University Press, 1986.

————. *Logic, Science, and Dialectic: Collected Papers in Greek Philosophy.* Edited by Martha Nussbaum. Ithaca: Cornell University Press, 1986.

————. *"Tithenai ta phainomena."* In *Logic, Science, and Dialectic: Collected Papers in Greek Philosophy*, 239–251.

Owens, Joseph. *Aristotle's Gradations of Being in Metaphysics E–Z.* South Bend, IN: St. Augustine's Press, 2007.

————. *The Doctrine of Being in the Aristotelian* Metaphysics, 2nd ed. Toronto: Pontifical Institute of Medieval Studies, 1963.

————. "The Universality of the Sensible in the Aristotelian Noetic." In *Aristotle: The Collected Papers of Joseph Owens*, edited by John R. Catan, 59–73. Albany: State University of New York, 1981.

Peirce, C. S. "How to Make Our Ideas Clear." In *Peirce on Signs*, edited by James Hooper, 160–179. Chapel Hill: University of North Carolina Press, 1991 [First published in *Popular Science Monthly* 12 (1878): 286–302].

————. "What Pragmatism Is." *Monist* 15, no. 2 (April 1905): 161–181.

Piepetas, S. A. *Science and Technology in Ancient Epics* (*History of Mechanics and Machine Science* 6). Dordrecht: Springer, 2008.

Preus, Anthony. *Science and Philosophy in Aristotle's Biological Works.* New York: George Olms Hildesheim, 1975.

Pritzl, Kurt. "Opinions as Appearance: *Endoxa* in Aristotle." *Ancient Philosophy* 14, no. 1 (Fall, 1994): 41–50.

Quine, Willard Van Orman. *Word and Object.* Cambridge: MIT Press, 1960.

Radcliffe, William. *Fishing from Earliest Times.* New York: B. Franklin, 1969 [1921 London: John Murray].

Reichenbach, Hans. "Rationalism and Empiricism: An Inquiry into the Roots of Philosophical Error." *The Philosophical Review* 57, no. 4 (July 1948): 330–346.

Rist, John. *The Mind of Aristotle: A Study in Philosophical Growth.* Toronto: University of Toronto Press, 1989.

Rose, P. L., and S. Drake. "The Pseudo-Aristotelian *Questions of Mechanics* in Renaissance Culture." *Studies in the Renaissance* 18 (1971): 65–104.

Salmieri, Gregory. "Aristotle's Non-'Dialectical' Methodology in the *Nicomachean Ethics.*" *Ancient Philosophy* 29 (2009): 311–335.

Schiefsky, Mark J. "Art and Nature in Ancient Mechanics." In *The Artificial and the Naural*, edited by Bernadette Bensaude-Vincent and William R. Newman, 67–108. Cambridge: MIT Press, 2007.

————. "Structures of Argument and Concepts of Force in the Aristotelian *Mechanical Problems.*" *Early Science and Medicine* 14 (2009): 43–67.

Schneider, Helmuth. *Das griechische Technikverständnis: Von den Epen Homers bis zu den Anfängen der technologischen Fachliteratur.* Darmstadt: Wissenschaftliche Buchgesellschaft, 1989.

Scriven, Michael. "Explanation, Predictions, and Laws." In *Readings in the Philosophy of Science*, edited by Baruch A. Brody, 88–103.

Sellars, Wilfrid. "Philosophy and the Scientific Image of Man." In *Science, Perception, and Reality*, 1–40. Atascadero, CA: Ridgeview Publishing, 1991.

Shute, Richard. *On the History of the Process by Which the Aristotelian Writings Arrived at their Present Form*. Oxford: Clarendon Press, 1888. Reprinted New York: Arno Press, 1976.

Sokolowski, Robert. *Phenomenology of the Human Person*. Cambridge: Cambridge University Press, 2008.

———. "Picturing." In *Pictures, Quotations, and Distinctions: Fourteen Essays in Phenomenology*, 3–26. Notre Dame: University of Notre Dame Press, 1992.

———. *Presence and Absence: A Philosophical Investigation of Language and Being*. Bloomington: Indiana University Press, 1978.

Solla Price, Derek de. "An Ancient Greek Computer." *Scientific American*. June 1959: 60–67.

———. "Automata and the Origins of Mechanism." *Technology and Culture* 5, no. 1 (1964): 9–23.

Sorabji, Richard. "Rationality." In *Rationality in Greek Thought*, edited by Gisela Striker and Michael Frede, 311–334. Oxford: Clarendon Press, 1996.

Sousa, David A. *How the Brain Learns Mathematics*. Thousand Oaks, CA: Corwin Press, 2008.

Steel, Carlos, ed. *Aristotle's Metaphysics A: Symposium Aristotelicum*, with a new critical edition of the Greek text by Oliver Primavesi. Oxford: Oxford University Press, 2012.

Stephenson, F. R. "Notes: A Lunar Occultation of Mars Observed by Aristotle." *Journal for the History of Astronomy* 31 (2000): 342–344.

Strawson, Peter. *Skepticism and Naturalism: Some Varieties*. New York: Columbia University Press, 1985.

Striker, Gisela, and Michael Frede, eds. *Rationality in Greek Thought*. Oxford: Clarendon Press, 1996.

Sylla, Edith. "The Status of Astronomy Between Experience and Demonstration in the Commentaries on Aristotle's *Posterior Analytics* of Robert Grosseteste and Walter Burley." In *Experience and Demonstration: The Sciences of Nature in the 13th and 14th Centuries*, edited by A. Fidora and M. Lutz-Bachmann, 265–291. Berlin: Akademie Verlag, 2007.

Sylla, Edith, and Michael McVaugh, eds. *Texts and Contexts in Ancient and Medieval Science: Studies on the Occasion of John E. Murdoch's Seventieth Birthday*. Leiden: Brill, 1997.

Thompson, D'Arcy. *On Growth and Form*. Abridged edition by John T. Bonner. Cambridge: Cambridge University Press, 1961.

Tiles, J. E. "Why the Triangle Has Two Right Angles *Kath'Hauto*." *Phronesis* 28 (1983): 1–16.

United States Bureau of Naval Personnel. *Basic Machines and How They Work*. New York: Dover, 1971.

Usher, Abbott Payson. *A History of Mechanical Invention,* rev. ed. New York: Dover, 1988.

Van Fraassen, Bas C. *Quantum Mechanics: An Empirical View*. Oxford: Clarendon Press, 1991.

———. *The Empirical Stance*. New Haven: Yale University Press, 2002.

———. *The Scientific Image*. Oxford: Clarendon Press, 1980.

Vatistas, Georgios H. "Floating Body Dynamics Inside Whirlpools Found in Mythology and Literature." *Second World Congress, Ancient Greece and the Modern World* (2002). University of Patras, Ancient Olympia, Greece. July 12–17, 2002. Also available at http://users. encs.concordia.ca/~vatistas/OlymbiaPaper.pdf (accessed December 13, 2013).

———. "Vortices in Homer's *Odyssey*: A Scientific Approach." In *Science and Technology in Ancient Epics,* edited by S. A. Piepetas, 67–76. Berlin: Springer, 2008.

Wallace, William A. *Galileo's Logic of Discovery and Proof*. Boston: Kluwer Academic Publishers, 1992.

Wardy, Robert. *The Chain of Change: A Study of Aristotle's* Physics VII. Cambridge: Cambridge University Press, 1990.

Wedin, Michael V. *Aristotle's Theory of Substance: the* Categories *and* Metaphysics Z. Oxford: Oxford University Press, 2000.

Weisheipl, James, O. P. "Classification of the Sciences in Medieval Thought." In *Nature and Motion in the Middle Ages,* edited by William E. Carroll, 203–237. Washington, D.C.: Catholic University of America Press, 1985.

West, Stephanie. "Archilochus' Message Stick." *Classical Quarterly* 38, no. 1 (1988): 42–48.

Whewell, William. *Novum Organum Renovatum, Being the Second Part of the Philosophy of the Inductive Sciences*. 3rd ed. London: John Parker and Son, 1858.

White, Michael J. *The Continuous and the Discrete: Ancient Physical Theories from a Contemporary Perspective*. Oxford: Clarendon Press, 1992.

Wians, William, ed. *Aristotle's Philosophical Development*. Lanham, MD: Rowman and Littlefield, 1996.

———. "Saving Aristotle from Nussbaum's *Phainomena*." In *Aristotle's Ontology: Essays in Ancient Greek Philosophy,* edited by A. Preus and J. Anton, vol. 5, 133–149. Albany: State University of New York Press, 1992.

Wiles, David. *Mask and Performance in Greek Tragedy: From Ancient Festival to Modern Experimentation*. Cambridge: Cambridge University Press, 2007.

Williams, Christopher G. *Origins of Form*. New York: Architectural Book
    Publishing, 1981.
Witt, Charlotte. *Ways of Being: Potentiality and Actuality in Aristotle's*
    Metaphysics. Ithaca: Cornell University Press, 2003.
Wittgenstein, Ludwig. *Tractatus Logico-Philosophicus*. German text with an
    English translation by C. K. Ogden. London: Routledge, 1992.
Zeeman, E. C. "Gears from the Greeks." *Proceedings of the Royal Institute of*
    Great Britain 58 (1986): 139–156.
Zhmud, Leonid. *The Origin of the History of Science in Classical Antiquity.*
    Translated by Alexander Chernoglazov. Berlin: Walter de Gruyter,
    2006.

Index Locorum

Index of Names and Subjects

• ALSO AVAILABLE FROM PARMENIDĖS PUBLISHING •

PRE-SOCRATICS

By Being, It Is: The Thesis of Parmenides by Néstor-Luis Cordero

Parmenides and the History of Dialectic: Three Essays by Scott Austin

Parmenides, Venerable and Awesome: Proceedings of the International Symposium edited by Néstor-Luis Cordero

The Fragments of Parmenides: A Critical Text with Introduction and Translation, the Ancient Testimonia and a Commentary by A. H. Coxon. Revised and Expanded Edition edited with new Translations by Richard McKirahan and a new Preface by Malcolm Schofield

The Legacy of Parmenides: Eleatic Monism and Later Presocratic Thought by Patricia Curd

The Route of Parmenides: Revised and Expanded Edition, With a New Introduction, Three Supplemental Essays, and an Essay by Gregory Vlastos by Alexander P. D. Mourelatos

To Think Like God: Pythagoras and Parmenides. The Origins of Philosophy. Scholarly and fully annotated edition by Arnold Hermann

The Illustrated To Think Like God: Pythagoras and Parmenides. The Origins of Philosophy by Arnold Hermann with over 200 full color illustrations

Presocratics and Plato: A Festschrift in Honor of Charles Kahn edited by Richard Patterson, Vassilis Karasmanis, and Arnold Hermann

PLATO

A Stranger's Knowledge: Statesmanship, Philosophy, and Law in Plato's Statesman by Xavier Márquez

God and Forms in Plato by Richard D. Mohr

Image and Paradigm in Plato's Sophist by David Ambuel

Interpreting Plato's Dialogues by J. Angelo Corlett

One Book, the Whole Universe: Plato's Timaeus Today edited by Richard D. Mohr and Barbara M. Sattler

Platonic Patterns: A Collection of Studies by Holger Thesleff

Plato's Late Ontology: A Riddle Resolved by Kenneth M. Sayre

Plato's Parmenides: Text, Translation & Introductory Essay by Arnold Hermann. Translation in collaboration with Sylvana Chrysakopoulou with a Foreword by Douglas Hedley

Plato's Universe by Gregory Vlastos

The Philosopher in Plato's Statesman by Mitchell Miller

ARISTOTLE

One and Many in Aristotle's Metaphysics—*Volume 1:*
Books Alpha-Delta by Edward C. Halper

One and Many in Aristotle's Metaphysics—*Volume 2:*
The Central Books by Edward C. Halper

Reading Aristotle: Physics *VII.3 "What is Alteration?" Proceedings of the*
International ESAP-HYELE Conference edited by Stefano Maso, Carlo Natali,
and Gerhard Seel

HELLENISTIC PHILOSOPHY

A Life Worthy of the Gods: The Materialist Psychology of Epicurus by David
Konstan

THE ENNEADS OF PLOTINUS
With Philosophical Commentaries
Series edited by John M. Dillon and Andrew Smith

Plotinus, Ennead *IV.8: On the Descent of the Soul into Bodies. Translation*
with an Introduction & Commentary by Barrie Fleet

Plotinus, Ennead *V.5: That the Intelligibles are not External to the Intellect,*
and on the Good. Translation with an Introduction & Commentary by Lloyd P.
Gerson

ETHICS

Sentience and Sensibility: A Conversation about Moral Philosophy by Matthew R.
Silliman

PHILOSOPHICAL FICTION

Pythagorean Crimes by Tefcros Michaelides

The Aristotle Quest: A Dana McCarter Trilogy. Book 1: Black Market Truth
by Sharon M. Kaye

AUDIOBOOKS

The Iliad (unabridged) by Stanley Lombardo

The Odyssey (unabridged) by Stanley Lombardo

The Essential Homer by Stanley Lombardo

The Essential Iliad by Stanley Lombardo

FORTHCOMING

The Imperial Plato: Albinus, Maximus, Apuleius.
Text, Translation, and Commentary
by Ryan C. Fowler

Plotinus, Ennead I.6: On Beauty.
Translation with an Introduction & Commentary
by Andrew Smith

Plotinus, Ennead II.4: On Matter.
Translation with an Introduction & Commentary
by Anthony A. Long

Plotinus, Ennead II.5: On What Exists Potentially and What Actually.
Translation with an Introduction & Commentary
by Cinzia Arruzza

Plotinus, Ennead II.9: Against the Gnostics.
Translation with an Introduction & Commentary
by Sebastian Ramon Philipp Gertz

Plotinus, Enneads IV.3–4, 29: Problems concerning the Soul.
Translation with an Introduction & Commentary
by John M. Dillon and H.J. Blumenthal

Plotinus, Enneads IV.1–2, IV.4, 30–45 & IV.5: Problems concerning the Soul.
Translation with an Introduction & Commentary
by Gary M. Gurtler

Plotinus, Ennead IV.7: On the Immortality of the Soul.
Translation with an Introduction & Commentary
by Barrie Fleet

Plotinus, Ennead V.1: The Three Primary Levels of Reality.
Translation with an Introduction & Commentary
by Eric D. Perl

Plotinus, Ennead V.8: On Intelligible Beauty.
Translation with an Introduction & Commentary
by Andrew Smith

Plotinus, Enneads VI.4 & VI.5: On the Presence of Being, One and the Same, Everywhere.
Translation with an Introduction & Commentary
by Eyjólfur Emilsson and Steven Strange

Plotinus, Ennead VI.8: On Free Will and the Will of the One.
Translation with an Introduction & Commentary
by Kevin Corrigan and John D. Turner

WQXR web site
Bach stork

Certainty, 72
 q index necessity

progressive science
   what to do to reform a sci discipline

EDS ranging over time seeing analogous ways of thinking
     pp340-41 CS Peirce

345 principles are not being
        de broot is philosophically more powerful
              than most historians
352 action as real in Greek theater
297 EDS from proportion to {equation
                                   {function

         adding change
302 notion of function
303 Review - Arist as qualitative
305 fluid divisions of mathematics
333 mechanics as experimental science
338 not qualitative

cite p. 6 re Aristotle / qualitative
deformation / equilibrium   (Kaye) 250

not flashy